AMERICAN IMMIGRATION

A Student Companion

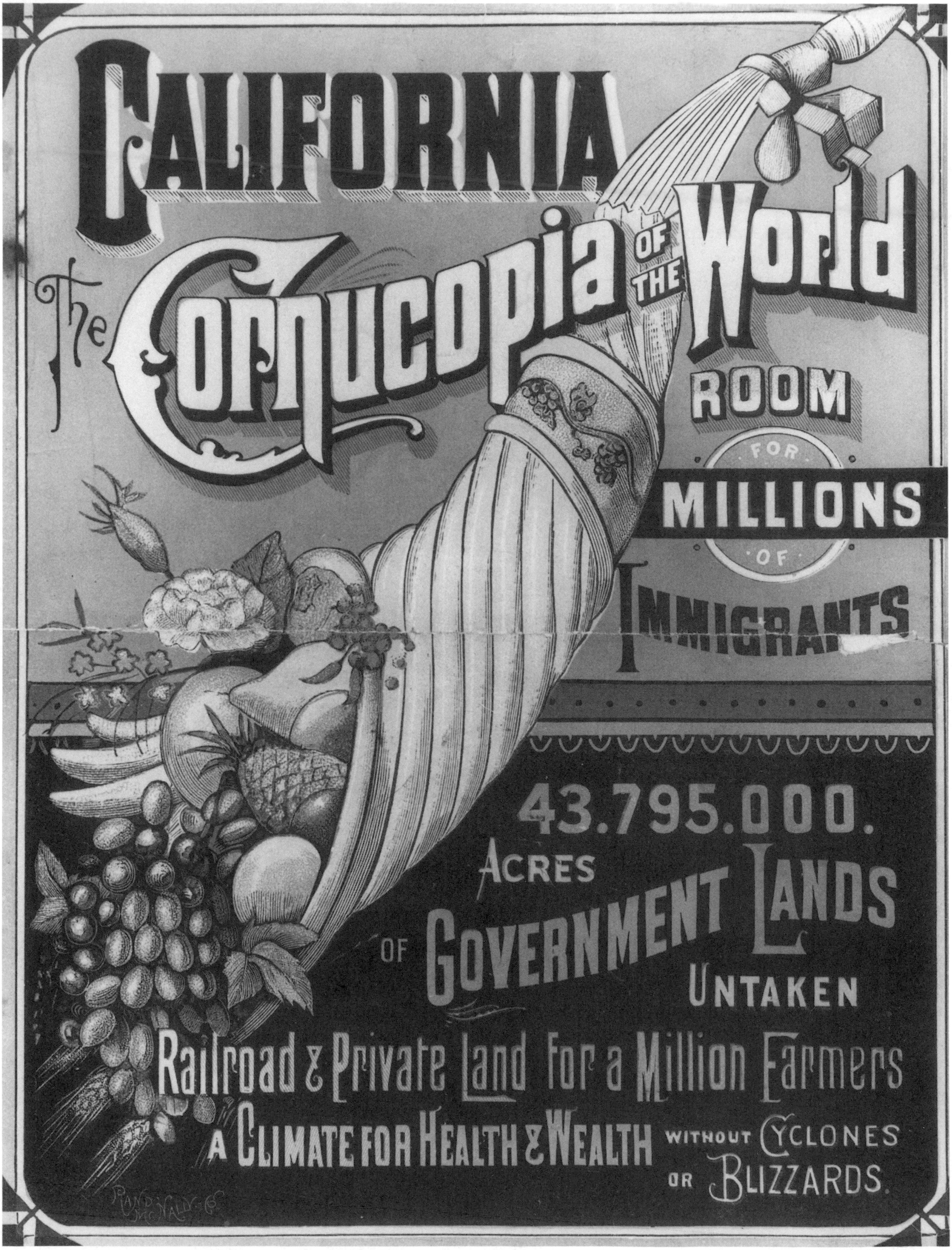

CALIFORNIA
The Cornucopia of the World
ROOM
FOR
MILLIONS
OF
IMMIGRANTS
43.795.000.
ACRES
OF GOVERNMENT LANDS
UNTAKEN
Railroad & Private Land for a Million Farmers
A CLIMATE FOR HEALTH & WEALTH without CYCLONES or BLIZZARDS.

OXFORD

Student Companions to American History
WILLIAM H. CHAFE, GENERAL EDITOR

AMERICAN IMMIGRATION

A Student Companion

Roger Daniels

OXFORD
UNIVERSITY PRESS

Oxford New York
Athens Auckland Bangkok Bogotá Buenos Aires Calcutta
Cape Town Chennai Dar es Salaam Delhi Florence Hong Kong Istanbul
Karachi Kuala Lumpur Madrid Melbourne Mexico City Mumbai
Nairobi Paris São Paulo Singapore Taipei Tokyo Toronto Warsaw
and associated companies in
Berlin Ibadan

Library of Congress Cataloging-in-Publication Data
Daniels, Roger.
American immigration: a student companion / Roger Daniels.
p. cm. – (Oxford student companions to American history)
Includes bibliographical references and index.
ISBN 0-19-511316-0
1. United States—Emigration and immigration—Encyclopedias.
2. Immigrants—United States—Encyclopedias. [1. United States—Emigration and immigration—
Encyclopedias. 2. Immigrants—United States—Encyclopedias.] I. Title. II. Series.
JV6465 .D257 2000
304.8'73'003—dc21

9 8 7 6 5 4 3 2 1

Printed in the United States of America
on acid-free paper

Design: Sandy Kaufman
Layout: Valerie Sauers
Picture Research: Lisa Kirchner and Lisa Barnett

On the cover: (top left) banner in a 1985 parade in New York City; (top right) 2000 swearing-in ceremony for new citizens; (bottom) the Statue of Liberty and boats in New York Harbor in an 1884 lithograph.

Frontispiece: California advertises for immigrants in a poster from 1870.

CONTENTS

HOW TO USE THIS BOOK

The articles in this *Companion* are arranged alphabetically, so you can look up the names of ethnic groups, concepts, and laws that you want more information about. You can also use the SEE ALSO list at the end of an article to find entries about related subjects. It may happen that you look up something that the *Companion* deals with under a different article name. For example, if you look up the Central American people called Garifuna, you will find the notice "Garifuna. SEE Hondurans." Under Hondurans you will find a definition of Garifuna.

This is *not* primarily a work about individuals, but many names of famous persons are mentioned. You can look these names up in the index.

You can use this *Companion* in a number of ways. To get an overall view of immigration, the introduction, "A Short History of Immigration to the United States," is a good place to start. The individual articles are much more focussed and are described below.

Ethnic groups: The articles on the various ethnic groups, large and small, are the most numerous. At the beginning of most such articles is a list of data. For example, the information about Danes is as follows:

- *1990 Ancestry: 1,634,669*
- *Immigration, 1986–96: 6,773*
- *Immigration, 1820–1996: 374,594*
- *Major periods of immigration: 1864–1924*
- *Major areas of settlement: Iowa, Wisconsin, Minnesota, Utah*

"1990 Ancestry" indicates how many people indicated on the 1990 census (the most recent data available) that at least one of their ancestors was Danish. Each person could list two ancestors but not everyone answered the question. Those who did could choose two groups. Since the census counts people of Asian ethnicity, entries such as Koreans will have a "1990 Census" listing. For some religious groups there are "1990 Population" estimates. The abbreviation "n.a." indicates that those statistics are not available.

"Immigration, 1986–96" indicates the number coming in that 10-year period only.

"Immigration, 1820–1996" indicates how many persons from Denmark were recorded as entering the United States since 1820, which is when the government began keeping those kinds of records. For earlier periods it is necessary to estimate. Many persons, even after 1820, were not recorded. In addition, these records indicate where a person came from, but not her or his ethnicity. A German person living in Denmark who came to the United States on a Danish passport would be recorded as Danish.

"Major periods of immigration" indicates when the largest number of persons came from Denmark.

"Major areas of settlement" indicates where most Danes settled in the period of heaviest immigration.

Immigration law: Articles on legislation such as the Chinese Exclusion Act, the Immigration Act of 1924, and the National Origins Act explain why each law was passed, state its provisions, and discuss it effects.

Concepts: This category of subjects describes how and in what ways such concepts as Acculturation, Assimilation, and Nativism have influenced immigration.

Categories of immigrants: Articles about certain categories of immigrants, such as Women, Children, Refugees, and War brides, explain their role in the immigration story.

Definitions: Particular aspects of the immigration process such as Circular migration, Push, Pull, and Return migration have their own entries, which define and explain these technical terms.

Immigration, ethnic, and refugee organizations: In Appendix 2 you will find a list of organizations, public and private, from which information about immigration and/or about certain ethnic groups may be obtained.

Further reading, museums, and websites: If you want to know more about a specific topic, you can use the FURTHER READING entries at the end of each article as well as the guide to further research at the end of the book. It lists general further reading titles, websites, and museums.

INTRODUCTION:
A SHORT HISTORY OF IMMIGRATION TO THE UNITED STATES

How important has immigration been in American history? One leading historian of immigration, Harvard's Oscar Handlin, wrote in 1951, "Once I thought to write a history of the immigrants in America. Then I discovered that the immigrants *were* American history."

Of course, Handlin was clearly exaggerating, but he was not exaggerating by very much. What he meant, at a time when the history of immigration was not highly thought of, was that it is not possible to understand American history without understanding America's immigrants.

Except for some 2 million American Indians, immigration in the past four centuries has been responsible for the presence of the more than a quarter of a billion people who now populate the United States. Immigrants and their descendants are the authors of American diversity, of what can be called the American mosaic. They have created a culture that, despite its largely European roots, is clearly not European, any more than it is African, or Amerindian, or Asian, or Caribbean, or Latino. Americans are, as the French sojourner Michel-Guillaume Jean de Crèvecoeur noted in 1782, new persons, who, over time, have been transformed by their new environment and ever changing heredity. It is impossible to imagine what America would be like if no immigrants had come; nor is it possible to imagine what it would have been like had only Europeans come, or only British, and so forth. The American people are a product of what they have been, and where they have come from, as well as of what has happened to them in the United States. When nativists—opponents of immigration—rant and rave about the dangers of being overrun by immigrants, or about losing control of our borders, or complain that immigrants and some of their children do not speak English well, they are denying the validity of an essential and enhancing part of the American

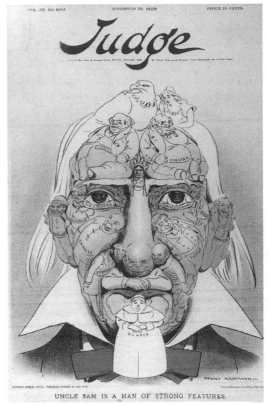

An 1898 Judge *magazine cover portrays immigrants as a source of strength. The left eye refers to the annexation of Hawaii, which took place earlier that year.*

experience. They are denying the vitalization that has come from the constant enrichment and reenforcement of American society by the muscles, brains, and hearts that every generation of immigrants has brought with them to America.

The history of immigration to the United States can be divided most conveniently into four distinct periods: the formative era, up to 1815; the so-called "long" 19th century stretching from 1815 to 1924; the era of restriction, 1924–1965; the era of renewed immigration, since 1965.

The Formative Period (1565–1815)
During the formative period, which begins with the settlement of St. Augustine, Florida, by Spanish in 1565 and ends with the conclusion of a series of wars between Britain and France in which Americans took part, the overwhelming majority of

immigrants came either from the British Isles or from Africa. We must remember, however, that the first permanent European settlements in what is now the United States were made by Spanish people at St. Augustine and in New Mexico in 1598, and that immigrants from other European countries, particularly France and Germany, were in almost every colony. Of the roughly 1 million people who came in this period, more than half were not free. All of the 350,000 Africans came in chains, and perhaps half of the 650,000 Europeans were indentured servants or convicts.

Most of the British who came were from England, and most of them were from the southern part of England. Smaller but still substantial numbers of Scots and Irish came, as did a yet smaller number of Welsh. Even in modern times, immigration statistics are often incomplete or unreliable, and they were less reliable in the 17th and 18th centuries. The most useful estimates come from the first United States census, taken in 1790, which found some 3.15 million white Americans and 750,000 African Americans. The 1790 census did not count most Native Americans, and the census takers did not try to do so until 1880. Scholars have analyzed the information contained in that first census and tried to estimate the number and percentage of the population represented by each ethnic group. The vast majority of the 3.9 million Americans had been born in what became the United States, as there had been relatively little immigration between the beginnings of the American Revolution in the mid-1770s and 1790.

The distribution of the members of the different ethnic groups was uneven. Most of the German Americans lived in Pennsylvania, where they were about one-third of the population. Similarly, most of the Dutch were in New York and adjoining states. By region, New England was the most heavily English, while the South was home to most African Americans, who, in some districts,

Estimated Non-Native American Population in 1790	
English	49%
African American	16%
Irish	7.6%
Germans	6.9%
Scots	6.5%
Dutch	2.5%
French	1.8%
Miscellaneous and unassigned	9.7%

American Historical Association, *Annual Report,* 1931

outnumbered whites. This clustering of ethnic groups in certain regions and smaller areas, called enclaves or neighborhoods, is typical of the immigrant experience everywhere in the modern world.

The United States Constitution, which went into effect in 1789, required that a census be taken every 10 years, but it said very little about immigration: in fact, the word *immigration* does not appear anywhere in the document. But the founding fathers clearly foresaw and encouraged continued immigration, as three separate provisions testify. In Article 1, Section 8, Congress was told to "establish a uniform Rule of Naturalization." The following section provided that Congress could not interfere with the African slave trade before 1808, and Article 2, Section 1 provided that the President— and by extension the Vice President— must be "a natural born Citizen." This left immigrants eligible for all other offices under the Constitution. From the beginning of the United States immigrants have filled these offices, serving in Congress, in the cabinet, and on the Supreme Court. For example, the first secretary of the treasury, Alexander Hamilton, was an immigrant from the island of Nevis in the West Indies and Madeline Albright, Secretary of State under Bill Clinton, was an immigrant from Czechoslovakia.

In the second year of the American republic, 1790, Congress passed a naturalization statute that provided for the naturalization of "free white persons." The law was intended to exclude Africans and indentured servants: later interpretation by the Supreme Court expanded the ban to include Asians, but for much of the 19th century some Chinese and Japanese were naturalized. In 1798, Congress passed the short-lived Aliens Act, which threatened to deport aliens who were involved in politics, but no one was deported.

Only two other laws passed in the first half of the 19th century affected immigration. In 1808, at the first legal opportunity, Congress abolished the slave trade but not slavery, and in 1819 it ordered that incoming immigrants be counted, but not those leaving the United States.

The "Long" 19th Century (1815–1924)
Historians sometimes define centuries not by the calendar, but by events: for American immigration two events define the 19th century more effectively than do the "normal" dates, 1801–1900. The first date, 1815, marks the end of a series of wars between Britain and France and our War of 1812 with Britain. The end of the fighting signaled a renewal of immigration. The second, 1924, denotes the enactment of a "permanent" restrictive immigration law by the United States. During that "long" 19th century, more than 36 million people immigrated to the United States. This is an absolute majority of all the immigrants who have ever come. The table on the right shows, by decade, how many came after 1819 and the rate of immigration in relation to the total U.S. population.

The mere numbers of immigrants do not tell the whole story. In the earlier part of the "long" century of immigration, the relative impact of immigration was higher than the table on the left seems to indicate because the population was much smaller. The table below shows the rate of immigration per thousand pre-existing inhabitants. Thus, for example, the rate for the 1850s is much higher than for the 1890s even though 42 percent more people came in the latter period. Immigration was discouraged in the 1860s by the Civil War and in the 1870s and 1890s by hard times in the United States.

This mass immigration was dominated by Europeans, and, to a lesser degree, the descendants of European immigrants coming from Canada. It also marked the beginnings of large-scale immigration from Asia, largely of Chinese and Japanese. Historians now believe that even though the international slave trade had been outlawed by Congress in 1808, perhaps 50,000 illegal slaves were brought into the United States between then and 1865, mostly from Caribbean islands. Toward the end of the 19th century, free Afro-Caribbeans began to come to the United States.

In the years before the Civil War (1861–65), immigration was dominated by Irish and Germans. Even before the dreadful

1820–1924 Immigration

	Immigration to the United States	Rate of Immigration per Thousand of U.S. Population
1820–30	151,824	1.2
1831–40	599,125	3.9
1841–50	1,713,251	8.4
1851–60	2,598,214	9.3
1861–70	2,314,824	6.4
1871–80	2,812,191	6.2
1881–90	5,246,613	9.2
1891–1900	3,687,564	5.3
1901–10	8,795,386	10.4
1911–20	5,735,811	5.7
1921–24	2,344,599	5.3
TOTAL	35,999,402	

U.S. Bureau of the Census

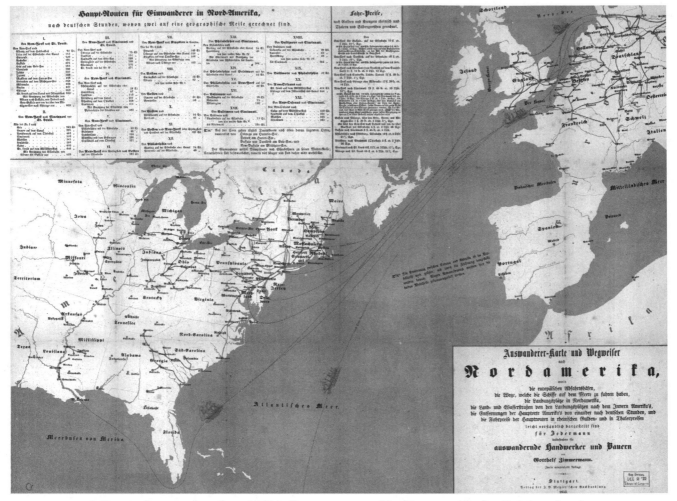

A German-language map from 1853 indicates routes used by German and other European immigrants coming to the United States in the 19th century.

potato famine of the 1840s, large numbers of Irish—mostly poor male laborers—came, and heavy Irish immigration of all kinds continued throughout the century, during which a total of 4.5 million Irish came. Almost all the Irish were Roman Catholics and most settled close to the northern Atlantic seaboard, particularly in New England.

Even more Germans—almost 6 million—came in the same period. No dreadful event pushed Germans out of Europe, and few were as poor as many of the Irish. Many Germans settled in eastern cities between New York and Baltimore but even more went to interior cities and farms, particularly in the so-called "Ger-

man triangle," the area bounded by Cincinnati, St. Louis, and Milwaukee. Most German immigrants were Protestants, but there was a sizable Roman Catholic minority and a smaller but substantial Jewish one.

Two other groups, Scandinavians and Chinese, began their mass migration before the Civil War. More than 2 million Scandinavians—Swedes, Norwegians, and Danes—came during the century. There were more than a million Swedes, 700,000 Norwegians, and 300,000 Danes. This was largely a migration of families, of whom an overwhelming majority settled in the upper Middle West, particularly in Nebraska, Iowa,

Minnesota, and the Dakotas. Most were farmers and practiced Protestant religions, chiefly variants of Lutheranism.

A smaller number of Chinese, perhaps 350,000, were the first large group of immigrants to cross the Pacific. They were, at first, chiefly gold miners and railroad workers in California and other western states and territories, and all but a few were single males who practiced Buddhism or Taoism. For both economic and cultural reasons they suffered from severe discrimination in both custom and law: the Chinese Exclusion Act of 1882 stopped the further immigration of Chinese laborers. This law began the systematic restriction of voluntary immigrants. Before 1882 there was no effective restrictive immigration legislation. Anyone not a slave who reached American shores or crossed a land border could enter legally.

After the Civil War the pace of migration increased, and, although British, Irish, German and Scandinavian immigrants continued to come from Europe, they were soon outnumbered by eastern and southern Europeans—Poles, eastern European Jews, Italians, southern Slavs and Greeks. The migration of these latter groups was aided by the improvement of European steamship lines and railroads. European shipping companies, such as the Cunard Line, based in Liverpool, England, and the German-based Hamburg-Amerika and North German Lloyd lines, built special ships for the immigrant trade and coordi-

THE SECRETARY OF THE STATE BOARD OF IMMIGRATION
Has recently published the following statement, showing the
COST OF COMING TO MINNESOTA.

Immigrants should procure Tickets and contract for the carriage of Extra Baggage through to their ultimate destination, if possible.

EUROPEAN
EMIGRANT RATES OF PASSAGE
TO ST. PAUL.
FROM

An advertisement from about 1872 shows how Minnesota, like California and other states, competed for immigrants. As the ad states, they got special reduced rates on transportation.

nated their sailings with railroad schedules. By the end of the century, a person in Poland could buy one ticket that would cover rail fare to Hamburg, an ocean passage, and a railroad ticket to an American city. Or, as often happened, a recent immigrant in an American city—Detroit, for example—could buy a ticket for a family member or friend in Krakow, Poland, for example, and have it delivered to that person in Poland. Similar conditions prevailed in the Pacific, where Japanese steamers, mostly of the NYK line, brought perhaps 275,000 Japanese to the United States. Historians call this kind of migration "chain migration," because immigrants send for and follow one another, like links in a chain.

Most of the members of these eastern and southern European immigrant groups had several things in common: almost all worked at industrial and urban occupations, they lived in American cities rather than in small towns or on farms, and very few were Protestants. Except for the Jews, and, after 1907, the Japanese, these populations were heavily male and large numbers of them, including Japanese, would work in the United States for a time and then return home. Such return migration was important in this era, because for every three immigrants, perhaps one went home, although, to be sure, many came back, sometimes more than once. Whereas Italian men worked largely in construction of all kinds, Polish and eastern European men worked at the dirtiest jobs in heavy industry, and Jewish and Italian immigrant women worked in the garment factories that clothed America. Large numbers of these folks would have preferred to work on their own farms, as many earlier immigrants had done, but the era of free land was long past. And even if free land had been available, few of these immigrants had the capital necessary to get started. The only immigrant group in this era that settled largely on

This cartoon from the 1860s attacks both Irish and Chinese. The Irishman (left) and the Chinese are devouring America, represented by Uncle Sam in his striped trousers; then the Chinese devours the Irishman.

the land was the Japanese, who did so in the expanding agricultural economy of the West Coast.

The restriction of immigration began with the passage of the Chinese Exclusion Act of 1882, which became the hinge on which the "golden door" of immigration began to swing closed. A whole succession of laws between 1882 and 1924 narrowed the opening through which immigrants came, although only in the 1920s did the total number of immigrants admitted begin to fall as a result of legislation.

The reasons that large numbers of Americans have supported immigration restriction are various and complicated, but two reasons stand out: fear of economic and cultural competition, and racial and ethnic prejudice. This was true in the mid-18th century when Benjamin Franklin and other English-speaking Pennsylvanians expressed fear that German immigrants and the German language would "take over" their colony. It was also true in the mid-19th century when many in the Northeast opposed the entry of Irish immigrants who were both poor and Roman Catholic. It was true again in the 1860s and in the following

decades, when many westerners insisted that "the Chinese must GO!", both because of their race and the fact that they, like many immigrants, were willing to work for very low wages. White workers feared that this would depress their own wages. And, in the late 19th and early 20th centuries many—perhaps most—Americans felt that too many eastern and southern Europeans were filling up American cities and competing for unskilled and semiskilled jobs.

These anti-immigrant notions were greatly stimulated by an official government commission, the U.S. Immigration Commission, whose 1911 report put forth many of the arguments used to justify drastic immigration restriction in the following decade. It argued that most of those then coming to the United States—what it called "new immigrants," people from eastern and southern Europe—were essentially different from and inferior to most of those who had come previously—what it called "old immigrants," people from the British Isles, Germany, and Scandinavia.

Similar kinds of arguments had been raised against Irish and German immigrants early in the 19th century and would be raised in the closing decades of the 20th century against Asians and Latin Americans.

These opponents of immigration, or nativists, were and are largely motivated by fears of all kinds, particularly fears about their economic well-being and about their culture being swamped by incoming strangers. Few noted that, although the number of immigrants rose steadily from about 230,000 a year in the 1860s to about a million a year in the early 20th century, the relative number of foreign-born people living in the United States remained remarkably constant. In every census between 1860 and 1920—a period of remarkable change in almost every aspect of American life—one significant social statistic remained constant:

This ship's manifest—a passenger list from January 2, 1892—shows nine immigrants and one returning American. Such lists are a major source of information about immigrants.

immigrants, persons who were foreign born, were just about 14 percent of the population. In other words, every seventh person was an immigrant. By 2000, for the sake of comparison, the figure was about 10 percent, or every 10th person.

The Era of Restriction, 1924–65

Although the beginning date of 1924 is commonly assigned to the era of restriction, the process had begun long before. Before 1882 there was nothing in American law to stop a free immigrant from entering the country. If you could get here, you were in. To be sure, many countries tried to prevent their inhabitants from leaving, but that is a different matter. The U.S. restriction of free immigration began in 1882 with the passage of the Chinese Exclusion Act, which barred the entry of Chinese laborers who had not been here before. Once that first restriction had been made, more restrictions followed.

The restrictions came piecemeal, as various categories of people were declared ineligible for entrance. By the end of World War I (1918), the once free and unrestricted immigration policy of the United States had been limited in seven

major ways as the following kinds of immigrants were barred from immigrating: Chinese laborers and other Asians, except for Japanese and Filipinos; certain criminals; people who failed to meet certain moral standards, including prostitutes and polygamists; people with various diseases; paupers; certain radicals, including anarchists and people advocating the overthrow of the government by force and violence; and illiterates.

Only the test to keep out illiterates caused significant political controversy. It was vetoed four times over a 20-year period by presidents as diverse as the conservative Democrat Grover Cleveland in 1897, the liberal Republican William Howard Taft in 1913, and the progressive Democrat Woodrow Wilson in 1915 and 1917. It was enacted in 1917 over Wilson's second veto. Unlike the 1901 Australian literacy test, which allowed government inspectors to choose the language or languages that immigrants had to read, the American law was reasonably fair. It allowed each immigrant to specify the language in which he or she would be tested. It also exempted close female relatives of any age and close male relatives over 55 years old joining

2674

Class No. 4   Serial Number   French

Tu tires le fondement de ta puissance de la bouche des petits enfants et de ceux qui tettent, à cause de tes adversaires, afin de confondre l'ennemi et celui qui veut se venger.

Out of the mouth of babes and sucklings hast thou ordained strength because of thine enemies, that thou mightest still the enemy and the avenger.

(Ps. 8 :2) (French Ps. 8 :3)

A number of the texts used for the literacy examinations of immigrants were drawn from the Bible. This one, from the eighth Psalm, is the copy the examiner used, which had the text in both French and English.

immigrants already in the United States, and it provided that if any adult member of an immigrating family was literate the whole family could be admitted.

Despite this impressive list of restrictions, nothing was done before 1920–21 to place any kind of numerical cap on immigration, and in no year before 1921 did the percentage of prospective immigrants turned away at Ellis Island and other ports of entry reach 2 percent. The fluctuations in the numbers of immigrants were due to either economic conditions—during hard times in the United States fewer immigrants came—or political ones: during the American Civil War (1861–65) and World War I (1914–18) immigration was significantly reduced.

Amid the political and social reaction of post–World War I—a period one historian has called the "tribal twenties" because of the many social and cultural issues that divided the American people—drastic immigration restriction became politically expedient. In 1920 the House of Representatives voted 296–42 to bar all immigration for one year. The Senate substituted a more rational bill, which Wilson vetoed in 1921 just before he left office. Within months Congress repassed it and President Warren G. Harding signed the Emergency Quota Act of 1921. A similar

but more restrictive measure was enacted three years later: the Immigration Act of 1924. Most of the provisions of that act remained in effect until 1965.

The thrust of the 1921 and 1924 laws was undisguised ethnic discrimination directed largely against people from southern and eastern Europe. It put numerical limits on the number of immigrants who could enter in any given year from each of more than a hundred countries and political entities. The number for each country was based on the presumed number of people from each place who were already in the United States. But when the 1920 census figures became available they showed what restrictionists in Congress thought were "too many" Italians, Poles, and Jews. So in 1924, Congress chose to base the new quotas on the 1890 census, taken nearly 35 years earlier, when fewer southern and eastern Europeans had been present. The quotas were relatively generous toward immigrants from the British Isles, Germany, and Scandinavia—in fact many of the "slots" for those countries went unused year after year—and stringent toward the rest of Europe. Asians were not allowed to immigrate, except for Filipinos, who were American nationals as long as the United States owned the Philippines, from 1898 until a law promising independence for the islands was enacted in 1934.

Yet it is an indication of how different American concerns were then from what they are today that the 1924 act placed no limits at all on immigration from Mexico or from any other independent country in the New World. It also allowed a very limited kind of family reunification: an immigrant who was the minor child, or spouse of a United States citizen could enter as a "nonquota immigrant."

Textbooks often illustrate the 1924 act by reprinting contemporary cartoons showing immigration reduced to a trickle. Those cartoons overstate the effect of the 1924 law. The new law did reduce annual immigration to about 300,000 annually. This was far below the 1 million a year that had been coming before World War I, but was hardly a trickle. In the 1930s immigration was really reduced to a trickle—an average of 50,000 a year. But it was not Congress but the worldwide Great Depression that slowed the traffic. Economic conditions were so poor in the United States that in two different years—1932 and 1933—more people left or were excluded from the United States than immigrated to it. This had not happened since the Loyalists (or Tories, as their opponents called them) fled the country in the 1780s after the successful American Revolution, and it has not happened since.

Late in the 1930s large numbers of refugees from Nazi Germany, most but not all of them Jews, tried to enter the United States, and, although eventually some 250,000 did find a permanent or temporary refuge in the United States, large numbers were turned away by consular and immigration officials, some of whom were prejudiced against Jews. Congress refused to pass a bill to let in several thousand Jewish refugee children. Some escaped elsewhere but others became part of the millions who were later sent to the death camps of the Holocaust. President Franklin D. Roosevelt, although sympathetic to the plight of the refugees, provided no significant leadership on this issue until late in the war. In 1944 he established, by executive order, the War Refugee Board, which brought about a thousand mostly Jewish refugees to the United States and set up camps for many others in Europe and Africa. Many years later, in 1979, Vice President Walter Mon-

This cartoon, entitled "The Only Way to Handle It," reflects what many people thought would happen after the passage of the Immigration Act of 1921. The restriction was actually much less severe.

dale described the situation well: in regard to the Jewish refugees from Nazism, he judged that the United States and other western democracies "failed the test of civilization."

Many of the refugees who did get to the United States made outstanding contributions both to the war effort and to American culture. Much of the research that developed the atomic bomb was done by refugee scientists such as the Italian Enrico Fermi, the Hungarian Leo Szilard, and the Austrian Lise Meitner. The moral authority of the German-born Albert Einstein, perhaps the greatest scientist of the 20th century, had been crucial in persuading President Roosevelt to consider establishing the project which led to the creation of the bomb. American culture was enormously enriched by the temporary or permanent residence of such composers as the German Paul Hindemith and the Hungarian Béla Bartók, the Italian conductor Arturo Toscanini, the German author

Thomas Mann, and a great number of painters, sculptors, and architects.

The years of World War II (1939–45) were, historians now agree, years of great social change in the United States. From the special point of view of immigration history a crucial turning point was reached in late 1943 when Congress, at the urging of President Roosevelt, repealed the Chinese Exclusion Act and, even more important, enabled Chinese, but not other Asians, to be naturalized. After the war was over and the United States began to exercise global influence more powerfully than ever before, it became apparent that U.S. naturalization and immigration policies were not congruent with American foreign policy. It was difficult to be "the leader of the free world" when much of the world's population was ineligible to immigrate to the United States. These peoples naturally resented the discrimination. Following the pattern of Chinese exclusion repeal, both Filipinos and "natives of India" were made eligible for naturalization and thus immigration in 1944, and in 1952 all ethnic and racial bars to naturalization were dropped.

In contrast to its refusal to make exceptions to the quota system for refugees during the war, in 1948 and 1950 Congress passed two bills that allowed some 450,000 "displaced persons" to enter without reference to quotas. Displaced persons were refugees in Europe who were unable or unwilling to be settled in their former homes, largely because the Soviet army had occupied their homelands and installed totalitarian regimes in them on the Russian model. Few of these refugees were Jews: most European Jews had perished in the Holocaust and most of the relatively few survivors went to Israel, not the United States.

In 1952 the McCarran-Walter Act, a major modification of immigration law, was passed over President Harry S. Truman's veto. In addition to its broadening of naturalization, it continued the quota

Immigration During the Era of Restriction	
1925–30	1,762,610
1931–40	528,431
1941–50	1,035,039
1951–60	2,515,479
1961–65	1,450,312
TOTAL	7,291,871

U.S. Bureau of the Census

system, applied new and more rigorous political tests on incoming immigrants and visitors, and greatly expanded the family reunification provisions of the law to include special preferences for brothers, sisters, and unmarried children of U.S. citizens and for spouses and children of resident aliens. Under its provisions, immigration began to climb steadily, so that during its 13-year existence nearly 3.5 million persons immigrated to the United States.

The Era of Renewed Immigration, 1965 to the Present

In 1965, at the high point of the period of social reform that President Lyndon B. Johnson called the "Great Society," Congress finally scrapped the quota principle and substituted an overtly two-track system that began the era of renewed immigration and is still our basic law. In place of national quotas, equal numerical caps were established for each hemisphere, and, at the same time, close relatives of both U.S. citizens and resident aliens were given preferred status; some could come in without regard to numerical restriction. The table on the next page compares the preference systems under the 1952 and 1965 acts.

The growth in the number of immigrants has increased sharply and steadily. There were 2.5 million in the 1950s, 3.3 million in the 1960s, 4.5 million in the 1970s, more than 7 million in the 1980s, and more than 8 million in the 1990s.

Even more important than the increasing numbers were the changes in the

Preference Systems: 1952 and 1965 Immigration Acts

Immigration and Nationality Act, 1952
Exempt from preference requirements and numerical quotas: spouses and unmarried minor children of U.S. citizens.
1. Highly skilled immigrants whose services are urgently needed in the United States and the spouses and children of such immigrants. *50 percent.*
2. Parents of U.S. citizens over age 21 and unmarried adult children of U.S. citizens. *30 percent.*
3. Spouses and unmarried adult children of permanent resident aliens. *20 percent.*
4. Brothers, sisters, and married children of U.S. citizens and accompanying spouses and children. *50 percent of numbers not required for 1–3.*
5. Nonpreference: applicants not entitled to any of the above. *50 percent of the numbers not required for 1–3 above, plus any not required for 4.*

Immigration Act of 1965
Exempt from preference requirements and numerical quotas: spouses, unmarried minor children, and parents of U.S. citizens.
1. Unmarried adult children of U.S. citizens. *20 percent.*
2. Spouses and unmarried adult children of permanent resident aliens. *20 percent (26 percent after 1980).*
3. Members of the professions and scientists and artists of exceptional ability. *10 percent: requires certification from U.S. Department of Labor.*
4. Married children of U.S. citizens. *10 percent.*
5. Brothers and sisters of U.S. citizens over 21. *24 percent.*
6. Skilled and unskilled workers in occupations for which labor is in short supply in the United States. *10 percent: requires certification from U.S. Department of Labor.*
7. Refugees from communist or communist-dominated countries, or the Middle East. *6 percent.*
8. Nonpreference: applicants not entitled to any of the above. *(Since there are more preference applicants than can be accommodated, this has not been used.)*

Immigration and Naturalization Service, *1997 Statistical Yearbook*

sources of immigration and the kinds of immigrants who were coming. Through the 1950s, Europe was the chief source of immigration to the United States, although the preponderance of Europeans was diminishing. By the 1960s, Europeans were only a third of all immigrants; in the 1970s they were less than a fifth; and in the 1980s and 1990s they were just over a tenth. Replacing them were persons from Latin America and Asia in roughly equal numbers. Between 1981 and 1996, about 13.5 million legal immigrants were admitted to the United States. Of the top 10 countries of origin, which accounted for 58 percent of all immigrants, half were in or around the Caribbean and half were in Asia.

In more recent years, partly because of the collapse of the Soviet Union and partly because of the diversity programs enacted in 1988, there has been a significantly wider distribution of immigrants. In 1996, for example, the top 10 countries accounted for a little less than half of all immigrants (49.5 percent) and two European countries, Ukraine and Russia, were numbers 8 and 9 of the top 10.

But it was not just the regional and national origin of immigrants that changed. Large numbers of recent immigrants have been very well educated and possessed of valuable entrepreneurial and

Leading Countries of Origin, 1981–96	
1. Mexico	3,304,682
2. Philippines	843,741
3. Vietnam	719,239
4. China	539,267
5. Dominican Republic	509,902
6. India	498,309
7. Korea	453,018
8. El Salvador	362,225
9. Jamaica	323,625
10. Cuba	254,193

U.S. Bureau of the Census

Spanish-speaking members of the International Ladies Garment Workers Union proclaim their loyalty in two languages at a New York City parade in 1985.

professional skills. Large numbers of others, however, including many refugees from Southeast Asia, had little education and few marketable skills.

The difference in treatment received by immigrants from two adjacent Caribbean islands, Cuba and Haiti, demonstrates the wide gulf that has existed between contemporary groups. The nearly 1 million Cubans who have been admitted since 1959 from Fidel Castro's Cuba as refugees from communism were given special status and relatively generous financial support by the United States government. The much smaller number of Haitians, whom the government refused to regard as refugees, were often rejected and returned to Haiti; those admitted received relatively little financial help.

By the 1980s, many Americans were again becoming nervous about "so many foreigners" coming to the United States. Many advocates of restricting immigration pointed out, correctly, that the total volume of immigration was approaching that of the peak years before World War I, when an average of about a million immigrants entered annually. But they rarely pointed out that the incidence of foreign-born people in the population was much lower than in those years. Despite much debate and many laws enacted by Congress since 1965, none has changed

significantly the volume of immigration. These laws have been aptly described as "thunder without lightning"— that is, laws without much effect. Although public opinion polls showed that, when asked, a majority of Americans was likely to say that there were too many incoming immigrants, when asked, in other polls what issues concerned them most, few put immigration high on the list. Many serious students of immigration believe that as long as the American economy remains reasonably prosperous, there is little likelihood that major bars against immigrants will be raised. A major reason for this is that immigrants in contemporary America, like their predecessors in other eras, come here to work. The work that they do, whether unskilled, semiskilled, or highly skilled, will continue to be a vital element in American economic growth.

AMERICAN IMMIGRATION
A Student Companion

Acadians

- *1990 Ancestry: 668,217 [Acadian/Cajun]*
- *Major period of immigration: 1765–1790s*
- *Major areas of settlement: Louisiana, northern Maine*

Acadia, the present-day Nova Scotia, Canada, was settled by France in 1605. One of the terms of the Treaty of Utrecht (1713), which ended the War of the Spanish Succession (Queen Anne's War), awarded Nova Scotia to Britain, although its inhabitants remained French in language and culture. In 1755, during another war between Britain and France, the Seven Years War (French and Indian War), British troops suddenly rounded up and deported 6,000 to 8,000 Acadians to Georgia, North and South Carolina, and Maryland. They also burned down many of their homes in Acadia to discourage the exiles from returning. A large number of Acadians remained in or returned to Nova Scotia, where their descendants still live in a mainly Francophone (French-speaking) society.

Many of the exiles eventually settled in the southwestern, French-speaking part of Louisiana, which had come under Spanish rule in 1762. The Acadians' exile was an atrocity accompanied by much suffering. It is immortalized in Henry Wadsworth Longfellow's long narrative poem "Evangeline" (1847). Longfellow's poem, once required reading for every American schoolchild, was such a pervasive cultural influence that the area of Acadian (shortened to Cajun in Louisiana) settlement in the bayous of southwest Louisiana is often called "Evangeline country."

Today one can visit the Longfellow-Evangeline Commemorative Area, a 157-acre site southwest of Baton Rouge,

This 1866 engraving shows descendants of Acadians in Louisiana. Their "Cajun" culture lasted for generations.

where the main attraction is a house built in 1765, and believed to have been the home of Louis Arcenaux, the prototype for Gabriel, Evangeline's lover.

Perhaps 20,000 to 25,000 Acadians found their way to Louisiana by the 1790s. A much smaller group moved to northern Maine. In both states the Acadians settled in isolated regions where few non-French speakers lived until well into the 20th century. Very large families were the rule—10 or 12 children were not unusual—so the Louisiana Acadian population grew from 35,000 in 1815 to perhaps 270,000 in 1880.

Cajuns developed a unique culture that featured celebrations such as Mardi Gras, the *easter-dodo,* or public country dance, and creole cooking, which prevailed for close to two centuries. A more recent cultural phenomenon is the distinctive music called zydeco, popular music that combines tunes of French origin with music of

Caribbean origin and the blues, typically performed with guitar, fiddle, accordion, and washboard. The key to the survival of this unique culture was the remarkable persistence of the French language, even though Cajuns lived surrounded by English speakers.

This "language maintenance," as experts call it, has been much studied. Cajun French has evolved very differently from the French spoken in France, or, for that matter, the French spoken in Canada. Anyone speaking "Cajun French" in Paris today would not be understood. In the second half of the 20th century the intrusion of highways into the once isolated bayou country, the spread of public schools taught in English, radio, and television, have combined to make Cajun French an endangered language.

Cajun culture, like other once vibrant immigrant cultures, now exists only as a sort of shadow culture, studied in universities, and celebrated in folk festivals aimed as much at tourists as at the descendants of the exiles.

SEE ALSO

Cajun; Language maintenance

FURTHER READING

Brasseaux, Carl A. *Acadian to Cajun: Transformation of a People, 1803–1877.* Jackson: University Presses of Mississippi, 1992.
Breton, Raymond, and Pierre User. *The Quebec and Acadian Diaspora in North America.* Toronto: Multicultural History Society of Ontario, 1982.
Browne, Turner. *Louisiana Cajuns/Cajuns de la Louisiane.* Baton Rouge: Louisiana State University Press, 1977.

Acculturation

Acculturation is the process by which individuals and groups adjust to another culture. Thus, immigrants coming to the United States must deal with, and are changed by, the ways that Americans do things. But immigrants, especially when they come in large numbers and when they settle densely in particular neighborhoods, sometimes called ethnic enclaves, also cause changes in American culture, which in turn has taken something from every major group that has come.

This modern view replaces the old notion of assimilation, sometimes called Anglo-conformity, in which immigrants were expected to conform, almost instantly, to American ways of doing things. The amount of acculturation that occurs varies with different groups and individuals. For example, a person coming from English-speaking Canada will need relatively little acculturation; anyone immigrating from Britain will, among other things, have to learn to drive on the "wrong" side of the street; someone coming from a country where the language spoken is not English will have to acculturate to the English language at least to some degree.

SEE ALSO

Americanization; Anglo-conformity; Assimilation; Cultural pluralism; Ethnic enclave; Melting pot; Mosaic; Salad bowl; Triple melting pot

FURTHER READING

Gordon, Milton M. *Assimilation in American Life: The Role of Race, Religion and National Origins.* New York: Oxford University Press, 1964.

Afghans

- *1990 Ancestry: 31,301*
- *Immigration, 1986–96: 28,106*
- *Immigration, 1820–1996: 41,393*
- *Major period of immigration: 1980+*
- *Major areas of settlement: San Francisco Bay Area; Los Angeles; New York City; Washington, D.C.; Portland, Ore.*

Afghanistan is a large mountainous country of 251,825 square miles in southwest Asia, nearly as large as Texas, with almost 24 million people. Its people are called Afghans. All but a few are Muslim. Although a few hundred Afghans had come to the United States before 1980, almost all of the perhaps 50,000 Afghans in the United States are refugees who have come since 1980 and their American-born children.

Since 1979, when the Soviet Union invaded Afghanistan, the country has been racked by war and civil war in which an estimated one million or more people have been killed. At one time perhaps as many as 6 million people, a quarter of the population, were living in refugee camps outside of the country. (For the Soviet Union, the Afghan War, 1979–89, was as disastrous as the Vietnam War was for the United States.)

Only a tiny fraction of Afghan refugees—fewer than 30,000—have been admitted to the United States. Most of them are members of the Afghan elite, with a large percentage coming from the capital city of Kabul. Yet even the best-educated Afghans have often had difficulty in adjusting to the United States. One man, a former official of Afghanistan's Ministry of Agriculture, told an interviewer:

> I thought I could get a good job because I was American-educated. I applied for every job I though was appropriate. The welfare department sent me letters saying I am capable of working and I should take any job. Honestly, taking a job in a fast food restaurant is very humiliating for me, but being on welfare is even more humiliating.

Most Afghans, fiercely independent, feel this way, yet many, perhaps most Afghan families in the United States need some kind of government assistance to survive. The major constant in the lives of Afghan Americans is Islam, their religion, and they have contributed to the growing Muslim population in the United States. Even the oldest Afghan Americans born in the United States are only teenagers, so it is very difficult to make generalizations about that community. We can assume that, like other recent refugee populations, most of the American-born generation of Afghans will successfully acculturate to some variant of the American way of life.

SEE ALSO

Acculturation; Muslims; Refugees

FURTHER READING

Leonard, Karen I. *The South Asian Americans*. Westport, Conn.: Greenwood, 1997.
Lipson, Juliene G., and Patricia A. Omidian. "Afghans." In David W. Haines, ed. *Refugees in America in the 1990s: A Reference Handbook*. Westport, Conn.: Greenwood, 1996.

African Americans
• *1998 Census estimate: 34 million*

Most of today's African American population—about 13 percent of the total U.S. population—are descended from the nearly 500,000 slaves brought from Africa and Caribbean before the end of the slave trade in 1808. Many also have some Caucasian and other ancestry, and an increasing minority are descended from the more than 500,000 persons of African birth or ancestry who have immigrated to the United States as free persons. Most of these immigrants have come since the 1980s.

A Sudanese refugee in Utica, New York, looks through donated clothing. Many refugees who come to the United States are sponsored and supported by churches and other religious institutions until they are able to take care of themselves.

Although the vast majority of African Americans are many generations removed from their African roots, many have strong sympathies with contemporary struggles of the new nations of Africa, particularly since the presidency of Nelson Mandela in South Africa beginning in 1991.

There have been, in the 19th and 20th centuries, several "back to Africa" movements, some sponsored by whites who wanted to rid the United States of its population of African origin, others by black leaders. In 1816 a prosperous free black, Paul Cuffe, sent seven black families to Sierra Leone. In that year white Americans organized the American Colonization Society which, between 1820 and 1840, sent about 12,000 African Americans, mostly freed slaves, to Liberia. The Society drew support from many prominent people, including the most prominent western politician, Henry Clay of Kentucky, and was opposed by abolitionists and most black leaders. For example, the black nationalist leader Martin R. Delany denounced it as "anti-Christian in its character" and called it "one of the negro's worst enemies."

There were numerically small back-to-Africa movements in the late 19th century and in the early 20th century. In 1914 an immigrant from Jamaica, Marcus Garvey, founded the Universal Negro Improvement Association, a truly mass organization which, however, did not result in numerically significant emigration. In addition, a few individual African Americans emigrated to Africa in the 20th century, the most prominent of whom was the leading African American intellectual of his era, W. E. B. Du Bois. African Americans, whose roots in the United States are older than those of most ethnic groups, even though they have been badly treated, have demonstrated a determined attachment to America.

SEE ALSO
Africans; Slave trade

FURTHER READING
Franklin, John Hope, and Alfred A. Moss, Jr. *From Slavery to Freedom: A History of African Americans.* 7th ed. New York: McGraw-Hill, 1994, 7th ed.
Kelley, Robin D. G., and Earl Lewis, eds. *To Make Our World Anew: A History of African Americans.* New York: Oxford University Press, 2000.

Africans
- *Immigration, 1986–96: 300,450*
- *Immigration, 1820–1996: 532,213*

Every eighth American is descended from someone who emigrated from Africa. Most of these 34 million people are descended from the nearly 500,000 who were brought in slavery to America prior to the prohibition of the slave trade in 1808. Since that time the immigration of persons from Africa or of African descent has continued.

Many more have come from the Caribbean than from Africa itself. American immigration records list 2,213 free African immigrants in the 19th century; 31,214 up to 1950; 123,825 between 1950 and 1980; and 353,429 between 1980 and 1996. Taking the Western Hemisphere as a whole during the colonial period—that is, up to about 1820—four or five Africans immigrated for every European who came. The impact of Africa and Africans on the Americas is incalculable—in their contributions to the culture, language, music, and soul of the nation, not to mention their (often unpaid) labor in the building of the national infrastructure—and it is impossible to imagine what the history of the Western Hemisphere would have been after Columbus and his European successors came, had no Africans come.

SEE ALSO

African Americans; Arabs; Cape Verdeans; Egyptians; Ethiopians and Eritreans; Slave trade

FURTHER READING

Berlin, Ira. *Many Thousands Gone: The First Two Centuries of Slavery in North America.* Cambridge, Mass.: Harvard University Press, 1998.

Hall, Gwendolyn Midlo. *Africans in Colonial Louisiana: The Development of Afro-Creole Culture in the Eighteenth Century.* Baton Rouge: Louisiana State University Press, 1992.

Klein, Herbert S. *The Atlantic Slave Trade.* New York: Cambridge University Press, 1999.

Albanians

- *Ancestry, 1990: 47,710*
- *Immigration, 1986–96: around 10,000*
- *Major periods of immigration: 1900–24, 1980+*
- *Major areas of settlement: Boston, Mass.; Bronx and Jamestown, N.Y.; Detroit, Mich.*

Albania is a small Balkan nation of 11,000 square miles on the Adriatic Sea. It has a population of 3.2 million, but some 500,000 to 600,000 Albanians lived in the Yugoslav province of Kosovo, which became one of the focal points of fighting in the late 1990s, resulting in United Nations occupation of the province. The first Albanian known to have come to the United States arrived in Boston in 1880. He, and most of the few thousand—primarily young men—who came before 1924, were Eastern Orthodox Christians, even though more than 70 percent of Albanians are Muslim.

In Boston, the focal point of Albanian American settlement, the first ethnic institutions were established, a coffeehouse and a meeting place both named after Scanderbeg, a 15th-century hero who led Albanians against the Ottoman

Albanian American bishop Fan S. Noli blesses his congregation. Priests and ministers were often major immigrant community leaders.

Turks. After World War II, when Albania became a very despotic communist state, many Albanians became refugees. Some of these eventually came to the United States. One of the most prominent Albanian American leaders was Bishop Fan S. Noli, who was a poet, a musicologist, and a translator of Shakespeare into the Albanian language.

SEE ALSO
Yugoslavia

FURTHER READING
Detroit Public Schools. *Multicultural Awareness for the Classroom: The Albanians*. Detroit: Detroit Public Schools, 1993.

Alien

In U.S. law, an alien is a person living in the United States who is not an American citizen. An alien who has entered the United States legally as an immigrant is a resident alien. A person who has entered the United States illegally is an illegal alien. The process of naturalization makes aliens citizens.

SEE ALSO
Citizen; Illegal emigrants; Illegal immigrants; Naturalization

Alien and Sedition Acts

Passed in 1798 during the undeclared naval war with France, the Alien Act empowered the President to order out of the United States all aliens regarded as dangerous to the public peace and safety or suspected of "treasonable or secret inclinations." The Sedition Act

called for a fine of not more than $2,000 and imprisonment for up to two years for persons convicted of publishing "any false, scandalous and malicious writing" attacking the U.S. government, Congress, or the President.

No one was ordered out of the country under the terms of the Alien Act, but 25 persons were charged under the Sedition Act. Ten of those people, many of them European refugees, were convicted. The two acts expired in 1800 and 1801. President Thomas Jefferson pardoned those convicted and Congress repaid the fines with interest.

SEE ALSO
Alien Enemies Act; Nativism; Naturalization

FURTHER READING
Smith, James M. *Freedom's Fetters: The Alien and Sedition Laws and American Civil Liberties*. Rev. ed. Ithaca, N.Y.: Cornell University Press, 1966.

Alien Enemies Act

The first Alien Enemies Act was passed in 1798, five months after the Alien and Sedition Acts, during the undeclared naval war with France. It authorized the President, in time of declared war, to arrest, imprison, or banish any alien national of an enemy power, that is, a person living in the United States who was a citizen or subject of an enemy power. A similar statute remains in force today and has been used in many declared wars. In the War of 1812, World War I, and World War II, many people who were nationals of nations with which the United States was at war were interned.

SEE ALSO
Alien; Alien and Sedition Acts; Internment

FIFTH *CONGRESS* OF THE UNITED STATES:

At the Second Session,

Begun and held at the city of *Philadelphia*, in the state of PENNSYLVANIA, on *Monday*, the thirteenth of *November*, one thousand seven hundred and ninety-seven.

An ACT *respecting alien enemies.*

The original copy of the Alien Enemies Act. President John Adams's signature is visible in the lower left-hand corner.

FURTHER READING

Smith, James M. *Freedom's Fetters: The Alien and Sedition Laws and American Civil Liberties.* Rev. ed. Ithaca, N.Y.: Cornell University Press, 1966.

Alien Land Acts

The first alien land acts were enacted in the late 19th century by a number of states and the federal government in order to limit the right of aliens to own land. These laws were aimed at foreign corporations, not individuals. In 1913, in the midst of an anti-Japanese furor caused by increased immigration of Japanese and anti-Asian racism, California passed an act prohibiting the ownership or sale of land to any "alien ineligible to citizenship." This act affected not only Japanese but all other Asians and limited the ability not only of Japanese but also of Chinese, Filipinos, Koreans, and Asian Indians to earn a living. Ten other western states, from Washington to Texas, passed similar laws, some of which also outlawed all or some leasing of land. These laws were all repealed after World War II, and existing federal civil rights statutes now bar their reenactment.

SEE ALSO

Aliens ineligible to citizenship; Japanese

Aliens ineligible to citizenship

Aliens ineligible to citizenship were persons who could not become American citizens because of their race. In the first naturalization law (1790), the right of naturalization was restricted to "free white persons." The Naturalization Act of 1870 extended the right of naturalization to "Africans" and "persons of African descent"; persons deemed Asians were ineligible for naturalization. In 1943 Chinese, but not other Asians, were made eligible for naturalization, and in 1946 the privilege was extended to Filipinos and "natives of India." The Immigration Act of 1952 ended all ethnic and racial bars to naturalization, and the category "aliens ineligible to citizenship" ceased to exist, although there are a number of other reasons for denying naturalization, chiefly relating to criminal activity.

SEE ALSO

Alien; Asian Indians; Asians; Chinese; Citizen; Japanese; Koreans; Naturalization; *Ozawa* v. *U.S.*; *U.S.* v. *Thind*

Alsatians

Alsatians are people from the region of Alsace (in German, Elsass) a long-disputed border area between France and Germany. In modern times it has been more often under French rule, except for the period 1870–1918 and during World War II, when it was a part of Germany. During periods of German rule, French-speakers were more likely to emigrate, while during periods of French rule, German-speakers were. Thus, Alsatian immigrants were sometimes recorded in American statistics as French, sometimes as Germans, depending on who ruled, not on their ethnic heritage.

SEE ALSO

French; Germans

A group of Alsatians in regional dress arrives at the St. Paul, Minnesota, Union Depot in 1908. Most immigrants quickly adopted American clothes.

Amerasian Acts

The Amerasian Acts are two laws passed in 1982 and 1987 that allow the immigration to the United States of certain Amerasian children. In order to qualify, the children must have been born after December 31, 1950, and before October 22, 1982, in Cambodia, Korea, Laos, Thailand, or Vietnam, and have been fathered by a U.S. citizen. Most of the fathers were American soldiers and the children were often discriminated against in Asia for that reason. After 1987 immediate relatives of Vietnamese children were also eligible. Between 1989 and 1996, 70,744 people, not counted elsewhere, immigrated to the United States under the provisions of these laws. They entered as family members of American citizens but received refugee benefits. Because their American fathers did not sponsor them, special legislation was necessary.

SEE ALSO
Amerasians; Asian Americans; Children; Vietnam War

FURTHER READING
Spickard, Paul R. *Mixed Blood: Intermarriage and Ethnic Identity in Twentieth-Century America*. Madison: University of Wisconsin Press, 1989.

Amerasians

Under U.S. law, Amerasians are children fathered by American soldiers while serving in Asia since 1945, and then abandoned by them. Their mothers are Asian women. These children are often treated badly in the race-conscious societies of East Asia, particularly in Japan and Korea. They have fared somewhat better in Southeast Asia, particularly in Vietnam. There are many thousands of these children—many now adults—but no one knows how many. Some have been able to come to the United States and be reunited with their fathers. Occasionally the term *Amerasian* has been used to describe some Asian Americans, but that is rare.

SEE ALSO
Amerasian Acts; Asian Americans; Children; Vietnam War

FURTHER READING
Spickard, Paul R. *Mixed Blood: Intermarriage and Ethnic Identity in Twentieth-Century America*. Madison: University of Wisconsin Press, 1989.

American nationals

Today American nationals are residents of certain U.S. Pacific territories, such as the Marshall Islands. American Nationals are *not* American citizens, but they have the right to immigrate to the United States and to live and work there. If they wish to become citizens they must become naturalized as though they were aliens. During the period of the American occupation of the Philippines (1900–1946), Filipinos were American nationals.

SEE ALSO
Filipinos; Samoans

American Party

SEE Know Nothing movement

American Protective Association (APA)

The American Protective Association (APA) was an anti-Catholic, anti-immigrant movement that, for a brief time in the 1890s, became an important political force. Founded in Iowa in 1887 by Henry F. Bowers, a pious but bigoted Protestant, it claimed a membership of more than 2 million people in the mid-1890s when an economic depression heightened fears about immigrants. It was strongest in the rural Midwest and in the Pacific Northwest. By 1900, when relative prosperity had returned, its influence was negligible. It had ceased to exist by 1911.

SEE ALSO
Nativism

FURTHER READING
Kinzer, Donald L. *An Episode in Anti-Catholicism: The American Protective Association*. Seattle: University of Washington Press, 1994.

Americanization

In the United States, Americanization has had two meanings, one general and the other specific and historical. The general meaning describes a person or institution becoming "more American," although there is no consensus as to what, exactly, "being American" means apart from the legal sense of possessing citizenship. The specific, historic use of the term refers to the movement in the first three decades of the 20th century in which immigrants were urged and sometimes coerced to use English and to adopt "American" patterns of behavior, what scholars now call Anglo-conformity.

The entry of the United States into World War I in April 1917 heightened American nationalism and induced an increase of nativism, opposition to foreigners. Private civic groups, some employers, the federal government, and many state and local governments all joined in putting on pageants stressing "Americanism," and numerous special educational programs were established to aid in the Americanization process, what is sometimes called acculturation or assimilation. By the late 1920s, with immigration reduced, most of these programs lapsed as what some scholars have called "the Americanization crusade" evaporated.

Outside the United States, the term *Americanization* is usually one of hostility, as many people abroad see the powerful American culture as a threat. As early as 1860, for example, a reporter for *The Times* of London wrote of Americanization "as the greatest of calamities."

SEE ALSO

Acculturation; Anglo-conformity; Assimilation; Cultural pluralism; Nativism

An Americanization poster from Cleveland during World War I presents the same text in English, Italian, Hungarian, Slovene, Polish, and Yiddish.

FURTHER READING

Alba, Richard. *Ethnic Identity: The Transformation of White America*. New Haven: Yale University Press, 1990.

Gordon, Milton M. *Assimilation in American Life: The Role of Race, Religion and National Origins*. New York: Oxford University Press, 1964.

Hartmann, Edward G. *The Movement to Americanize the Immigrant*. New York: Columbia University Press, 1948.

Americans for Responsible Immigration (ARI)

Americans for Responsible Immigration (ARI) was founded by Alan C. Nelson, who was Commissioner of Immigration and Naturalization from 1982 to 1989. The organization outlines a clear anti-immigrant program in its "Mission Statement and Goals":

A.R.I. is a non-partisan organization of people from all ethnic backgrounds working for the common purpose of protecting American citizenship and our heritage of legal immigration.

A.R.I. supports a responsible legal immigration policy for those who desire to become American citizens and make a positive contribution to our society and believes that illegal immigration undermines that policy.

A.R.I.'s purpose is to develop and promote public policies regarding the control of legal and illegal immigration, and to protect American citizens from the burden of supporting illegal aliens, and to educate the public and elected representatives at all levels of government about the problems caused to our society by uncontrolled legal immigration.

Goals

1. To restore the integrity of our borders and ensure that illegal immigration is brought under control through the increase of border law enforcement resources, and ensuring that immigration is a priority issue in all diplomatic negotiations with sending countries.

2. To restore an interior immigration enforcement program designed to locate and, through due process, cause the deportation of the five million illegal aliens currently residing in the United States.

3. To require immigration legislation that will end the current family reunification program (chain migration) and to place higher priority on skill and educational based immigrants.

4. To require legislation that will deny automatic citizenship to children born in the United States of illegal alien parents.

5. To require the issuance of a tamper resistant social security card designed to sharply reduce the number of fraudulently obtained jobs and benefits by illegal aliens.

6. To separate the border patrol from the Immigration and Naturalization Service and expand its function to include all immigration and drug interdiction responsibilities on our borders, between ports of entry.

7. To require a strong national drug control policy designed to curb the cross border trafficking of narcotics and dangerous drugs from Mexico and other countries.

A.R.I. has had its chief influence in California, where it has sponsored numerous anti-immigrant ballot propositions, some of which have been approved by the voters but voided by the courts as unconstitutional.

SEE ALSO

Immigration policy; Nativism

FURTHER READING

Reimers, David M. *Unwelcome Strangers: American Identity and the Turn Against Immigration.* New York: Columbia University Press, 1998.

Amish

Amish are a small Protestant religious group more properly known as Old-Order Amish Mennonites. Mennonites are followers of the 16th-century Dutch Anabaptist religious reformer Menno Simons, who advocated adult rather than infant baptism and absolute pacifism. The Amish are descended from Germanic Swiss followers of Jacob Ammann, who broke away from the larger Mennonite group in the 1690s. They began settling in Pennsylvania in

Many Amish do not drive cars, so this boy in 1957 had to take his date for a buggy ride—and bring his sister along as a chaperon.

the 18th century, when about 500 came from Europe. They settled and have remained in tightknit farming communities. Most Amish still speak the German language of their ancestors, a form of German that sounds "peculiar" to modern Germans. They tend to refer to all other Americans as "English." In outward appearance Amish are distinctive. The men wear broad-brimmed black hats, beards but not moustaches, and plain, homemade clothes usually fastened with hooks and eyes (rather than zippers or buttons). The women wear bonnets, long dresses with capes or shawls, and black shoes and stockings. They avoid jewelry. The Amish believe that in dressing as they do they are following Biblical injunctions, but historians of clothing note that they wear the common dress of 17th-century Germanic Europe.

Amish artifacts, especially quilts, are quite marketable. Some Amish shun all modern technology and travel by horse and buggy; others use tractors. Some refuse to have telephones; others have them but keep them outside of their homes; while still others have them inside their houses. Amish do not believe in "advanced"—that is, high school—education for their children. Some parents have gone to jail because they have

refused to obey compulsory education laws. They are staunch pacifists.

Because of a relatively high birthrate and an insistence that their children follow in Amish traditions, as most do, Amish settlements, once confined to southeastern Pennsylvania, now exist in at least 20 states, particularly Ohio, Indiana, and Illinois, and the Canadian province of Ontario, and comprise more than 100,000 believers. The Amish communities in Europe have been absorbed by larger Protestant denominations.

SEE ALSO

Anabaptist sects; Germans; Hutterites; Mennonites; Pennsylvania Dutch; Religion; Swiss

FURTHER READING

Hostetler, John. *Amish Society*. 4th ed. Baltimore: Johns Hopkins University Press, 1993.

Amnesty

SEE Immigration Act of 1986

Anabaptist sects

Anabaptism (from a Greek word meaning "rebaptizers"), the doctrine that only adult baptism is valid, arose among some Dutch, German, and Swiss Protestants in the 16th century. Some Anabaptist groups, often collectively described as Pennsylvania Dutch, emigrated to America beginning in the 17th century. The most important are Amish, Hutterites, and Mennonites.

SEE ALSO

Amish; Hutterites; Mennonites; Pennsylvania Dutch

Angel Island

Angel Island, a 740-acre island in San Francisco Bay, was the main western immigration station from 1910 to 1940, when it was closed because it was unsanitary and unsafe. Unlike its eastern counterpart, Ellis Island, whose function was to make it easier for immigrants to enter the United States safely, the purpose of Angel Island was to enforce the terms of the Chinese Exclusion Acts and to make it as difficult as possible for Chinese and other Asian immigrants to get in. Prospective Chinese immigrants were subjected to detailed examinations that usually lasted for weeks. One man was kept waiting for two years. Perhaps 50,000 Chinese did gain admission; some 9,000 were sent back. Many of the latter were so-called paper sons, men and boys who falsely claimed relationships with American citizens in order to gain entrance to the United States. The detention barracks on Angel Island, which are now open to visitors, have poems in Chinese characters carved into the soft wood of its walls. One such poem may be translated:

> Lin, upon arriving in America,
> Was arrested, put in a wooden
> building,
> And made a prisoner.
> I was here for one Autumn.
> The Americans did not allow me
> to land.
> I was ordered to be deported.
> When the news was told,
> I was frightened and troubled
> about returning to my country.
> We Chinese of a weak nation
> Can only sigh at the lack of freedom.

The detention barracks were declared a National Historic Landmark in 1997.

SEE ALSO
Chinese Exclusion Acts; Ellis Island; Paper sons

FURTHER READING
Daniels, Roger. "No Lamps Were Lit for Them: Angel Island and the Historiography of Asian American Immigration." *Journal of American Ethnic History* 17 (Fall 1997): 4–18.
Lai, Him Mark, Genny Lim, and Judy Yung. *Island: Poetry and History of Chinese Immigrants on Angel Island, 1910–40.* Seattle: University of Washington Press, 1991.

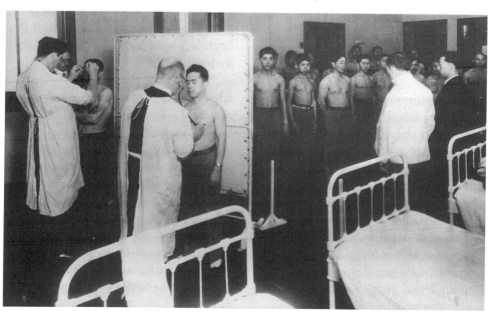

During the medical examination at Angel Island, immigrants were checked for ailments such as syphilis, hookworm, and trachoma, a common eye disease. It was only one of many hurdles to pass before being declared eligible to enter the country.

of vandalism against synagogues and other Jewish institutions, and Jews were a secondary target of such organizations as the second Ku Klux Klan. As nasty and vicious as American anti-Semitism could be, however, it only rarely resulted in homicides.

The establishment of the federal Fair Employment Practices Committee (FEPC) in 1940, the passage of state fair employment acts during and after World War II, and the growing awareness of the horrific dimensions of the Holocaust have tempered and reduced American anti-Semitism, but it still exists in a variety of forms, including vandalism against synagogues and cemeteries, and exclusion from private social organizations.

SEE ALSO

Discrimination; Jews; Ku Klux Klan; Nativism; Prejudice; Restrictive covenant; Stereotype

FURTHER READING

Dinnerstein, Leonard. *Antisemitism in America.* New York: Oxford University Press, 1994.
Jaher, Frederick C. *A Scapegoat in the New Wilderness.* Cambridge: Harvard University Press, 1994.

Arabs

- *1990 Population: not available*
- *Major periods of immigration: 1900–24, 1948+*
- *Major areas of settlement: Northeast, Detroit*

Although the vast majority of the world's Arabs are Muslim, until the 1970s by far most of the Arabs living in the United States were Christians. They came primarily from what are now Lebanon and Syria, areas that, before World War I, were part of the Ottoman (Turkish) Empire. Christian Arabs emi-

grated to West Africa and Latin America as well as to the United States.

Although in the United States and Canada Arabs were generally called "Syrians," in the other regions they were usually called "Turks." In the United States after about 1920, when the region from which they had come became the country of Lebanon, most began to refer to themselves as Lebanese, and sometime after World War II they—along with the growing Muslim population—began to refer to themselves as Arab Americans.

The earliest immigrants in the late 19th century were almost exclusively young men, but large numbers of women and children soon followed. The major economic niche that the early Arab immigrants made for themselves was in peddling. As many as 90 percent of male immigrants before 1914 did some kind of peddling.

As with many immigrant occupations, peddling was one that they developed in the United States, not in their homeland. Some were city peddlers who slept at home every night, while others criss-crossed the entire country on trips that lasted for weeks or even months. Initially most peddlers sold rosaries, other religious items, and knickknacks: things that could be carried in a pack. Most soon learned enough English to claim that they came from "the Holy Land" (although few were actually from Palestine), which gave a special appeal to their religious items. As peddlers became more prosperous, they progressed to using horse and wagon, and later the automobile, and could carry larger and more varied items. Many if not most peddlers eventually became store owners or operators.

The 1930 census identified 7,500 "Syrians" in New York City, which was then the largest concentration. By 1970 there were 70,000 persons who identified themselves as Arab Americans living in and around Detroit, which has become the "capital" of Arab America.

There were a few Muslim Arabs in the United States before World War II, but it was very difficult to practice their religion, as there were only a few mosques before the 1950s. One scholar has reported that upon discovering that America was *bilad kafur*—a land of unbelief—one prospective immigrant immediately got off the ship to the United States, because he did not want to live among unbelievers.

That has all changed. There are at least half a million Arab American Muslims in the United States and the nation is dotted with mosques. The Arab immigrants who have come have been students, refugees, and ordinary immigrants, and, like other immigrants in contemporary America, they practice chain migration, in which relatives or friends follow each other to a new country. In the 1990 Census, 355,000 Americans reported that they spoke Arabic at home.

Contemporary Arab immigrants range from rich and well-to-do businessmen and students from Saudi Arabia to poor Yemeni farm workers in California. Most live in large cities and work at urban occupations and professions.

Many Arab Americans have experienced discrimination and even hate crimes, both because of their religion and because of American conflicts with some Arab nations. Mosques have been vandalized and burned. (Arab Americans experienced discrimination and hate crimes during times of American conflicts with Iran, even though Iranians, while largely Muslim, are not Arabs.) In the 1990s, when there were serious terrorist atrocities against Americans in both the United States and abroad—most tragically, the bombings

of New York's World Trade Center in 1993 and the American embassies in Kenya and Tanzania in 1998—committed by individuals who were Arabs, the negative stereotype of Arabs was heightened, and transferred to Arab Americans who were innocent.

As their numbers have increased, Arab Americans have found more acceptance in American society. A few of the public service billboards and media spot announcements, which once urged Americans to "Attend the church of your choice," and were then amended to include synagogues, now say "Attend the church, synagogue or mosque of your choice."

In 1996, perhaps 20,000 Arabs were recorded as entering from Iraq,

Arab men perform the act of Wudhu—purification by washing before prayer—in the male washing room (there is a separate one for women) of Philadelphia's Al-Aqsa Islamic Society School and Mosque in 1999.

Israel, Jordan, Lebanon, Kuwait, Oman, Qatar, Saudi Arabia, Syria, United Arab Emirates, and Yemen. One says "perhaps 20,000" because the census records nationality, not ethnicity, and Iraq and Lebanon are Arab countries with significant non-Arab populations, while Israel is a Jewish country with a sizable Arab minority.

SEE ALSO

Chain Migrations; Eastern Rite churches; Muslims; Nativism; Prejudice; Stereotype

FURTHER READING

Naff, Alixa. *Becoming American: The Early Arab Immigrant Experience.* Carbondale: Southern Illinois University Press, 1985.
Orfalea, Gregory. *Before the Flames: A Quest for the History of Arab Americans.* Austin: University of Texas Press, 1988.

Argentinians

- *1990 Ancestry: 63,176*
- *Immigration, 1986–96: 28,651*
- *Immigration, 1932–96: 149,995*
- *Major period of immigration: since 1960*
- *Major areas of settlement: California, New York, Florida, New Jersey*

Argentina, a large country at the southern end of South America, contains a little more than a million square miles. It is one-third larger than Alaska, more than twice the size of Texas, and has a population of 36 million people. Like the other two nations of South America's southern cone, Uruguay and Chile, the overwhelming majority of its population is of European descent. Argentina drew its people primarily from Spain and Italy. Many more people have immigrated to Argentina than have emigrated from it. Its people speak Spanish and some 90 percent of the population

is Roman Catholic. Perhaps 2 percent of the population is Jewish: these 700,000 people constitute the largest Jewish group in Latin America and the fifth largest in the world.

The Spanish settled Argentina in the 16th century and it remained a Spanish colony until independence in 1810. Its developing economy, based on cattle ranching and wheat farming, produced the same kinds of products as the United States did, so that Argentina's export trade was typically with Europe.

Numerically significant immigration from Argentina to the United States began in the 1950s, when nearly 20,000 came. The peak was reached in the 1960s, when nearly 50,000 came. In no decade since have more than 30,000 come. Argentinian immigration has been propelled by several periods of political instability and by periods of economic uncertainty marked by very high inflation. Since that time, while skilled and largely middle-class Argentineans have emigrated to the United States and, to a lesser degree to Europe, unskilled immigrants have come to Argentina from neighboring countries. Little has been written about Argentinean Americans, but the Census Bureau's data, which probably missed some of the poorest recent immigrants, showed that just over half of them have some higher education and that 7.8 percent of their households were below the poverty line.

SEE ALSO

Hispanics; South Americans

Armenians

- *1990 Ancestry: 308,096*
- *Immigration, 1992–96: 20,848*
- *Major period of immigration: 1880–1924*
- *Major areas of settlement: Northeast; California, especially Fresno*

The region known as Armenia, the homeland of the Armenians, was, during most of modern times, divided among three powers: Turkey, Russia (the Soviet Union), and Persia (Iran). Since the dissolution of the Soviet Union in 1991, there has been an independent Republic of Armenia, where some 3.5 million Armenians live. Only since 1992 have American immigration records listed Armenians separately.

The Armenians are an ancient people who, unlike most of their neighbors, were converted to Christianity early in the Christian era. Numerically significant Armenian immigration to the United States did not begin until about 1880, although at least one came to America very early: the records of the Jamestown colony list a "Martin the Armenian" who came in either 1618 or 1619.

Although, as is the case with other ethnic groups that did not have a country of their own, it is not always easy to recognize Armenians in the immigration and census records, most authorities believe that about 100,000 Armenians came between 1880 and 1924. Much of that immigration was "pushed" by the persecution of Armenians, particularly but not exclusively in Turkey. The worst persecution was a horrible series of events in 1915 which few Armenians have been able to forget: the massacres—many would say genocidal massacres—of some 600,000 Armenian men, women, and children by Turks. These events had been preceded by outbreaks of severe persecutions and killings in 1894–96 and in 1909.

The 50,000 Armenians who came to the United States before World War I arrived by two different routes and

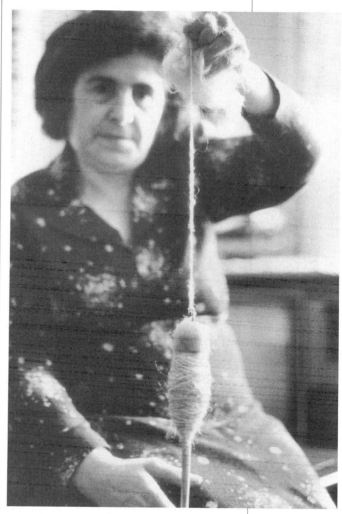

This Armenian woman is practicing a traditional craft. She is spinning wool, in this case for a rug, on a spindle rather than on a spinning wheel.

established very different communities. The larger group came from Turkey, landed in New York, and worked in northeastern and midwestern factories, as did most of the immigrants of that era. The 1909 persecutions intensified this migration: in 1913 alone some 10,000 came.

The second and smaller stream was a migration from Russian Armenia to the Prairie Provinces—Manitoba, Saskatchewan, and Alberta—of Canada. Most Armenians did not find the Canadian prairies to their liking, and moved from Canada to California—particularly around Fresno. Perhaps 2,500 were settled in Fresno by 1914. Unlike the Armenians in the eastern United States, and unlike most other 20th-century immigrants generally, they settled on the land.

The Armenians of the Fresno region, who were celebrated by Fresno-born William Saroyan, the best-known Armenian American author, have a rich history. By 1930 some 30,000 foreign-born Armenians lived there as opposed to 7,000 in New York City, the second largest center. Here some established the only all-Armenian town in America: Yettem ("Eden" in Armenian).

Ironically, it was only in the Fresno region that special discrimination against Armenians developed, because it was the only place where Armenians were numerous enough to be seen as a special threat. The most enduring discrimination was in the form of restrictive covenants that prevented persons of Armenian ancestry from buying houses in most of Fresno's better neighborhoods. They were also barred from social clubs, the YMCA, and some churches.

Most Armenian immigrants were members of the Armenian Apostolic Church, which in 1992 claimed 150,000 members. In the five years after the 1991 dissolution of the Soviet Union, some 20,000 Armenians immigrated to the United States.

SEE ALSO
Eastern Orthodox churches; Push; Restrictive covenants

FURTHER READING
Mirak, Robert. *Torn Between Two Lands: Armenians in America, 1890 to World War I.* Cambridge: Harvard University Press, 1983.
Saroyan, William. *My Name is Aram.* New York: Harcourt, Brace, 1940.

Artists, immigrant

Before 1700, the fine arts were largely nonexistent in the North American colonies, but after 1700 increased wealth and leisure attracted a number of portrait painters from Europe, including John Smibert from England and Gustavus Hesselius and Pieter Vanderlyn from Holland. These men helped set artistic standards and taught and inspired budding American artists. By the late 18th century it was the American-born artists who became immigrants, studying and sometimes settling in foreign capitals, especially London. The most important of these were John Singleton Copley and Benjamin West, who became painter to the king and president of the Royal Academy, never returned to America.

In the 19th century few important immigrant painters came to the United States, but two of the most important American painters, James Abbott McNeil Whistler and John Singer Sargent spent most of their professional lives in London or Paris. In the middle and late 19th century, American artists were drawn to the European continent. Frank Duveneck made Munich, Germany, an important place for the training of American artists, but it was Paris, particularly after the development of impressionism, which drew the most and the most important artists, such as Mary Cassatt, who went there to study and work.

By the 20th century, although American artists still studied abroad, immigrant artists were again drawn to the United States: some, such as the Russian-born sculptor Alexander Archipenko, came fleeing political upheavals; others, such as the Polish-born sculptor Elie Nadelman, were drawn by American opportunities. In addition, some immigrants, such as the Lithuanian William Zorach, developed into important artists after they came to the United States. The rise of fascism in Europe in the 1920s and 1930s and World War II sent many famous artists into exile in the United States, large numbers of whom were Jewish. Many of the exiles returned to Europe after the war, while others remained permanently. A few of the most prominent were the Russian Marc Chagall, the Spaniard Salvador Dalí, the German Max Ernst, the Lithuanian Jacques Lipchitz, the Dutch Piet Mondrian, and the French Yves Tanguy. Perhaps even more important was the influence of a number of important refugee art historians, the most eminent of whom was the German Erwin Panofsky, who spent more than three decades at the Institute for Advanced Study in Princeton, New Jersey. As a group, the refugee art historians established the discipline in American universities.

SEE ALSO
Refugees

FURTHER READING
Fleming, Donald, and Bernard Bailyn, eds. *The Intellectual Migration: Europe and America, 1930–1960.* Cambridge: Harvard University Press, 1969.
Taylor, Joshua C. *The Fine Arts in America.* Chicago: University of Chicago Press, 1979.

Aryan

The term *Aryan* was used most narrowly to describe some of the ancient languages of India and Iran, of which Hindi is the most widely spoken direct descendant. More broadly it is used to describe a family of languages, often called Indo-European, which include not only the languages noted above but also Greek, Latin, Celtic, Teutonic, and Slavic. A few 19th-century European nationalists and racists began to speak about an "Aryan" and superior "race,"

a misconception taken up by Adolf Hitler and his Nazi followers, who wanted first to expel and then exterminate "non-Aryans," chiefly Jews but also Gypsies. In the contemporary U.S. a few racist and extremist white supremacist groups called themselves Aryan, for example, the Aryan Nation.

Asia-Pacific triangle

The "Asia-Pacific triangle" is a term used in U.S. immigration law between 1952 and 1965 to describe a large area comprising much of Asia apart from China, India, Japan and the Philippines, to which was assigned a minimal and discriminatory quota of 100 per year. In 1952 the "Asia-Pacific triangle" replaced the "Asiatic barred zone" of earlier legislation, which had forbidden immigration from that area. It was replaced, in 1965, by the hemispheric admissions policy of the relatively nondiscriminatory Immigration Act of 1965.

SEE ALSO
Asiatic barred zone; Immigration Act of 1917; Immigration Act of 1952; Immigration Act of 1965

Asian Americans

Asian American is a term used since the 1960s to describe Americans of Asian birth or ancestry, but rarely used to describe those of Middle Eastern birth or origin. The 1990 census recorded about 7 million such persons. Formerly the term "Oriental" was used.

SEE ALSO
Asian Indian; Chinese; Filipinos; Japanese; Koreans; Vietnamese; and other specific ethnic groups

Asian Indians

- *1990 Population: 786,694*
- *Immigration, 1986–96: 378,608*
- *Immigration, 1820–1996: 680,969*
- *Major period of immigration: 1965+*
- *Major area of settlement: New York–New Jersey*

The term *Asian Indian* was adopted by the U.S. Census Bureau in 1980 to describe immigrants from India and their descendants because of confusion with American Indians and with Pakistanis and Bangladeshis. Previously the terms "East Indian" and "native(s) of India" had been used. While a few Asian Indian seamen were probably in the United States in the late 18th and early 19th century, the first numerically significant immigration from India came to the United States around 1900 as part of a larger movement that brought thousands of Asian Indians to western Canada.

Between 1900 and 1917, when American law virtually stopped Indian immigration for four decades, perhaps 10,000 came to America, a large percentage of whom were Sikhs. All but a few hundred of these were male laborers who worked on the West Coast as laborers in the northwestern timber industry and on railroad construction gangs.

Eventually most Asian Indians went into agriculture. Many became agricultural proprietors in two regions of California, the Imperial and the Sacramento valleys. Almost all were from the Punjab and most were Sikhs. The remainder were college students and merchants who were widely dispersed.

The general western prejudice against Asian immigrants quickly attached itself to Asian Indian immigrants, whom the ignorant public usually called "Hindoos" or "rag-heads" (the latter term refers to the turbans that the Sikh religion requires all men to wear). Indian immigration was brought to a stop by three separate aspects of American law: the so-called LPC provision, first adopted in 1882, which barred the admission of anyone immigration authorities deemed "likely to become a public charge"; the more specific "Asiatic barred zone" of 1917 which excluded most non-Chinese Asians by barring immigrants from parts of Asia designated by degrees of latitude and longitude; and the Immigration Act of 1924 which barred the immigration of "aliens ineligible to citizenship." Merchants and students could still enter on temporary visas. In addition, those few thousand Asian Indians who were permanent residents were, like all other Asians, ineligible to naturalization.

Asian Indian immigration resumed after a 1946 law made "natives of India" eligible for naturalization, and by 1970 there were perhaps 70,000 Asian Indians in the United States. From then on, under the liberal provisions of the Immigration Act of 1965, Asian Indian immigration grew rapidly. In the 15-year period between 1981 and 1996, nearly half a million came to the United States, making them the sixth most numerous immigrant group of those years.

The vast majority of these post-1965 immigrants, like most residents of India, have been Hindus: over 300,000 persons told the census taker in 1990 that they spoke one of two major languages of India, Hindi or Urdu, although most recent immigrants from India have a good command of English when they come.

Dalip Singh Saund (far right), the first Asian elected to the U.S. Congress, visits government officials in his native India with his wife in 1957. California elected Saund to the House of Representatives in 1956 and he served three terms.

Contemporary Asian Indian immigrants are extremely well educated. Nearly two-thirds of the men and almost half the women are college graduates. They have pursued professional and entrepreneurial occupations. A prominent occupation often mentioned in the press is in the computer industry, for instance, as software engineers, and, increasingly, as entrepreneurs. One interesting "niche" that a surprising number of Asian Indians have found is running motels. So many immigrants from the Indian state of Gujarat, where the most common surname is Patel, have entered this business that a community joke speaks of "hotel, motel, Patel." Obviously this was not an occupation back in Gujarat. (See, for instance, the film *Mississippi Masala*.)

Small motels require relatively little capital and a large amount of unskilled labor, and most Asian Indian immigrants have relatives who can help supply both capital and much of the labor. The Patel name is so common that an Asian Indian traveling salesman developed a formula for finding an Indian restaurant in a strange town, if none are listed in the yellow pages. He counts the number of Patels in the white pages. If there are fewer than 10, there will be no restaurant. If there are more than 10 he calls one up, says he is from India, and asks where a restaurant is.

Asian Indian Americans, like other dark-skinned foreigners, have encountered sporadic discrimination and violence in recent years. The worst instances were in Jersey City, New Jersey, in the late 1980s where Indian men and women were regularly harassed on the street. One young man, an executive of a New York City bank, was beaten so badly by a group of youths that he died in the hospital. Most of those committing violent act seem to have been young, native-born, lower-class whites who resented the obvious economic success of many Indians who seemed to them to be taking over what they regarded as "their" neighborhood.

Despite these and other setbacks, Asian Indians as a group seem to be doing well. Hindu temples are being built all over America, often in places not usually associated with Asian immigration. For example, a Hindu temple and community center was built in 1998 in Pelham, Alabama, outside Birmingham. Most Asian Indians have been in the United States only a very short time. About a quarter, mostly children, are American-born, and more than two-fifths of those here in 1990 had arrived during the previous 10 years. In 1996 the INS and the Census Bureau estimated that there were 33,000 Asian Indians illegally in the United States, which placed India 17th as a source of illegal immigrants.

SEE ALSO

Aliens ineligible to citizenship; Asiatic barred zone; Gujaratis; Hindus; Illegal immigrants; Immigration Act of 1924; Immigration Act of 1965; LPC clause; Nativism; Naturalization; Sikhs

FURTHER READING

Kitano, Harry H. L., and Roger Daniels. *Asian Americans: Emerging Minorities.* 2nd ed. New York: Prentice-Hall, 1995.
Leonard, Karen I. *The South Asian Americans.* Westport, Conn.: Greenwood, 1997.

Asians

- *Immigration, 1986–96: 3,412,989*
- *Immigration, 1820–1996: 7,894,571*

Most scholars believe that today's Native Americans are descended from peoples who emigrated to North America tens of thousands of years ago. In modern times, only handfuls of Asians, most of them seamen, had crossed the little-traveled Pacific to the United States by the end of the 1840s. Soon after Asians began to come, discriminatory laws were enacted against them. First Chinese, and then all alien immigrants were barred, and Asians were forbidden to become naturalized citizens. During World War II and afterward, discriminatory laws were gradu-

ally repealed, and after 1965 Asians were able to immigrate to the United States without specific discrimination.

SEE ALSO

Afghans; Asian Americans; Asian Indians; Bangladeshis; Cambodians; Chinese; Filipinos; Hmong; Indonesians; Japanese; Koreans; Laotians; Pakistanis; Taiwanese; Thais; Tibetans; Vietnamese

FURTHER READING

Chan, Sucheng. *Asian Americans: An Interpretive History.* Boston: Twayne, 1991.
Kitano, Harry H. L., and Roger Daniels. *Asian Americans: Emerging Minorities.* 2nd ed. New York: Prentice-Hall, 1995.
Takaki, Ronald. *Strangers from a Different Shore: A History of Asian Americans.* Boston: Little, Brown, 1989.

Asiatic barred zone

The Asiatic barred zone was created by Congress in 1917. It was a part of the Asian exclusion policies that prevailed between 1882 and 1952. It prohibited the immigration of Asians not already otherwise excluded by delimiting a broad geographic area, using degrees of latitude and longitude but without naming countries or ethnic groups. The barred zone included all of Southeast and southern Asia, but not the countries west of what are now Pakistan and Afghanistan.

SEE ALSO

Immigration Act of 1917

Assimilation

Assimilation is a term used by many to describe the adjustment of immigrants to the host country's culture. Many scholars

now prefer the term *acculturation*. Others, like Alejandro Portes and Min Zhou, have recently proposed a model of "segmented assimilation . . . three possible patterns" likely to occur in present-day immigrant families. "One of them replicates the time-honored portrayal of growing acculturation and parallel integration into the . . . middle-class; a second leads straight into the opposite direction to permanent poverty and assimilation into the underclass; still a third associates rapid economic advancement with deliberate preservation of the immigrant community's values and tight solidarity." It is possible to imagine a large immigrant family in which some individuals take each path.

SEE ALSO

Acculturation; Americanization; Anglo-conformity; Assimilation; Cultural pluralism; Ethnic enclave; Melting pot; Mosaic; Salad bowl; Triple melting pot

FURTHER READING

Gordon, Milton M. *Assimilation in American Life: The Role of Race, Religion and National Origins.* Oxford University Press: New York, 1964.
Portes, Alejandro, and Min Zhou. "The New Second Generation: Segmented Assimilation and Its Variants among Post-1965 Immigrant Youth." In *The Annals* (1993): 74–98.

Asylees

An *asylee* is a refugee who applies for asylum—that is, legal entry as a refugee—even though he or she is already in the country, either as a legal visitor or illegally. The Refugee Act of 1980, passed in an attempt to regularize American refugee policy, was the first recognition of "the right of asylum" in American law. An asylee must be a person unable or unwilling to return to his or her country of nationality because of persecution or a well-founded fear of persecution. Persecution or the fear of persecution may be based on the person's race, religion, nationality, membership in a particular social group, or political opinion. Between 1980 and 1996 asylum was granted to 112,638 applicants, and to some 18,000 in 1996 alone.

SEE ALSO

Asylum; Refugee Act of 1980; Refugees

Asylum

Asylum, in modern times, is protection offered by one nation to exiles or refugees from another nation. Until 1980 there was no right of asylum in the United States. The Refugee Act of that year, which used criteria set by the United Nations, established that right, which was successfully claimed by 112,638 applicants between 1980 and 1996, including some 18,000 in 1996 alone.

SEE ALSO

Asylees; First asylum; Refugees

Australians

- *1990 Ancestry: 52,133*
- *Immigration, 1986–96: 19,249*
- *Immigration, 1820–1996: n.a.*
- *Major periods of immigration: 1849–50, 1945–48*
- *Major area of settlement: California*

Australia, itself a continent settled by immigration, has never sent very many immigrants to the United States, nor attracted many Americans as permanent settlers. A vast nation of nearly 3 million square miles (the United States has 3.5 million square miles) Australia has about the same population, about 18 million, as the state of New York.

Immigration to the United States was statistically significant in only two widely separated periods. The first was in 1849–50, when perhaps 6,000 persons from Australia, perhaps 10 percent of its European population, participated in the California gold rush. When, in 1851, gold was discovered in Australia, most of them returned, along with a large number of others who had been seeking gold in California.

The second period of relatively heavy immigration came just after World War II, when some 10,000 Australian war brides—women who married American soldiers stationed in Australia—emigrated to the United States. The two most prominent Australian immigrants in the 20th century have been the labor leader Harry Renton Bridges and the newspaper magnate Rupert Murdoch. In addition, a relatively large number of professional athletes have come, particularly tennis players, and, to a lesser degree, basketball players. Because they acculturate very easily and there are so few of them, there are no special Australian enclaves in the United States.

SEE ALSO
War brides

FURTHER READING
Monaghan, Jay. *Australians and the Gold Rush: California and Down Under, 1849–1954.* Berkeley: University of California Press, 1966.

Austrians
- *1990 Ancestry: 864,783*
- *Immigration, 1986–96: 5,596*

- *Immigration, 1820–1996: n.a.*
- *Major periods of immigration: 1880–1914, 1920s, 1938–41*
- *Major areas of settlement: New York, Midwest*

American immigration statistics list 1.8 million "Austrians" as having immigrated to the U.S. since 1820, but these figures reflect the fact that the multinational Austro-Hungarian Empire, which was broken up after World War I, was the eighth largest source of immigrants. Most of these were subject nationalities, and most are treated under their ethnic group names: Poles, Czechs, Slovaks, Hungarians, Italians, Croats, etc. Modern Austria is small (32,000 square miles) and has a population of 8 million. Some 85 percent of modern Austrians are Roman Catholics. This essay will treat (1) Austrian immigrants of Germanic extraction during the period of the Empire and (2) any citizen of Austria after that. Contemporary Austria, and particularly its capital, Vienna, is highly multicultural. Many Austrian immigrants to the United States have simply been treated as if they were Germans.

A few Austrians came in the colonial period, most important of whom were about fifty families of the approximately 30,000 Protestant Salzburgers who became refugees after the Catholic Bishop-prince of Salzburg began persecuting them in the 1730s. These families settled in Georgia and became so well acculturated that one of their number became the first elected governor of the state.

In the 19th and early 20th centuries, Austrian immigrants were all but indistinguishable from other German speakers: they went to the same Catholic churches, joined the same social and athletic organizations, and read the same German-language newspapers. One historian has examined Wisconsin, the most German of American states, and found that according to the state census of 1905, for example, the 2,319 family heads born in Austria were evenly divided between rural and urban residences, and lived in the same places as most other German-speakers. Within Austria the heaviest area of emigration was Burgenland, a poor province south of Vienna.

The annexation of Austria by Nazi Germany in 1938 created intolerable conditions for the many Austrian Jews, most of whom were Viennese. Most perished in the Holocaust, but a small minority escaped, including some 30,000 who came to the United States. These were mostly middle-class professionals who settled primarily in New York City. Included among them were a number of cultural luminaries including pianist Artur Schnabel, composer Arnold Schoenberg, conductor Bruno Walter, author Franz Werfel, economist Ludwig von Mises, and psychiatrist Theodor Reik. Some found asylum elsewhere, such as Sigmund Freud (in England) and the physicist Lise Meitner (in Sweden). After the war additional refugees came.

In recent years few Austrians have immigrated, but Vienna has served as an important transit point for refugees coming from the Soviet Union.

SEE ALSO

Austro-Hungarian Empire; Refugees

FURTHER READING

Höebling, Walter, and Reinhold Wagnleitner, eds. *The European Emigrant Experience in the U.S.A.*. Tübingen: Gunter Narr Verlag, 1992.

Spaulding, E. Wilder. *The Quiet Invaders: The Story of the Austrian Impact on America*. Vienna: Österreichischer Bundesverlag, 1968.

Austro-Hungarian Empire

The Austro-Hungarian Empire, or Dual Monarchy, existed between 1867 and 1918 and was one of the great sources of immigrants to the United States. The Austro-Hungarian Empire, like the Hapsburg Austrian Empire that preceded it, was the home of many subject nationalities, including Poles, Czechs, Slovaks, Ukrainians, southern Slavs, and Italians, as well as the ruling Austrians and Hungarians. American immigration data recorded more than 4 million immigrants from the empire.

Azerbaijanis

- *1990 Population: 2,000 (est.)*
- *Immigration, 1986–96: n.a.*
- *Immigration, 1890–1920: n.a.*
- *Major periods of immigration: 1950s, since 1991*
- *Major area of settlement: New York–New Jersey*

Azerbaijanis, also known as Azeri Turks, number about 9 million in their homeland, which is divided between the Russian Federation and Iran. The first Azerbaijanis in the United States we know about came from Germany in the 1950s. They were prisoners of war captured by the Germans in Russia who chose not to return to the Soviet Union. They came to the United States under provisions of the Displaced Persons Acts of 1948 and 1950, which made special provisions to admit victims of World War II to the United States. At about the same time, a second small group came from Turkey, to which they had fled from the Soviet Union in the 1920s. The 1991 collapse of the Soviet Union set off sporadic warfare between them and neighboring Armenians, which may result in other refugees coming here. The Azerbaijanis are Muslims, divided between Shiite and Sunni branches.

SEE ALSO

Displaced persons; Displaced Persons Acts; Muslims; Refugees

Azoreans

SEE Portuguese

Bahais

Bahais are members of a religion founded in Persia (now Iran) by a religious leader, Baha Ullah, and promulgated by his eldest son Abdul Baha. The father had been an adherent of Babism, a religious movement that broke away from Islam in Persia in the middle of the 19th century. Bahais believe that Baba Ullah is but the most recent in a line of prophets that includes Abraham, Moses, Christ, and Muhammad. They hold that all religions are one and believe in universal education, world peace, and the equality of men and women.

The Bahai faith has spread from Iran and has today perhaps 5 million adherents, about a fifth of whom lived in Iran before the revolution of 1979. Heavily persecuted there since then, many have emigrated to the United States. In the United States the center of worship is the great temple at Wilmette, Illinois, a northern suburb of Chicago.

SEE ALSO

Iranians

FURTHER READING

Smith, Peter. *The Bahá'i Religion*. Oxford: Oxford University Press, 1988.

Bahamians

- *1990 Ancestry: 21,081*
- *Immigration, 1986–96: 8,978*
- *Immigration, 1820–1996: n.a.*
- *Major periods of immigration: since 1965*
- *Major area of settlement: Florida*

The Bahamas consist of nearly 3,000 islands and islets, none of them large, and only 29 of them inhabited. The islands extend almost 800 miles, from about 50 miles off the Atlantic coast of southern Florida running south and east nearly to Haiti. About 260,000 people live on them, most on New Providence Island where the capital city, Nassau, is located. About 85 percent of the people are of African descent, with most of the rest Euro-Americans. English is the official language and most inhabitants are Protestants.

When Columbus "discovered" America in 1492, his first landfall was in the Bahamas. The islands were then inhabited by a group of native Americans, Arawaks, who were wiped out by the Spanish and their diseases. The Spanish never colonized the Bahamas, so the islands were uninhabited, except for occasional pirates, until British settlement began in the mid-17th century. After the American Revolution, many American loyalists emigrated to the Bahamas, bringing their African and African American slaves with them. The British ruled the Bahamas until 1973, when it became an independent nation and member of the British Commonwealth.

Barbadians

- *1990 Ancestry: 35,455*
- *Immigration, 1986–96: 14,485*
- *Immigration, 1820–1996: n.a.*
- *Major periods of immigration: 1900–24, 1940–45, 1965+*
- *Major area of settlement: New York City, especially Brooklyn*

Barbados is a small Caribbean island, 166 square miles, whose population of more than 250,000 makes it the most densely populated nation in the Western Hemisphere. It was uninhabited when the first British settlers arrived in 1627. Barbados was a British colony until 1966, when it became independent. Its linkages to the United States stretch back to the 17th century.

The first immigrants from Barbados were white settlers, some of them former indentured servants, who were displaced by African slaves brought to Barbados in vast numbers for its booming sugar industry after 1650. Almost as many African slaves were brought to the tiny island as to all of British North America, what is now the United States. Later in the colonial period some Barbarian slave owners immigrated to the Carolinas, where they purchased plantations and made other investments. Some brought African or Afro-Caribbean slaves with them.

Numerically significant free Afro-Caribbean migration to the United States began around 1900 and was largely halted by the Immigration Act of 1924 and the Great Depression of the 1930s. During World War II, a large number of Barbadians were among the West Indians (perhaps 50,000 in all) brought to the United States under government contract to do agricultural labor in the eastern United States. Almost all of this heavily male contingent returned to Barbados.

The Immigration Act of 1952 made it much more difficult for Barbadians and other black West Indians to come to the United States.

The distinctive culture of Barbadian immigrants in Brooklyn is described in Paule Marshall's 1959 novel, *Brown Girl, Brownstones*. The Immigration Act of 1965 again encouraged immigration, and since that time there has been a steady migration, largely to New York City and environs.

A majority of these immigrants have been women. Many of them, coming at a time when married American women with young children were moving rapidly into the work force, found initial employment opportunities in domestic work and child care. Many of these immigrants left their own children in Barbados in the care of grandparents. By the 1990s, however, only about a quarter were in service industries and more than half were in white- or pink-collar jobs. Barbadians, along with others from the West Indies, have shown a penchant for American politics. Herbert Bruce, who became the first black elected Democratic district leader in Manhattan was a Barbadian, and Shirley Chisholm, a black woman who was elected to the House of Representatives and who competed for the Democratic Presidential nomination in 1968, is a second-generation Barbadian American.

SEE ALSO

Immigration Act of 1924; Immigration Act of 1952; Immigration Act of 1965; Indentured servants; Slave trade; West Indies

FURTHER READING

Chisholm, Shirley. *Shirley Chisholm: Unbought and Unbossed*. New York: Houghton, Mifflin, 1970.

Barred Zone

SEE Asiatic barred zone

Barrio

A barrio is a Spanish-speaking ethnic neighborhood, usually but not always Mexican American or Puerto Rican American.

SEE ALSO
Ethnic enclave

Basques

- *1990 Ancestry: 47,956*
- *Major periods of immigration: intermittent since mid-19th century*
- *Major areas of settlement: Nevada, Idaho, and California*

Basques generally do not appear in the census or the immigration reports because Basques are divided between two nations, Spain and France. The Basque homeland runs along the Atlantic Coast of both countries from Bilbao to Bayonne. Of the roughly 2.5 million people of this region, only about 200,000 are French. Basques tend to refer to themselves as *Euskaldunak*, "speakers of *Euskera*" as the Basque language is called. Only about a quarter of the people who now live in the Basque homeland are speakers of that language. There has been, for the last decades, a strong movement for Basque independence or autonomy, and some of its supporters have resorted to terrorism.

Basques, who may represent one of the oldest surviving peoples in Europe, have a long migratory tradition. Many have been seamen and fishermen; many members of Columbus's crew were Basques, and so was Ferdinand Magellan's first mate, Juan Sebastián de Elcano, who completed the circumnavigation of the globe after Magellan was killed in the Philippines. Many Basques participated in the Spanish conquests in Latin America and in the administration of the Spanish Empire. The first Basques to come to the United States were attracted by the California gold rush of 1849, and since that time Basque immigration has focused on the Far West. Immigration patterns developed so that the French Basques went largely to California, while the more numerous Spanish Basques tended to settle in Nevada and Idaho.

Not gold but sheep and cattle ranching have been the main attraction for most Basque immigrants since the

American-born children of Basque descent with sheep on an Idaho ranch during the 1930s. Although most Basques began as shepherds, today they are in all walks of life.

gold rush. For a long period in the late 19th and early 20th centuries there was severe hostility to Basque ranchers and sheepherders. An Idaho newspaper complained in 1909, "These Bascos . . . are on a par with the Chinaman. . . . They are filthy, treacherous and meddlesome . . . clannish and undesirable . . . and unless something is done will make life impossible for the white man."

As the 20th century progressed, the image of the Basques changed. Basque sheepherders became greatly prized, so much so that Congress, at the urging of Nevada senator Patrick McCarran, passed special legislation enabling western ranchers to bring in sheepherders as contract laborers. Well into the 1970s the majority of the several thousands thus brought to the United States were Basques, but the relative prosperity of contemporary Spain has caused the program to shift its focus to Latin America. In addition, a number of second- and third-generation Basques have become prominent politicians in several western states, most notably Paul D. Laxalt, who served Nevada as both governor and U.S. senator.

A special institution that western Basques developed was the "Basque hotel" or boardinghouse. Normally run by a European-born Basque well acculturated to American ways, the hotels served as permanent addresses for nomadic sheepherders, and the owner served as an intermediary between newly arrived Basques and American society. Since the hotels usually recruited Basque young women to work, the hotels served as a kind of marriage broker for the male ranchers. The wives often returned to the hotels from their isolated ranches for the last weeks of their pregnancies. Eventually the best hotels drew local non-Basques looking for a good meal, and, in more recent years, they have become minor tourist attractions.

There have been smaller concentrations of Basques in the eastern United States, sometimes caused by the presence of jai alai, the Basque national sport, which is played on elaborate courts, called frontons. In Miami jai alai has been established as a spectator sport since before World War II. People gamble via pari-mutuel machines on the results of matches. In the 1970s jai alai spread to Connecticut and Rhode Island. Wherever it is played, professional players are recruited from the Basque region.

In addition, many people of Basque ancestry have come to Miami from Fidel Castro's Cuba, where Basques have settled since the 16th century.

SEE ALSO
Spaniards

FURTHER READING
Douglas, William, and Jon Bilbao. *Amerikanuak: Basques in the New World*. Reno: University of Nevada Press, 1975.

Belgians

- *1990 Ancestry: 380,498*
- *Immigration, 1986–96: 6,765*
- *Immigration, 1820–1996: 215,107*
- *Major period of immigration: 1900–24*
- *Major area of settlement: Great Lakes states*

The nation of Belgium, created by international treaty in 1830, covers about 12,000 square miles in Western Europe and has more than 10 million people. The Belgians are largely of two ethnic groups, the Flemings and the Walloons. The Walloons, the larger of the two groups, speak French, while the Flemings speak Flemish, a language very much like Dutch. The Walloons are mostly Catholic and the Flemings largely Protestant. A few Walloon individuals played significant roles in early American history. Several Protestant Walloon families, whose most prominent member was Peter Minuit, were among the earliest settlers of Manhattan island and the Hudson River Valley, and a number of Catholic priests accompanied early explorers, including Father Louis Hennepin, who was a member of La Salle's Mississippi River expedition in 1675.

Of the 200,000+ immigrants listed above, about 63,000 came in the 19th century, some 75,000 between 1900 and 1924, and some 70,000 since then. (Perhaps another 18,000 emigrated to Canada and then remigrated across the border without being counted.) About 7,000 came between 1986 and 1997. Although some Protestants of both groups emigrated for religious reasons, until all but the most recent period, most Belgian immigrants came seeking agricultural work.

The same fungus that caused the dreadful Irish potato famine of the 1840s, *Phytophthora infestans*, had dire effects on Belgian agriculture as well, although Belgium was not as dependent on the potato as Ireland was. The emigration of poor Belgian farmers was often aided by the Belgian government, which subsidized emigration to Algeria and Guatemala as well as to the United States. During the American Civil War some Belgians were recruited in Europe to fight in the Union army.

Each ethnic group concentrated in a different area of the Great Lakes states. Both Flemings and Walloons settled heavily in Michigan, and Walloons settled in Wisconsin, Illinois, and Indiana.

In most cases neither group established separate identities: Protestant Flemings tended to interact and assimilate with Dutch immigrants, while Walloons tended to mix with French and French Canadians. But Catholic Flemings in southern Michigan found themselves unacceptable to the militantly Protestant Dutch Reformed Church. Neither Belgian group suffered significant discrimination as Belgians from American nativists, although Belgian Catholics of both groups would be affected by any anti-Catholicism in their area of settlement. The only joint Walloon-Flemish settlement was in Mishiwaka, Indiana, a suburb of South Bend, where there were a number of Belgian American secular organizations.

In recent decades Belgian immigrants, like most nonrefugee immigrants, have been largely professionals who have constituted a small part of the "brain drain" that, while diminishing the country of origin, has enriched American life since World War II.

SEE ALSO
Dutch; French; French Canadians

FURTHER READING
[Belgian Ministry of Foreign Affairs]. *Belgians in the United States*. Brussels, 1976.
Lucas, Henry S. *Netherlanders in America: Dutch Immigration to the United States and Canada, 1789–1950*. Grand Rapids, Mich.: Eerdmans, 1989.

Belorussians

- *1990 Ancestry: 4,277*
- *Immigration, 1992–96: 21,414*
- *Immigration, 1820–1996: perhaps 250,000*
- *Major periods of immigration: 1880–1914, 1945–52*
- *Major areas of settlement: Northeast and Midwest, especially New Jersey and Cleveland*

Belorussians (sometimes Byelorussians) are a Slavic people who had no national state in modern times until the emergence of the Republic of Belarus when the Soviet Union broke up 1991.

Belarus has a population of 10 million in a territory of 80,000 square miles, a little smaller than Utah. Belorussians are sometimes called "White Russians," a literal translation of *Belarusy*. (This should not be confused with the political term White Russian, used during and after the Russian Revolution of 1917, when opponents of the communist or "Red" Russians were called "White Russians," regardless of their ethnicity.) Belorussians were never singled out by either American census takers or immigration officials before 1992, so their number can only be roughly estimated. Probably between 175,000 and 200,000 persons who could be called Belorussians immigrated to the United States in the years before World War I, but many of them had little sense of ethnic identity and thought of themselves as Russians, Poles, or Lithuanians. As the ancestry figures for the 1990 census show, very few American are conscious of a specifically Belorussian identity. This may change, however, now that Belarus is an independent nation.

The Belorussians who came before World War I did the same kind of hard, low-paying industrial work that most of their fellow immigrants did in those years, and they settled generally in the cities and factory towns of the Northeast and Midwest.

SEE ALSO
Slavs

FURTHER READING
Kipel, Vitaut. *Belarusans in the United States*. Lanham, Md.: University Press of America, 1999.
Magocsi, Paul Robert. "Belorussians." In Stephan Thernstrom, ed., *The Harvard Encyclopedia of American Ethnic Groups*. Cambridge: Harvard University Press, 1980.

Bilingual education

SEE Education

Birthright citizens

Birthright citizens are people whose citizenship comes from their place of birth as opposed to parentage or naturalization. The United States has had birthright citizenship since the adoption of the 14th Amendment to the Constitution in 1868, which provides that "All persons born or naturalized in the United States . . . are citizens of the United States and the state in which they reside." Thus, a child born in the United States is an American citizen regardless of the citizenship or status of its mother.

SEE ALSO
Citizen; Naturalization

Boat people

Boat people is a term first applied to Vietnamese fleeing their country after the Vietnam War ended in 1975. It has also been applied to some Haitians and Cubans trying to reach the United Sates in small boats.

SEE ALSO
Cubans; First asylum; Haitians; Refugees; Vietnamese

These Mexican workers were caught in the United States by the Border Patrol and are being returned to Mexico at a crossing point at Calexico, California.

Border Patrol, United States

In 1924 Congress created the Border Patrol as a component of the Immigration and Naturalization Service "to patrol the land border and stop smuggling." By 1950 most of the Border Patrol's resources had shifted to the U.S.–Mexican border to prevent illegal immigration.

The Border Patrol has steadily expanded, and numbered more than 6,300 agents in 1997. During the 1996–97 fiscal year 1,549,876 apprehensions were recorded, although many individuals were apprehended more than once. Despite this record number, a much larger number of persons is believed to have entered the United States illegally.

The places where the largest numbers of apprehensions were made are all on the border with Mexico. Much smaller numbers of persons were apprehended at other points, as the list at right shows.

Apprehensions at Top Border Sectors, 1996–97	
Mexican Border	
San Diego, Cal.	483,815
Tucson, Ariz.	305,348
McAllen, Tex.	210,553
El Paso, Tex.	145,929
Laredo, Tex.	131,841
Del Rio, Tex.	121,137
Elsewhere	
New Orleans, La.	8,642
Miami, Fla.	8,250
Buffalo, N.Y.	2,090
Spokane, Wash.	1,342

Immigration and Naturalization Service, *1997 Statistical Yearbook*

The Border Patrol has been the subject of much criticism by national and international civil rights organizations, including Amnesty International. The Immigration and Naturalization Service, while admitting some instances of civil rights violations, including homicides, by Border Patrol agents, insists that, in the overwhelming number of instances, proper procedures are observed.

SEE ALSO

Illegal immigrants; Immigration and Naturalization Service

FURTHER READING

Heyman, Josiah McC. "United States Surveillance at the Border: Snapshots of an Emerging Regime." *Human Organization,* Vol. 54, no. 4 (Winter 1999): 430–38.

Human Rights Watch/Americas. *Crossing the Line: Human Rights Abuses along the U.S. Border with Mexico Persist amid Climate of Impunity.* New York: Human Rights Watch/Americas, 1995.

United States Immigration and Naturalization Service. *The Border Patrol: Its Origin and Its Mission.* Washington, D.C.: Government Printing Office, 1978.

Bosnian Muslims

- *1990 Ancestry: n.a.*
- *Immigration, 1992–96: 11,255 [Bosnia-Herzegovina]*
- *Immigration, 1820–1996: around 35,000*
- *Major periods of immigration: 1900–14, 1945–52*
- *Major area of settlement: Chicago*

Bosnian Muslims are people who speak the Serbo-Croatian language but are adherents of Islam. Most are descendants of persons who were converted from Christianity during the long Ottoman occupation of their homeland in Bosnia and Herzegovina, which began in the 15th century and lasted until 1878. The 1971 census in the former Yugoslavia listed nearly 1.8 million Muslims, about 8 percent of the population. Perhaps another 100,000 live in Turkey, to which they emigrated after the Ottomans were ousted. Bosnian Muslims are ethnically indistinguishable from most of their neighbors, who are either Roman Catholic or Orthodox; in fact, before the terrible civil war in the former Yugoslavia in the 1980s and 1990s, many persons called themselves either Muslim Serbs or Muslim Croats, depending on where they lived.

Bosnian Muslims began to immigrate to the United States around 1900. Most of the few thousand who came were single males, many if not most of them sojourners. They worked at various industrial employments and in construction of highways and tunnels. The largest concentration was in the Chicago–Gary, Indiana area, and Chicago remains the major center of Bosnian Muslim population. For a time a number of Bosnian Muslims worked in the copper mines of Butte, Montana, but there is no longer a community there.

After World War II several thousand Bosnian Muslims came as displaced persons, and there has been a small immigration since the 1960s. This more recent immigration, although predominantly male, contains more women than that earlier in this century. These immigrants are better educated than their predecessors and they have come intending to remain.

The Bosnian Muslims of Chicago founded a fraternal benefit society in 1906 and set up two cemeteries, one for bachelors and one for married members and their families. They did not have enough money to establish a mosque, but prayer meetings were held in individual homes. In 1955 a mosque largely for Bosnians was established in Chicago, and in 1976 a large Islamic center was built in Northbrook, a Chicago suburb. As has been true of many recent institutions for Muslims in the United States, the Northbrook Islamic center was built with substantial financial subsidies from Saudi Arabia and Kuwait.

During and after the wars spawned by the breakup of Yugoslavia, Bosnian immigration, largely of the family variety, increased, although relatively few people were involved.

SEE ALSO

Displaced persons; Muslims; Refugees; Sojourners; Yugoslavia

FURTHER READING
Lockwood, William G. "Bosnian Muslims." In Stephan Thernstrom, ed., *The Harvard Encyclopedia of American Ethnic Groups*. Cambridge: Harvard University Press, 1980.
St. John, Warren. "The Talk of the Town: A Bosnian Diaspora in Astoria" [New York City]. *The New Yorker,* Sept. 11, 1995, 31–32.

Bracero program

The Bracero program was a cooperative effort between the United States and Mexican governments that brought hundreds of thousands of male Mexican workers to fill labor shortages in the United States between 1942 and 1947 and between 1951 and 1959. Although not officially counted as immigrants, many braceros stayed in the United States or returned later. The term *bracero,* (literally, "one who swings his arms"), derives from *brazo,* the Spanish word for arm, and refers to someone who does manual labor, in this case usually harvesting fruit and vegetables, although a number of braceros also did maintenance work on American railroads.

SEE ALSO
Mexicans

FURTHER READING
Craig, Richard B. *The Bracero Program: Interest Groups and Foreign Policy.* Austin: University of Texas Press, 1971.
Driscoll, Barbara A. *The Tracks North: The Railroad Bracero Program of World War II.* Austin: University of Texas Press, 1999.

Brain drain

The term *brain drain* was coined in 1963 to describe the emigration of highly skilled and educated people from one country to another, typically from a lesser developed country to a highly developed one such as the United States. While there have always been some highly educated immigrants to the United States—there were a large number of college graduates, for example, in the Puritan "great migration" of the 1630s and 1640s, and an extraordinary number of outstanding intellectuals and artists came to the United States as refugees in the 1930s and during World War II—only in the years after the 1960s have there consistently been a high percentage of very well educated immigrants year after year. Silicon Valley in California, and other centers of high-tech enterprise, have attracted computer scientists

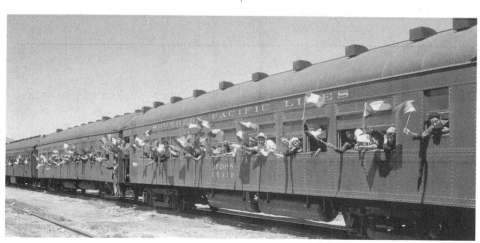

Some Braceros, like these waving Mexican flags, worked on railroad tracks during World War II.

and technicians from all over the world, especially from India and Taiwan.

SEE ALSO

Artists, immigrant; Canadians; Exiles; Musicians, immigrant; Scientists, immigrant; Refugees

Brazilians

- *1990 Ancestry: 65,875*
- *Immigration, 1986–96: 47,461*
- *Immigration, 1820–1996: n.a.*
- *Major period of immigration: since 1980*
- *Major areas of settlement: New York, Boston, southern Florida*

Brazil is the largest country in South America, whose 3.3 million square miles make it larger than the lower 48 American states. Most of its 164 million people speak Portuguese and are descended from immigrants from Africa, Portugal, Spain, Italy, Japan, and a number of other nations. Brazil, which did not abolish slavery until 1888, imported more than 3.6 million enslaved Africans, some 38 percent of all the slaves brought to the New World. Perhaps 44 percent of Brazil's people can trace some of their ancestors to Africa. There is a sizable Native American population as well.

Brazilians use the slang Portuguese term *Brazucas* to describe Brazilians in the United States. Some authorities believe than there were as many as 300,000 Brazilians in the United States toward the end of the 1990s, several times more than the recorded immigration. Most of these are persons who entered legally as tourists and deliberately overstayed their visas. Although it is illegal for such people to work, most manage to do so.

Many Brazilians are engaged in what scholars call circular migration—that is, they go back and forth—but Brazilians call it "yoyo" migration. Recent immigrants report that they are "economic refugees" or "economic prospectors" fleeing Brazil's recent economic problems, low wages, high unemployment, and inflation. Most Brazilian immigrants have low-wage, low-skill jobs, often in the service sector, which is typical for recent immigrants without extensive education. Few black Brazilians—about 44 percent of the nation's population—have immigrated to the United States, almost certainly because anti-black prejudice is much more apparent in the United States than in Brazil.

SEE ALSO

Illegal immigrants; Portuguese; Slave trade; South Americans

FURTHER READING

Margolis, Maxine L. *Little Brazil: An Ethnography of Brazilian Immigrants in New York City.* Princeton, N.J.: Princeton University Press, 1994.

British

SEE Cornish; English; Irish; Manx; Scotch-Irish; Scots; Welsh

Buddhists

Buddhists are adherents of Buddhism, a religion founded in India by Siddhartha Gautama, called the Buddha ("the enlightened one"), sometime around 525 B.C. It is one of the world's great religions, with an estimated 300 million followers throughout the world. Although it has all but disappeared in India, it is particularly strong in Tibet,

Immigration from Asia after 1965 led to the establishment of many Buddhist temples, such as this one in Chicago, as well as many mosques.

Japan, Southeast Asia from Vietnam to Burma, and in Sri Lanka.

In the United States until the second half of the 20th century, almost all of the Buddhists were immigrants from Japan and their descendants, although the first Buddhist temple was located in San Francisco in 1853, before any significant number of Japanese were in America. Since 1965 relatively large numbers of Buddhists have come to the United States as refugees from Vietnam, Laos, and Cambodia so that Southeast Asian Americans are now the majority among American Buddhists who may number, all told, perhaps 2 million persons.

Buddhism, once seemingly alien to American culture, is now so well established that the U.S. Army has recognized Buddhist chaplains and more than 1,500 Buddhist centers of one kind or another have been established.

SEE ALSO

Religion

FURTHER READING

Kashima, Tetsuden. *Buddhism in America.* Westport, Conn.: Greenwood. 1977.

Layman, Emma McCloy. *Buddhism in America.* Chicago: Nelson-Hall, 1976.

Seager, Richard H. *Buddhism in America.* New York: Columbia University Press, 2000.

Tweed, Thomas A. *The American Encounter with Buddhism, 1844–1912: Victorian Culture and the Limits of Dissent.* Bloomington: Indiana University Press, 1992.

Bulgarians

- *1990 Ancestry: 29,595*
- *Immigration, 1986–96: 5,074*
- *Immigration, 1820–1996: around 100,000*
- *Major periods of immigration: 1900–10, 1989+*
- *Major area of settlement: Great Lakes states, especially Michigan*

Modern Bulgaria is a nation of 8.6 million people in a territory of nearly 43,000 square miles, much of it mountainous. Its people are about 85 percent Orthodox and 13 percent Muslim. Emigration from Bulgaria began around 1900 and, initially, was composed almost exclusively of single young men who worked in unskilled and semi-skilled jobs in American industry. The majority of these young men, perhaps 50,000 in number, like millions of other young male immigrants of that era, were primarily sojourners who intended to work for a while in the United States, save some money, and return home. Those who decided to remain in the United States often sent for "mail order" or "picture" brides from Bulgaria.

Most Bulgarians are Eastern Orthodox in religion, and at one time, early in the 20th century, there were at least 31 Bulgarian Orthodox churches in the United States, but by the post–World War II era there were many fewer. Most Bulgarian churches in the United States are affiliated with the Orthodox Church.

Before World War II many Bulgarian Americans were affiliated with left-wing organizations, both socialist and communist. Conversely, many of the numerically fewer postwar refugees and displaced persons were militantly anti-communist. In recent years, after the disintegration of the Soviet Union and the Warsaw Pact, immigration from Bulgaria has increased a little, and may be expected to grow modestly in the foreseeable future. The contemporary immigration is largely economic in nature and consists of families.

SEE ALSO

Displaced persons; Eastern Orthodox churches; Sojourners

FURTHER READING

Carlson, Claudia, and David Allen. *The Bulgarian Americans.* New York: Chelsea House, 1990.

This 1908 photo shows a group of immigrants in Chicago identified as "unemployed Bulgarians." Immigrants, especially recent immigrants, are often the first to be laid off during hard times.

Cajuns

The word *Cajun* was originally a Louisiana corruption of *Acadian,* the name for the French Canadians who were exiled from their home in Nova Scotia by the British in the 1750s. Now the term is often used not only for Acadians but also for any person from Louisiana, certain types of Louisiana cooking, etc.

SEE ALSO
Acadians

Cambodians

- *1990 Ancestry: 134,955*
- *1990 Population: 149,047*
- *Immigration, 1986–96: 58,772*
- *Immigration, 1970–96: around 120,000*
- *Major period of immigration: since 1975*
- *Major areas of settlement: California, Massachusetts, Washington*

Only in the aftermath of the Vietnam War did significant numbers of Cambodians come to the United States. Almost all came as refugees. Relatively few were westernized, and, except for a small number of elite escapees, most were almost totally without material possessions when they came. The census figures from 1990 showed that more than 42 percent of Cambodians in America lived in poverty, that their per-capita income was barely over $5,000 a year, that more than three-quarters did not speak English very well, and that more than half lived in households in which no one spoke English very well. Of persons over 25, only 1 in 12 of the

males and fewer than 1 in 25 of the females was a college graduate.

In addition to the horrors of the Vietnam War, Cambodians suffered through the murderous regime of the Cambodian leader Pol Pot which deliberately massacred an estimated 1 million Cambodians—including most of the intelligentsia—who did not agree with his fanatical regime. Journalist Sydney Schanberg's Pulitzer Prize–winning reports from the "killing fields" (and the film of the same title made from them) grippingly describe the atrocities of Pol Pot's reign of terror, which lasted for nearly four years, 1975–79.

Cambodians, like Laotians and Hmong, have been in the United States for such a short time that it is difficult to make meaningful generalizations about their experiences except to note their poverty and their lack of the kinds of skills which make for success in a high-tech society. Much will depend on what happens to the American-born generation. As of 1990, there were 30,000 of the American-born, or one Cambodian American in five. The oldest cohort among them were of college

A Cambodian refugee attends a cosmetology class in a vocational high school in 1994. Her goal was to be an actress, though her parents strongly objected.

age in the middle of the 1990s. The fate of this cohort and its descendants will be crucial for the status of the Cambodian American community.

SEE ALSO

Refugees; Vietnam War

FURTHER READING

Hein, Jeremy. *From Vietnam, Laos, and Cambodia: A Refugee Experience in the United States.* New York: Twayne, 1995.
Schanberg, Sydney H. *The Death and Life of Dith Pran.* Viking: New York, 1985.

Campanilismo

Since Italy became a unified nation only in 1870, many Italian immigrants before 1930 at first tended to think of themselves as from a village or a region rather than a country. This phenomenon is known as *campanilismo*, from the notion that only those who lived within earshot of the local bell tower (*campanile*) were truly one's fellow countrymen. Believing this, many Italian immigrants, even in large cities, tried to recreate village and small-town clustering. One scholar identified 17 such mini-neighborhoods within early 20th-century Chicago's Little Italy. Campanilismo can be seen even in the ways that Italian Americans have practiced religion. Unlike immigrant Catholics from Ireland or Poland, their loyalty was not so much to a national church as to the local patron saint or madonna, and the special feast day, or *festa*, was the most important cultural celebration of the year.

SEE ALSO

Italians

FURTHER READING

Orsi, Robert. *The Madonna of 115th Street: Faith and Community in Italian Harlem, 1880–1950.* New Haven: Yale University Press, 1985.

Canadians

- *1990 Ancestry: 549,990*
- *Immigration, 1986–96: 154,351*
- *Immigration, 1820–1996: 4,423,066*
- *Major periods of immigration: 1860–1900, 1920s, 1950s–70s.*
- *Major areas of settlement: the northern tier of states west of New England; Florida*

[This entry treats all immigrants from Canada except for French Canadians. The immigration data, but not the ancestry data, do include French Canadians, who consider themselves as a distinct people.]

Modern Canada has 28 million people in a vast nation of 3.8 million square miles, an area slightly larger than the United States. From the time of the American Revolution there has been a constant mingling of the Canadian and American peoples. In addition, from 1820 to 1965, large numbers of immigrants from other places used Canada as a stopping-off place on a journey to the United States. The bulk of the traffic has been from north to south, from Canada to the United States. In 1937 the official Canadian statistician reported wistfully that "if we count all of Canadian stock perhaps a third of us are south of the [border], while certainly not more than 1 percent of the Americans are north." Half a century later Statistics Canada "guesstimated" that of perhaps a million Canadians living abroad, 84 percent of them were in the United States.

But in four distinct periods there has been significant south-to-north traffic, emigration from the United States to Canada. The first of these periods came in the aftermath of the American Revolution, when 80,000 American Loyalists left the new United States whose breakaway from England they had opposed. Half of them, about 40,000, settled in Canada, where they became a key element in the then-minority Anglophone (English-speaking) population of Canada. In Canada they are known as United Empire Loyalists.

The second period of U.S. emigration to Canada came in the decades before World War I, when thousands of Americans, some of them recent immigrants, chose to settle on the Canadian prairies where there was still free or nearly free farming land to be had. The third period was during the Great Depression of the 1930s, when many recent immigrants from Canadian farms to American cities lost their jobs and returned home. The fourth and latest period of emigration was during the Vietnam War in the 1960s and 1970s, when perhaps 50,000 young Americans went to Canada to avoid military service in a war they did not support. In addition, as long as slavery existed in the United States, small numbers of African Americans found sanctuary in Canada. These men and women were the founders of Canada's black population.

Although a few handfuls of Canadian sympathizers with the American Revolution had moved south during and just after the war, numerically significant Canadian immigration to the United States began in the decades after the Revolution. Most of the several thousand in the 18th century were American Loyalists re-emigrating. After 1815, to encourage emigration to Canada rather than to the United States, the British government artificially lowered the prices of ship tickets to Canada from British ports, making them substantially cheaper than fares to the United States. Many immigrants took advantage of the low fares and then moved south, sometimes on foot, to the United States. One historian has pointed out that much of "the second colonization of New England" by Irish immigrants was accomplished by way of Canada and that the routes by which they traveled can be identified by looking for the earliest Catholic churches founded in northern New England.

This kind of transitory migration was often not reflected in the immigration statistics of either country, as border crossing was not closely monitored. Such immigration continued throughout the 19th and into the 20th century until restrictive U.S. immigration statutes made such entries by non-Canadian citizens difficult, though not impossible. Many of the earliest immigrants from India, for example, entered North America through Victoria and Vancouver and quickly moved south.

The attraction of the United States for Canadians was largely economic. Between 1860 and 1900 nearly 2.5 million people left Canada, the vast majority of them for the United States. These decades are the only ones in Canada's history as a nation in which more people emigrated than immigrated. While many of these emigrants took jobs at the lower end of the economic ladder, other migrants were well trained and well educated, and offer one of the first examples of "brain drain" migration to the United States.

Canada has often lost some of its best and brightest sons and daughters who saw greater economic opportunity south of the border. The distinguished American economist John Kenneth Galbraith is just one example of this continuing phenomenon. For a short time, in the 1950s and 1960s, as Canadian universities were expanding, there was a "brain gain" to Canada's benefit, as a significant number of American academics found teaching positions in Canada, but protective Canadian legislation has largely stemmed that flow.

The restrictive American immigration legislation in the 1920s, the so-called Quota acts of 1921 and 1924, created opportunities for Canadian immigrants, especially those seeking industrial jobs, because Canadians—as long as they were not of Asian ancestry—were not affected by numerical limits. This advantage ended with the Immigration Act of 1965, and the end of that advantage probably accounts for the ending of the relative boom in Canadian emigration between 1950 and 1970. While most Anglophone Canadian immigrants to the United States, like their British counterparts, have been "invisible immigrants," in recent times two small but highly visible groups of Canadians, motion picture stars such as Raymond Massey and John Candy, and hockey players such as Gordie Howe and Paul Kariya, have been highly visible. And, in a relatively recent development, significant numbers of Canadians, largely retirees, have been attracted by the warmer southern and southwestern American climate and settled in Florida and in the desert Southwest of the United States. This partly accounts for the presence of professional hockey teams in those unfrozen climes.

Although discussions of illegal immigrants rarely feature Canadians, the INS and the Census Bureau estimate for 1996 made Canada, with 120,000 such persons, as the fourth most numerous source of illegal immigrants. Canadians were not, however, high on the list of those illegal immigrants who availed themselves of the opportunity to gain citizenship under the 1986 Immigration Act, as only 6,312 persons did so. Neither of these last statistics distinguishes between Canadians and French Canadians.

SEE ALSO

Brain drain; French Canadians; Illegal immigrants; Immigration Act of 1921; Immigration Act of 1924; Immigration Act of 1965; Immigration Act of 1986

FURTHER READING

Hansen, Marcus Lee, and John Bartlett Brebner. *The Mingling of the Canadian and American Peoples.* New Haven: Yale University Press, 1940.
Thompson, John H., and Stephen J. Randall. *Canada and the United States: Ambivalent Allies.* 2nd ed. Athens: University of Georgia Press, 1997.

Canadians, French

SEE French Canadians

Cape Verdeans

- *1990 Ancestry: 50,772*
- *Immigration, 1986–96: 9,819*
- *Immigration, 1820–1996: around 55,000–65,000*
- *Major periods of immigration: 1900–1920; since 1965*
- *Major areas of settlement: New Bedford, Mass.; southeastern New England*

The 15 Cape Verde islands are some 350 miles off the shore of Senegal in West Africa. Uninhabited when Portuguese navigators discovered them in the mid-15th century, they were ruled by Portugal for half a millennium until the Republic of Cape Verde was established in 1975. The earliest Portuguese settlers brought relatively large numbers of African slaves to the island, and persons of mixed European and African ancestry, called Creoles, comprise 71 percent of the present population of nearly 400,000. While the official language is Portuguese, most Cape Verdeans speak Crioulo, a language

Cape Verdeans pick cranberries in a Massachusetts bog. This is stoop labor of the back-breaking variety.

that evolved from Portuguese and several West African languages.

The initial immigration of Cape Verdeans to the United States began after American whalers stopped to take on drinking water in the islands signed on Cape Verdeans as crew members toward the end of the 18th century. This pattern became traditional, and some Cape Verdeans made New Bedford, Massachusetts, the center of the American whaling industry, their home. Thus, Cape Verdeans were the first Africans to sail to America voluntarily.

By the end of the 19th century, as the whaling industry died, some Cape Verdean entrepreneurs bought American vessels and sailed between the islands and New England ports, bringing goods one way and immigrants the other. Other Cape Verdeans became pickers in the cranberry bogs of New England, and a few have become bog-owning cranberry farmers. The color line in the United States resulted in some Cape Verdeans being classified, on the basis of appearance, as "white," while others were accounted "black." Many of the former,

and their descendants, came to identify themselves as Portuguese rather than Cape Verdean, so that the ancestry numbers reported in the census are well below the 350,000 that some specialists believe is the actual number of persons of Cape Verdean birth and ancestry living in the United States.

The Catholic faith of almost all Cape Verdeans and their initial lack of English tended to separate them from most Protestant, English-speaking African Americans. The most famous Cape Verdean immigrant however, was the Protestant evangelist who took the name of "Sweet Daddy" Grace. Born Marceline Manoël da Graça on Brava in the Cape Verdes, he immigrated to New Bedford in 1900 and, by the late 1930s, had founded hundreds of "United House of Prayer for All People" congregations, which claimed a total of 500,000 communicants. In 1952 *Ebony* magazine identified Daddy Grace as "America's richest Negro minister."

SEE ALSO

Africans; Portuguese

FURTHER READING

"America's Richest Negro Minister." *Ebony*, Jan., 1952, 17–23.
Halter, Marilyn. *Between Race and Ethnicity: Cape Verdean American Immigrants, 1860–1965*. Urbana: University of Illinois Press, 1993.

Caribbeans

• *Immigration, 1986–96: 1,176,554*
• *Immigration, 1820–1996: 3,351,660*

Caribbeans, or West Indians as they are sometimes called, are persons from the islands of the Caribbean Sea. The region takes its name from one the aboriginal peoples of the region, the Caribs. The vast majority are descendants of

Catholics

SEE Eastern Rite churches; Polish National Catholic Church; Roman Catholics

Celts

A Celt is a person who speaks a Celtic language—such as Gaelic in Ireland, Cornish or Welsh in Britain, and Breton in France—or whose ancestors were native to an area where the Celtic language was spoken. One often speaks of the Celtic fringe or circle surrounding England, which includes the Scottish Hebrides and Highlands of Scotland, the Isle of Man, Ireland, Wales, Cornwall, and Brittany in northwestern France.

There is a broader use of the term *Celt* or *Celtic* to describe a group of peoples of the 2nd millennium B.C. who spread out from parts of what are now Germany and France into much of southern Europe and Asia Minor. When speaking of modern peoples, Celt or Celtic (pronounced "kelt," "keltic") almost always refers to the first definition.

Census

The U.S. Constitution, Article 1, Section 2, requires that a census—an "actual enumeration" or counting of the people—be taken every 10 years for the purpose of allocating seats in the House of Representatives. But, since the first one was taken in 1790, the census has provided all kinds of other statistical information and, every 10 years, has given us a series of snapshots of the ever-changing American people.

Beginning in 1850, the census began keeping records of persons born outside of the United States, and, for a time, made special counts of "foreign stock," the native-born children of immigrants as well as immigrants. Recent censuses, although they still count foreign-born persons, do not provide as much detailed information. Prior to 1990, people could list only one ethnicity, or race, or ancestry. Beginning in 1990, people were allowed to list two, and in the 2000 Census people were allowed to list an unlimited number of ancestries. Since 1902 the Census has been administered by the Bureau of the Census, now a part of the Department of Commerce.

SEE ALSO
Foreign stock

FURTHER READING
Margo Anderson. *The American Census: A Social History*. New Haven: Yale University Press, 1988.

Central Americans

- *Immigration, 1986–96: 678,451*
- *Immigration, 1820–1996: 1,163,575*

Central America, the long isthmus between Mexico and South America, consists of the present nations of Belize, Costa Rica, El Salvador, Guatemala, Honduras, Nicaragua, and Panama. Although the site of advanced civilizations in pre-Columbian times, today it has the very low standards of living typical of so-called Third World countries. Most Central American immigrants work at low-skill, low-wage jobs.

SEE ALSO
Guatemalans; Hondurans; Nicaraguans; Panamanians; Salvadorans; Third World

FURTHER READING
Repak, Terry A. *Waiting on Washington: Central American Workers in the Nation's Capital.* Philadelphia: Temple University Press, 1995.

Chain migration

Chain migration occurs when individuals, often related by blood, but sometimes by friendship, follow one another in the immigration process. Chain migration is sometimes called serial migration.

Chamorros

SEE Guamanians

Chicanas/Chicanos

Derived from the Mexican Spanish word *mexicano*, meaning Mexican, this term came into use in the late 1940s to describe an American of Mexican ancestry. The first form is for females; the second, for males.

SEE ALSO
Latinos; Mexicans

Children

Although the photographs of immigrants used in books often focus on

women with children, the facts of the matter are that until the 1950s, women were a distinct minority of those who immigrated to the United States, and there have always been fewer children among those immigrating than among the general population either in the places from which immigrants came or in the United States. The chief reasons for this are, first of all, that large numbers of immigrants have been sojourners, people intending to come for a short time, earn some money, and return. Second, immigrants have been predominantly young adults, many of whom have come unmarried so that their children are born after they have settled in the new country.

However, millions of children have immigrated to the United States. What is often crucial in the acculturation of immigrant children is the age at which they immigrate. Very young children learn a language quickly, and it has been almost universally noted that young immigrant children tend to acculturate faster than their immigrant parents. However, children who immigrate as teenagers often have serious problems adjusting to the new country. If they are unable to speak English—or do not speak it well—they often have great difficulty in attending school at the "normal" grade level. Those who enter public school in preschool or at the first-grade

Immigrant children of detained immigrants play, under supervision, on the roof of the main building at Ellis Island. The wagon, labeled "Uncle Sam," and the flags were provided by patriotic Americanizing organizations.

Thousands of American families adopt children in foreign countries every year. These two children, from Russian Siberia, now live in Ithaca, New York.

HAPPY HOLIDAYS

Shendy. John. Stasi & Misha

age level have fewer difficulties with language and concept comprehension. Scholars have observed that in many immigrant families, the older children have been encouraged by their parents to leave school as early as possible so as to earn money to help the family, and that younger children in the same families have been able to go to school longer.

Since 1970, a significant number of children from foreign countries, mostly orphans and usually infants, have been adopted by Americans and brought to the United States. In 1997, for example, 13,621 such child immigrants were recorded by the INS. Almost half (47.6 percent) came from Asia, and most of the rest, 38 percent, came from Europe. Most were under one year of age, and almost 90 percent were under five. Among the Asian adoptees, girls outnumbered boys by more than 3 to 1, while those from Europe were almost evenly divided by gender, reflecting the lesser value placed on female babies in Asian cultures. More than three-quarters of the children came from just five nations: Russia (3,816); the People's Republic of China (3,597); the Republic of Korea (1,654); Guatemala (788); and Romania (621).

Under certain circumstances, foreign-born children adopted by U.S.-citizen parents may immediately acquire derivative U.S. citizenship.

SEE ALSO

Acculturation; Citizen; Education; Sojourner

FURTHER READING

Berrol, Selma Cantor. *Growing Up American: Immigrant Children in America, Then and Now.* New York: Twayne, 1995.

Brooks, Devon Barth, et al. "Adoption and Race," *Social Work* (March 1999): 167–78.

Hutchinson, Edward P. *Immigrants and Their Children, 1850–1950.* New York: Wiley, 1956.

Zucchi, John. *The Little Slaves of the Harp: Italian Child Street Musicians in Nineteenth-century Paris, London, and New York.* Montreal: McGill–Queen's University Press, 1992.

Chinese

- *1990 Ancestry: 1,505,245*
- *1990 Population: 1,648.696*
- *Immigration, 1986–96: 412,437*
- *Immigration, 1820–1996: 1,176,660*
- *Major periods of immigration: 1850–82, 1965+*
- *Major areas of settlement: California, Hawaii, New York*

China, with an estimated 1.25 billion people, is the most populous nation on earth. It contains nearly 3.7 million square miles and is only slightly larger than the United States. Millions of Chinese live in other parts of Asia, and the Chinese diaspora has spread Chinese peoples to almost every country in the world. A significant minority of the Chinese who have come to the United States in recent years have emigrated from places other than China, most of them from Southeast Asia; many of these were refugees from the Vietnam War.

Although a few Chinese sailors were in U.S. east coast ports as early as the 1780s, the large-scale immigration of Chinese began in 1850 and centered on San Francisco. Between 1850 and 1882, some 250,000 Chinese entered the United States. Almost all were men from the Pearl River Delta of Guangdong Province in southern China. Originally attracted by the gold rush of 1849—the Chinese characters for California can also be translated "gold mountain"—most of the immigrants found other work.

Many of the men were married, but their wives usually remained in China both because of Chinese cultural customs and, after 1875, American law. The Chinese came to call these women "living widows," because their husbands were alive but absent. During the building of the transcontinental railroads (1860s–90s) Chinese did most of the work. Like most immigrants, they took whatever jobs were available and were willing to work long hours for low pay. This, and the fact that they were not "white," led many, particularly other workers, who feared that their standard of living would be lowered, to oppose the presence of Chinese: riots in western cities from Los Angeles to Denver destroyed Chinatowns, the ethnic enclaves where all Chinese were forced to live, and dozens of Chinese were killed.

Many state laws and local ordinances discriminated against them, prohibiting them from owning land, barring them from certain jobs—mining, especially—and even denying them the right to testify in court cases. At the national level, Chinese—and other Asians—were aliens ineligible to citizenship and denied the right to be naturalized until the middle of the 20th century. In 1882 the Chinese Exclusion Act stopped the entry of Chinese workers. This was the beginning of significant restriction of the immigration of free persons in American history.

Because the vast majority of the 125,000 Chinese then in the United

Chinese workers did most of the heavy construction work in the Far West in the decades just after the Civil War of 1861–65, such as this trestle built in 1877.

A Chinese American nuclear family at home around 1900. The father was most likely a treaty merchant; the mother probably would rarely have left the home to go out in public.

States were males, the Chinese American population dropped steadily, so that by 1930 there were fewer than 60,000. Most lived in urban Chinatowns and were engaged in service occupations and small businesses, particularly laundries and restaurants. In 1943, during World War II, when China and the United States were allies, the Chinese Exclusion Act was repealed.

Chinese immigration to Hawaii is a very different story. Beginning in 1852, Chinese contract laborers were brought to the then independent Kingdom of Hawaii. Between 1852 and 1898, when the annexation of Hawaii by the United States made both contract labor and the immigration of Chinese laborers illegal, some 46,000 Chinese contract laborers came as well as a much smaller number of free immigrants. Chinese Hawaiians have been a significant element in the Hawaiian population for almost 150 years—in 1990, 68,000 Chinese Americans were 10 percent of the state's population—and the first person of Chinese ancestry to win a major political office in the United States was the Honolulu banker Hiram Leong Fong, who served in the U.S. Senate from 1959 to 1977.

The repeal of the Chinese Exclusion Act opened a new chapter in Chinese American history. Renewed immigration since that time, plus natural increase, has seen a steady growth in Chinese American population. The immigrant population since the 1965 Immigration Act has been diverse, including large numbers of women and children, persons drawn from many parts of mainland China as well as Taiwan, and from many countries of Southeast Asia.

While, as in the past, many recent Chinese immigrants have been poor workers, there have been increasing numbers of businesspeople and highly educated technicians and scientists. More and more of these Chinese Americans live outside of the still bustling Chinatowns of many large American cities; many of them live in new suburban Chinatowns, of which Monterey Park, California, is the predominant example.

SEE ALSO

Angel Island; Chinese Exclusion Acts; Contract labor; Diaspora; Ethnic enclave; Hawaiians; Immigration policy; Nativism; Naturalization; Paper sons; Students; Taiwanese; Vietnam War

FURTHER READING

Glick, Clarence E. *Sojourners and Settlers: Chinese Migrants in Hawaii.* Honolulu: University Press of Hawaii, 1980.

Kitano, Harry H. L., and Roger Daniels. *Asian Americans: Emerging Minorities.* 2nd ed. New York: Prentice-Hall, 1995.

Saito, Leland. *Race and Politics: Asians, Latinos and Whites in a Los Angeles Suburb.* Urbana: University of Illinois Press, 1998.

Shih-shan, Henry Tsai. *The Chinese Experience in America.* Bloomington: Indiana University Press, 1986.

Yung, Judy. *Unbound Feet: A Social History of Chinese Women in San Francisco.* Berkeley: University of California Press, 1995.

Chinese Exclusion Acts

The Chinese Exclusion Acts, the earliest of which went into effect in 1882, were the first statutes to exclude free immigrants—that is, immigrants who were neither slaves nor contract laborers—from entering the United States. The acts were thus the hinge on which all American immigration policy turned. The 1882 act barred the entrance of Chinese laborers for 10 years, but allowed the entrance of merchants, scholars, students, and their families, as well as "travelers for pleasure." The prohibition was extended for another 10 years in 1892, and made "permanent" in 1902.

The Immigration Act of 1924 ended the exceptions for all but students and tourists. In 1943, as a gesture to a wartime ally, the 15 statutes and parts of statutes that had enforced Chinese exclusion were repealed. This repeal was another turning point in U.S. immigration policy. Prior to the passage of the 1882 law, the Page Act of 1875 made it difficult, but not impossible, for Chinese women to enter the United States.

SEE ALSO

Chinese; Contract laborers; Immigration policy

FURTHER READING

Peffer, George Anthony. *If They Don't Bring Their Women Here: Regulating Chinese Female Immigration, 1875–1882.* Urbana: University of Illinois Press, 1999.

Riggs, Fred W. *Pressures on Congress: A Study of the Repeal of Chinese Exclusion.* New York: King's Crown Press, 1950.

Circular migration

Circular migration is the term used to describe a migration in which the immigrant goes to another country to work and then returns home, often to come again, and return home again. In the 19th century many Europeans participated in such migration: today it is primarily practiced by some immigrants—often called sojourners—from Mexico, the West Indies, and Canada. Agricultural laborers, for example, often come at harvest time and return home after the crops have been gathered.

SEE ALSO
Sojourner

Cities

Cities have been centers of immigrant populations throughout American history, but of course not all immigrants have gone to cities. The historian

Peddlers, mostly Jewish, sell goods from crates along Chicago's Maxwell Street in 1906. Such scenes could be seen in immigrant neighborhoods all over America.

Richard Hofstadter liked to point out that the United States was born in the country and only later moved to town.

But even in the colonial period, when perhaps 5 percent of the people lived in an urban area, its cities, almost all of which were seaports, were filled with immigrants. In 1643, when New York was still New Amsterdam and had only two or three thousand people, a visiting Jesuit priest reported that 18 different languages could be heard on its streets. New York was certainly the most polyglot (many-tongued) American city in the 17th century, but there were more immigrants, mostly Germans, in 18th-century Philadelphia than in New York.

Early in the 19th century, New York probably regained its supremacy as the nation's leading city of immigrants. But for a number of years there were more Irish in Boston than anywhere else in the nation. In the decades before the Civil War, Irish and German immigrants far outnumbered all the rest of the nation's immigrants. Moving westward, they began to fill up interior cities such as Cincinnati, St. Louis, and Milwaukee, and, after 1850, Chicago, which became the interior center for urban immigrant America. By 1870 Milwaukee was more than 30 percent German-born, and with a growing second generation it had a clear German-American majority; Cincinnati was the second most German city, with about 25 percent German-born, while Buffalo and St. Louis came in at just under 20 percent.

The most Irish city in 1870 was Lawrence, Massachusetts, which was more than 25 percent Irish-born. Of the larger cities in 1870, New York was about 16 percent German-born and about 22 percent Irish-born, while Chicago had about 17 percent German-born and 13 percent Irish-born. If we tabulate the percentages for all the large American cities combined in 1870, their mean percentage was 11.5 percent German and 14.5 percent Irish.

These proportions tended to shrink as immigrants from southern and eastern Europe began to predominate. By 1910 the German-born mean was down to 5.4 percent and the Irish dropped to 3.6 percent. At the same time, Italians and Russians combined were nearly 9 percent of the largest cities, and those from the Austro-Hungarian Empire about 4 percent.

The census of 1920, which, for the first time, found a bare majority of Americans living in urban areas, also showed that 75 percent of the foreign-born lived in cities. In addition, while many native-born Americans lived in middle-sized and small cities and towns, the overwhelming majority of the foreign-born urbanites lived in the largest cities. In those cities immigrants tended to live in ethnic enclaves, "Little Italies," "Chinatowns," "Greektowns," or Cincinnati's "Over the Rhine," that were centers of immigrant living and culture.

In the four decades after the passage of the Immigration Act of 1924, the incidence of foreign-born people in the population, which had hovered around 13 or 14 percent in every census between 1860 and 1920, dropped steadily until it reached a mere 4.7 percent in 1970.

Since then, renewed immigration, largely from Asia and Latin America, has created new urban immigrant enclaves, such as the Mexican and Central American barrios of the West Coast, the Puerto Rican barrios of East Coast cities, the "Little Saigon" of California's Orange County, and Miami's Little Havana. Even more than their predecessors, recent immigrants have been urban dwellers as more than 90 percent live in cities.

SEE ALSO

Barrio; Ethnic enclave; Immigration Act of 1924

FURTHER READING

Garcia, Maria Christina. *Havana USA: Cuban Exiles and Cuban Americans in South Florida, 1959–1994*. Berkeley: University of California Press, 1996.
Ward, David. *Cities and Immigrants: A Geography of Change in Nineteenth-Century America*. New York: Oxford University Press, 1971.

Citizen

People may become citizens of the United States in three ways:

(1) by being born in the United States (which is called birthright citizenship);

(2) by being born anywhere to parents who are American citizens (which is called derivative citizenship);

(3) by naturalization.

Under certain circumstances citizenship may be acquired through naturalization of parents, by marrying a U.S. citizen, or by being adopted by U.S. citizen parents. Citizenship is now governed by the 14th Amendment to the U.S. Constitution and by subsequent statutes. Naturalization is administered

A group of immigrants takes the oath of allegiance in a ceremony in Detroit, Michigan, in 1995. Michael Adeyoju (foreground) came to the United States from Nigeria in the early 1980s.

by the Immigration and Naturalization Service, but new citizens must take their oaths before a federal judge.

SEE ALSO

Birthright citizens; Denaturalization; 14th Amendment; Naturalization

Civil Liberties Act of 1988

During World War II, shortly after the December 7, 1941, Japanese attack on Pearl Harbor, President Franklin D. Roosevelt signed Executive Order 9066, which resulted in more than 120,000 Japanese-American men, women, and children living on the West Coast of the United States being incarcerated in concentration camps for as long as three years. More than two-thirds of them were native-born American citizens. Although this action was accepted by most Americans at the time, and, in effect, sanctioned by the Supreme Court of the United States in 1944 and 1945, more and more Americans became convinced that it had been a gross miscarriage of justice. Some even called it an American war crime.

In 1983, a Presidential commission, the Commission on Wartime Relocation and Internment of Civilians (CWRIC), reported to Congress that, contrary to the wartime claim of military necessity, the wartime incarceration of Japanese Americans (1942–46) was "not justified by military necessity" and that the "broad historical causes that shaped [that decision] were race prejudice, war hysteria, and a failure of political leadership." The CWRIC recommended that Congress issue a formal apology and award each survivor $20,000 in compen-

sation. After much debate, Congress enacted and President Ronald Reagan signed the Civil Liberties Act of 1988. By 1999, more than 80,000 Japanese American victims had been compensated.

SEE ALSO
Internment

FURTHER READING

Daniels, Roger. *Prisoners Without Trial: Japanese Americans and World War II.* New York: Hill & Wang, 1993.
Maki, Mitchell, Harry H. L. Kitano, and S. Megan Berthold. *Achieving the Impossible Dream: How Japanese Americans Obtained Redress.* Urbana: University of Illinois Press, 1999.

Colombians

- *1990 Ancestry: 351,717*
- *Immigration, 1986–96: 154,523*
- *Immigration, 1932–96: 375,479*
- *Major period of immigration: since 1980*
- *Major areas of settlement: New York, Florida*

Colombia, conquered by Spain in the 1530s, gained its independence in 1819. Its 37 million people live in a nation of 440,000 square miles, a little larger than Texas and California combined. It has sea coasts on both the Caribbean Sea and the Pacific Ocean. Its territory once included Panama, which it lost in a revolution organized by Americans and supported by the U.S. government in 1903. More recent issues between the United States and Colombia revolve around the illegal drug trade: Colombians are among the major producers and Americans their primary customers.

Colombia, partly because of its Caribbean location, has become the major South American source of immigrants to the United States. Like most other South American immigrant

Many immigrants dress up in fancy clothes for special occasions. This dancer, a member of the troupe Estampas Colombianas, performed at a festival in Philadelphia in 1991.

ual income shows the same pattern: Colombian Americans tend to earn more than other Hispanics and less that the average Americans.

The INS and the Census Bureau estimated that 65,000 Colombians were illegally in the United States in 1996, the 11th largest group from any nation.

SEE ALSO

Hispanics; Illegal immigrants; South Americans

FURTHER READING

Tomás Rivera Policy Institute. *America's Newest Voices: Colombians, Dominicans, Guatemalans, and Salvadoreans in the United States.* Claremont, Calif.: Tomás Rivera Policy Institute, 1998.
U.S. Bureau of the Census. *Persons of Hispanic Origin in the United States.* Washington, D.C.: Government Printing Office, 1993.

groups, Colombians have been little studied and most are first-generation: an estimated 74 percent of the Colombians living in the United States in 1990 were foreign-born. Half of them live in just two states: New York had 28 percent and Florida 22 percent. Another 28 percent lived in three other states: 11 percent lived in California, 13 percent in New Jersey, and 4 percent in Texas. Within those states, most Colombians lived and worked in large cities, particularly New York City, Miami, and Los Angeles.

Government data shows that Colombians are better educated than are Hispanics generally, and that they are somewhat less educated than the general American population. For example, 67 percent of all Colombian Americans over 25 years of age have high school diplomas, as do 50 percent of American Hispanics generally and 75 percent of the total population. The government data on family and individ-

Contract labor

Contract labor evolved from slavery on the one hand and the European apprentice system on the other. During the colonial period of American history a special form of contract labor called indentured servitude was a major means of bringing Europeans to America. Most indentured servants had their transportation to America paid, and, in return, were obligated to work without pay for a fixed term that could be as long as seven years. Less important, but significant, was the exile of thousands of convicts from England to America.

The worldwide contract labor system arose in the 19th century as the African slave trade was being outlawed. Most of the hundreds of thousands of such workers were Asian Indians and Chinese. This system was most important in the Caribbean and other tropical plantation areas. It was never significant in the mainland United States, where all forms of contract labor were outlawed after the Civil War. It was significant in the Kingdom of Hawaii from 1852 until American annexation in 1898, and resulted in tens of thousands of Asian workers, mostly Japanese and Chinese, being brought there. In the years before World War I a surreptitious form of contract labor, the padrone system, exploited the labor of immigrant children.

SEE ALSO

Convicts; Coolies; Indentured servants; Padrone system; Redemptioners; Slave trade

FURTHER READING

Tinker, Hugh. *A New System of Slavery: The Export of Indian Labor Overseas, 1830–1920.* London: Oxford University Press, 1974.

Convicts

In the 18th century and well into the 19th, Great Britain exported a considerable number of convicts to her colonies. These were people who had been con-

victed of a whole range of offenses, criminal and political, and who were sentenced to "transportation for life," that is, to permanent exile. Before the American Revolution perhaps 20,000 such convicts actually arrived in what is now the United States, while perhaps half that number were sent to West Indian colonies. The convicts were scattered throughout the colonies. For a short time, starting in 1732, a penal colony was established in Georgia. The whole practice of sending convicts was greatly resented in America. Benjamin Franklin proposed, satirically, to send one live rattlesnake to England for each convict sent to America.

After the American Revolution the independent United States were no longer available, so the bulk of Britain's transported convicts were sent to Australia where, for some years, they formed the bulk of the European population. The title character of Daniel Defoe's novel *Moll Flanders* (1722) is sent to Virginia as a convict, and the young hero of Charles Dickens's *Great Expectations* (1861) has a benefactor who is a convict who managed to return to England, illegally, from Australia.

A British cartoonist in 1770 shows some of the leading men of England as if they were convicts being sent to the penal colony in Georgia. The real convicts were almost all poor and obscure men and women.

SEE ALSO

Africans; Contract labor; Coolies; Indentured servants; Slave trade

FURTHER READING

Ekirch, A. Roger. *Bound for America: The Transportation of British Convicts to the Colonies, 1718–1775.* New York: Oxford University Press, 1987.
Smith, Abbot E. *Colonists in Bondage: White Servitude and Convict Labor in America, 1607–1776.* Chapel Hill: University of North Carolina Press, 1947.

Coolies

The term *coolie*, originally a Hindi word, was applied, in the 19th and early 20th centuries, to Asian contract laborers, mostly Chinese and Indian. Large numbers of these Asian workers were brought to the Caribbean as replacements for African slaves after the slave trade was outlawed. No coolies were ever brought to the U.S. mainland, although many Chinese and Japanese were brought to Hawaii in the 19th century, mostly to work on sugar cane plantations by the Hawaiian Sugar Planters Association. After their contracts expired some returned to their homelands but most either stayed in Hawaii or migrated to the U.S. mainland.

SEE ALSO

Contract labor; Hawaiian Sugar Planters Association; Indentured servants

Copts

Copts are Egyptian Christians, members of the Coptic church. They are not an ethnic group but rather people of various ethnicities who were never converted to Islam, as the majority of Egyptians did. In Egypt Copts, who have often been persecuted, are estimated to be 5 to 10 percent of its 63 million people. A number of Copts have come to the United States since 1966, when persecution in Egypt grew severe. Several dozen Coptic churches have been established in American cities, including New York and Los Angeles.

SEE ALSO

Egyptians; Muslims; Refugees; Religion

FURTHER READING

Abdelsayed, Gabriel. "The Coptic-Americans: A Current African Contribution." In Barbara Cunningham, ed., *The New Jersey Ethnic Experience.* Union City, N.J.: W. H. Wise, 1977.

Cornish

- *1990 Ancestry: 3,991*
- *Major period of immigration: 1830–1920*
- *Major area of settlement: Wisconsin*

The Cornish were a Celtic people who migrated to the extreme southwest of England from France sometime in the 1st century B.C. Their separate language survived into the 17th century. Since Cornwall is a part of the United Kingdom there are no separate listings for Cornish in immigration, census, and linguistic statistics. And, although fewer than 4,000 people listed "Cornish" in the 1990 census ancestry questionnaire, most authorities believe that something over 100,000 Cornish people migrated to the United States, most of them between the 1830s and World War I.

Cornwall has been famous for mining, especially for tin and copper mining, since ancient times, but by the 19th century Cornish mines were running out of ore. Cornish miners were widely sought after by American mine owners and one can still see, in the little museums in what are now Cornish resort towns, like St. Ives, yellowing posters and handbills urging Cornish miners to come to this or that mine in America. Cornish miners were a significant presence on every 19th-century American mining frontier. They were called "Cousin Jacks," supposedly because the Cornish were always interested in finding work for their kith and kin. As the story goes, whenever there was a vacancy, a Cornish immigrant would volunteer that he had a "Cousin Jack" who would be willing to take it.

The first Cornish miners in America worked in iron mines in Pennsylvania, New Jersey, and other eastern states. But the focal point for Cornish migration was the small town of Mineral Point, Wisconsin, in the Wisconsin–Illinois–Iowa lead mining district. By 1850 there were perhaps 10,000 Cornish there, many of them combining mining and farming, as had been traditional in Cornwall for centuries. The Cornish presence is still celebrated in Mineral Point and restaurants there feature Cornish meat pies, called pasties.

The Cornish moved on to other mining frontiers and were particularly important in the Michigan copper fields and in the California gold rush. There, and on later frontiers, they specialized in underground, hard-rock mining as opposed to surface sluice mining of alluvial deposits. They mined not only on other western American frontiers but also in Australia, British Columbia, and South Africa. On their journeys to these far-flung mines, many miners left families back in Wisconsin. It is said that when a Cornish miner struck it rich in one of these places, he would return to Wisconsin and buy more land. Unlike many other British miners, the Cornish did not usually

join unions. Cornish miners traditionally worked in groups of three to six men who would bid on a contract to work a "pitch," or section of a mine, for a percentage of the yield.

FURTHER READING

Rowe, John. *The Hard-Rock Men: Corning Immigrants and the North American Mining Frontier*. New York: Barnes and Noble, 1974.
Rowse, A. L. *The Cousin Jacks: The Cornish in America*. New York: Scribners, 1969.

Croatians

- *1990 Ancestry: 544,270*
- *Immigration, 1992–96: 2,277*
- *Major period of immigration: 1890–1914*
- *Major areas of settlement: Northeast and Midwest, particularly Pittsburgh, Chicago, and Cleveland*

Although more than half a million Americans identify themselves as Croatians by ancestry, Croatians do not appear in American immigration records before 1992, and Croatian was listed as a separate tongue in only four censuses. Prior to 1918, Croatians immigrants entered as Austro-Hungarians. After the creation of Yugoslavia just after World War I, Croatians entered as Yugoslavs until that nation broke up in 1992. Only then was the modern Croatia created.

Croatians, or Croats, are a southern Slavic people closely related to two other southern Slavic groups, the more numerous Serbs and the less numerous Slovenes. All three peoples speak a closely related language usually called Serbo-Croatian, but are deeply divided by religion and history. Most Croatians and Slovenes are Roman Catholics, but most Serbs are Eastern Orthodox. Thus

A peaceful demonstration of Croatian Americans on the grounds of the Capitol in Washington, D.C., in the mid-1990s. They are demonstrating for recognition of Croatia by the U.S. government.

Croats and Slovenes use the Latin alphabet, while Serbs use the Cyrillic. In both World Wars, Croat and Slovene leaders in Europe were largely on the side of the Austrians and the Germans, while most Serb leaders opposed them.

Croatian sailors and others, including missionaries, came to America in the 17th and 18th century but only in the 19th century was there regular traffic between Dubrovnik and other Adriatic ports and the United States. By mid-century a few thousand Croatians were settled in the United States, chiefly around the ports of San Francisco and New Orleans.

Partly because a Croatian had been present when James Marshall discovered gold at Sutter's Mill in California in 1848, thousands of his countrymen were drawn to California. These and most of the other Croatians who came before the 1880s were from the Dalmatian coast of the Adriatic and were men with trades and professions. After 1880 Croatian immigrants came largely from the interior and were mainly peasants. These, like many other late-19th-century immigrants, were drawn to the American northeast and Midwest to do

hard, dirty, dangerous, and low-paying work in coal mines, steel mills, and other heavy industries.

A very high percentage of these immigrants were male, and half or more of them returned to Europe after years of work in the United States. For those who remained, a typical pattern was for young men to emigrate first, establish themselves, and then send for other family members. Only in the 20th century did large numbers of Croatian women emigrate to America. Before that, most Croatians who married in the United States married women from other Catholic Slavic groups. Only in 1901, when there were perhaps 100,000 Croatians in the United States, was the first Croatian Catholic parish established, in Allegheny City, Pennsylvania. From 1924 until after World War II, relatively few Croatians came to the United States.

After the establishment of a communist government in Yugoslavia under Marshal Tito after World War II, several thousand anticommunist refugees and exiles came from Croatia and other parts of Yugoslavia, and nationalist politics, which had long been a staple of Croatian American cultural life, became even more intensified as the vast majority of Croatian Americans opposed Tito's regime. The relationships between Croatian Americans and the new Croatian state are still being worked out, but there is every reason to believe that it will strengthen Croatian American identity.

SEE ALSO
Austro-Hungarian Empire; Serbs; Slovenes; Yugoslavia

FURTHER READING
Prpic, George J. *The Croatian Immigrants in America.* New York: Philosophical Library, 1971.
Rasporich, Anthony W. *For a Better Life: A History of the Croatians in Canada.* Toronto: McClelland and Stewart, 1982.

Cubans

- *1990 Ancestry: 859,739*
- *Immigration, 1986–96: 168,749*
- *Immigration, 1921–96: 840,093*
- *Major period of immigration: 1959+*
- *Major areas of settlement: southern Florida, New Jersey*

Cubans have been coming to the United States for economic and political reasons since the 19th century. Early in that century, a Cuban Catholic priest, Father Féliz Varela, ministered to a New York City flock composed largely of Irish and German immigrants. By mid-century there were small groups of Cubans, mostly cigar makers, in Key West and Tampa, Florida, and New York. During the long struggle for Cuban independence from Spain, from 1868 to 1898, many exiles, including José Martí, who is sometimes called Cuba's George Washington, used the United States as a base of operations.

Yet despite its closeness—only 90 miles of water separate Cuba and the United States—there were probably not more than 50,000 Cuban Americans before Fidel Castro's Cuban Revolution of 1959. In the decades that have followed, some 750,000 Cubans have fled to the United States and have made their presence felt, culturally, economically, and politically. The vast majority of these were almost automatically granted refugee or asylee status, more than from any other nation. During some periods, as during the Mariel boatlift of 1980, Castro's government encouraged many dissidents to leave, but more often it made emigration difficult. Many recent exiles have crossed the dangerous waters in flimsy boats and rafts, and some have perished at sea.

The first post-Castro refugees were members of the upper and middle classes; subsequent exiles have been less elite, but the very poor and Afro-Cubans have been underrepresented. At first, almost all assumed that Castro would soon be overthrown, but after the failed Bay of Pigs invasion of 1961, backed by the United States and manned by Cuban exiles, and the Cuban Missile Crisis of 1962, Cas-

Cigar workers, mostly Cuban, rolling cigars in Tampa, Florida, 1929. The man on the platform was paid to read aloud to the workers.

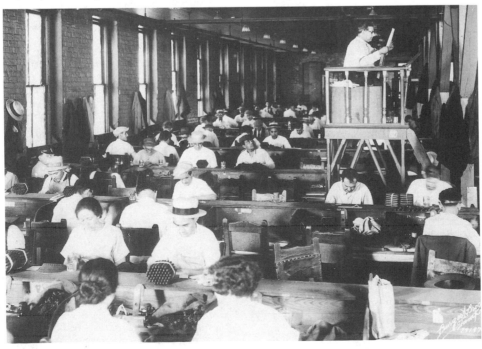

In one of the post–Bay of Pigs exchanges in 1963, Cuban prisoners released by Fidel Castro are checked by U.S. Customs officials in Havana. The men standing behind the chairs are Cuban soldiers and police. The United States ransomed these 751 refugees with goods, including tractors, worth $3.75 million.

tro's survival was assured by an informal agreement between the United States and the Soviet Union. Ironically, Castro has outlasted the Soviet Union.

Many exiles still believe that they will migrate to Cuba, but now most experts agree that, despite what many of them say, most will continue to live in the United States even, as they say, "when Castro falls." One scholar differentiates between "Cuban exiles" and "Cuban Americans"; to her, a Cuban American is an exile who no longer thinks of remigrating to Cuba. And of course, many of today's Cuban Americans are American-born children and grandchildren of the exiles. But even most grandchildren maintain some Cuban customs.

As with some other middle-class Latin American families, Cubans in the United States have a special celebration for the daughters at or close to their 15th birthday. Called a *quinceañera*, the party is similar to the "sweet sixteen" parties celebrated by many other Americans.

The exiles and their skills have helped to transform Miami and southern Florida from a region dependent on tourism and agriculture to an important center of finance and trade with Latin America. Whole sections work and play in Spanish. The major street

of Miami's "Little Havana" is now called "Calle Ocho," Spanish for Eighth Street. The Cuban presence has helped to attract many other Spanish-speaking groups to southern Florida, particularly Puerto Ricans and Central Americans, so that in 1990, 62.5 percent of Miami's population was of Hispanic heritage, as was 49.2 percent of Dade County's 1.9 million people.

SEE ALSO

Asylees; Mariel boatlift; Refugees

FURTHER READING

Garcia, Maria Cristina. *Havana USA: Cuban Exiles and Cuban Americans in South Florida, 1959–1994.* Berkeley: University of California Press, 1996.
Mormino, Gary, and George E. Pozzetta. *The Immigrant World of Ybor City: Italians and Their Latin Neighbors in Tampa, 1885–1985.* Urbana: University of Illinois Press, 1987.

Cultural pluralism

Cultural pluralism is a term developed in the 1920s by the American philosopher Horace M. Kallen in opposition to the strong Anglo-conformity and nativism then being expressed. Kallen's cultural pluralism emphasized the notion that the United States was a land of many cultures, and that, unlike the notion of the melting pot (or the triple melting pot), in which foreign cultures were melted into a distinctive American culture, he expected some aspects of many cultures to remain. Some adherents of multiculturalism are, essentially, echoing Kallen.

Although the term "cultural pluralism" was new, the recognition of diversity was not. The American geographer Jedidiah Morse had argued in 1789 that "Intermingled with Anglo-Americans, are the Dutch, Scotch-Irish, French, Germans, Swedes and Jews; all these, except the Scotch and Irish, retain, in a greater or lesser degree, their native language, in which they perform their public worship, converse and transact business with each other. The time, however, is anticipated . . . when the language, manners, customs, political and religious sentiments of the mixed mass of people who inhabit the United States, shall have become so assimilated as that all nominal distinctions shall be lost in the general and honourable names of Americans."

More than 200 years later, the degree of assimilation that Morse expected has not occurred, so that the reality is closer to Kallen's notions than to his.

SEE ALSO

Acculturation; Americanization; Anglo-conformity; Ethnic enclave; Melting pot; Multiculturalism; Triple melting pot

FURTHER READING

Alba, Richard D. *Ethnic Identity: The Transformation of White America.* New Haven: Yale University Press, 1990.
Gordon, Milton M. *Assimilation in American Life: The Role of Race, Religion and National Origins.* New York: Oxford University Press, 1964.
Kallen, Horace M. *Culture and Democracy in the United States.* 1924. Reprint, New York: Arno, 1970.

Cypriots

- *1990 Ancestry: 4,879*
- *Immigration, 1986–96: 2,837*
- *Immigration, 1820–1996: n.a.*
- *Major periods of immigration: n.a.*
- *Major areas of settlement: n.a.*

Cypriots are natives of an island of 4,867 square miles in the Eastern Mediterranean, home to persons of Greek and Turkish ethnicity and scene of intermittent fighting between these groups since 1974. Since that time the island has been divided politically between Greek and Turkish republics with a cease-fire policed by the United Nations. The larger Greek republic has a population of about 750,000, 78 percent Greek and 18 percent Turkish; the smaller Turkish republic has a population of about 135,000, 99 percent Turkish. Prior to World War II Cyprus had a long and complicated history: between 1878 and 1960 it was ruled by Great Britain. Greek dominance of an independent Cyprus produced a secession movement by the island's Turks supported by Turkish government troops which led, after 14 years of fighting, to the present partition.

In earlier times Cyprus had been ruled by the Byzantine Empire and Venice. Shakespeare's play, *Othello,* takes place on Cyprus. Until the 1970s almost all Cypriots who have come to the United States were Greeks who blended into the larger Greek American community. Current immigration data does not differentiate Cypriots of Greek and Turkish ethnicity.

SEE ALSO

Greeks; Turks

FURTHER READING

Saloutos, Theodore. *A History of the Greeks in the United States.* Cambridge, Mass.: Harvard University Press, 1964.

Czechs

- *1990 Ancestry: 1,611,696 [includes 315,285 who answered Czechoslovakian]*
- *Immigration, 1994–96: 248*
- *Major period of immigration: 1848–1914*
- *Major areas of settlement: Chicago, New York City, Cleveland, Wisconsin, and Texas*

The Czechs are the most western branch of the Slavic peoples. They come from

three contiguous areas, Bohemia, Moravia and southern Silesia. Because more Czechs lived in Bohemia than anywhere else, they were often called Bohemians until the creation of the Czechoslovak Republic after World War I. This nation of Czechs and Slovaks endured until 1993 when it peacefully divided itself into separate nations: a Czech Republic and a Slovak Republic. The Czech Republic, created in 1993, has a population of 10 million people in a territory of some 30,000 square miles. Most of the several hundred thousand Czechs who emigrated to the United States did so while the Czech or largely-Czech lands were part of the Austro-Hungarian Empire.

Although a few Czechs came to America in the colonial period—one Czech man is known to have lived in New Amsterdam in 1633—probably no more than 500 came before 1850. The immigration that began about that time was a largely peasant family migration to rural America. Events in Europe—the revolutions of 1848, the Austro-Prussian War of 1866, poor

agricultural conditions—and events in America, such as the Homestead Act of 1862, which promised free land to settlers, and letters home from successful immigrants, combined to create what was the first large-scale migration of a Slavic people to America. In addition, the creation of regular steamship service from the north German ports of Hamburg and Bremen brought Czech immigrants to New York and to Galveston, Texas.

In this era, Czech rural settlements were founded from Wisconsin to Texas. The great Czech composer, Antonín Dvořák, who was a guest conductor and director of a music conservatory in New York for two years, spent his summers in the tiny Czech settlement of Spillville, Iowa, and wrote some of his most important music there.

Around 1890 the nature of Czech immigration changed: skilled workers rather than farm laborers began to predominate and Czechs, like most immigrants of that era, migrated to cities, particularly to Chicago, New York, and Cleveland. A few professionals

Although most Czech immigrants settled in cities, many settled in rural areas, as this sign outside the country town of Wilbur, Nebraska, testifies.

migrated as well: a large percentage of them were musicians, perhaps following Dvorák's example. It was also a migration in which adult males predominated, but not overwhelmingly so.

World War I, of course, cut off Czech and most European migration, and the existence of the new Czechoslovak Republic attracted the return of some Czechs who had settled in America. A few thousand a year came to the United States until the Immigration Act of 1924 all but cut off Czech migration. Only a few hundred Czech refugees found their way to the United States during and after World War II, but the 1948 communist coup sent about 25,000 Czechs, many of them professionals and highly skilled workers and their families, to the United States. A smaller group of refugees, about 10,000, came as a result of the brutal Soviet suppression in 1968 of the "Prague Spring" movement toward democratization.

Religion in the Czech American community is a complicated affair. In Europe the Protestant Reformation of the 16th century had made great gains in the Czech lands, but was soon overcome by the ultra-Catholic Austrian monarchy. Thus, many Czechs associated Catholicism with their foreign rulers and were, at best, nominal Catholics, although many others were devout believers. Some authorities believe that anywhere from a half to two-thirds of

the Czechs in 19th-century rural America had left the Catholic church. Some became Protestants, but more became secular (nonreligious) freethinkers. Many of the Czechs' rural neighbors in America were aghast that so many of them did not go to church and that they often had parties on Sundays.

The most dynamic Czech American social organizations were the sokols, gymnastic organizations that had important social and patriotic functions, first organized in St. Louis in 1865. As was the case with other ethnic groups, Czechs quickly organized death benefit societies which evolved into life insurance companies. One such surviving organization is CSA Fraternal Life.

Music of all kinds has been important in Czech American lives—a Czech saying goes, "If he's a Czech, he's a musician"—and one historian reports that if a Czech immigrant took anything from home other than a feather quilt and some food for the journey, it was a musical instrument. Czech folk tunes, particularly polkas, were heard everywhere.

The Czech American press was sharply divided between secular and religious, largely Catholic publications, but now has largely died out. Much Czech American political energy was focused for a long time on homeland goals, and the establishment of the Czechoslovak Republic in 1918 was, in part, a result of that energy. No Czech American has been a national political figure, but Czech-born Adolph Sabath represented a Chicago district in the U.S. House of Representatives from 1907 to 1952 and was an important advocate for immigrants.

SEE ALSO

Austro-Hungarian Empire; Czechoslovakia; Immigration Act of 1924; Refugees; Slovaks; Sokols

FURTHER READING

Habenicht, Jan. *History of Czechs in America*. St. Paul, Minn.: Czechoslovak Genealogical Society International, 1996.

Saxon-Ford, Stephanie. *The Czech Americans*. New York: Chelsea House, 1999.

Danes

- *1990 Ancestry: 1,634,669*
- *Immigration, 1986–96: 6,773*
- *Immigration, 1820–1996: 374,594*
- *Major period of immigration: 1864–1924*
- *Major areas of settlement: Iowa, Wisconsin, Minnesota, Utah*

The Danes in America are much less numerous than their Scandinavian immigrant neighbors the Norwegians and Swedes: mass Danish immigration came later, was spread out more widely, and Danes were less concerned with maintaining their ethnic identity than were the others. Denmark itself has some 5 million people in less than 17,000 square miles. Two Danish explorers led expeditions in the European probing of North America: Jens Munk sailed to Hudson's Bay in 1619 looking for a shortcut to Asia, and Vitus Bering, sailing for Russia, was the first European to reach Alaska. The first Danish immigrant we know of in America was Jonas Bronck, for whom the New York borough of the Bronx is named. A few individual Danes came to North America from the West Indies, where Denmark maintained a colony in the Virgin Islands from 1672 until 1917, when it was sold to the United States.

The first Danish families to come to America were small groups who had been converted to pietistic Protestantism in Denmark and settled among the German pietists around Bethlehem, Pennsylvania, in the mid-18th century. A second and much more numerous family migration of Danes began in the 1850s, when Mormon missionaries from America began converting Danes, loaning them money to emigrate, and settling them on what became their own land. Between 1850 and 1930 some 18,000 Danish Mormons

Danish women attend the anniversary meeting, around 1930, of the Danish Ladies Aid Society of an ethnic settlement in Danevang, Texas. Ethnic women's groups were important preservers and transmitters of immigrant culture.

emigrated to America, most of them before 1887. Almost all settled in Utah.

Large-scale migration of other Danes followed the defeat of Denmark by Prussia in 1864 and the subsequent loss of almost a quarter of Danish territory. Most of these Danes, like the Danish Mormons, came seeking farmland—as late as 1900 two-thirds of the Danes in America were rural—and a minority came as part of group migrations. both religious and secular.

Almost all Danes were Protestants, and the overwhelming majority of those belonged to the state church, which was Lutheran. Danish Lutherans in America were divided into two groups and one of the issues that divided them was the question of continued ethnic identity. One group, the Grundtvig wing (Grundtvig was a Danish bishop), believed that Danish Americans should settle together in colonies, establish Danish schools, and maintain as much Danish culture as possible. The other wing, the Inner Mission wing, thought that Danish Americans should encourage their children to Americanize.

Danes in America were and have remained widely dispersed, particularly when compared to their fellow Scandinavians. They also seem to have intermarried, both with Norwegians and Swedes and with people of other backgrounds, to a greater degree and earlier, than their Scandinavian contemporaries. Where there were considerable concentrations of Danes, a foreign-language press developed and at one time or another, nearly 100 newspapers have been published in Dano-Norwegian (the two languages were all but identical in the 19th century, although they have diverged somewhat in the 20th).

Given the relatively wide dispersion of Danes in America, it is not surprising that Danish American voting blocs have not developed, although individual Danish-born politicians have been elected governors of five states: Iowa, Minnesota, and South Dakota, each of which had significant numbers of Danes, and New Jersey and Wyoming, which did not. The most famous Danish immigrant was Jacob Riis, the journalist and reformer whom Theodore Roosevelt once called "New York's most useful citizen."

In recent years, as part of the ethnic revival in the United States, and because of the increasing economic value of tourism, Danish folk customs have been revived and celebrated in a number of places, the most well known of which is Solvang, California, where an annual "Danish days" festival is held.

SEE ALSO
Mormons; Scandinavians; Swedes; Triple melting pot

FURTHER READING
Hale, Frederick, ed. *Danes in North America*. Seattle: University of Washington Press, 1984.
Hvidt, Kristian. *Flight to America: The Social Background of 300,000 Danish Emigrants*. New York: Academic Press, 1975.

Denaturalization

Denaturalization is the process by which a person loses citizenship. Today, an American citizen can lose citizenship only in two ways: by voluntarily giving it up or as part of a punishment for crime. For a number of years in the early 20th century American women, native-born or naturalized, could lose their citizenship by marrying an alien. No American man ever lost citizenship merely by marriage.

SEE ALSO
Birthright citizen; Citizen; Naturalization

Deportation

Deportation is the formal forced removal of an alien from the United States. Deportation is usually ordered by an immigration judge, who is an administrative, not a judicial, officer. Most persons apprehended by immigration officials are not formally deported, but, in the words of the Immigration and Naturalization Service (INS), depart while "physically observed" by an INS official. In 1996, for example, 50,064 people were "deported" while there were 1,572,798 "voluntary departures" of people in custody. Many people have been required to make "voluntary departures" more than once. Between 1892 and 1996 the government deported 1,269,817 people and observed 31,388,325 "voluntary departures," a ratio of about 25 to 1.

SEE ALSO

Illegal aliens; Immigration and Naturalization Service (INS); Immigration policy

Deportee

Deportees are, technically speaking, only persons who have been formally deported by the government. In practice, however, the term can also be used to describe the much larger number of persons required to make "voluntary departures."

SEE ALSO

Deportation

Diaspora

The word *diaspora* derives from a biblical term meaning "dispersion," and originally referred only to the scattering of the Jews in the centuries after the Roman conquest of Palestine in the first century B.C. But by the late 20th century it had also become to be a synonym for migration, so that one speaks of the African diaspora, the Chinese diaspora, the Irish diaspora, the Japanese diaspora, etc.

Dillingham Commission

SEE United States Immigration Commission

Discrimination

Discrimination of an ethnic or racial nature was a major factor in American immigration policy between 1882 and 1965 and in naturalization policy between 1790 and 1952. In immigration policy the first such discrimination came in 1882 with the Chinese Exclusion Act. Additional discrimination came with the Gentlemen's Agreement of 1907–08, and the Immigration Acts of 1917, 1921, and 1924. The lessening of such discrimination began with the repeal of Chinese exclusion in 1943. Several acts, culminating in the Immigration Act of 1965, removed direct ethnic and racial discrimination in immigration from the statute books.

In naturalization policy the very first naturalization statute in 1790 limited naturalization to "free white persons." In 1870 "persons of African descent," were added, as were Chinese in 1943 and Filipinos and "natives of India" in 1946. In 1952 all ethnic and racial bars were lifted. To be sure, other kinds of discrimination still exist. Immigration policy, for example, favors persons with close relatives in the United States, and naturalization policy favors those who can pass a citizenship test.

Apart from discrimination in immigration and naturalization, there are many other, informal kinds of discrimination practiced in the United States, many of them against native-born citizens, including African Americans and Native Americans.

SEE ALSO

Aliens ineligible to citizenship; Chinese Exclusion Acts; Gentlemen's Agreement; Immigration Act of 1917; Immigration Act of 1921; Immigration Act of 1924; Immigration policy; Nativism; Naturalization policy; Prejudice; Stereotype

Displaced persons

Displaced persons (DPs) were a special group of refugees. The term was coined toward the end of World War II to describe the more than 7 million people from all over Europe who were found by the Allied armies as they liberated and conquered territory from Nazi Germany. These included former slave laborers brought to work in German factories, former concentration camp inmates and prisoners of war, and eastern Europeans who had either come to Germany voluntarily or who had fled

there before advancing Soviet armies. Almost 6 million of these were refugees who had countries to return to: they were repatriated by Allied forces between May and September 1945. There remained about 1.5 million who refused to, or could not, return to their former homes.

The resettlement of these displaced persons, and others who became displaced persons, was largely accomplished, with great difficulty, over the next seven years. A special body of the United Nations, the International Refugee Organization (IRO), administered the DP camps, the first of many kinds of temporary refugee camps operated by the IRO. The UN body defined DPs as "persons who . . . for reasons of race, religion, nationality, or political opinion . . . have been deported from, or obliged to leave their country of nationality or of former residence." In the United States the resettlement of DPs was aided by both government and voluntary agencies, or VOLAGS.

SEE ALSO

Displaced Persons Acts; Holocaust; International Refugee Organization; Refugees; VOLAGS

Huddled displaced persons (DPs) in Berlin in 1945 wait for a train to take them to a camp. Nearly 450,000 DPs came to the United States between 1948 and 1952.

FURTHER READING

Dinnerstein, Leonard. *America and the Survivors of the Holocaust.* New York: Columbia University Press, 1982.

United States Displaced Persons Commission. *Memo to America: The DP Story.* Washington, D.C.: Government Printing Office, 1952.

Displaced Persons Acts

The Displaced Persons Acts were two separate acts of Congress passed in 1948 and 1950 at the urging of President Harry S. Truman. They allowed the admission of displaced persons without regard to the limitations of the immigration quota system then in force. A vocal nativist minority in Congress opposed their passage as a breach of the quota system. By the time the acts expired in 1952, some 450,000 people, perhaps 140,000 of whom were Jewish survivors of the Holocaust, gained refuge in the United States. Most of the remaining 310,000 were people who had been displaced by the Soviet takeover of Eastern Europe, particularly Poles and persons from the Baltic republics of Estonia, Latvia, and Lithuania.

SEE ALSO

Displaced persons; Holocaust; International Refugee Organization; Nativism; Quota system; Refugees; VOLAGS

FURTHER READING

Dinnerstein, Leonard. *America and the Survivors of the Holocaust.* New York: Columbia University Press, 1982.

United States Displaced Persons Commission. *Memo to America: The DP Story.* Washington, D.C.: Government Printing Office, 1952.

Diversity programs

Diversity programs are a part of American immigration law. They began in 1988 with special provisions that were placed in the immigration laws providing visas for nationalities which would not otherwise be entitled to them, later called a diversity program. Their proponents have said that these provisions were designed to promote fairness in the allocation of visas, and opponents have said they were designed to enable more Europeans, especially Irish, to come to the United States.

There is some truth in both claims. The 1988 law called for 10,000 visas a year to be allocated to natives of "underrepresented countries" for 1990 and 1991. Underrepresented countries were defined as those that had received fewer than 5,000 visas in 1988. As part of the Immigration Act of 1990, Congress established a diversity program that came in two phases, a transitional program for the three years, 1992–94, and a "permanent" program for subsequent years. Under the transitional program, 40,000 visas a year were set aside for "diversity immigrants," with 40 percent of them, 12,000 a year, reserved for natives of Ireland.

From 1995 on, the law allocated 55,000 visas annually for diversity. Countries that have had 50,000 or more admissions over the previous five years are excluded from any year's program, and no nation may receive more than 3,850 diversity visas in any one year.

SEE ALSO

Immigration Act of 1990; Immigration policy

Dominicans

- *1990 Ancestry: 505,690*
- *Immigration, 1986–96: 405,239*
- *Immigration, 1931–96: 764,968*
- *Major period of immigration: 1961+*
- *Major areas of settlement: New York, Puerto Rico*

Dominicans come from the Dominican Republic, which comprises the eastern two-thirds of the Caribbean island called Hispaniola; Haiti occupies the other third. The Dominican Republic has a population of 8,228,151 in an area of 18,726 square miles, about twice the size of New Hampshire. The explorer Christopher Columbus landed on Hispaniola in 1492, and Santo Domingo, founded in 1496, is the oldest European-founded city in the New World. The colony remained Spanish until 1795, when it was ceded to France.

The successful revolution in Haiti in 1803 was followed by a Haitian conquest of Santo Domingo, the first of many bloody clashes between Haitians and Dominicans. Spanish rule was reestablished in 1809. The Dominicans expelled the Spanish in 1821 but were reconquered by Haitians the next year. The Haitians were expelled in 1841 and a republic established. A long, turbulent, and bloody history followed, which included an occupation by the U.S. Marines from 1916 to 1924. This history was capped by the ruthless and bloody dictatorship of Rafael Trujillo Molina, who ruled from 1930 until 1961. Trujillo's assassination in 1961 and the resultant chaos, including another American military intervention in 1965, triggered what has become a massive immigration to the United States.

In the 1950s just under 10,000 Dominicans immigrated to the United

Latin American baseball players, such as home run king Sammy Sosa, have become very important in the major leagues.

States. In the 1960s, 93,000 came; 148,000 arrived in the 1970s, 252,000 in the 1980s, and, through 1996, 334,000 had come in the 1990s. In 1995 Dominicans were the fourth largest national group to immigrate to the United States, and in 1996 the fifth largest. Dominicans are Spanish-speaking and mostly Roman Catholics.

About 75 percent of all the Dominicans who now live in the United States live in greater New York. About half of these live in Manhattan, mainly in two enclaves, the larger on the Upper West Side and the smaller on the Lower East Side. About 10 percent of Dominican Americans live in Puerto Rico, chiefly in its capital, San Juan. Nothing more clearly demonstrates the poverty of the Dominican Republic that this fact: although Puerto Ricans flee poverty at home for the better conditions in the United States, many Dominicans find the conditions in Puerto Rico better than at home. In addition, many Dominicans use Puerto Rico—which is "right next door," across the narrow Mona Passage—as a stepping-stone to the United States. For a long time relatively few Dominicans became naturalized citizens. As late as 1987 only 4,257 did. Naturalization has increased steadily since that time: in 1996 27,293 Dominicans became American citizens.

Most Dominican Americans, whether naturalized or not, continue to maintain close relations with their homeland. At one time or another most Dominican immigrants have participated in circular migration between their island and the United States. As with Puerto Ricans, relatively inexpensive air fares enable Dominicans to make holiday and vacation visits "back home," and the coming and going of these "Dominican Yorkers" is a significant factor in the Republic's tourist industry. In addition, it is estimated that current remittances from immigrants in the United States to their relatives run at about $1 billion annually. The INS and the Census Bureau estimated that, in 1996, there were 50,000 Dominicans illegally in the United States. The island ranked 13th among the sources of illegal immigrants migrants.

Two aspects of Dominican American culture have spread widely in the United States. The first is an import, the stylish music and dance form, in 2/4 time, called the *merengue*, which was native to their home island and has become popular among many Americans who are not Dominicans. The second is baseball. This American game has become immensely popular in the entire Caribbean region, but nowhere more enthusiastically than in the Dominican Republic, where sandlot and club baseball is played virtually everywhere. Latin American baseball players—the most famous of whom was the Puerto Rican–born Roberto Clemente—have made a major impact on major league baseball and many Dominicans, such as the pitcher Juan

Marichal, and the new home-run hitter, Sammy Sosa, have become stars in the United States and idols in the Dominican Republic.

SEE ALSO

Caribbean; Circular migration; Haiti; Hispanics; Illegal immigrants; Puerto Ricans

FURTHER READING

Grasmuck, Shirley, and Patricia Pessar. *Between Two Islands: Dominican International Migration.* Berkeley: University of California Press, 1991.
Torres-Saillant, Silvio, and Ramona Hernández. *The Dominican Americans.* Westport, Conn.: Greenwood Press, 1998.

Dutch

- *1990 Ancestry: 6,227,089*
- *Immigration, 1986–96: 14,452*
- *Immigration, 1820–1996: 382,960*
- *Major periods of immigration: Colonial period, 1830–1857, 1880–93, 1900–14, 1945–65*
- *Major areas of settlement: New York, Michigan, Wisconsin*

The initial settlement of the Dutch in North America was due to the commercial activities of Dutch trading and colonizing companies, the most important of which in the New World was the Dutch West India Company, chartered in 1621. These companies were modeled on the fabulously profitable Dutch East India Company, but none achieved economic success. The West India Company's major goal was to wrest Brazil from the Portuguese, but its colony there was lost after three decades in 1654. It also seized colonies in Guiana and on several West Indian islands, which remained Dutch well into the 20th century.

The first Dutch settlement in North America was in 1619 on the Hudson River near what is now Albany, New

The earliest surviving view, from 1651, of New Amsterdam, now New York, was incorrectly engraved and should be reversed. The ships are anchored about where the Statue of Liberty and Ellis Island are today.

York. In 1626 the Dutch West India Company founded New Amsterdam at the mouth of the Hudson, which, after the British conquered it in 1664, was renamed New York. At that time New Netherland had about 10,000 people of European ancestry, 30 percent of whom were non-Dutch.

From the point of view of the merchants who ran the West India Company, New Netherland, as the whole Dutch settlement area in New York and adjoining Connecticut and New Jersey was called, never turned a profit. But the Dutch had founded one of the world's great cities. During New Netherland's 50-year life span, a total of perhaps 6,000 Dutch emigrated to North America. There was only a scattered migration of Dutch during the rest of the colonial period. Nevertheless, by the time of the first census in 1790, there were about 100,000 people of Dutch ancestry in the United States, almost all of them American-born. Eighty percent of them lived within 50 miles of New York City.

These Dutch Americans, and their descendants, can be called "Old Dutch." They have had great influence in American life and the group has produced three presidents—Martin Van Buren and the distant cousins Theodore Roosevelt and Franklin Delano Roosevelt—and a number of other national and regional political and cultural leaders. The most prominent Dutch American businessman, Cornelius Vanderbilt, a 19th-century railroad entrepreneur, founded one of the great American fortunes. His descendants are still wealthy and socially prominent. The Holland Society of New York is the best known of several organizations devoted to preserving the "Old Dutch" heritage.

The overwhelming majority of Dutch who have come to America have been Hollanders who speak the Dutch language; most of the rest have been Frisians, a minority group in both the Netherlands and Germany, whose language is related to but distinct from both Dutch and German. The Flemings, whose language is almost the same as Dutch, are discussed under Belgians. Since Dutch and German are related languages, other Americans have long had trouble distinguishing between them. In a vain effort to end this confusion, the Dutch in America have often referred to themselves as "Hollanders" or "Netherlanders."

No further significant immigration of Dutch occurred until about 1830, when movements that eventually brought some 250,000 Dutch to the United States began. This first "New Dutch" immigration was caused by a number of factors, including population pressure, the infestation of the fungus *Phytophthora infestans*, which destroyed the potato crop, and religious differences, sometimes called a pietistic revolt. Two separate Protestant groups, each led by its own pastor, founded settlements in Holland, Michigan, and Pella, Iowa, while a Catholic group, led by its priest, settled in the Fox River Valley of Wisconsin. This communal migration, which brought some 20,000 Dutch to the United States, was largely stopped by the financial panic of 1857 in the United States.

During the American Civil War and for decades afterward, the Dutch migration was largely family migration. Most of these migrated to the areas in Michigan and elsewhere already settled by Hollanders. This and subsequent Dutch migration was sensitive to economic conditions in both the Nether-lands and the United States and to wars. Migration was greatly spurred by an agricultural crisis in the Netherlands in the 1880s, which sent about 75,000 to the United States until the depression of 1893 slowed it perceptibly. Another 75,000 came in the decade and a half before World War I, and another 20,000 in the 1920s. Few came during the Great Depression and World War II, although 3,000 to 4,000 Dutch refugees from the Nazis immigrated to the United States.

Prior to World War II, the Dutch government policy neither hindered nor encouraged emigration. But after World War II the Netherlands, which had suffered badly during World War II, was considered overpopulated, and the Dutch government subsidized emigrants. Perhaps 400,000 Dutch emigrated in the 20 years after World War II, Only about a fifth of them went to the United States, because of existing American immigration policies; more than a third went to Canada and nearly 30 percent to Australia. These later Dutch immigrants, unlike most of their predecessors, were not attracted to the traditional Dutch settlement areas in the Middle West, but tended to settle in

A Dutch mother and her 11 children on the way to Minnesota were photographed on Ellis Island in 1908. There seem to be two sets of twins.

metropolitan New York and in California. Very few were farmers.

Throughout the 19th century the Dutch immigrants in the United States remained predominantly rural, with relatively few living in urban areas. In the 20th century more and more of the immigrants followed urban, nonagricultural pursuits. The midwestern Dutch settlement areas, particularly those in Michigan and Iowa, have remained heavily Dutch in ethnic composition. As the Netherlands was neutral during World War I, the Dutch suffered somewhat from nativism, since many believed them, falsely, to be pro-German. The state laws that outlawed foreign-language preaching helped to end that practice in many Dutch American churches. Some 80 percent of the New Dutch have been Calvinist Protestants, and most of the Dutch settlement areas have been socially conservative and strongly Republican since the Civil War.

SEE ALSO

Belgians; Immigration Act of 1924; Immigration Act of 1952; Nativism; Pennsylvania Dutch; Protestantism; Refugees

FURTHER READING

Goodfriend, Joyce D. *Before the Melting Pot: Society and Culture in Colonial New York City* Princeton, N.J.: Princeton University Press, 1992.
Lucas, Henry S. *Netherlanders in America: Dutch Immigration to the United States and Canada.* Ann Arbor: University of Michigan Press, 1955.
Swierenga, Robert P., ed. *The Dutch in America: Immigration, Settlement, and Cultural Change.* New Brunswick, N.J.: Rutgers University Press, 1985.

East Indians

SEE Asian Indians

Eastern Orthodox churches

Christian Eastern Orthodox churches are usually known in America by their national names such as Greek, Russian, Armenian, Serbian, Syrian, or Ukrainian. Altogether the so-called Orthodox Communion, for which there is no overall spiritual leader, includes 21 different national bodies. All derive more or less from the split, which began more than a thousand years ago, between churches that continued to owe their allegiance to Rome, and those that owed allegiance to Constantinople, culminating in a formal schism in 1054. The breakup of empires after World Wars I and II also affected many of the national churches and created others.

The first Eastern Orthodox parish in the United States was founded in New Orleans in 1866, but most of the American parishes were established following the growth of immigration from eastern Europe and the Mediterranean in the 20th century. The largest of the Eastern Orthodox churches in America is the Greek Orthodox, followed by the Russian Orthodox. All told, there are perhaps 4 million Eastern Orthodox communicants in the United States.

SEE ALSO

Armenians; Eastern Rite churches; Greeks; Serbs; Syrians; Russians; Ukrainians

FURTHER READING

Ahlstrom, Sydney E. *A Religious History of the American People.* New Haven: Yale University Press, 1972, (See especially the chapter on "The Ancient Eastern Churches in America.")
Erickson, John H. *Orthodox Christians in America.* New York: Oxford University Press, 1999.

Ware, Kallistos. "Eastern Christendom."
In John McManners, ed. *The Oxford
Illustrated History of Christianity*. New
York: Oxford University Press, 1990.

Eastern Rite churches

Eastern Rite churches, unlike the more
numerous Eastern Orthodox churches,
date from the 15th and 16th centuries
and owe their allegiance to the Pope in
Rome, although much of their ritual is
different. These churches are sometimes
called Eastern, Byzantine, or Greek
Catholics, although few if any Greeks
are members. Much less numerous
than Eastern Orthodox, the largest
groups in the United States are called
Ruthenians according to most Catholic
directories, and include many Carpatho-
Rusyns, Croats, Hungarians, and Slovaks. The second largest group consists
of Ukrainians, while two Arab groups,
Melchites and Maronites, have few
members in the United States.

SEE ALSO

Arabs; Carpatho-Rusyns; Croats; Hungarians; Roman Catholics; Ukrainians

FURTHER READING

Ahlstrom, Sydney E. *A Religious History
of the American People*. New Haven:
Yale University Press, 1972. (See especial-
ly the chapter on "The Ancient Eastern
Churches in America.")
Erickson, John H. *Orthodox Christians in
America*. New York: Oxford University
Press, 1999.

Ecuadorians

- *1990 Ancestry: 197,374*
- *Immigration, 1986–96: 79,073*
- *Immigration, 1932–96: 201,195*
- *Major period of immigration: 1960+*
- *Major area of settlement: New York*

Ecuador, a mountainous country on the
Pacific coast of South America, contains 109,483 square miles and is
about the size of Colorado. It is named
after the equator, which passes through
it. It has more than 11.5 million people, 55 percent of whom are *mestizo*
("mixed blood," that is, largely of
indigenous and other ancestry). Twenty-
five percent are of indigenous ancestry,
and those of African and European
ancestry each constitute 10 percent of
the population. Spanish is the official
language, and 95 percent of the population is Roman Catholic.

Before conquest by the Spaniards
in the 16th century, Ecuador was a part
of the Incan empire. It remained a
Spanish colony until 1822; for eight
years it was part of Colombia. Since
1830 it has been an independent country. Ecuador has had a turbulent political history, and, despite the presence of
major deposits of petroleum, the country and most of its people are poor.

Few Ecuadorians immigrated to the
United States until the 1960s, when
36,000 came. Another 50,000 immigrated in the 1970s and 1980s, and
even more arrived during the 1990s.
The U.S. government estimated that
there were 55,000 Ecuadorians in the
country illegally, the 12th largest number from any nation. In addition,
between 1986 and 1996, under the provisions of the Immigration Reform and
Control Act of 1986 (IRCA), nearly
15,000 Ecuadorians who had entered
illegally went through the complex
process of legalization and became
United States citizens.

Ecuadorians are concentrated in
New York City, which is said to be
Ecuador's third largest city, as only two

Ellis Island

Ellis Island is a small, largely man-made island in New York harbor, now 27.5 acres, which from 1892 to 1932 served as the chief American immigration station through which more than 12 million immigrants passed. It was used chiefly for deportees after 1932 and during World War II it served as an internment camp for enemy aliens. It was vacated by the Immigration and Naturalization Service in 1954 and for almost 30 years was abandoned, although in 1965 it was made a national monument along with the neighboring Statue of Liberty. The main building was restored in the 1980s and now houses a magnificent museum of immigration which opened in 1990 and is run by the National Park Service.

A Supreme Court decision in 1989 awarded jurisdiction over most of Ellis Island, but not the museum, to the state of New Jersey.

It has become an important icon of immigration to America, second only to the Statue of Liberty.

These detained immigrants are spending Christmas 1906 on Ellis Island. Most immigrants were processed within a single day. The man at the far right is Robert Watchorn, an English immigrant and commissioner of immigration from 1905 to 1909.

The restored main building on Ellis Island has housed, since it opened in 1990, the world's most important museum of immigration history.

Most of the 12 million immigrants who passed through Ellis Island did so very quickly and did not even spend a night there. They were given largely cursory medical examinations, provided with directions and sometimes aided in the purchase of railroad tickets, and ushered on to boats to either New York City or the New Jersey shore. For those who had become ill, there was a hospital, and there were volunteer social workers to give advice. A very tiny percentage were refused admittance for one reason or another and were held on Ellis Island until they could be placed on a ship to return to where they came from.

SEE ALSO

Angel Island; Castle Garden; Deportation; Internment; Statue of Liberty

FURTHER READING

Pitkin, Thomas M. *Keepers of the Gate: A History of Ellis Island.* New York: New York University Press, 1975.
Shapiro, Mary J. *Ellis Island: An Illustrated History of the Immigrant Experience.* New York: Macmillan, 1991.
Yans-McLaughlin, Virginia, and Marjorie Lightman. *Ellis Island and the Peopling of America: The Official Guide.* New York: W.W. Norton, 1997.

El Salvadorans

SEE Salvadorans

Emigrant

An emigrant is a person migrating *from* one country to another. From the point of view of the country of origin, that person is an emigrant, but from the point of view of the receiving country, an immigrant. Thus, when Albert Einstein came to the United States in 1933 he was an emigrant from Germany but an immigrant to the United States.

SEE ALSO
Immigrant

Emigration from the United States

Emigration from the United States refers to the departure of American residents for permanent residence elsewhere. Millions of Americans live abroad, but most retain their citizenship. Although the U.S. government now keeps no statistics on the emigration of citizens, it did do so between 1918 and 1950. In that period 789,000 citizens were recorded as emigrating permanently, about 25,000 a year.

In certain times of crisis there has been mass expatriation, most notably after the American Revolution, when perhaps 80,000 Americans who opposed independence left the country.

Many settled in Great Britain and Canada, particularly in Ontario, where they are known as United Empire Loyalists. Other large-scale movements to Canada occurred in the years around 1900, when thousands of Americans went to the Canadian to get agricultural land when good land was no longer cheap in the United States, and at the height of the Vietnam War in the late 1960s and early 1970s, when many thousands of young men emigrated to avoid military service in a war they opposed.

In addition, millions of people who temporarily came to the United States eventually returned home. These returned migrants, sometimes called sojourners, are not really emigrants from America.

SEE ALSO

Canadians; Emigrant; Return migration; Sojourners

FURTHER READING

Brown, Wallace, and Hereward Senior. *Victorious in Defeat: The American Loyalists in Exile.* New York: Facts on File, 1984.

Norton, Mary Beth. *The British-Americans: The Loyalist Exiles in England, 1774–1789.* Boston: Little, Brown, 1972.

Enemy aliens

SEE Alien Enemies Act

English

- *1990 Ancestry: 32,651,788*
- *Immigration, 1986–96: 165,436 (United Kingdom)*
- *Immigration, 1820–1996: 5,225,701 (United Kingdom)*
- *Major period of immigration: Colonial period*
- *Major area of settlement: Atlantic seaboard*

No group is more difficult to write about with precision than the English because they became, as far as most Americans were concerned after the colonial period, what one historian calls "invisible immigrants." That is because so many of them were so much like many Americans that they blended into the population almost imperceptibly. (The same may be said for many 20th-century Canadians.) The English are "invisible" in another way: American immigration statistics do not differentiate between English and the other ethnic groups native to Britain: the Cornish, Irish, Scotch-Irish, Scots, and Welsh. All are now listed under United Kingdom.

Although representatives of two other European nations, Spain and France, founded prior settlements in what is now the United States, the English, because of their much larger numbers and political power, became what some historians call the "charter group" in the European conquest of the United States.

This means that the English language and English institutions—law, customs and religion—predominated, although they were modified by the very different conditions that prevailed in the new settlements. These environmental differences were not just between England and America, but differences between, say, New England and the southern colonies. The English immigrants of the colonial period were not drawn evenly from all parts of England but were predominantly from the southeast counties around London and the southwestern counties around Bristol. Those two cities were the major ports for immigrants to America in those years.

English settlers were predominant in all the North American colonies south of

NOVA BRITANNIA.
OFFERING MOST
Excellent fruites by Planting in
VIRGINIA.
Exciting all such as be well affected to further the same.

LONDON
Printed for SAMVEL MACHAM, and are to be sold at his Shop in Pauls Church-yard, at the Signe of the Bul-head.
1 6 0 9.

Although by 1609 English colonists in Virginia were dying in large numbers, advertisements such as this broadside did not tell the truth.

Embarking with your Family for America—
Taking Leave of Albion's White Cliffs—
No more Taxes—

Landing at an American Port, more dead than
alive— The Cholera raging — Coffins as common as packing cases — half a mind to go
back again — !!

Strolling in the Woods — & having an In-
terview with the Natives!

Your Hut on Fire for the 3rd time. Goods & chattels included— No engines no Water nor Neighbourly assistance, not having had no prospect or a subscription or Poor
Relief— sit down unable to do any thing & witness
the destruction of your little all— until the dry grass catch-
es fire & compells you to run off your own Estate—

Extracts from an 1834 narrative called "Emigration! Detailing the Progress and Vicissitudes of an Emigrant" illustrate the difficulties faced by English emigrants on their way to and once arriving in North America, including disease, snakes, and fire. The aim of the narrative seems to be to discourage emigration. One picture, not shown, shows immigrants about to be eaten by cannibals.

Canada, but, after the 17th century, they were not quite a majority. The best estimate we have, based on the first United States census (taken in 1790), is that persons of English ancestry were 49 percent of the non-Indian population. (The census did not bother to count Indians then.) African Americans were the next largest group, at 16 percent, followed by Irish, Germans, Scots, and Dutch.

By region, New England was the most heavily English, and Massachusetts, with some 80 percent, was the most English state in 1790. Of course the English language and English law prevailed in each of the original thirteen states, as did some form of Protestant Christianity. Because English persons were so numerous, they seldom formed specifically ethnic organizations. In Pennsylvania, for example, the first organization of English immigrants, the Society of the Sons of St. George "for the Advice and Assistance of Englishmen in distress" was not founded until 1772, 23 years after the Scots, 13 years after

the Irish, and 8 years after the Germans of Pennsylvania had formed societies for similar purposes. Two other branches of the St. George Society were later formed in New York City and in Charleston.

Although some English immigrants in the colonial period, such as the Pilgrims and many of the Puritans, came for religious reasons, and, after the return of the Stuart monarchy in the 1660s a few others came for political reasons, most English immigrants in the colonial period, and after, came for economic reasons. A goodly number of them were only semi-free: ten of thousands of English immigrants came as indentured servants, bound to work for a master for a term of years. Indentured servants were a majority of the English immigrants to Virginia and Maryland in the colonial period, and some indentured servants were present in all the colonies. In addition, about 20,000 English convicts were sent to the 13 colonies. These were persons sentenced to "transportation for life" for both criminal and political offenses and were forbidden to return to England.

After the end of the Revolutionary War in 1783, immigration from Britain to America, cut off during the war, resumed. Immediately after the war a few English sympathizers with the American Revolution immigrated to the new nation, most notably the noted English chemist and reformer, Joseph Priestley, one of the rare pre-20th-century immigrants who was famous *before* coming to America. For about three decades after the Revolution the British government tried to limit emigration. It was particularly concerned with the emigration of skilled workers—what were called artisans and mechanics—who knew at first hand the "secrets" of the machines of the first industrial revolution. These efforts proved fruitless: encouraged by rewards offered by American entrepreneurs and by the greater economic and social opportunities available, many Englishmen with the "secrets" managed to come to America.

The most well known of these immigrants involved in what we now call "technology transfer" was Samuel Slater. As first an apprentice and then a mill foreman, Slater had learned all about the new textile machines. He emigrated illegally from England in 1789 and helped to establish the cotton textile industry in New England and became a very prosperous owner of a number of factories. Dozens of other English workmen brought the first industrial revolution to America a generation or so after it began in Britain.

During the War of 1812 between the United States and Great Britain, all British aliens were required to register, and at least 10,000 did so. A small number of these, mostly merchants and their employees, were eventually interned in centers at least 40 miles from the seacoast. Those from New York City, for example, were interned in Fishkill, New York.

After 1820 immigration of English increased as did the immigration of the other British ethnic groups. Large numbers of these immigrants were skilled workingmen, particularly members of the building trades and miners of all kinds, and English workmen were particularly important in the beginnings of the American trade union movement. Most of those stayed, but some workmen regularly crossed and recrossed the Atlantic for seasonal work, such as the English house painters who worked in America every spring and then returned to Britain to work for the rest of the year.

Throughout the 19th century English immigrants established dozens of colonies, most of them short-lived, in the midwestern United States. Some were religious in nature, others secular and sometimes socialist. The most famous of the latter was established by Robert Owen at New Harmony, Indiana, in 1825. Although it soon collapsed, some 30 of its buildings have been restored and are open to the public. English immigrants also established a number of fraternal benefit associations, some of which, like the Odd Fellows, survive today, but without specific ethnic connotations. Other ethnic associations formed in the 19th century, such as the Sons of St. George, which had more than 30,000 members, failed to survive. Many of the British ethnic organizations had nativist overtones, and many English immigrants were associated with the anti-Catholic American Protective Association in the late 19th century.

There were a number newspapers and magazines founded to appeal to English immigrants in the 19th century, but only one, *Albion* (New York, 1827–63), lasted very long. More successful were a few publications aimed at British rather than just English immigrants: three of them lasted for 25 years or more, but none exist today.

In the 20th century English immigration has been less significant, both in number and cultural impact, than in previous times. As opposed to the 19th-century situation when more British emigrants came to the United States than to the entire British Empire, in the 20th century British emigration to Canada alone was greater than that to the United States. Some historians believe that the reduction in enmity between the United States and Great Britain that began in the 1890s and developed into an Anglo-American alliance in the two World Wars was a significant factor in the lowering of English immigrant self-consciousness.

English actors have long been prominent on the American stage, and with the development of the movies, in Hollywood as well. This included the greatest moviemaker of them all, Charlie (later Sir Charles) Chaplin. During World War II, when England underwent sustained aerial bombardment, thousands of English children, most from the middle and upper classes, were given temporary homes by American families. In the immediate aftermath of that war, 70,000 British women, mostly English, came to the United States as war brides of American soldiers they had married overseas during and after the war.

SEE ALSO

Aliens; American Protective Association; Convicts; Cornish; Indentured servants; Internment; Irish; Scotch-Irish; Scots; War brides; Welsh

FURTHER READING

Bailey, Anthony. *America, Lost & Found.* 1980. Reprint, Chicago: University of Chicago Press, 2000. (A memoir of a World War II child in the United States)

Berthoff, Rowland T. *British Immigrants in Industrial America.* Cambridge: Harvard University Press, 1953.

Erickson, Charlotte. *Invisible Immigrants.* Miami: University of Miami Press, 1972.

Van Vugt, William E. *Britain to America: Mid–Nineteenth-Century Immigrants to the United States.* Urbana: University of Illinois Press, 1999.

Virden, Jenel. *Good-bye Piccadilly: British War Brides in America.* Urbana: University of Illinois Press, 1996.

Eritreans

SEE Ethiopians and Eritreans

Estonians

- *1990 Ancestry: 26,762*
- *Immigration, 1986–96: 1,231*
- *Major periods of immigration: 1890–1914, 1948–65*
- *Major areas of settlement: northeastern cities, especially New York*

Estonia is a small country that has existed independently in modern times only between 1918 and 1940 and since 1991. German Teutonic knights conquered Estonia in the 13th century, and their descendants became an entrenched upper class. During most of the modern period it was a part of the Swedish, Russian, and Soviet empires. Today about 1.5 million persons live there, some 60 percent of them ethnically Estonian. The Estonian language is linguistically close to Finnish, and most Estonians have been Lutherans since the Protestant Reformation of the 16th century.

There were a few Estonians in colonial North America, but little is known about them. Estonians began coming to the United States in discernible numbers in the late 19th century. Experts employed by Congress in the 1920s to set quotas estimated the

Estonian American population at just over 5,000 in 1890 and nearly 70,000 in 1920. Perhaps 3,000 more came before World War II.

Although the earliest Estonian institutions were all in the rural Midwest and religious—a Lutheran congregation near Ft. Pierre, South Dakota, in 1897, a church in Bloomville, Wisconsin, and community buildings near Chester, Montana—the bulk of the pre–World War I Estonian immigrants were urban, socialist-oriented workers. A number of radical Estonians fled to the United States after the failure of the 1905 Russian Revolution in which they had participated. Estonian workers' societies were organized in a number of American cities, most importantly in New York and San Francisco.

All Estonian Americans welcomed the Russian Revolution of 1917 but for quite different reasons. Most saw the revolution as a chance for an independent Estonia, which did emerge, but the extreme radicals wanted Estonia included in the new Soviet Union. A whole variety of new, nonradical Estonian American organizations developed. The chief of these was the Estonian Educational Society, which established a cultural center in New York City.

After World War II, when Estonia had been amalgamated into the Soviet Union as the Estonian Socialist Soviet Republic, some 15,000 Estonians came to the United States as displaced persons or under other refugee programs. A wide variety of communal organizations were established by these immigrants and their children, some of them jointly with the two other subject Baltic groups, the Latvians and Lithuanians. The reemergence of the Estonian nation has made some of these organizations obsolete, but many Estonian and other Baltic Americans have organized to support their newly freed former homelands.

SEE ALSO

Displaced persons; Latvians; Lithuanians; Refugees

FURTHER READING

Pennar, Jaan, et al., eds. *The Estonians in America, 1627-1975: A Chronology and Fact Book* Dobbs Ferry, N.Y.: Oceana, 1975.

Ethiopians and Eritreans

- *1990 Ancestry: 34,851*
- *Immigration, 1986-96: 73,036*
- *Immigration, 1820-1996: n.a.*
- *Major periods of immigration: since 1976*
- *Major areas of settlement: Washington, D.C., Los Angeles, New York, and Dallas*

Ethiopia is an ancient land on the east coast of Africa, part of the so-called Horn of Africa. Its 60 million people live in a country of 471,776 square miles. Although there are traditions and myths claiming that King Solomon's son by the Queen of Sheba founded the first Ethiopian kingdom in the 10th century B.C., the earliest kingdom that can be documented dates from the 2nd century B.C. Many Ethiopians were converted to Christianity in the 4th century A.D., and two centuries later some converted to Judaism. The rise of Islam in the 7th century cut Ethiopia off from easy contact with Byzantine civilization, and for more than a thousand years Ethiopia was racked by internal struggles.

The opening of the Suez Canal in 1889 made Ethiopia strategically significant to European powers, and the Italians achieved prominence in the area. Italy seized Eritrea in 1890 and defeated Ethiopia in 1898. In 1935, in what is now regarded as a prologue to World War II, the Italian dictator Benito Mus-

How this group of Ethiopians came to Ellis Island in 1910 is not clear. Perhaps they were imported for theatrical or display purposes.

solini conquered Ethiopia and drove its emperor, Haile Selassie, into exile. The emperor made a dramatic appeal before the League of Nations in Geneva, but received sympathy instead of aid. Britain liberated Ethiopia and restored Haile Selassie to the throne and united Eritrea with Ethiopia.

In 1974 Haile Selassie, who had assumed power in 1930, was deposed, an event that set off a series of rebellions and civil wars, including a 30-year struggle by Eritreans for independence, which they finally achieved in 1973. Many authorities argue that Ethiopians and Eritreans are one people, and that is the way they are treated in the United States, as the INS does not list Eritreans separately.

Significant immigration from Ethiopia grew out of these political and military struggles. Initially a few elite students and exiles came, but, beginning in 1976, refugees began to come in fairly large numbers, especially after passage of the Refugee Act of 1980.

Between 1976 and 1996, 33,648 Ethiopian and Eritrean refugees were admitted to the United States and 6,603 others were granted asylum. More than three-fifths of these immigrants have been men, and the Ethiopian American community remains heavily male.

American officials, guided in part by the notion that the selection should favor those most likely to make a success in the United States, have shown a bias toward selecting Christians and well educated members of the elite. One study reported that while among Ethiopian refugees in Africa only 4 percent had attended a university, but that almost 20 percent of the Ethiopian family heads admitted to the United States had done so. As is typical of non-technologically trained elites, most refugees experience downward economic and social mobility after coming to the United States. University graduates may become taxi drivers, as many in Washington have done. A significant number have acquired enough capital to establish Ethiopian restaurants in cities that attract up-scale customers, as opposed to, say, the restaurants opened by Greek immigrants earlier in the century, which catered to workingmen.

SEE ALSO

Africans; Asylum; Refugee Act of 1980

FURTHER READING

Koehn, P. H. *Refugees from Revolution: U.S. Policy and Third World Migration.* Boulder, Colo.: Westview, 1991.
Schnapper, LaDena. *Teenage Refugees from Ethiopia Speak Out.* New York: Rosen, 1997.

Ethnic enclave

An ethnic enclave in the United States is an area, usually but not always in a city, in which members of a particular ethnic group live in close proximity to one another. These enclaves are usually also inhabited by some people who are not members of the group. They are sometimes termed "ghettos," but this is an inappropriate term. Ghettos, historically speaking, were districts in European cities in which Jews were compelled by law to live and work. Ethnic enclaves in the United States have been largely voluntary, although in some parts of the United States, in the past, residential segregation was enforced by law, and in many places is still encouraged in practice.

The first ethnic enclave in the American colonies was at Germantown, outside of Philadelphia, established in 1683. There have been—and are—"Chinatowns" in many cities, "Little Italies" in Manhattan, Chicago, and elsewhere, a "Greektown" in Detroit, a "Little Tokyo" in Los Angeles, and a "Little Havana" in Miami, to name only a few.

Critics of ethnic neighborhoods usually stress the negative factors of cultural isolation from the mainstream of American life, the promotion of clannishness, and the continuation of the use of ethnic languages. They ignore the positive factors. The following, from a memoir by a Swedish-American journalist written in 1890 about Swede Town in Chicago, describes the positive aspects well:

> The liveliest section of the busy Chicago Avenue shows, its entire length, a large mass of exclusively Swedish signs, that Andersen, Petterson, and Lundstrom were here conducting a Swedish general store, a Swedish bookshop, a Swedish beer saloon . . . and so on. And wherever one goes one hears Swedish sounds generally, and if one's thoughts are somewhat occupied, one can believe one has been quickly transported back to Sweden.

SEE ALSO

Cities

FURTHER READING

Kwong, Peter. *The New Chinatown*, rev. ed. New York: Hill & Wang, 1996.
Ward, David. *Cities and Immigrants: A Geography of Change in Nineteenth Century America*. New York: Oxford University Press, 1971.

Ethnicity

A person's ethnicity depends on the culture that he or she acquires. This is different from nationality, which depends upon the individual's citizenship but, sometimes ethnicity and nationality are the same. A Norwegian immigrant from Norway would be recorded in the American census and by immigration officials as having Norwegian nationality or national origin, and would also have Norwegian ethnicity. But a Polish immigrant, arriving at a time when a Polish state did not exist, would be listed in American records as having the nationality of the nation he or she came from— usually Russia, Austria or Germany— but would have Polish ethnicity. If these immigrants became naturalized both would acquire American citizenship and nationality and be considered as Norwegian American or Polish American.

SEE ALSO

Citizenship; Nationality; Naturalization

Eurocentric

Eurocentric is a term used by some scholars to describe the tendency in many histories of the United States to overemphasize the undoubted major contribution of European people and ideas in American life, with a resulting underemphasis on the contributions of Native Americans, Africans, Asians, and Hispanics.

SEE ALSO
Stereotypes

Europeans

- *Immigration, 1986–96: 1,259,337*
- *Immigration, 1820–1996: 38,071,793*

Europeans dominated American immigration until after World War II. Since the crumbling of the Soviet bloc in Eastern Europe and the dissolution of the Soviet Union have caused European immigration to increase. Although still a minority of all immigrants, Europeans accounted for more than 10 percent of immigrants in the period 1986–96.

SEE ALSO

Albanians; Alsatians; Austrians; Basques; Belgians; Belorussians; British; Bosnian Muslims; Bulgarians; Carpatho-Ruysins; Celts; Cornish; Croatians; Cypriots; Czechs; Danes; Dutch; English; Estonians; Finns; Flemings; French; Frisians; Georgians; Germans; Greeks; Gypsies; Hessians; Huguenots; Hungarians; Icelanders; Irish; Italians; Latvians; Lithuanians; Little Russians; Lusatian Sorbs; Luxembourgers; Macedonians; Magyars; Manx; Montenegrins; Norwegians; Poles; Portuguese; Romanians; Roms; Russians; Rusyns; Ruthenians; Scandinavians; Scotch-Irish; Scots; Serbs; Slavs; Slovaks; Slovenes; Sorbs; Spaniards; Swedes; Swiss; Ukrainians; Vikings; Walloons; Welsh; Wends

Exiles

Exiles are, in the simplest sense, persons who are absent from their homes, and, in that sense, all immigrants are exiles. In fact, the term "Mother of Exiles" is one of the names sometimes given to the Statue of Liberty. However, the term is more often used to describe a forced exile, particularly one that focuses on a particular individual or group for political, religious, or ideological reasons. In modern times, the word refugee is often used instead.

SEE ALSO
Refugees; Statue of Liberty

Expatriation

Expatriation is the act of voluntarily giving up one's nationality, a kind of denaturalization. The act of immigration is not necessarily expatriation: many immigrants live most of their lives in a new country without changing their citizenship or nationality. In the United States such persons are classified as "resident aliens." An immigrant to the United States expatriates when he or she becomes a naturalized American citizen.

The word *expatriate* is also used to describe Americans living in foreign countries (for example, Ernest Hemingway and other American writers who lived in Paris in the 1920s), but the vast majority of these persons do not give up their American citizenship and thus do not really expatriate.

SEE ALSO
Denaturalization; Naturalization

Fenian Brotherhood

The Fenian Brotherhood was founded in New York in 1858. It was the American version of the Irish Revolutionary Brotherhood founded in Dublin, Ireland, in the same year. Both were dedicated to Irish independence from Great Britain. The American organization was intended to raise money and volunteers to be sent to Ireland to help in the struggle. But after the Civil War, with a membership of 250,000, many of them war veterans, the American organization decided to invade sparsely defended Canada, conquer some of it, and hold it "hostage" until Britain granted Ireland freedom. Two abortive invasions—raids, really—took place in 1866 and 1870 and were easily put down by American and British armed forces. After 1870 the organization collapsed.

SEE ALSO
Irish

FURTHER READING

Jenkins, Brian. *Fenians and Anglo-American Relations during Reconstruction.* Ithaca, N.Y.: Cornell University Press, 1969.

Filipinos

- *1990 Population: 1,419,711*
- *Immigration, 1820–1996: around 1,500,000*
- *Major periods of immigration: 1903–34, 1965+*
- *Major areas of settlement: California, Hawaii, Illinois, New York*

The earliest Filipinos that we know of in what is now the United States were a few handfuls who came, via Mexico, to Louisiana early in the 18th century. There is no direct connection between them and the Filipinos who began to come to the United States after the American conquest of their home islands in 1898. The first post-1898 group of immigrants were several hundred elite students, called *pensionados*, who were chosen, sponsored and financed by the U.S. government to be educated at American universities in a brief program that lasted from 1903 to 1910. Most returned to the Philippines, and many held important government positions there.

Other Filipinos followed their example, without either sponsorship or financing: one scholar estimates that 14,000 Filipinos studied at U.S. colleges and universities between 1910 and 1938. For one reason or another, however, most did not complete their studies.

The second and much larger group was of farm laborers. After the Gentlemen's Agreement of 1907–8 cut off the supply of Japanese laborers, the Hawaiian Sugar Planters Association brought 119,470 Filipinos to work on the sugar and pineapple plantations. Many of these workers eventually moved on to the United States. By 1940 there were 45,000 Filipinos in Hawaii and 30,000 on the American mainland. Only about 6 percent of latter were female. Most of the immigrant Filipinos were either farm laborers or employed in casual occupations in American cities. Some found niches as pullman porters and post office employees.

In addition, a number of Filipino writers and other intellectuals were attracted to the United States where most experienced disappointment. The most distinguished of them, Carlos Bulosan, wrote: "Do you know what a Filipino feels in America? . . . He is the

Filipino American servicemen and friends gather in downtown Los Angeles to celebrate the end of World War II.

loneliest thing on earth. There is much to be appreciated . . . beauty, wealth, grandeur. But is he part of these luxuries? He looks, poor man, through the fingers of his eyes. . . . He is betrayed."

From 1924 to 1943, Filipinos were the only Asian laborers able to immigrate to the United States. This was because, since the Philippines belonged to the United States as a result of the Spanish-American War (1898), the courts ruled that Filipinos were American nationals and could not be kept out of the United States. On the other hand, they were not, as Hawaiians were, U.S. citizens, and since they were not "white," were not eligible for naturalization. Filipinos born in Hawaii or on the American mainland were birthright citizens. This second stage of Filipino migration was all but stopped by two events: the onset of the Great Depression of the 1930s, and the passage of a law in 1934 which both promised the Philippines independence in 1945 and limited further Filipino immigration to 50 in any one year. As was the case with other Asians, Filipinos were violently opposed by American nativists, especially in California.

A 1935 federal statute shows how unwanted Filipinos were. That law gave a free trip to the Philippines to any Filipino who would return there. Only about 2,000 accepted the offer.

In 1946, after World War II, during which many Filipinos fought with Americans against Japan, Congress passed a law enabling Filipinos to be naturalized, but did not increase their token immigration quota.

The passage of the Immigration Act of 1965 set off the third and continuing phase of Filipino immigration. In recent years, Filipinos have been the second most numerous national immigrant group. Unlike most of their predecessors, perhaps two-thirds of the post-1965 Filipino immigrants have been of the professional classes, very large numbers of them health professionals. Nurses from the Philippines play an important role in providing health care to all Americans, and their presence has helped to make women a majority, 53 percent, of all Filipino Americans. Although Filipinos of both genders are well educated, theirs is one of the few groups in which women have more higher education than men: in 1990,

41.6 percent of Filipino women had bachelor's degrees, as opposed to 36.2 percent of Filipino men. In addition to the large number of legal immigrants, the INS and the Census Bureau have estimated that there are 95,000 Filipinos in the United States illegally, the sixth-largest national total.

SEE ALSO

Birthright citizens; Gentlemen's Agreement; Hawaiian Sugar Planters Association; Illegal immigrants; Immigration Act of 1965; Nativism; Naturalization

FURTHER READING

Bulosan, Carlos. *America Is in the Heart: A Personal History*. Seattle: University of Washington Press, 1973.
Posadas, Barbara M. *The Filipino Americans*. Westport, Conn.: Greenwood, 1999.

Finns

- *1990 Ancestry: 658,870*
- *Immigration, 1986–96: 4,688*
- *Immigration, 1820–1996: around 350,000*
- *Major period of immigration: 1880–1920*
- *Major areas of settlement: Michigan and Minnesota*

The first Finns in North America were perhaps 200 members of the small and short-lived Swedish colony along the banks of the Delaware River. Founded in 1638, New Sweden had fewer than 500 inhabitants when it was conquered in 1655 by the Dutch, who, in turn, were conquered by the British in 1664. Most Swedes and Finns remained there or in neighboring New Jersey, but by the end of the 18th century, the only traces of them were a few place names.

It was the Finns and the Swedes who brought the log cabin to America, a form of housing that came to be regarded as the typical pioneer American home. It was natural for Finns to be part of a Swedish colony, as Finland was then a duchy of Sweden. After 1808, however, Finland was ruled by Czarist Russia, so after that time Finns were not recorded separately in the American immigration data.

After the colonial period and until the 1860s, only a very few Finns came to the United States, most of them sailors who left their ships in American ports. Beginning in the 1860s, Finns who had been living and working in Norway were recruited to come to Michigan as miners, and at about the same time other Finns from Norway began settling farmland in Minnesota. In the 1870s perhaps 3,000 Finns immigrated, most of them directly from Finland. The volume of emigration increased after that and, according to Finnish statistics, more than 330,000 Finns emigrated between the 1880s and 1920, the vast majority of them to the United States.

Overwhelmingly these Finns were from rural areas, and perhaps 7 in 10 were unmarried young males. The motives for immigration were largely economic, but some came to avoid Russian military service and others came as political exiles. Most of the Finns who came to the United States did so via other European countries: at first they went largely through Sweden, but later they traveled via Germany or England. Perhaps 30 percent of those who came before 1920 eventually returned to Finland. Since 1920 very few Finns have come to America. Under the quota system that prevailed between 1924 and 1965, the annual Finnish quota was never larger than 566: in only one year, 1928, was that quota filled.

Following the example of earlier migrants, most of the Finns settled in

Although Suomi College—now Finlandia University—was established to preserve the Finnish immigrant heritage, it taught everyday commercial subjects as well. The class shown is doing bookkeeping exercises.

states close to the Canadian border. In 1900 almost half of the 63,000 Finns counted by the American census lived in just two states, Michigan and Minnesota. The census figures for 1910 and 1920 show that most Finns married other Finns: in 1910 more than 90 percent of the 80,000 American-born children of Finns had two Finnish-born parents, and 10 years later the figure was almost as high for the 145,000 such children recorded then. By 1920 the second generation of Finns was almost as numerous as the first, and by 1930 the second generation outnumbered the first.

As few of the Finns who came were skilled workmen, Finns took largely unskilled and semiskilled work in mines. They were particularly prominent in iron mining on the Mesabi Range in northern Minnesota and as seamen and dock workers in the iron ore trade on the Great Lakes.

In both Finland and the United States, most Finns were Lutherans, although many of the immigrants were hostile to the Lutheran state church which levied taxes on everyone. In 1904 Finns founded Suomi College—

now Finlandia University—in Hancock, Michigan, to train clergymen, something American ethnic groups had been doing since the Puritans founded Harvard College in 1636.

Relatively large numbers of Finns were active in labor and socialist organizations, and after the Russian Revolution, many Finnish American socialists became associated with American Communist parties. The most prominent historian of Finnish Americans has estimated that around 1916, when some 33,000 Finns were in organized Lutheran synods, nearly 13,000 were members of the Finnish Socialist Federation. The Federation was not just a political organization; its 260 local chapters sponsored social, cultural, and athletic events and in 1907 took control of the Work People's College near Duluth, Minnesota, which had been founded by Lutheran organizations. During World War I, the Finnish American labor movement, like most American radical movements suffered heavy blows. It was divided over whether to support the American entry into World War I and even more by the Russian Revolution (both took place in 1917). Conversely, large number of Finnish immigrants and their American-born children served in the American armed forces.

The lack of substantial immigration since World War I has gradually weakened Finnish American cultural institutions, and no such mass institutions survive today. However, many third- and fourth-generation Finnish Americans actively study and promote the Finnish American heritage.

SEE ALSO

Immigration Act of 1924; Quota system

FURTHER READING

Hoglund, A. William. *Finnish Immigrants in America, 1820–1920*. Madison: University of Wisconsin Press, 1960.

1868, has been significant for immigrants for two reasons.

(1) It established birthright citizenship: "All persons born or naturalized in the United States . . . are citizens of the United States and of the State wherein they reside."

This has meant that children born in the United States, even those of illegal immigrant mothers, or mothers who were ineligible to citizenship, were themselves citizens of the United States.

(2) Its "due process" and "equal protection" clauses have often protected immigrants, and others, from unfair treatment by national, state, and local laws and ordinances: "nor shall any State deprive any person of life, liberty, or property, without due process of law; nor deny to any person within it jurisdiction the equal protection of the laws."

Many immigrants, but particularly Chinese during the "exclusion era," 1882–1943, were protected by the courts from unjust state laws and municipal ordinances.

SEE ALSO

Aliens ineligible to citizenship; Birthright citizen; Citizenship

Franco-Americans

SEE French; French Canadians

Fraternal benefit societies

Fraternal benefit societies were usually the first secular, or, nonreligious, institutions established by immigrant groups in the United States. They typically began as local organizations, though some became regional or national in scope. The societies had both social and mutual benefit functions. They provided a place for immigrants to meet with one another, and their membership dues, which were usually small, provided cash benefits to the sick and tried to guarantee a proper burial for their deceased members. Some examples of national benefit societies that have survived are the Czech CSA Fraternal Life, the Irish Ancient Order of Hibernians, and the Ukrainian National Association. (See Appendix 2.)

FURTHER READING

Beito, David T. *From Mutual Aid to the Welfare State: Fraternal Societies and Social Services.* Chapel Hill: University of North Carolina Press, 2000.
Weisser, Michael R. *A Brotherhood of Memory: Jewish Landsmanshaftn in the New World.* Ithaca: Cornell University Press, 1989.

French

- *1990 Ancestry: 10,320,935*
- *Immigration, 1986–96: 29,908*
- *Immigration, 1820–1996: 810,682*
- *Major period of immigration: 1849–50s*
- *Major areas of settlement: California, Louisiana (esp. New Orleans)*

[The data on French immigration to the United States are particularly unsatisfactory and misleading. The best authorities believe that the immigration figures are perhaps one-third too large because they include many ethnic Germans from Alsace, many ethnic Italians from Savoy, Basques from the Pyrenees, and many others who emigrated from France but were not French. (France has long been a magnet for other Europeans, and, more recently for Africans and Asians.) In addition, large but unknown numbers of French who emigrated to America returned. The 1990 census figure of 10 million people claiming French ancestry obviously contains many people who are descendants of people who were from Canada, both French Canadians and Acadians.]

The first French immigrants to North America were the primary European settlers of Canada, beginning in 1541, and many of the French who came to what is now the United States in the colonial period, came by way of Canada. The French did start colonies in what is now South Carolina and Florida in 1562 and 1564, but the first was soon abandoned and the second soon captured by the Spanish, who killed most of the several hundred colonists.

Other French, using Canada as a base, reconnoitered both sides of the Great Lakes and the Ohio–Mississippi River system in the 17th and early 18th centuries, founding a number of cities and forts that became cities. These include Duquesne (now Pittsburgh),

Louisville, Detroit, St. Louis, and New Orleans. When the United States acquired these places, after the American Revolution and the Louisiana Purchase of 1803, it acquired small pockets of French and French Canadian populations.

More numerous were French who emigrated to the United States as religious refugees. The first group came mostly after the revocation of the Edict of Nantes by Louis XIV in 1685, which ended religious toleration in France, although there had been an unsuccessful attempt to found a Huguenot (French Protestant) colony in South Carolina and Florida in the 1560s. Fewer than 3,000 Huguenots came as refugees to the British colonies in North America, and so successful was their acculturation that within a generation or so they were all but indistinguishable from other settlers in South Carolina, New York, and Massachusetts.

There is a paradox here: the Huguenots and their descendants were so successful, economically and socially,

A 16th-century lithograph shows the Timuca Indians of Florida joyfully greeting the French. Although the initial greetings were sometimes joyful, Native Americans soon learned that the Europeans intended to take their land.

French religious helped establish Catholicism in the United States. This 1892 painting shows French Ursuline nuns landing in New Orleans in 1727. They ran a hospital, a school, and the first convent within the present United States.

in integrating into American society that their self-conscious presence lasted only a generation or so. As a historian of Huguenots has noted, "everywhere they fled, everywhere they vanished," not only in America, but also in England and Germany. Conversely, the French-speaking Acadians, who were relatively isolated socially as well as geographically, and who did not enjoy conspicuous economic success, have survived as an American ethnic group to the present day.

Though some French Catholic clergy had participated in French exploration, hundreds of French Catholic priests, nuns, and monks fled to the United States in the aftermath of the French Revolution of 1789. As there were only a few dozen Catholic clergy in the United States at that time, these French religious were, for a time, dominant in the Catholic Church in America. As late as 1833, 6 of the 12 American Catholic bishops were French-born. One French-born priest, Father Gabriel Richard, was elected to Congress in 1832 and was a co-founder of the University of Michigan.

Most of the approximately 10,000

French-speaking people who came to the United States in the aftermath of the French Revolution came from French colonies in the Caribbean, including some 3,000 of mixed French and Afro-Caribbean ancestry. Among the latter was Mother Louise Noël, the leader of the Oblate Sisters of Baltimore, a Catholic religious order.

The 1789 Revolution also sent political exiles to America, as has every other political upheaval in modern French history. Napoleon Bonaparte himself considered fleeing to America, and some of the Bonaparte family did. The most illustrious French refugees in America came during World War II: they included artists like Jacques Lipchitz, the composer Darius Milhaud, and the statesman Pierre Mendes-France, who returned to France and became premier.

Over the years, thousands of French have come from France as "normal" immigrants rather than as refugees—and are still coming—but they have been, almost exclusively, middle-class individuals and families. In the 19th century there were two large concentrations of French-born people: one in Louisiana that, in 1860, contained 15,000, and the other in California, where 30,000 French participated in the gold rush of 1849–50.

In recent years French have not engaged in group settlement. Many French immigrants, like many of the refugees, have returned to France or gone elsewhere. Those who have remained have largely been assimilated. The largest French organizations in the United States, the Club Français d'Amerique and the Alliance Française, are devoted to the perpetuation of French language and culture rather than the typical immigrant organization's concerns.

SEE ALSO

Acadians; Alsatians; Basques; French Canadians; Huguenots; Refugees; Swiss

FURTHER READING

Butler, Jon. *The Huguenots in America: A Refugee People in New World Society.* Cambridge: Harvard University Press, 1983.

Morrice, Polly A. *The French Americans.* New York: Chelsea House, 1988.

French Canadians

- *1990 Ancestry: 2,167,127*
- *Immigration, 1986–96: n.a.*
- *Immigration, 1820–1996: n.a.*
- *Major periods of immigration: 1845–95, 1923–30*
- *Major areas of settlement: New England, Great Lakes region*

The French Canadians are the descendants of the perhaps 30,000 French who immigrated to Canada before 1759 when the British conquered Canada. The French Canadians continued to exist as a subject people, concentrated in the present-day province of Quebec,

until the Durham Report of 1839 instituted reforms that gave the French language equal status with English throughout Canada. Canadians now often speak of three kinds of persons: Anglophones (speakers of English); Francophones (speakers of French); and Allophones (immigrants who speak other languages). Products originating in Canada have labels in the two official languages, English and French, and all Canadian government documents are printed in both languages.

At the time of the British conquest (1759), there were perhaps 60,000 Quebeckers; a century later, when the French Canadian migration to the United States set in, there were perhaps a million. Three main causes of that migration were:

(1) A shortage of desirable agricultural land in Quebec. Although Quebec is very large—twice the size of Texas or France—much of it was not fit for agriculture due to the poor soil and harsh climate.

(2) The closeness of Quebec to the United States and the good transportation

Members of two French Canadian families, workers in the filling bay at Appleton mill, Lowell, Massachusetts, in the late 19th century.

between the two. The French Canadians are the only ethnic group ever to migrate to the United States principally on railroad trains.

(3) The availability of large numbers of jobs for entire families in the expanding New England textile mills and boot and shoe factories.

Although French Canadian immigration before the Civil War was largely that of male, seasonal agricultural workers who went back to Canada after the crops were picked, after the war it was very much a family immigration. Though large numbers of Quebeckers returned to Quebec, and others went back and forth in what is called circular migration, by 1890 the U.S. census reported more than half a million first- and second-generation French Canadians, and by 1910 there were nearly a million.

The first French Canadian–American novel, *Jeanne la Fileuse* (Jeanne the Mill Girl), published in 1878 by an immigrant journalist, Honoré Beaugrand, tells the story of one such family. The family gets on a train in Montreal at 4 P.M. one afternoon and arrives in Fall River, Massachusetts, which became the "capital" of French Canadian America, at 2 P.M. the next day. A 17-year-old son, who has been working there in a textile mill for some time, has arranged jobs for the whole family and a place for them to live in a company apartment house. The father and several older children go to work the next day. The younger children, aged 8 to 12, must under Massachusetts law attend school for at least 20 weeks a year, but once that minimum requirement is satisfied, they too go to work in the mills. The mills run for 10 hours a day, 6 days a week, and even small children are expected to put in 60 hours. Grown-up mill workers were paid $1.22 a day; children as little as

28 cents. Yet, the novel tells us, by the third month, even before the three younger children can go to work, the family is putting money in the bank, money they hope will eventually buy them a better farm in Quebec.

French Canadians quickly imported many institutions from Quebec. Many priests from the province soon joined them, and largely French Canadian parishes sprang up all over New England, but especially in the mill towns of Massachusetts and Rhode Island. The immigrants from Quebec established other institutions, including French-language newspapers: one of them, *L'Echo du Canada* (News of Canada), published *Jeanne la Fileuse* as a serial, though today it would be a TV soap opera.

The proximity of Canada was both an advantage and a disadvantage. It was easy to get to the United States and to return home, either permanently or for a visit. That proximity, and the fierce loyalty to their language developed by French Canadians since their conquest by the English, also aided in the retention of the French language. According to 1990 census data, French was the third most-spoken language in American homes (after English and Spanish): 1.7 million persons told the census that they habitually spoke French at home. Many of them were second- and third-generation Americans. Although discussions of illegal immigrants rarely feature Canadians, the INS and the Census Bureau estimate for 1996 estimated that Canada, with 120,000 such persons, was the fourth most numerous source of illegal immigrants. The estimate made no distinction between French Canadians and others.

SEE ALSO
Acadians; Canadians; Circular migration; French; Illegal immigrants; Language maintenance

FURTHER READING

Brault, Gerard J. *The French-Canadian Heritage in New England*. Hanover, N.H.: University Presses of New England, 1986.

Frisians

SEE Dutch

Gadar Party

The Gadar Party (*Gadar* is an Urdu word that may be translated as "revolution" or "mutiny") was an organization formed in San Francisco in 1913 with the ambitious goal of overthrowing the British rule in India. Its plan to send arms to India and to begin an uprising was foiled and many of its adherents were captured and killed by the British. Those members who remained in the United States were convicted of violating the Neutrality Acts. It is but one of many examples of a "freedom movement" begun in the United States by exiles.

SEE ALSO

Asian Indians; Exiles

FURTHER READING

Jensen, Joan M. *Passage from India: Asian Indian Immigrants in North America*. New Haven: Yale University Press, 1988.

Gamsaanhaak

Gamsaanhaak is a Chinese word meaning "Gold Mountain guest," referring to the presumably transient or sojourn-er nature of early Chinese immigration to the United States. "Gold Mountain" was the Chinese term for California.

SEE ALSO

Chinese; Gold Mountain; Sojourners

Garifuna

SEE Hondurans

Genealogy

Genealogy is the study of family ancestry and history, or a record or account of a person or family's line of descent. Researching letters, documents, family bibles, and other records can be useful in tracing family histories and a good way to find immigrant ancestors and where they came from.

Genealogical information can be displayed in simple diagrams or in decorative family trees, such as this one from 1867. A fragment of a much larger image, the trunk indicates that this tree starts with the children of Isaac Collins and Rachel Budd, who married in 1771.

Genealogists use a variety of sources, including birth and baptismal records, death certificates, military pension records, passenger lists, Social Security records, and naturalization records. The Church of Latter Day Saints (Mormons) maintains the largest collection of genealogical records in the world and makes much of it available to all users in its Reading Rooms spread all across the United States. There is also much useful genealogical information on the World Wide Web (See Further Reading, Museums, and Websites at the back of the book).

FURTHER READING

Gilmer, Lois C. *Genealogical Research and Resources: A Guide for Library Use.* Chicago: American Library Association, 1988.
Schaefer, Christina K. *Genealogical Encyclopedia of the Colonial Americas.* Baltimore: Genealogical Publishing, 1998.

Gentlemen's Agreement

The Gentleman's Agreement was a series of notes exchanged between the United States and Japan in 1907–8 to calm the furor in Japan and California over Japanese immigration during the administration of Theodore Roosevelt. Japan agreed to stop issuing passports valid for the United States to laborers, and the United States agreed not to enact overtly anti-Japanese immigration legislation. Other sections provided ways for Japanese already living in the United States to be reunited with family members left behind. It also led to the so-called picture bride immigration, which brought thousands of Japanese women to the United States. The United States unilaterally ended the Gentlemen's Agreement with the Immigration Act of 1924, which blocked the immigration of "aliens ineligible to citizenship."

SEE ALSO

Aliens ineligible to citizenship; Immigration Act of 1924; Japanese; Picture brides

FURTHER READING

Daniels, Roger. *The Politics of Prejudice: The Anti-Japanese Movement in California and the Struggle for Japanese Exclusion.* 1962. Reprint, Berkeley: University of California, 1999.

Georgians

- *1990 Ancestry: n.a.*
- *Immigration, 1992–96: 3,374*
- *Immigration, 1820–1996: 7,142,393*
- *Major period of immigration: 1992–96*
- *Major area of settlement: New York*

Georgians are a people of the Caucasus Mountains who were converted to Christianity in the 4th century. Their homeland, once a part of the Soviet Union, is now an independent republic of some 5 million people. It covers nearly 27,000 square miles, less than half the size of the southern American state of the same name. The Georgians' language belongs to the Kartvekian group of Caucasian languages. The Georgian Orthodox Church is a largely autonomous institution with close ties to other Eastern Orthodox churches.

Very few Georgians have ever come to the United States. The 3,000 who entered between 1992 and 1996 outnumber all those who came before them. Perhaps the first Georgians were 15 skilled horseback riders who came to join Buffalo Bill's Wild West show in 1890. A few years later, some 30 men and women equestrians came to join American circuses, and perhaps 50 others came to work on railroads. About half of these pre–World War I immigrants returned home.

After World War I about 150 upper-class Georgian exiles from the Russian Revolution came to America and settled permanently. In 1931 or 1932 they formed the Georgian Association in the United States of America, which has served as the voice of the Georgian American community ever since. After World War II perhaps 250 more immigrated, largely under terms of the Displaced Persons Acts of 1948 and 1950.

Between 1971 and 1976 some 300 Georgian Jews came to the United States, largely as families. They were assisted by the Hebrew Immigrant Aid Society. These Jews have continued to interact with other Georgians in the United States as well as with other Jews. Almost all of the post–World War I immigrants, including those who began to come regularly after the dissolution of the Soviet Union, have been relatively well educated and have had at least modest economic success in their new home.

SEE ALSO

Displaced persons; Hebrew Immigrant Aid Society

German-American Bund

The German-American Bund, and a predecessor organization, Friends of the New Germany (1933–35), were American organizations created to support Adolf Hitler's Nazi Germany. They received support and secret financial assistance from the German government. The Bund (German for "alliance" or "league") appealed to a tiny minority of German Americans, many of them unnaturalized recent immigrants, and to anti-Semitic and pro-Nazi elements of other ethnicities. Its members wore uniforms modeled on Nazi ones. As the debate about whether the United States should enter World War II grew, the Bund also drew support from groups opposed to American intervention. At its peak it had perhaps 20,000 members. When the United States entered World War II the Bund collapsed and many of its unnaturalized members were interned.

SEE ALSO

Germans; Internment

FURTHER READING

Canedy, Susan. *America's Nazis: A Democratic Dilemma: A History of the German American Bund*. Menlo Park, Calif.: Markgraf, 1990.
Diamond, Sander A. *The Nazi Movement in the United States, 1929–1941*. Ithaca, N.Y.: Cornell University Press, 1974.

Germans

- *1990 Ancestry: 57,947,374*
- *Immigration, 1986–96: 79,224*
- *Immigration, 1820–1996: 7,142,393*
- *Major periods of immigration: 1840s–1850s, 1880s*
- *Major areas of settlement: Midwest, New York*

Nearly 7 million German speakers have come to America, more than any other group of continental European immigrants. They have come for economic, religious, and political reasons, settled both on farms and in cities, and worshipped in the three major American faiths, Protestant, Catholic, and Jewish.

Though a few Germans came in the early 17th century—largely to Virginia and New York—organized settlement

began in 1683 when a Protestant congregation from Krefeld in the Rhineland arrived in Philadelphia seeking farms and religious liberty. Misnamed the Pennsylvania Dutch, many thousands followed in the next 90 years so that, by the time of the first census of 1790, one-third of Pennsylvania's population and nearly 9 percent of all white Americans—some 280,000 persons—were of German birth or descent.

Many of them had come originally as indentured servants, or what the Germans called "redemptioners." Unlike British indentured servants, who were overwhelmingly single males, many German indentured servants came as families. Sometimes only part of the family came as servants; in such cases other family members often paid off and thus "redeemed" their indebtedness as soon as they earned enough money to do so.

Few Germans came between the American Revolution and 1830, although perhaps 3,000 German mercenary soldiers in the British Army, usually called Hessians, deserted and stayed in America. For the 60 years after 1830, Germans were never fewer than a quarter of all immigrants. Four and a half

million Germans came in those years. The focus of their settlement was the so-called German triangle, an imaginary region created by later analysts who noted that most Germans settled in an area delimited by the cities of Cincinnati, Milwaukee, and St. Louis. A secondary area of settlement was in eastern cities between New York and Baltimore. The overwhelming majority of Germans came for economic opportunity, but a few were political refugees after the failed revolutions of 1848. Though many of these "forty-eighters" became outstanding citizens—many, like General Franz Sigel, served in the Union army during the American Civil War—their influence on the nation as a whole has been overemphasized in German American folklore.

Most Germans, like most immigrants generally, came to cities, but a substantial minority were farmers. But among one particular group of German immigrants—Germans who had settled in Russia for generations before migrating to America—farmers were the overwhelming majority. Most of them had previously settled in southern Russia and the Ukraine, and in the United States they settled mainly in the wheat farming belt between Kansas and the Dakotas.

Most German immigrants were Protestants, chiefly Lutherans, but a large minority were Catholics, and a smaller minority, perhaps a quarter of a million persons in the 19th century, were Jews. Although most Germans did well in America, they were singled out for attack during three specific periods. In the mid-18th century, a nativist attack in Pennsylvania, led by Benjamin Franklin, claimed that they were trying to "take over" and displace English. In the 1840s and 1850s, the so-called Know Nothing movement attacked all immigrants, and particularly Irish and German Catholics.

And during 1917–19, as a side effect of American participation in World War I and with the encouragement of federal and state governments, everything German came under attack. The names of streets and towns were changed (in Cincinnati German Street became English Street); "hamburger" and "sauerkraut" had to be called "salisbury steak" and "liberty cabbage"; the music of long-dead German composers, including Beethoven, was shunned; and dachshunds became very unpopular.

More seriously, many Germans were assaulted—one German immigrant was lynched in Illinois—and many high schools and some universities simply stopped teaching the German language. One state, Nebraska, went so far as to bar anyone from teaching in a language other than English and prohibited the study of *any* foreign language, including Latin, before the eighth grade. After the war these and other laws were declared unconstitutional in the cases of *Meyer* v. *Nebraska* and *Pierce* v. *Society of Sisters*.

Despite these periodic attacks, German immigrants as a group were generally well regarded. German farmers and artisans contributed significantly to

American prosperity, as did engineers such as John A. Roebling, designer of the Brooklyn Bridge, an important symbol of American technical superiority. Germans were also important in American wars: during the Civil War entire regiments were composed of Germans, with German-born officers giving commands in German, and in World War II a general of German descent, Dwight D. Eisenhower, was the Supreme Allied Commander of the forces in Europe that defeated Nazi Germany. He was later elected president in 1952 and 1956. German Americans created a vast cultural apparatus, much of which was crippled by nativist attacks during World War I. The German-language press included 74 daily and some 400 newspapers; in much of the Midwest many public schools taught all subjects in the German language. Nowhere was the German cultural influence more important than in classical music; practically speaking, for much of the late 19th and early 20th centuries German music *was* classical music.

German immigrants brought the kindergarten ("children's garden") to America and their social and athletic

Recruiters sign up German and Irish immigrants at Castle Garden for the Union Army in 1864. The bounty sign on the wall at the left is in German.

organizations, called "turnverein," flourished throughout German America. More controversial were the German beer gardens, places to which whole families would go on Sundays and holidays, which came under attack from the Temperance Movement that opposed alcoholic beverages, particularly during the decades before the adoption of national Prohibition in 1919.

Further German immigration took place in the decades before and after World War II. In the late 1920s, Germans trying to avoid dire postwar economic conditions dominated European immigration and in the 1930s thousands of refugees from Nazi Germany, most of them Jewish, found asylum in the United States. After World War II the latest group of Germans entered as displaced persons. Most of these were ethnic Germans from countries that had been occupied by the armies of the Soviet Union. In recent years fewer than 10,000 Germans have immigrated annually.

SEE ALSO

Alsatians; Amish; Displaced persons; Forty-eighters; German-American Bund; German triangle; Hessians; Hutterites; Indentured servants; Jews; Know Nothing movement; Mennonites; *Meyer* v. *Nebraska*; Nativism; Pennsylvania Dutch; *Pierce* v. *Society of Sisters*; Revolutions of 1848; Turnverein

FURTHER READING

Hoobler, Dorothy, and Thomas Hoobler. *The German American Family Album.* New York: Oxford University Press, 1996.

Kamphoefner, Walter D., Wolfgang Helbich & Ulrike Sommer, eds. *News from the Land of Freedom: German Immigrants Write Home.* Ithaca, N.Y.: Cornell University Press, 1991.

Luebke, Frederick C. *Germans in the New World: Essays in the History of Immigration.* Urbana: University of Illinois Press, 1990.

Rippley, LaVern J. *The German-Americans.* Boston: Twayne, 1976.

German triangle

The geographical term *German triangle* refers to the imaginary triangle created by drawing straight lines on a map to connect the midwestern cities of St. Louis, Milwaukee, and Cincinnati. Many German immigrants landed at Gulf ports and then moved up the Mississippi, first on steamboats and then on railroads, to this area of the Midwest. The area thus enclosed was a major destination for German immigrants in the 19th and 20th centuries, and the three cities were main centers of German American culture. It is no accident that much of the lager beer industry started in German triangle cities, as German craftsmen made the beer and, initially, German Americans were its primary consumers.

Ghetto

SEE Ethnic enclave

Golden door

The golden door is a symbolic term for entrance to the United States through New York harbor. The words are taken from the poem "The New Colossus" by Emma Lazarus, which is inscribed on a plaque on the base of the Statue of Liberty: "I lift my lamp beside the Golden Door."

SEE ALSO

Statue of Liberty

Gold Mountain

The Chinese characters for California may also be translated as "Gold Mountain," referring to the 1849 gold rush. When gold was discovered in Australia in 1851, the characters for that country read "New Gold Mountain." These Chinese called themselves *Gamsaanhaak* or "Gold Mountain guests."

SEE ALSO
Chinese; *Gamsaanhaak*

Greeks

- *1990 Ancestry: 1,110,373*
- *Immigration, 1986–96: 22,878*
- *Immigration, 1820–1996: 718,798*
- *Major period of immigration: 1890–1924*
- *Major areas of settlement: New York, Illinois, California*

A few Greeks were present in the New World in the colonial period, but no significant number of Greeks came to the United States or other parts of the New World before the 1890s. Although Greece was the creator of a kind of democracy in the ancient world, in modern times Greece was a part of Ottoman (Turkish) Empire until 1829. The Greek struggle for independence was admired by many Americans, and several American towns were given Greek names early in the 19th century—for example, Ypsilanti, Michigan—but had few or no Greek residents. Even after Greek independence in 1829–32, more Greeks lived outside of Greece than in it: most of these lived in Turkey and on islands off the coast of

Turkey. Many of these Greeks of the diaspora immigrated to the United States but are counted as Turks, so that the immigration figures listed above seriously understate the number of Greeks who entered the United States. In the late 19th and very early 20th century, a very large majority of Greek immigrants were men, and probably about half of them returned to Greece.

One of the best ways to discover when a Greek American community developed is to find out when the first Greek Orthodox church was established there. Although the earliest Greek immigrants found and attended already established Eastern Orthodox churches—that church was first brought to North America in 1794 by Russian monks doing missionary work among the Aleuts and Tinglit Indians of Alaska—the Greeks wanted churches in which Greek was spoken. The first of these was founded in New Orleans in 1864 by a small community of cotton merchants, but no others existed until the 1890s, when churches were established in New York, Chicago, and Lowell, Massachusetts. By 1909 there was a chain of Greek Orthodox churches from coast to coast. A large number of

Mr. Boosalis (far left), a Greek immigrant, poses with two employees in his spacious "Ice Cream and Candy Emporium" in Minneapolis, 1905. Many Greek immigrants went into the ice cream and candy business but few of their shops were as fancy as this one.

them were in New England, whose textile mills employed many Greeks.

Greeks could be found in many industries, including both coal and hard-rock mining in the American West, railroad construction gangs, and meat packing. Others were organized by padrones, or labor contractors, and ran shoeshine stands, and sold popcorn and candy in theaters and at outdoor entertainments. But a relatively high percentage of them opened small businesses. Most numerous were small restaurants. These did not specialize in Greek cuisine, but catered to workingmen and women. In Cincinnati, Ohio, one of the most successful such restaurateurs invented "Cincinnati chili"—which is totally unlike Mexican chili—and developed a large local chain of restaurants.

The most prominent Greek businessmen of the immigrant era were Alexander Pantages and Spyros Skouras and his brothers, all of whom established themselves in the infant motion picture industry, which was dominated by immigrant Jews. Pantages developed one of the earliest chains of theaters, and the Skouras brothers founded the Twentieth Century-Fox studio.

None of these occupations, of course, was a part of the Greek heritage. The movies were brand-new in the early 20th century, and most Greeks who immigrated had not been running restaurants or shining shoes in the old country, any more than Italians had run barbershops or Chinese had run laundries before coming to America. These were all economic opportunities or niches that immigrants filled.

But Greek workers did bring one special skill to America, and from it has developed a most interesting Greek American enclave in Tarpon Springs, Florida. By the first decade of the 20th century Greek immigrants, who had

experience in diving for sponges in their Mediterranean homeland, established the sponge fishing industry in this Gulf of Mexico port. Although the number of Greeks there is small, it is an important and highly visible community. Its blessing of the boats ceremony every January 6 has become a significant tourist attraction. In what historians call an "invented tradition," a Greek Orthodox prelate conducts the blessing, after which a large Greek cross is thrown into the water and dived for by young Greek men, 15 to 18 years of age. Recently there has been much controversy in the community about whether young men who are of partly Greek ancestry are eligible to dive for the cross or not.

For a long time the political energies of most Greek immigrants in America were centered on Greece rather than on America. This was especially true after Greek victories in the Balkan Wars of 1912–13 created rivalries between monarchists and republicans, and many Greek Americans actively supported one faction or the other. Other organizational energies of the community—a historian of Greek Americans speaks of their "mania" for forming groups—were devoted to keep-

Greek fishermen examine their catch of sponges in Tarpon Springs, Florida, in 1944. Greeks brought skills learned in the Mediterranean to the United States.

ing Greeks aware of their classical heritage and of making other Americans aware of it. The most persistent Greek American organization has been the American Hellenic Educational Progressive Association (AHEPA). In the post–World War II years, much of the Greek American political energy went into helping to reconstruct the war-ravaged Greek homeland, and, after the Turkish invasion of Cyprus in 1974, into support for the Greek Cypriots. In these postwar years, however, as second-generation Greek Americans began to outnumber their parents' generation, more and more of the community emphasis switched to American politics. One second-generation Greek American, Spiro T. Agnew, was twice elected Vice President, and another, Michael Dukakis, won the Democratic nomination for President in 1988.

SEE ALSO

Diaspora; Eastern Orthodox churches; Padrone system

FURTHER READING

Leber, George J. *The History of the Order of Ahepa (The American Hellenic Educational Progressive Association) 1922–1972; Including the Greeks in the New World, and Immigration to the United States.* Washington, D.C.: Order of Ahepa, 1972.
Saloutos, Theodore. *A History of the Greeks in the United States.* Cambridge: Harvard University Press, 1964.
Scourby, Alice. *The Greek Americans.* Boston: Twayne, 1984.

Green card

A green card is an identification card, once green in color, issued to an alien permitting him or her to work in the United States. Green cards are held both by resident aliens, and, along the land borders of the United States, by persons who live in Mexico or Canada and commute daily to the United States. The cards of resident aliens are "permanent," whereas those of others usually have a fixed term. Currently "green" cards are pink in color.

SEE ALSO

Immigration policy; Passport; Resident alien; Visa

Guamanians

• *1990 Census: 49,345*

Guamanians, the people of Guam, are United States citizens but do not participate in federal American elections. They do send a nonvoting delegate to Congress. About half the population are called Chamorros and are of mixed Spanish, Filipino, and Micronesian descent, reflecting the island's history. The Spanish explorer Ferdinand Magellan seized the island for Spain in 1521, and Spain controlled it until 1898, when the United States took it as a prize of the Spanish-American War. Japan attacked and seized the island in 1941, and the United States took it back three years later.

Guam, the most populous, and southernmost of the Mariana Islands, is in the Central Pacific and contains 217 square miles. Its population in 1990 was 156,974. The estimated ethnic mix in 1994 was 47 percent Chamorro, 25 percent Filipino, 10 percent Caucasian, and most of the rest Japanese, Chinese, or Korean. The majority of the population, about 52 percent, were born elsewhere, 48 percent in Asia and 40 percent in the U.S. The small population of Guamanians in the United States is primarily in Hawaii and California.

SEE ALSO
Pacific Islanders

Guatemalans

- *1990 Ancestry: 241,559*
- *Immigration, 1986–96: 138,245*
- *Immigration, 1820–1996: n.a.*
- *Major period of immigration: late 1970s+*
- *Major areas of settlement: Indiantown, Florida; Houston, Phoenix, Los Angeles*

Guatemala, with a population of more than 11 million in a country of 42,042 square miles, is the largest nation of Central America. The vast majority of Guatemalans who have immigrated to the United States, although classified as "Hispanics," are actually Maya whose first language is not Spanish, but one of the 31 Maya languages. Most of them, however, have an understanding of Spanish.

The conquest of Guatemala by Spain began in 1523, and it became one of the centers of Spanish civilization in the New World. The University of San Carlos de Guatemala, established in 1676 in Guatemala City, is the oldest university in Central America. When Central America became independent of Spain in 1821, Guatemala was initially a part of Mexico, but has been independent since 1839.

In modern times Guatemala has been dominated by foreign economic interests, primarily investors in banana and coffee plantations. A left-wing government was elected in 1951. It was overthrown in 1954 by a right-wing coup aided by the U.S. Central Intelligence Agency. This began a turbulent

period that continues more than 40 years later. It is this internal disorder with attendant economic misery that has motivated most of the Maya immigrants to the United States.

Large numbers of Maya in the United States are illegal immigrants. In 1996 the Immigration and Naturalization Service (INS) and the Census Bureau estimated that there were 165,000 illegal Guatemalan immigrants in the country, the third highest national total. Similarly, between 1986 and 1996, under the provisions of the Immigration Reform and Control Act of 1986 (IRCA), more than 63,000 Guatemalans who had entered illegally went through the complex process of legalization and became U.S. citizens, also the third highest national total. Because the United States supported the Guatemalan government for a long time, no significant number of Guatemalans have been granted refugee or asylee status.

Many if not most Guatemalans in the United States are or have been involved in migratory farm labor. The largest Guatemalan Maya enclave in the United States is in Indiantown in southern Florida near Lake Okeechobee, where some 3,000 have settled

This Guatemalan store, near downtown Los Angeles, is typical of immigrant businesses. Although its main business is selling music imported from Guatemala, it also performs a variety of services recent immigrants need, including filling out immigration and income tax forms.

permanently. Smaller enclaves have developed in many American cities, particularly in Houston, Phoenix, and Los Angeles. A recent and poor immigrant group, none of the Guatemalans have yet become prominent, but one Guatemalan Mayan woman who has visited the United States, Rigoberta Menchú, a Quiché Indian human rights advocate, was awarded the Nobel Peace Prize in 1992.

SEE ALSO

Asylees; Central Americans; Ethnic enclave; Illegal immigrants; Immigration Act of 1986; Maya; Refugees

FURTHER READING

Burns, Allan F. *Maya in Exile: Guatemalans in Exile.* Philadelphia: Temple University Press, 1993.
Malone, Michael. *A Guatemalan Family.* Minneapolis: Lerner, 1996.

Gujaratis

Gujaratis, people from the large Indian state of Gujarat, are very prominent in the Asian Indian migration to the United States. Almost all are Hindus. Many of them share the surname Patel, and members of this clan have come to specialize in the ownership and management of hotels and motels in the United States. A community joke goes, "Hotel, motel, Patel."

SEE ALSO

Asian Indians

Gypsies

- *1990 Ancestry: n.a.*
- *Estimated population, 1990s: 60,000*
- *Immigration, 1986–96: n.a.*
- *Immigration, 1820–1996: n.a.*
- *Major periods of immigration: 1850s, 1880–1924, 1970+*
- *Major areas of settlement: widely distributed*

Gypsies are a nomadic people who now live on every continent. They call themselves Rom or Roma. The word *Gypsy* was coined in the 16th century and stems from the false belief that they had originated in Egypt. Actually Gypsies began to migrate out of northern India more than a thousand years ago, first to Persia and then into Europe in the 15th century. Their language, Romany, belongs to the Indo-Iranian family and is closely related to the languages of northwest India.

Gypsies usually traveled in small wagons and made their living as metal-workers, singers, dancers, musicians, and horse dealers. A modern adaptation finds many of them working as itinerant auto mechanics. Gypsy women are famous as fortune-tellers. Most gypsies are dark-complexioned and short, with slight physiques. Although they have kept their language and many of their customs, most Gypsies have adopted Christianity, particularly Roman Catholicism or Eastern Orthodox. They are largely governed by elders and have

These Gypsies were photographed at a roadside on the Jefferson Highway in Minnesota during the Great Depression in 1933.

their own informal courts to settle disputes between themselves.

They have been subjected to persecution by many nations. During the Nazi regime perhaps 500,000 Gypsies were murdered in concentration camps. Lesser persecutions continue in many eastern European countries. In the United States they are subject to much suspicion and are often accused of sharp and often illegal economic practices and of performing shoddy work.

The first Gypsies in North America came from the British Isles beginning in the 1850s and called themselves Romnichels. A second group, the Rom, began to come from Germany and other parts of western Europe. A third group, the Ludar, came from southern European ports beginning in 1882. Within each group there are a number of extended families or lineages. Within the United States the Gypsies have been migratory, moving often within a regular sequence of locales, although most have developed particular bases to which they return.

Gypsy "economics" vary from host society to host society and have varied over time. Some have noted that they opportunistically exploit the host society. In other words, like many other ethnic groups, they try to find a niche in which they can comfortably and profitably operate. While many at one time were horse traders and tinkers (repairers of pots and pans), in recent years Gypsies are more likely to be selling used cars and trailers, blacktopping driveways, and roofing. Women still use fortune-telling as a means of earning money. Gypsies have maintained a strong ethnic identity and have largely been quite reluctant to associate with non-Gypsies, except on an economic basis.

FURTHER READING
Sutherland, Anne. *Gypsies: The Hidden Americans*. New York: Free Press, 1975.

Haitians

- *1990 Ancestry: 289,521*
- *Immigration, 1986–96: 210,636*
- *Immigration, 1932–96: 754,968*
- *Major period of immigration: 1965+*
- *Major areas of settlement: Miami, New York*

Haiti, which shares the Caribbean island of Hispaniola with the Dominican Republic, is the poorest country in the Western Hemisphere. Nearly 7 million people live in its 11,000 square miles. Its small upper and middle classes practice Roman Catholicism and speak standard French. The vast majority of the population is poor, and more than 80 percent are illiterate. Most of the poor practice *Vodun* (Voodoo)—a religion derived from African ancestor worship involving escapist trances and magical practices—and speak a variety of French known as Creole.

Haiti, home of the only successful slave rebellion in history, expelled its French colonists and abolished slavery during its revolution, which ended in 1803 and made Haiti the second independent country in the New World. Perhaps 50,000 Haitians, largely whites and their slaves but including some free blacks, came to the United States as refugees after the Haitian Revolution. Before that, a Haitian mulatto, Jean Baptiste Point du Sable, a fur trader with an Indian wife, founded the city of Chicago.

Numerically significant immigration from Haiti occurred during the period 1915–34, when United States troops occupied Haiti. Perhaps 500 people, most of them well educated and involved in Haitian politics, lived in New York. Some developed businesses, while others taught languages in

This sailing vessel jammed with Haitian "boat people" reached Florida safely in 1980, but many vessels were lost at sea and hundreds, perhaps thousands, of Haitians drowned trying to reach the United States.

the public schools. After World War II hundreds of Haitian women migrated to a number of American cities to serve as live-in maids for middle- and upper-class families. The brutal Duvalier dictatorships in Haiti—those of François Duvalier ("Papa Doc") and his son Jean-Claude ("Baby Doc"), who became president for life at age 19—terrorized Haiti from 1957 to 1986. In the early Duvalier years many prominent Haitian politicians went into exile, largely in New York.

Beginning in the later 1960s a desperate migration of Haitians to the United States began and continues. Often they came by boat and without visas. Before 1980 such immigrants could simply be called "illegal" and sent back. But since the Refugee Act of 1980, these immigrants have been able to claim asylum. For a long time it was official government policy, except in very unusual circumstances, to deny applications from Haitians, ruling that they were fleeing from poverty and not from persecution. Cubans, on the other

hand, fleeing from Fidel Castro's communist dictatorship, received almost automatic admission and government benefits. Many Americans argued that this was discrimination. Cubans found at sea by the U.S. Navy and Coast Guard were usually brought to American ports; Haitians were usually returned to Haiti.

Representative Bruce Morrison, a Connecticut Democrat who chaired a House of Representatives subcommittee on immigration, said in 1989, "[T]here's been a lot of discrimination with Haitians. They are black, they are from a nation close to ours, and their country isn't Communist." Conversely, an INS official in Miami fantasized, "I wish a boatload of blue-eyed Anglo-Saxon Protestants tried to enter the U.S. illegally" so he could keep them out too and show that he was not prejudiced.

Beginning in 1993 the Clinton administration, partly because of court decisions, liberalized admissions policy, as the data show. In the last three years before the Clinton Presidency, more than

300,000 refugees were admitted: just 54 of them were Haitians. From 1993 through 1996 almost 400,000 refugees were admitted, of whom nearly 7,000 were Haitians. As of 1996 the INS and the Census Bureau estimated that there were 105,000 illegal Haitians in the country, the fifth largest national number.

SEE ALSO

Asylees; Caribbeans; Cubans; Dominican Republic; Illegal immigrants; Refugee Act of 1980

FURTHER READING

Catanese, Anthony V. *Haitians: Migration and Diaspora.* Boulder, Colo.: Westview, 1999.

Laguerre, Michel S. *Diasporic Citizenship: Haitian Americans in Transnational America.* New York: St. Martin's, 1998.

Hawaiian Sugar Planters Association

The Hawaiian Sugar Planters Association was an organization responsible for bringing tens of thousands of contract laborers, largely Asians, to Hawaii to work on sugar and pineapple plantations. The Association began this practice with Chinese in the mid-19th century, and then brought in Japanese, Koreans, and, finally, Filipinos. It continued this practice even after American annexation in 1898, when such contracts became illegal.

SEE ALSO

Contract labor

FURTHER READING

Dorita, Mary. *Filipino Immigration to Hawaii.* San Francisco: R & E Research Associates, 1975.

Patterson, Wayne. *The Korean Frontier in America: Immigration to Hawaii, 1896–1910.* Honolulu: University of Hawaii Press, 1988.

Hawaiians

- *1990 Ancestry: 256,081*
- *1990 Census: 211,014*
- *Major areas of settlement: Hawaii, California*

Although Hawaiians have been U.S. citizens since the annexation of the Hawaiian Islands in 1898, it is appropriate to say something about their history here. In 1990 ethnic Hawaiians were a small minority in the islands where nearly 140,000 of them lived. They were outnumbered by whites (about 370,000), Japanese (about 247,000), and Filipinos (about 169,000). Some 72,000 Hawaiians live on the mainland of the United States, almost half of them (34,000) in California.

Scholars believe that the Hawaiian Islands were first settled about 1,500 years ago by Polynesian voyagers from the Marquesas Islands more than 2,000 miles away, and that other Polynesian settlers came from Tahiti somewhat later.

When the British explorer Captain James Cook "discovered" the islands in 1778, there were perhaps 300,000 ethnic Hawaiians. By 1910 their numbers had decreased to fewer than 40,000. Many scholars thought that Hawaiians would "vanish," as they thought, erroneously, was happening to the American Indians, but this has not been the case, and their numbers have increased steadily during the 20th century. Since the 1970s many Hawaiians have participated in what anthropologists call a "revitalization movement," which calls for a reassertion of the rights of ethnic Hawaiians, the return of land, and certain other rights.

SEE ALSO
Hawaiian Sugar Planters Association;
Polynesians

FURTHER READING
Fuchs, Lawrence. *Hawaii Pono: A Social
History*. San Diego: Harcourt Brace
Jovanovich, 1983.
Native Hawaiians Study Commission.
*Native Hawaiians Study Commission:
Report on the Culture, Needs, and Con-
cerns of Native Hawaiians*. Washington,
D.C.: U.S. Department of the Interior,
1983.

Hebrew Immigrant Aid Society (HIAS)

The Hebrew Immigrant Aid Society
(HIAS), founded in 1880, is one of the
largest immigrant aid organizations in
the nation, with a staff of about 150.
Originally devoted to helping poor
immigrant Jews, it now helps both Jewish and Gentile refugees and migrants
from Europe, North Africa, the Middle
East, and other areas resettle in the
United States, Canada, Latin America,
and Australia. (The term Hebrew was
often used as a synonym for Jews in
the 19th century.) It maintains offices
and committees around the world to
help locate relatives and friends, to help
in the preparation of documents, to
arrange transportation, and to provide
reception and resettlement services.
Like other such voluntary agencies, or
volags, it works with the U.S. government. It also has a speakers' bureau,
compiles statistics, and has a reference
library. It has absorbed a number of
similar organizations, including the
Hebrew Sheltering and Immigrant Aid
Society, the Migration Department of
the American Jewish Joint Distribution
Committee, and the United Services for
New Americans.

SEE ALSO
Georgians; Jews; VOLAGS

Hessians

A Hessian is a person from Hesse, a
region in southwest Germany, much
of it currently a state of the Federal
Republic of Germany. The significance
of the term Hessians in American history comes from the German mercenary
soldiers who were hired by the British
to fight with them against the Americans in the Revolutionary War. Many
"Hessians" were in fact not from
Hesse, and perhaps 3,000 accepted free
land and citizenship and remained in
America, most of them in Pennsylvania.
George Washington's famous Christmas victory at Trenton, New Jersey, in
1776 was largely fought against Hessian troops.

SEE ALSO
Germans

FURTHER READING
Atwood, Rodney. *The Hessians: Mercenar-
ies from Hessen-Kassel in the American
Revolution*. Cambridge: Cambridge University Press, 1980.

*A contempo-
rary British
illustration
depicts Ger-
man merce-
nary soldiers
in a British
army regiment
during the
Revolutionary
War. Some,
but by no
means all,
were Hessians.*

Hinduism

Most of the Asian Indian immigrants in the United States Practice Hinduism, the majority religion of India. Hinduism is one of the world's great religions and has an estimated 750 million adherents. Thus, a little more than one-eighth of the earth's population is Hindu. Most in live in India and adjoining countries. The religion originated in the Indus Valley perhaps 3,000 years ago. It is polytheistic (worships "many gods") and has a highly differentiated caste system, which in India regulates almost every aspect of daily life, but which cannot be effectively practiced outside of South Asia. Although the government of India has tried to abolish or modify some of the more restrictive aspects of the caste system—it was once all but impossible for members of the lowest castes to get an education—in rural India where most of the population lives, it still largely prevails.

Many Hindus are vegetarians, and all are forbidden to eat beef. In the United States Hindu temples, many of them quite elaborate, have been built everywhere significant numbers of Asian Indians have settled. Since almost all of those who practice Hinduism in the United States are very recent arrivals and their native-born children, it is not clear how the practice of Hinduism in America will evolve, but it is already clear that there will be many changes, as has been true with other immigrant religions, including Christianity.

SEE ALSO

Asian Indians; Muslims; Religion; Sikhs

FURTHER READING

Kinsley, David R. *Hinduism: A Cultural Perspective.* Englewood Cliffs, N.J.: Prentice-Hall, 1982.

Tweed, Thomas A., and Stephen Prothero, eds. *Asian Religions in America: A Documentary History.* New York: Oxford University Press, 1999.

Hispanics

Hispanics is a Census Bureau term used to describe all persons of Hispanic heritage. In 1940 the census identified 1.6 million "persons of Spanish tongue." In 1950 and 1960 it enumerated 2.3 million and 3.5 million persons, respectively, of "Spanish surname." The censuses of 1970, 1980, and 1990 have asked about origins: in 1970, 9.1 million people were listed as Hispanic; in 1980 the number was 14.6 million; and, in 1990, 22.4 million.

Of the 22.4 million identified as Hispanic in 1990, 13.5 million were of Mexican birth or ancestry, 2.7 million of Puerto Rican birth or ancestry, 1 million of Cuban birth or ancestry, and 5 million of other Hispanic birth or ancestry. In 1990, 7 out of 10 Hispanics lived in just four states: California had 34.4 percent, Texas had 19.4 percent, New York had 9.9 percent, and Florida had 7 percent. Those in California and Texas were mainly Mexican Americans, in New York largely Puerto Ricans, and chiefly Cubans in Florida. Hispanics

Hispanics in the 50 States, 1990 Census

Birth/ Ancestry	Number, in millions
Mexican	13.5
Puerto Rican	2.7
Cubans	1.0
Other	5.0

U.S. Census, 1990

may be of any race. Most are classified as either white or black, but a few, largely Cubans of Chinese or part-Chinese ancestry, are classified as Asians.

Many terms are currently used for some or all of the Hispanic population. The most common is "Chicano," (the feminine form is "Chicana"), derived from *mexicano* (Mexican). Increasingly popular is "Latino" for all New World Spanish speakers. In 1990, 7 out of 10 Hispanics lived in just four states: California, Texas, New York, and Florida.

SEE ALSO

Central Americans; Chicanos; Colombians; Cubans; Latin Americans; Latinos; Mexicans; Puerto Ricans; South Americans; Spanish surname

FURTHER READING

Smith, Carter, and David Lindroth, eds. *Hispanic-American Experience on File.* New York: Facts On File, 1999.
U.S. Bureau of the Census. *We, the American Hispanics.* Washington, D.C.: Government Printing Office, 1992.

Historiography of American immigration

Historiography is the study of history-writing. Thus the historiography of immigration is the study of what historians and others have written about immigration. Until the 1920s, serious historians had not concerned themselves much with immigration. What immigration history had been written was what is often called "filio-pietism," a fancy term for ancestor worship. Thus, for example, a filio-pietistic history of the Irish in America might claim that the Irish won the Civil War; such a history of the Jews might claim

that they financed the American Revolution, and so forth. Historians who wrote about British America talked about colonists, not immigrants.

This perspective began to change in the 1920s when a historian named George M. Stephenson wrote *A History of American immigration,* (1926), the first textbook on the subject, and the man who is usually called the father of American immigration history, Marcus Lee Hansen, published an essay in the *American Historical Review* (April 1927) entitled "The History of American Immigration as a Field for Research." Hansen, not surprisingly, was the son of immigrants—his mother was from Denmark and his father from Norway—and his emphasis was on immigrants from Europe.

The second major figure in immigration historiography was the Harvard historian Oscar Handlin, whose many works include the most popular serious book ever written about American immigration, *The Uprooted: The Epic Story of the Great Migrations that Made the American People.* At a time when the history of immigration was not highly thought of, he argued that it is not possible to understand American history without understanding America's immigrants.

Handlin switched the focus of immigration history from immigrants from western Europe to those from eastern Europe, but he did not stress those from Africa, Asia, and Latin America, as many historians of immigration currently do. By 1965, there were enough immigration historians to make possible the founding of a learned organization, the Immigration and Ethnic History Society, and in 1981, the society began publishing its own learned journal, the *Journal of American Ethnic History.* Given the vogue for social history and the current prominence of immigration in American political debate, the historiography of immigration is sure to become even more interesting and complex in the foreseeable future.

FURTHER READING

Daniels, Roger. *Coming to America: A History of Immigration and Ethnicity in American Life.* New York: Harper-Collins, 1990.

Handlin, Oscar. *The Uprooted: The Epic Story of the Great Migrations that Made the American People.* Boston: Little, Brown, 1951.

Hmong

- *1990 Census: 90,823*
- *Immigration, 1986–96: around 20,000*
- *Immigration, 1820–1996: around 100,000*
- *Major period of immigration: 1975+*
- *Major areas of settlement: California, especially Fresno, and Minneapolis.*

[There is a certain amount of confusion about Laotians and Hmong in American data. The Immigration and Naturalization Service, which records nationality, includes both groups as "Laotians." The Bureau of the Census, which records ethnicity and asks people what they are, separates the two.]

The Hmong are an ancient people who originated in China at least 3,000 years ago. In books about China they are usually referred to as Miao, and in books on Laos they are often called Meo, which means "savage," a name the Hmong understandably resent. In their language, *Hmong* means "free." In the early 19th century, in response to political and cultural persecution by Chinese authorities, some Hmong moved south into Laos, northern Burma, Thailand, and Vietnam. Most, however, still live in China: estimates of

their numbers there range from 2.8 million to 6 million.

All of the Hmong who have come to the United States since 1975 have come as refugees from Laos, where there may have been 300,000 Hmong in 1960. In Laos the Hmong were one of perhaps 60 ethnic groups. They had no written language until American missionaries created one for them in 1950. They practiced an animistic form of religion, although many have been converted to Christianity. They were what anthropologists call a premodern people, who lived by slash-and-burn agriculture and whose chief crops were corn for their livestock and opium poppies for cash.

As the name Meo ("savage") suggests, the Hmong had a long tradition of fighting against authority in China, against the French colonizers in Laos,

Some Hmong, like these women in Liverpool, New York, in 1992, came to the United States from Laos soon after U.S. military forces began to leave Vietnam. The Hmong had allied themselves with the United States and as a consequence faced particularly vicious repression by the communist governments.

and later against local governments. It is therefore not surprising that in 1960 they were recruited by the Central Intelligence Agency (CIA) to fight against the North Vietnamese, who were using Laos as a base for their war against the South Vietnamese (and, increasingly, the Americans). The Hmong fought long and hard, and it is estimated that some 15,000 were killed during the next 15 years.

With the end of the Vietnam War in 1975, many Hmong were forced to flee to refugee camps, largely in neighboring Thailand. From these camps perhaps some 150,000 have been resettled: about 100,000 of them in the United States and the rest in France, Australia, and Canada.

In the United States their adjustment has been difficult. An agricultural people, they have been resettled in cities. Some of their customs—polygamy (men having multiple wives), bride purchase, and bride kidnapping—are illegal in America. According to the 1990 census, Hmong were the poorest ethnic group enumerated: whereas whites on average earned a per-capita annual income of $15,265, and blacks $9,017, Hmong had a per capita annual income of just $2,692. Almost two-thirds of the Hmong—63.6 percent—were below the poverty line. Yet many Hmong, especially the young, are making the same kinds of successful adjustments to American life as members of other immigrant groups have done.

More than a third of the Hmong in the United States in 1990 were native-born, as opposed to only a fifth of Cambodians and Laotians. Sucheng Chan, author of the most insightful book about the Hmong in America, used four young Hmong college students to transcribe interviews with other Hmong refugees. All had successful careers at the University of California, Santa Bar-bara, where they majored in law and society, biological sciences, French, and sociology. In 1992, a Hmong woman, Choua Lee, was elected to the St. Paul, Minnesota, school board, the first refugee from the wars in Vietnam to become an elected American official.

SEE ALSO

Cambodians; Laotians; Refugees; Vietnam War

FURTHER READING

Chan, Sucheng. *Hmong Means Free: Life in Laos and America.* Philadelphia: Temple University Press, 1994.
Hein, Jeremy. *From Vietnam, Laos, and Cambodia: A Refugee Experience in the United States.* New York: Twayne, 1995.

Holocaust

The word Holocaust is now generally used to describe the attempt of Hitler's Germany and its collaborators during World War II to exterminate the Jews of Europe. Many of the survivors of the Holocaust came to the United States as displaced persons. Some 6 million European Jews were deliberately murdered, mostly in death camps, as were other victims including Gypsies, the physically handicapped, homosexuals, Poles, and political opponents. The original meaning of the word *holocaust*, as used in the biblical books of Genesis and Exodus, was "a sacrifice consumed by fire; a whole burnt offering." The United States Holocaust Museum in Washington, D.C., opened in 1993.

SEE ALSO

Displaced persons; Gypsies; Jews; Refugees

FURTHER READING

Bauer, Yehuda. *A History of the Holocaust.* New York: Franklin Watts, 1982.

Dinnerstein, Leonard. *America and the Survivors of the Holocaust*. New York: Columbia University Press, 1982.

Hondurans

- *1990 Ancestry: 116,635*
- *Immigration, 1986–96: 75,142*
- *Immigration, 1820–1996: n.a.*
- *Major period of immigration: since 1980*
- *Major areas of settlement: New York, New Orleans, Los Angeles, Houston*

Honduras, the second largest Central American nation, has a racially and ethnically diverse population of about 6 million in a nation of 43,277 square miles, about the size of Virginia. Conquered by Spain in the 1520s and 1530s, it broke from Spain in 1821, was first a part of Mexico and then of the Central American Federation until 1838, and has been nominally independent ever since. Like most nations in the region, Honduras has had a turbulent history and has been subjected to domination by foreign economic interests, in particular the United Fruit Company, a U.S. firm.

In the late 1960s several hundred thousand Salvadorean refugees illegally immigrated to Honduras; many were forcibly expelled. Honduras and El Salvador fought an inconclusive five-day war about this in 1969 which had dire economic consequences for both countries. During the 1980s Honduras served as a base for the so-called Contras, who were attempting to overthrow the left-wing Sandinista government of Nicaragua. The Contras were financed and otherwise supported by covert American government operations of dubious legality. Since 1990, Honduras and its neighbors have been at peace and the economy has greatly improved.

The Honduran people are perhaps 90 percent mestizo—that is, of mixed European and indigenous ancestry—who speak Spanish and are largely Roman Catholic. The remaining 10 percent are composed of a number of ethnic groups including Maya, Garifuna, and Afro-Caribbeans who came as free immigrants. (*Garifuna* is a Central American term for persons of African and Carib descent, sometimes called Black Caribs, who were brought to the region by the British as slaves.)

The Maya largely adhere to their indigenous language and culture, while the black groups speak English and are largely Protestant. Immigration from Honduras to the United States began during World War II and was largely a result of economic channels developed by the United Fruit Company and other American firms whose banana plantations dominated the economies of Honduras and other Central American countries.

As it did for other ethnic groups, the World War II labor shortages opened doors that had previously been closed. Honduran men were hired as sailors and other Hondurans, men and women, came to the United States as domestic servants of returning managers. Many settled in ports used by the company: particularly in New Orleans, New York, New Jersey, and Boston. In the 1960s and 1970s most Hondurans came from relatively elite backgrounds as students, tourists, and as part of the family reunification process. The regionwide political crises in the late 1970s and 1980s stimulated the first large-scale immigration of Hondurans, both legal and illegal. The INS and the Census Bureau estimated in 1996 that there were 90,000 Hondurans illegally in the United States, the seventh largest group from any nation.

As is the case with most Central American immigrants, their employment is largely in the service sector. Although they do not seem to have created any neighborhoods that are particularly Honduran, it is sometimes the case that a Honduran will become the building superintendent of an apartment house and, over time, that building will become largely Honduran.

SEE ALSO

Central Americans; Illegal immigrants; Maya; Mestizo

FURTHER READING

Gonzalez, Nancie L. *Sojourners of the Caribbean.* Urbana: University of Illinois Press, 1988.

Huguenots

Huguenot is a word of disputed origin used to describe the French Protestant followers of the theologian John Calvin, who were very powerful in 16th- and 17th-century France. The revocation of the Edict of Nantes by Louis XIV in 1685, which ended religious toleration of Protestantism in France for a century, resulted in the dispersion and emigration of many Huguenots within Europe and to British colonies in the New World. Their faith was so similar to that of some American Protestant churches that Huguenots in America soon "disappeared," an interesting case of near total assimilation.

SEE ALSO
Assimilation; French; Religion

FURTHER READING
Butler, Jon. *The Huguenots in America: A Refugee People in New World Society.* Cambridge: Harvard University Press, 1983.

Hungarians

- *1990 Ancestry: 1,582,302*
- *Immigration, 1986–96: 11,976*
- *Immigration, 1820–1996: 1,673,579*
- *Major periods of immigration: 1899–1914, late 1950s*
- *Major areas of settlement: Midwest, Cleveland*

Hungary and Hungarians have had a complex history. Hungarian culture comes from the Magyars, an ancient people who are distinct in language and culture from most of Hungary's Slavic neighbors. A thousand years ago, in 1001, Hungary crowned its first king, Stephen, a Christian Magyar. In 1526 the Ottoman Turks conquered Hungary and were not driven out until 1699. Hungary then became a part of the Austrian Empire, and, after 1867, it was given some self-rule as the Austrian emperor took the title of King of Hungary. The Hungary of that era was almost twice as large as present-day Hungary and contained large numbers of non-Magyar peoples.

Hungary has been independent since the breakup of the Austro-Hungarian Empire at the end of World War I, although it was under Soviet Russian control for some 35 years after World War II. Today Hungary has 10 million people and covers nearly 36,000 square miles, so it is a little larger than South Carolina.

A few Hungarians came to the United States in the 18th century—some fought in the Revolution—and a few more came in the early 19th century. One of these, Agoston Haraszthy, settled for a while in Wisconsin and then joined the gold rush to California. He did not find much gold, but he became one of the founders of the California wine industry.

This formal portrait of Colonel Julius Stahel was taken before he was promoted to major general during the Civil War. Hundreds of thousands of immigrants, some of them with European military experience, fought for both the Union and the Confederacy during the Civil War.

The first sizable group of Hungarians to come to America, some 4,000 or 5,000, came as refugees after the failed revolution of 1848. Most of these young political and military leaders were still in the United States when the Civil War broke out in 1861, and about 800 served in the Union army, many of them as officers. The most celebrated was Major General Julius H. Stahel, who organized a regiment, was wounded, and received the Congressional Medal of Honor. As late as 1870 the few thousand Hungarians in America, who were mostly middle-class and politically active, were scattered across the country.

Then, between 1871 and 1914, more than a million Hungarians came to the United States, nearly 90 percent of them in the 15 years before World War I. In just one year, 1907, some 185,000 Hungarians came to the United States, about 1 percent of Hungary's total population. Not all of these were ethnic Hungarians: many were Slovaks, Romanians, or Jews. These were not middle-class revolutionaries and soldiers in exile, but peasants and workers seeking to earn a living wage. A large number of them were sojourners who wanted to return to Hungary with enough money to buy a new farm or improve an existing one. Although most had been agricultural workers in Europe, in America they worked largely in heavy industry and in coal mining.

With the outbreak of World War I in Europe in 1914, many Hungarians who might have gone home decided to stay, and Hungarian settlements grew larger. Many Hungarian immigrants and their children served in the U.S. Army after 1917, when the United States entered the war. Both before and after the war, the number of women immigrants increased, and Hungarian-American families began to develop in many towns and cities, particularly in the Midwest.

The largest Hungarian ethnic neighborhood was in Cleveland, centered on Upper Buckeye Road. At its peak it covered an area 30 blocks long and as much as 15 blocks wide. Not only Hungarians lived there, but they and their culture predominated for a couple of generations.

As was true of other immigrant groups of the era, Hungarians established religious, fraternal, and cultural associations. Because Hungarians were quite fragmented religiously—its Christians were divided among Protestant, Roman Catholic, and Greek Orthodox denominations—strictly ethnic churches have been less prominent among them than is the case for many other nationalities. Many Hungarians worshipped in churches that were not primarily Hungarian.

The 1924 Immigration Act ended mass immigration from Hungary (as it did for would-be immigrants from most countries) for 30 years. Only about 15,000 came between 1925 and 1945. Many of these were refugees, the most famous of whom was the com-

A musical Hungarian family, the Jánossys, formed a quintet in the 1930s. The man in the center is playing a cembalo, an instrument popular in Hungary.

poser Béla Bartók, who died in the United States but was reburied in Hungary in 1988 as a national hero. After World War II, much larger numbers of refugees immigrated. Nearly 25,000 came as displaced persons between 1945 and 1952.

Then, in October 1956, the doomed Hungarian uprising against Soviet domination was quickly crushed by Soviet troops and tanks, with heavy casualties. Some 200,000 Hungarians escaped to the West, mostly across the Austrian border. Under a special Hungarian Refugee Program authorized by the administration of President Dwight D. Eisenhower, about 38,000 of these "freedom fighters" were admitted to the United States in a program that ignored the tiny Hungarian quota. Since that time, relatively few Hungarians, about a thousand a year, have come to America.

SEE ALSO
Austro-Hungarian Empire; Displaced persons; Eastern Rite churches; Jews; Refugees; Romanians; Slovaks; Sojourners

FURTHER READING
Lengyel, Emil. *Americans from Hungary.* Philadelphia: J.B. Lippincott, 1948.
Széplaki, Joseph, ed. *The Hungarians in America, 1583–1974: A Chronology and*

Fact Book. Dobbs Ferry, N.Y.: Oceana, 1975.
Várdy, Stevan Béla. *The Hungarian-Americans: The Hungarian Experience in North America.* New York: Chelsea House, 1990.

Hutterites

The Hutterite Brethren, an Anabaptist sect, are the largest and, some say, the most successful Christian communal group in the United States. Unlike the better known Amish and Mennonites, they adhere strictly to common ownership of real property and communal living patterns. The Hutterites originated in what is now Austria and Czechoslovakia in the 16th century and took their name from their leader, Jacob Hutter, who was burned at the stake in 1536. Most of their settlements in Europe were destroyed in the late 16th and early 17th centuries, and they fled to several eastern European regions before settling in Russia in 1770.

A hundred years later, threatened with forced military service, almost 1,300 fled to the United States. About a third of them maintained their communal practices in South Dakota. During World War I, the Hutterite and other conscientious objectors (C.O.'s) were treated brutally by the American military. As a result most Hutterites fled to Canada. Today there are more than 200 Hutterite colonies in North America with some 75 of them, with 6,000 inhabitants, in the United States.

SEE ALSO

Amish; Anabaptist sects; Germans; Mennonites

FURTHER READING

Hostetler, John. *Hutterite Society*. Baltimore: Johns Hopkins University Press, 1974.

Icelanders

- *1990 Ancestry: 40,529*
- *Immigration, 1986–96: 1,428*
- *Immigration, 1820–1996: around 7,500*
- *Major period of immigration: 1880–1900*
- *Major areas of settlement: northern Great Plains*

Iceland is a large island, almost 40,000 square miles, about the size of Virginia, with just 270,000 people. Most of the territory is mountainous, with many glaciers and volcanoes. Located on the edge of the Arctic Circle, its temperature is mitigated by both the warm Gulf Stream and many volcanic hot springs. Although Iceland is usually considered part of Europe, some geographers argue that since it is closer to Greenland, it ought to be considered part of North America. President Franklin D. Roosevelt used this as an excuse to institute a friendly military occupation of Iceland during World War II.

Iceland was first settled in A.D. 874 by Vikings, who were later joined by Celts from Ireland. Around 1000 Leif Eriksson, who was born in Iceland, sailed from Greenland and founded a short-lived colony called Vinland, which was probably on Labrador. Iceland was independent until the 13th century, when it came under the dominion of Norway, then of Denmark. In 1874 Iceland was granted autonomy under the Danish crown and in 1944 it became an independent republic.

The first Icelanders we know about who emigrated to the United States were a few dozen who, like some 18,000 Danes, were converted to Mormonism and settled in Utah beginning in Utah in 1855. Larger numbers of Icelanders settled in the northern Great Plains, particularly in Minnesota and the Dakotas in the 1880s and 1890s. Since American immigration officials counted Icelanders as Danes until 1930, the numbers of Icelanders who came must remain approximate. The best estimate is that some 5,000 immigrated to the United States before World War II; about twice as many went to Canada.

Like most Scandinavian immigrants, Icelanders are predominantly Lutheran, and an Icelandic Lutheran synod was created in America in 1885. Practically all Icelanders were literate and supporters of public education. In addition to observing typical American holidays (though the Icelandic Christmas lasts 13 days), many Icelandic Americans celebrate June 17 as Icelandic Independence Day.

SEE ALSO

Celts; Danes; Mormons; Scandinavians; Vikings

FURTHER READING

Arnason, David, and Vincent Arnason, eds. *The New Icelanders: A North American Community*. Winnipeg, Manitoba, Canada: Turnstone Press, 1994.

Walters, Thorstina J. *Modern Sagas: The Story of Icelanders in North America.* Fargo: North Dakota Institute for Regional Studies, 1953.

Illegal emigrants

Illegal emigrants are those whose departure violates the laws of the nations from which they migrate. Many of the immigrants to America, from colonial times to the present, have left their homelands illegally. In European nations that had feudal systems, the rural poor were not legally free to leave the land. In the 18th and early 19th centuries, Britain tried to restrict the emigration of skilled workers who understood the "secrets" of her industrial revolution.

In the 19th and early 20th centuries, many Europeans emigrated to avoid compulsory military service, which in some cases involved serving as much as 25 years. In the 20th century many communist nations in Europe, Asia, and the Caribbean have made it illegal for their people to emigrate to the United States or other noncommunist countries. The United States has generally ignored such restrictions on free movement; it has actively encouraged the illegal emigration of political exiles from failed European revolutions in the 19th century, and in many cases it has actively encouraged illegal emigrants, especially from communist nations. The current laws on asylum, which enable victims of persecution elsewhere to enter the United States, are an example of this encouragement.

SEE ALSO

Asylum; Illegal immigrants

Illegal immigrants

Illegal immigrants are those whose immigration violates the immigration laws of the nation to which they migrate. In the United States, the first illegal immigrants were some 50,000 slaves, mostly Afro-Caribbeans, who were brought in after the slave trade was made illegal in 1808. After American immigration became restrictive, with the passage of the Chinese Exclusion Act of 1882, more and more categories of people have been declared ineligible to come to the United States.

Today there are two distinct kinds of illegal immigrants. The more publicized "border crossers," people who enter the United States without the proper documents, are fewer in number than the less publicized "visa abusers," people who enter the United States on visitor or student visas and simply do not leave. No one knows how many illegal immigrants there are in the United States—one scholar writes of the impossibility of "counting the uncountable"—but the number is surely several million. Many of the "border crossers" are involved in circular migration and do not intend to stay permanently. The usual penalty for illegal entry is deportation or removal from the United States. The Immigration Act of 1986 eventually legalized more than 2 million illegal immigrants.

Some people do not like the phrase "illegal immigrants" and use the term "undocumented persons" instead. The following table represents the official "guess" by the Immigration and Naturalization Service (INS) about the number and origin of illegal immigrants in the United States, according to the Census Bureau and the INS as of 1996.

Contemporary maps show how the 1924 act was expected to work. However, because of non-quota immigration, many more than the projected number of 161,990 immigrants were admitted.

quota numbers was moved back from 1910 to 1890.

These two changes drastically reduced the quotas for eastern and southern European countries. The annual quotas for Italy and Poland, for example, were about 42,000 and 31,000 under the 1921 law. Under the 1924 law they were reduced to about 4,000 Italians and some 6,000 Poles annually. The total number of quota spaces was reduced to about 180,000 from 380,000.

By this act, Congress broke the Gentlemen's Agreement with Japan by barring all "aliens ineligible to citizenship." In addition, some kinds of people were declared "Non-Quota" immigrants, who, if they were otherwise eligible, could enter without numerical restriction. The most numerous groups were wives and children under 18 years of age of American citizens, and natives of independent nations of the Western Hemisphere and Canada. The first of these provisions meant that when an alien became a naturalized citizen, his wife and minor children were automatically admissible without numerical limitation. College professors and clergymen and their immediate families could enter without reference to quotas.

With the Immigration Act of 1924, Congress created a fantastically complicated National Origins System, which did not go into effect until 1930. Congress mandated a "scientific" study of the origins of the American people as of 1920 to serve as a base for a new "national origins system" that would govern immigration after July 1, 1929. The total number of quota spaces from then on was to be reduced to about 150,000. Based on that study, the President was to promulgate national quotas by executive order. In one section of the law, the method of making that determination seems reasonably fair; "national origin" was to be determined by calculating "the number of inhabi-

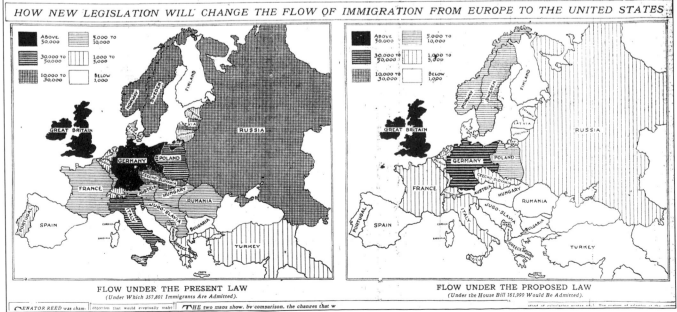

AMERICA OF THE MELTING POT COMES TO END

Effects of New Immigration Legislation Described by Senate Sponsor of Bill—Chief Aim, He States, Is to Preserve Racial Type as It Exists Here Today

HOW NEW LEGISLATION WILL CHANGE THE FLOW OF IMMIGRATION FROM EUROPE TO THE UNITED STATES

FLOW UNDER THE PRESENT LAW
(Under Which 357,801 Immigrants Are Admitted).

FLOW UNDER THE PROPOSED LAW
(Under the House Bill 161,990 Would Be Admitted).

You can't come in. The quota for 1620 is full.

This 1924 cartoon, by a noted Dutch immigrant, pretends that Native Americans had an immigration quota and that the Pilgrims were kept out by it.

tants in continental United States in 1920 whose origin by birth or ancestry" is attributable to each nation. But the next section, not usually cited, excludes from "inhabitants in the United States in 1920" the following: any immigrants from the New World and their descendants; any Asians or their descendants; the descendants of "slave immigrants"; and the descendants of "American aborigines," that is, Native Americans. Some aspects of this system remained in effect until 1965. The laws' purpose was to curtail immigration to the United States and it was effective.

SEE ALSO

Aliens ineligible to citizenship; Gentlemen's Agreement; Immigration Act of 1921; Immigration policy

FURTHER READING

Hutchinson, E. P. *Legislative History of American Immigration Policy, 1798–1965.* Philadelphia: University of Pennsylvania Press, 1981.

Immigration Act of 1952

The Immigration Act of 1952, also called the McCarran-Walter Act, was essentially an extension and updating of the Quota and National Origins Systems as established in the acts of 1921 and 1924. For this reason it was vetoed by President Harry S. Truman, who called the act unfair, but Congress overrode his veto. It did, however, contain some significant reforms, and it can

now be argued that it was a stepping-stone to the present, more liberal policy. The act embodied three major changes.

The most important change was the elimination of the racist provisions of naturalization and immigration law, which had barred certain races from naturalization, and denied permission to immigrate to many Asians on the ground that they were "aliens ineligible to citizenship." Since 1952 American naturalization policy has been "color blind": neither race nor ethnicity is any longer a bar to immigration or naturalization. However, the new quotas established for Asian nations were tiny, so the law still discriminated against them. In addition, persons of Asian ancestry—say a person of Chinese ethnicity born in Canada—would have to find space in the small Chinese quota. Other Canadians could enter without limit as natives of the Western Hemisphere.

Second, immigrants from colonies were now to be charged to the quotas of the mother country, but only 100 per year from any single colony could enter as immigrants. This provision chiefly affected black people from Caribbean islands, such as Jamaica, who had been able under previous legislation to enter the United States relatively freely.

Third, the non-quota classification—those who could enter without numerical limitation—was broadened to include all children and spouses of American citizens, and aliens and their families, if the family head had worked for the U.S. government abroad for at least 15 years.

Reflecting the prevailing cold war atmosphere, in which conflict with the Soviet Union was all-pervasive, the law expanded the grounds for deportation and contained several provisions that were designed to keep persons with ideas and associations that Congress deemed "subversive" from coming to the United States.

SEE ALSO

Aliens ineligible to citizenship; Immigration Act of 1921; Immigration Act of 1924; Immigration policy; Quota system

FURTHER READING

Hutchinson, E. P. *Legislative History of American Immigration Policy, 1798–1965*. Philadelphia: University of Pennsylvania Press, 1981.

Immigration Act of 1965

The Immigration Act of 1965, which ended the era of the Quota and National Origins Systems, has remained the basis of American immigration policy ever since. It replaced the quota system and the criteria of race and ethnicity with a preference system, based first of all on family reunification—which has been an element of every major bill since 1921—and, to a lesser degree, on the qualifications of individual immigrants in terms of education and skills.

The 1965 act, whose passage was in great part due to the effective leadership of President Lyndon B. Johnson, was seen by its supporters as returning fairness to American immigration policy. In addition, at a time when the United States was striving for world leadership, it was important to end the visible and open discrimination against peoples who composed the majority of the world's population. The 1965 act was not a complete break with the past, but rather a reorientation of basic immigration policy. Largely as a result of the 1965 act, the major sources of immigration have shifted from Europe. Since

1965 the major providers of immigrants to the United States have been nations of Latin America and of Asia.

SEE ALSO

Immigration Act of 1952; Immigration policy; Preference system; Quota system

FURTHER READING

Reimers, David M. *Still the Golden Door: The Third World Comes to America*. 2nd ed. New York: Columbia University Press, 1992.

Immigration Act of 1986

The Immigration Act of 1986, known as the Immigration Reform and Control Act (IRCA), made a number of changes in immigration law. The most significant change provided a process by which immigrants who had either entered the country illegally or had entered legally on tourist or other visas and overstayed their authorized stay, *and* had been in the United States since January 1, 1982, could legalize their stay and eventually be eligible to become naturalized citizens of the United States.

This process is often called an "amnesty" program, but that term does not appear in the law. Under its provisions 2,684,892 persons had legalized their status under IRCA's provisions between 1989 (the first year of eligibility for citizenship) and 1996. All of these people have become naturalized citizens. Just over 2 million of those naturalized under IRCA provisions, 74.7 percent of the total, were natives of Mexico. The following tables show, by regions, the number of persons so naturalized and list the countries with 10,000 or more legalizations.

Legalizations under IRCA, 1989–96, by Region

Region	Number	Percent
Africa	39,634	1.5
Asia	128,634	4.8
Caribbean	112,321	4.2
Central America	259,387	9.7
Europe	34,844	1.3
Oceania	5,355	0.2
North America	2,011,883	74.9
South America	92,661	3.5
Unknown	*173*	*0.0*
TOTAL	2,684,892	100.1

Legalizations under IRCA, 1989–96, by Country

Region	Number	Percent
China*	15,352	0.6
Colombia	30,862	1.1
Dominican Rep.	24,411	0.9
Ecuador	14,854	0.6
El Salvador	153,447	5.7
Guatemala	63,885	2.4
Haiti	57,053	2.1
Honduras	16,212	0.6
India	20,863	0.8
Iran	13,250	.5
Jamaica	17,038	0.6
Korea	10,146	0.4
Mexico	2,005,531	74.7
Nicaragua	15,426	0.6
Nigeria	14,454	0.5
Pakistan	17,215	0.6
Peru	17,802	0.7
Philippines	26,542	1.0
Poland	16,131	0.6
Other	*134,418*	*5.0*
TOTAL	2,684,892	100.0

* "China" includes The People's Republic of China (9,392); Hong Kong (2,271), and Taiwan (3,689).

Immigration and Naturalization Service, *1997 Statistical Yearbook*

SEE ALSO
Immigration policy

FURTHER READING
Reimers, David M. *Still the Golden Door: The Third World Comes to America*. 2nd ed. New York: Columbia University Press, 1992.

Immigration Act of 1990

The Immigration Act of 1990 consisted of a significant set of amendments to the 1965 Immigration Act. It established a "flexible cap" at 675,000 beginning in 1995, to be divided into 480,000 family-sponsored, 140,000 employment-based, and 55,000 in a new category, "diversity" immigrants. The diversity program reserved spaces for citizens of countries that, for one reason or another, had not been awarded many spaces in previous years. It should be noted that these caps have been exceeded with regularity: in 1995, 720,461 immigrants were admitted; in 1996, 915,900.

Other changes in the law included a relaxation of the ideological bars to admission, and an authorization for the attorney general to grant temporary protected status to undocumented alien nationals subject to armed conflict and natural disasters. This later category included Tibetans, who were being persecuted by the People's Republic of China, which ruled their homeland. This was a way of allowing them to stay in the United States even though they had entered illegally.

SEE ALSO
Diversity programs; Immigration Act of 1965; Immigration policy; Refugee Act of 1980; Tibetans

FURTHER READING
Reimers, David M. *Unwelcome Strangers: American Identity and the Turn Against Immigration*. New York: Columbia University Press, 1998.

Immigration and Naturalization Service (INS)

A part of the Department of Justice, the Immigration and Naturalization Service is the federal government agency that regulates immigration, administers naturalization certification, and is responsible for deportation. It is headed by a commissioner who reports to the attorney general. The Border Patrol, created in 1924, whose mission is to keep illegal immigrants and drugs out of the country, is also part of the INS.

The INS was created in 1933 by combining two separate bureaus, one for immigration and one for naturalization. The two bureaus had been created in 1891 and 1906, respectively. The INS was originally part of the Department of Labor, but was moved to the Department of Justice in 1940 in a reorganization intended to provide closer control over aliens in a time of preparation for war (World War II). The first federal immigration office, which had been created in 1864 and abolished four years later, was intended to encourage immigration. But the service created in 1891 had an opposite purpose: to keep out Chinese laborers, contract laborers, and others declared inadmissible by Congress.

Administrating immigration policy once involved very few people. In 1891 the superintendent of Immigration had just 27 subordinates, including one at each of 24 inspection stations around the country. In 1995 the commissioner of the INS had more than 20,000 subordinates: 14,000 of them were employed to keep people out, 2,800 to help people who have been admitted. Its yearly operating budget was more than $2 billion, of which $640 million came from fees collected from immigrants and visitors.

During the 1990s the INS was harshly criticized as an incompetent, "broken agency" by many members of Congress and the press. A survey by the Maxwell School of Government at Syracuse University rated it as the "least efficient" federal government bureaucracy. A number of proposed restructurings of the agency were made—some by the agency itself—but none were adopted. Many scholars argued that Congress, increasingly concerned about illegal immigration, kept increasing the responsibilities of the INS without a proportionate increase in its budget, and so was at least partly to blame for the agency's gross inefficiency. For example, some people who had met all of the requirements for naturalization had to wait years because the INS was behind in its paperwork.

SEE ALSO
Border Patrol; Illegal immigrants; Immigration policy

FURTHER READING
Masanz, Sharon D. *History of the Immigration and Naturalization Service*. Washington, D.C.: Congressional Research Service, Library of Congress, 1981.

Immigration policy

The original immigration policy of the United States was to encourage as

Sheet music for a 1923 song, "O! Close the Gates," represents the anti-immigrant sentiment of the time. Uncle Sam is enlisted to lend patriotic appeal to the cover.

much immigration as possible. The United States, at the time of its formation, was a largely empty country, and everyone was aware of the need for greater population. Although the Constitution does not mention immigration directly, it did instruct Congress "to establish a uniform system of naturalization" [Art. 1, Sec. 8] and made it possible for naturalized immigrants to hold any office under the Constitution except that of President and Vice President [Art. 2, Sec.1].

In 1790 Congress passed a naturalization act that limited the privilege to "free white persons." The Constitution also enabled Congress to end the immigration of slaves after 1807, which Congress did in 1808. The Supreme Court later ruled in the *Passenger Cases* of 1849 that immigration was "commerce with foreign nations" and thus, under Article 1, Section 8, a federal prerogative; therefore only the federal government, and not the states, could regulate it.

After the Civil War and the 13th Amendment ended slavery, and the 14th Amendment established birthright citizenship, Congress amended the naturalization law in 1870 to permit the naturalization of "persons of African descent," but refused to include Asians among those eligible.

No significant federal regulation occurred until the passage of the Chinese Exclusion Act of 1882, which marked the beginning of a period of special restriction of Chinese that lasted 61 years, and of a policy of regulating immigration that continues to the present day.

Until 1921 the restriction was bit by bit, as various kinds of restrictions were legislated by Congress. By 1920 the once free and unrestricted immigration

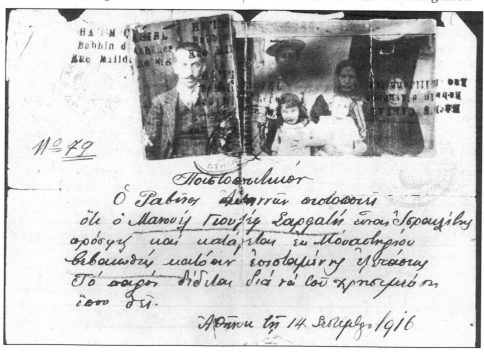

Haim Castel, who may originally have been from Poland, came to Ellis Island in 1916 from Greece. Like many immigrants then, he had no passport. The endorsement on his identification document in Greek asserts that he is a "rabbinic Jew" and that he has significant funds to support himself. Since "likely to become a public charge" was the most frequent cause for exclusion in before 1917, this was a significant statement.

policy had become limited in eight different ways: contract laborers, Asians (except for Japanese and Filipinos), criminals, persons who failed to meet certain moral standards, persons with various diseases, persons likely to become a public charge, certain types of political radicals, and illiterates had all been barred from immigrating.

By 1920, although the United States was not nearly as crowded as other industrial nations, it was no longer an "empty" country. In addition, many Americans felt that too many of the "wrong" kinds of people were entering. Thus Congress passed the notorious immigration acts of 1921 and 1924. These acts, often called the Quota Acts, not only deliberately reduced immigration, but also intentionally discriminated against immigrants from eastern and southern Europe. The 1924 act also contained a clause that ended all immigration of Japanese.

These policies remained unchanged until 1943, when a period of easing restrictions began. In that year, in the midst of World War II, the Chinese Exclusion Act was repealed and Chinese were given a minimal quota and made eligible for naturalization. This was done as a gesture of solidarity toward China, an ally against the Japanese. Congress passed similar acts for Filipinos and "natives of India" in 1946. The quota system for Europeans was breached in 1948 and 1950 as two Displaced Persons acts were passed to admit victims of World War II. But the quota system was only slightly modified by the Immigration Act of 1952, which ended all racial and ethnic bars to naturalization.

During the 1950s and 1960s numerous special refugee acts were passed to admit Hungarians, Cubans, Southeast Asians, and many others. The

Immigration Act of 1965 ended the quota system first established in 1921 and made immigration truly global in its reach. The Refugee Act of 1980 consolidated policies that had evolved on a case-by-case basis and, for the first time in American law, provided the right of asylum. Most acts since 1980 have stressed problems of illegal immigration without seriously changing either the composition or volume of immigration. The Immigration Act of 1986, however, by establishing a "one-time" amnesty, created pressures for and the likelihood of subsequent amnesties.

In the 1990s there occurred what has been called a "turn against immigration," and Congress enacted a series of punitive laws—some of which have since been declared unconstitutional—

This vicious 1881 cartoon was part of the campaign for Chinese exclusion. Many Chinese were employed in cigar making, so the white workers' trade union, which barred Chinese, invented the union label so that consumers could tell which cigars were made by white unionists.

restricting benefits to immigrants who were already permanent residents of the United States. By the end of the 1990s that turn against immigration had been at least partly reversed, as evidenced not only by judicial decisions but also by changes in public opinion and the repeal of some of the punitive legislation passed earlier in the decade.

SEE ALSO

Birthright citizens; Chinese Exclusion Act; Displaced persons; Federation for Immigration Reform; Immigration Acts of 1921, 1924, 1952, 1965, and 1986; Japanese; Naturalization; *Passenger Cases*; Refugee Act of 1980; Slave trade

FURTHER READING

Hutchinson, E. P. *Legislative History of American Immigration Policy, 1798–1965*. Philadelphia: University of Pennsylvania Press, 1981.
Reimers, David M. *Still the Golden Door: The Third World Comes to America*. 2nd ed. New York: Columbia University Press, 1992.
Reimers, David M. *Unwelcome Strangers: American Identity and the Turn Against Immigration*. New York: Columbia University Press, 1998.

Immigration Restriction League

The Immigration Restriction League was a nativist organization founded by a small group of Harvard graduates in Boston in 1894. Its primary purpose was to advocate the restriction of immigration. A lobbying organization rather than one of mass membership, it was instrumental in the passage of the literacy test (1917) and of the immigration acts of 1921 and 1924. After the passage of the 1924 act its activities were no longer significant.

SEE ALSO

Immigration Act of 1917; Immigration Act of 1921; Immigration Act of 1924; Literacy Test; Nativism

FURTHER READING

Hall, Prescott F. *Immigration and Its Effects upon the United States*. New York: Holt, 1907.
Solomon, Barbara Miller. *Ancestors and Immigrants*. Cambridge: Harvard University Press, 1956.

Immigration stations

SEE Angel Island; Castle Garden; Ellis Island

Indentured servants

Indentured servants were people who, in exchange for passage to America, obligated themselves to work without wages for as long as seven years. Before the widespread introduction of African slavery in the 18th century, white male indentured servants, chiefly English and Irish, were the chief source of plantation labor in the southern colonies. Among non-British groups, indentured servitude was most common among Germans, who often referred to indentured servants as "redemptioners" because many were "redeemed" by their families before their term of service had run out.

The original indenture, or contract, was usually to a ship captain in Europe who expected to sell the servant to someone in America for a profit. The use of indentured servants died out about 1830 because it seemed no longer appropriate for white persons to be in bondage, and many forms of contract labor were outlawed by the 13th Amendment to the Constitution, which

This ad for "indented" (indentured) servants gave those who needed workers an opportunity to buy them for a term of several years.

abolished both slavery and "involuntary servitude, except as punishment for crime."

SEE ALSO

Africans; Contract labor; Convicts; Germans; Peru; Redemptioners; Slave trade

FURTHER READING

Salinger, Sharon V. *"To Serve Well and Faithfully": Labor and Indentured Servitude in Pennsylvania, 1682–1800.* New York: Cambridge University Press, 1987.
Smith, Abbot E. *Colonists in Bondage: White Servitude and Convict Labor in America, 1607–1776.* Chapel Hill: University of North Carolina Press, 1947.

Indians

SEE Asian Indians

Indo-Chinese

Indo-Chinese is an obsolete term for several peoples of South Asia, including Cambodians, Hmong, Laotians, and Vietnamese. What the French colonizers called *Indo-Chine* (Indo-China) has, since the late 1950s, been generally known as Vietnam.

SEE ALSO

Cambodians; Hmong; Laotians; Vietnamese

Indonesians

- *1990 Ancestry: 43,969*
- *Immigration, 1986–96: 19,167*
- *Immigration, 1820–1996: n.a.*
- *Major periods of immigration: 1950s–60s, 1980+*
- *Major area of settlement: southern California*

Indonesians, whose nation of islands contains more than 200 million people and is the fourth most populous country in the world, are the least represented of all the major peoples of the earth among the population of the United States. The reasons are to be found in both geography and history. Indonesia is at the other side of the world. It comprises more than 13,000 islands that extend for 3,000 miles—farther than from New York to San Francisco—on both sides of the equator between Southeast Asia and Australia and between the Indian and Pacific Oceans.

Indonesians are ethnically diverse. The largest immigrant minority group is the Chinese, who number between 2 and 3 million. Chinese Indonesians are economically important well beyond their numbers, and have been subjected to nativist attacks with occasional massacres since the 18th century. The most recent was in 1998.

More than 300 languages are spoken in Indonesia but an official language, Bahasa Indonesia, is said to be understood in all but the most remote villages. English is considered to be the country's second language. The vast majority of the population, 87 percent, is Muslim, less than 10 percent is Christian (largely Protestant), 2 percent is Hindu, and perhaps 1 percent Buddhist.

In the 16th and early 17th centuries, the colonial powers of Portugal, England, and the Netherlands struggled for control. By 1623 the Dutch had won, leaving the Portuguese with only part of one island, Timor, and ousting the English completely. The Dutch ruled the islands as the Dutch East Indies until World War II, when the islands were briefly conquered by Japan. When Japan surrendered in 1945, Indonesia leaders proclaimed independence which the Dutch contested. After four bitter years of warfare, the Dutch recognized Indonesian independence.

A few Indonesian seamen "jumped ship" or otherwise settled in the United States during and just after World War II. In the two decades after the Indonesian revolution of 1949, a number of Indonesian refugees of mixed Asian and European ancestry, often called Indos, settled in the United States, after first being resettled in the Netherlands. The Dutch government claimed that there were as many as 60,000, but this figure seems very high.

Most other Indonesians who have come to the United States have arrived since 1980. Most of the Indonesians who have settled in California are of Indonesian-Chinese ancestry. Many of them operate small businesses in the vicinity of Monterey Park in suburban Los Angeles, often called "the first suburban Chinatown." Many of these and other Indonesian Americans living in southern California are Protestants who worship in one of more 30 Indonesian churches there. There are also several Roman Catholic churches in the region where Indonesian priests hold services. A few Indonesian ethnic groups that are predominantly Christian there, such as the Amboinese, are heavily represented in southern California.

Since the 1960s, large numbers of university students from Indonesia have studied in the United States, most of them on government scholarships. The majority of these are Muslim. In 1997 there were more than 13,000 Indonesian students studying in the United States. An unknown but growing number either do not return to Indonesia or return to the United States later. The unsettling political and economic events in Indonesia in 1998, with the ousting of the long-established Suharto government, will almost certainly lead to increased Indonesian immigration to the United States.

SEE ALSO
Asians; Refugees; Students

FURTHER READING
Kwik, Greta. *The Indos in Southern California*. New York: AMS Press, 1989.

Indos

SEE Indonesians

INS

SEE Immigration and Naturalization Service

International Refugee Organization (IRO)

The International Refugee Organization was a temporary agency of the United Nations that existed from 1946 to 1952. It was responsible for the physical well-being and eventual repatriation or resettlement of refugees, mostly European displaced persons, who had been made homeless by World War II (1939–45). It took over duties that had been performed by the United Nations Relief and Rehabilitation Administration (UNRRA), and was superseded by the United Nations High Commissioner for Refugees in 1952. During its existence the IRO resettled about 1 million people, many of whom eventually came to the United States. It was replaced by the United Nations High Commission for Refugees.

SEE ALSO

Displaced persons; Refugees; United Nations High Commission for Refugees, Office of; United Nations Relief and Rehabilitation Administration

FURTHER READING

Holborn, Louise W. *The International Refugee Organization: A Specialized Agency of the United Nations: Its History and Work, 1946–1952.* New York: Oxford University Press, 1956.

Internment

Internment is a legal process commonly used by nations at war. During several wars, people living in the United States who were still nationals of a country with which the United States was at war, were placed in confinement, presumably for national security. Internment has been carried out under statutes that go back to the War of 1812 and which constituted, in 1941—when the United States entered World War II—Sections 21–24 of Title 50 of the United States Code.

The first internment by the United States was during the War of 1812, when all British aliens were required to register with the federal government, and at least 10,000 did so. A small number of these aliens, mostly merchants and their employees, were even-

tually interned in centers at least 40 miles from the seacoast. Those from New York City, for example, were interned in Fishkill, New York.

In both World Wars I and II the United States interned only a tiny fraction of its enemy aliens. In World War I some 3,000 people, largely Germans and nationals of the Austro-Hungarian Empire, were interned, mostly on Army posts. In World War II some 10,000 people—about 8,000 Japanese, 2,300 Germans, and a few hundred Italians—were interned in military installations and in camps run by the Immigration and Naturalization Service. In addition, several thousand Japanese, Germans, and Italians living in Peru and other Latin American countries were brought, with the permission of these governments, to the United States and interned.

Because the other American wars in the 20th century—Korea, Vietnam, and the Persian Gulf War—were not declared, no internment took place. Since 1925 the conditions in internment camps have been regulated by an international agreement known as the Geneva Convention. Although there were some injustices in the World War II internment program, each person interned had presumably done something to merit internment. However, military and civilian intelligence officers, who chose those to be interned, often chose people who were not a threat to the United States. Any person interned could get a special hearing to reexamine the reasons for internment.

Internment should not be confused with the World War II incarceration of 120,000 Japanese Americans, more than two-thirds of whom were American citizens, in concentration camps run by the War Relocation Authority. The reasons that they were locked up were that they were of Japanese ancestry, and they lived on the West Coast of the United States. The incarceration did not follow due process of law, and in 1988 the federal government admitted its wrongful action, apologized, and awarded each survivor $20,000.

SEE ALSO

Alien Enemies Act; Austro-Hungarian Empire; Civil Liberties Act of 1988; Germans; Italians; Japanese; Peruvians

FURTHER READING

Fiset, Louis. *Imprisoned Apart: The World War II Correspondence of an Issei Couple.* Seattle: University of Washington Press, 1998.

Iranians

- *1990 Ancestry: 235,521*
- *Immigration, 1986–96: 171,747*
- *Immigration, 1925–96: 222,624*
- *Major period of immigration: since 1965*
- *Major areas of settlement: California, New York*

Almost all of the nearly quarter million Iranian Americans are either immigrants who have come to the United States since 1950, or their descendants. Large numbers are people who came as nonimmigrants, especially as college students, and then became immigrants when Iran was racked by political turmoil culminating in the Iranian Revolution of 1979. The Islamic revolution transformed Iran from a moderately westernized ally of the United States to an "enemy," though the two nations have never been at war.

Iran, now officially the Islamic Republic of Iran, is a large country of nearly 650,000 square miles, nearly as large as Alaska. It has a population of almost 70 million. It was the heart of the ancient Persian Empire and was called Persia until 1935, when it was renamed Iran.

Persia was the home of Zoroastrianism and other religions. Conversion to Islam began in the 7th century, and now all but a tiny segment of the population are Muslims, 95 percent of them Shiite Muslims. Perhaps 1 percent are Bahais and there are smaller numbers of Christians and Jews, although most of the latter have emigrated either to Israel or to the United States since

An Iranian singer, Gharib-Afshar Parviz, performs at the University of California in Los Angeles in 1963. Los Angeles is one of the centers of Iranian American population.

1948. The Bahais, who numbered perhaps 1 million before 1979, have been persecuted in recent years and many have left Iran. As Persia was a region of much internal migration, the population is far from homogeneous; there are many minority ethnic groups including Kurds and Arabs.

The Iranians who have come to the United States are largely of the business and professional classes and represent a considerable brain drain from Iran. As early as 1976, one scholar reported that there were more than 2,000 Iranian doctors on the rolls of the American Medical Association. Iranian Americans, like other Middle Eastern groups, have been discriminated against in the United States in retaliation for anti-American actions by Iran or by terrorist groups.

SEE ALSO

Arabs; Bahais; Brain drain; Kurds; Muslims; Refugees; Zoroastrians

FURTHER READING

Ansari, Mabound. *The Making of the Iranian Community in America.* New York: Pardis, 1992.
Bozorgmehr, Mehdi. "Iranians." In David W. Haines, ed., *Refugees in America in the 1990s: A Reference Handbook.* Westport, Conn.: Greenwood, 1996.

Iraqis

SEE Arabs

IRCA

SEE Immigration Act of 1986

Irish

- *1990 Ancestry: 38,746,539*
- *Immigration, 1986–96: 82,136*
- *Immigration, 1820–1996: 4,778,159*
- *Major periods of immigration: 1840s–90s, 1965+*
- *Major areas of settlement: New York, New England, Midwest*

["Irish," in American immigration history, means Irish Catholics. The migration of perhaps 2 million Irish Protestants is treated in the essay "Scotch Irish," a term not used outside of the United States. Only after the creation of what is now Ireland (Eire) in 1922 is there a nation called Ireland in American immigration statistics. Conversely, many Irish, both Catholic and Protestant, have migrated to the United States from the United Kingdom, which includes Northern Ireland, and appear in immigration statistics as British. Ireland, that is, Eire, has 3.5 million people in a territory of 27,000 square miles. The population is 93 percent Catholic. Northern Ireland, part of the United Kingdom of Great Britain and Northern Ireland, has 1.6 million people in a territory of less than 6,000 square miles. The population is 58 percent Protestant and 42 percent Catholic.]

One American colony, Maryland, was founded as a refuge for Catholics. From its beginnings in 1634 it had a sizable minority of English and Irish Catholics, many of them elite and one of whom, Charles Carroll of Carrollton, signed the Declaration of Independence. Elsewhere in colonial and early national America most of the few Irish were lower class, many of them indentured servants. As there were few priests, many Catholics were simply lost to the faith.

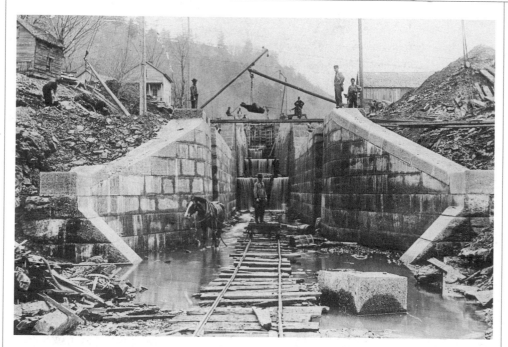

Most of the workers on this canal construction site in the mid-19th century were Irish immigrants. The rails are for wheeled carts, not trains.

Irish immigration began in earnest in the 1820s as a largely male phenomenon. Irish dug the Erie Canal and worked on other "internal improvement" projects, what we call today public works. Much of that migration came via Canada as British trade patterns made the fare to Canada much cheaper; most then walked south in what one historian called "the second colonization of New England." This migration grew until the mid-1840s, due largely to the rapid increase in Ireland's population (from 4.8 million in 1791 to 8.2 million in 1841) and its lack of economic opportunity. Ireland was a classic case of "push" migration even before a natural disaster changed dramatically the volume and character of Irish immigration. Because of the harshness of their experience at home, relatively few Irish ever remigrated, although many who found success went back to visit.

By the mid-19th century the poor in Ireland had come to depend on potatoes as their basic food. (Potatoes are part of what is called the "Columbian Exchange," referring to things and peo-ple who moved between the Old World and the New after 1492. Potatoes originated in South America and were unknown in Europe.) An acre and a half of potatoes could feed a family of six, and perhaps a third of the Irish ate almost nothing else. Thus, when a fungus, *Phytophthora infestans*, destroyed much of the crop in 1844, 1845, and 1846, the results were devastating and created the last great peacetime famine in Western European history. One Irishman wrote that "the land blackened as if the frown of God had passed across it."

The British government, which then ruled all of Ireland, provided no significant relief, an atrocity for which the British prime minister apologized—in 1997. More than a million Irish—one person in six—died in the famine era (1845–55). They died not just from starvation but from diseases that defeated weakened bodies. In the same period, some 2 million emigrated, 1.5 million of them to the United States. Ireland's population continued to decline: the 1891 census found only 4.7 million people, about 57 percent of the 1841 figure.

In the famine years immigration, which had been largely male immigration, now became family immigration, and even the British government helped to "shovel out the paupers" onto what contemporaries called "coffin ships" bound for Canada. In one terrible year, 1847, 100,000 Irish men, women and children were put on ships to Canada: 17,000 of them died at sea and 20,000 more died shortly after arriving in Canada. Most of those who survived came to live in cities in the northeastern United States. The Irish became the most urban 19th-century immigrant group.

By 1870 Irish-born people were almost 15 percent of the population of the 50 largest American cities; if we count their U.S.–born children, the figure would be one-third or more. Their relatively large numbers and their "foreignness" inspired nativists to protest against them.

Although there were professionals among them—in 1850 nearly a tenth of Boston's physicians were Irish-born—the vast majority of Irish men worked in jobs at the bottom of the economic ladder, and most of the numerous Irish working women were domestic servants. As the century progressed, Irish immigrants and their children came to dominate many of the new urban occupations: the Irish cop or fireman or trolley car driver is more than a stereotype. Irish Americans "got in on the ground floor" when many of these new urban occupations were being created and have maintained their presence in them for generations.

Irish were also the first immigrant group successfully to play the game of immigrant–ethnic group urban politics, and they played it well, often to the disadvantage of groups that arrived later. In cities like Boston and New York, Irish-American politicians dominated local politics for decades.

There were also significant physical clashes between Catholic Irish and Protestant Scotch-Irish. These often took place on one of two parading holidays, the Irish St. Patrick's Day, March 17, and the Scotch-Irish celebration of the 1660 battle of the Boyne every July 12. The worst instances of this ethnic violence occurred in New York City in 1870 and 1871. During the 1870 riot 8 persons were killed and 13 seriously wounded. The next year it was worse: 33 persons were killed, including 2 policemen. Although never again resulting in as many fatalities, this sectarian violence continued in America well into the 20th century.

Many Irish in America, both of the immigrant and later generations, engaged in politics in Ireland, sometimes violently. For a century and a half American organizations have struggled, first for Irish independence and then for Irish reunification. The Fenian Brotherhood was briefly important just after the American Civil War, when its estimated 250,000 followers, many of them veterans of the Union army, spoke of invading Canada, or part of it, and holding it hostage until Britain granted Ireland independence. Two short-lived invasions of Canada actually occurred, in 1866 and 1870, but both were easily repelled by British and U.S. armed forces, and the Fenian movement collapsed. There were several other organizations involved in Irish nationalism, the most moderate of which (and the only survivor) is the Ancient Order of Hibernians, which has become essentially a fraternal insurance organization that also promotes Irish American issues. In the 1980s and 1990s, a shadowy and controversial organization called Northern Aid collected money for the relief of Catholic victims of sectarian warfare in Northern Ireland, but it has been implicated in the purchase

Irish immigrant priests were vital to the Catholic church in America. Here they lead a Roxbury, Massachusetts, procession in 1954.

and shipment of arms to the Irish Republican Army (IRA).

In addition to urban occupations and politics, Irish took control of the Catholic church in America, which came to be an immigrant church. Irish-born clergy—men such as John Hughes, bishop and archbishop of New York between 1838 and 1864, and John Ireland, bishop and archbishop of St. Paul, Minnesota, between 1875 and 1918—led the American church.

By the end of the 19th century the nature of Irish immigration changed again; women immigrants began to outnumber men both because of the declining opportunities for women in post-famine Ireland and the presence of economic and other opportunities in America. One immigrant, Mary Brown from County Wexford, wrote inviting a girlfriend back home to come to where there was "love and liberty."

Although legal Irish immigration was not large between 1965 and 1990, in the years after 1965 many young and well-educated Irish came to the United States illegally. Though it is not possible to count illegal immigrants accurately, in the 1990s experts "guesstimated" that as many as 350,000 illegal Irish immigrants were living in the "metropolis" that stretches from Boston to just south of Washington, D.C. In 1990 Congress began a "diversity program" to provide visas to immigrants from countries where few individuals could qualify under the family preference system. For the first three years of the program, 1992–94, a provision of the law allocated 12,000 visas per year, 40 percent of the total, to natives of Ireland. After 1995 a maximum annual visa limit of 3,850 for any one county was set.

SEE ALSO:

Catholics; Diversity programs; Fenian Brotherhood; Illegal immigrants; Indentured servants; Nativism; Preference system; Push; Scotch-Irish; Stereotype

FURTHER READING

Crosby, Alfred W. *The Columbian Exchange: Biological and Cultural Consequences of 1492.* Westport, Conn.: Greenwood, 1972.

Diner, Hasia R. *Erin's Daughters in America.* Baltimore: Johns Hopkins University Press, 1983.

Miller, Kerby A. *Emigrants and Exiles: Ireland and the Irish Exodus to North America.* New York: Oxford University Press, 1985.

Miller, Kerby A., and Paul Wagner. *Out of Ireland: The Story of Irish Emigration to America.* Washington, D.C.: Elliot and Clark, 1994. (This text accompanies a video, "Out of Ireland." Alexandria, Va.: American Focus, 1995.)

IRO

SEE International Refugee Organization

Israelis

- *1990 Ancestry: 81,677*
- *Immigration, 1986–96: 42,890*
- *Immigration, 1949–96: 165,009*
- *Major period of immigration: 1965+*
- *Major areas of settlement: New York, California*

Israel, which obtained independence in 1948, is a small country of less than 8,000 square miles at the eastern end of the Mediterranean, a little smaller than Vermont. In 1995 it had almost 5.5 million inhabitants; about 82 percent are Jewish, and most of the rest are Palestinian Arabs. Most Israeli immigrants to the United States have been Jewish, but a significant number are Arabs. Many Israelis have dual citizenship, and many authorities believe that the 1990 census ancestry figure of 81,000 understates significantly the number of persons born in Israel who live in the United States.

SEE ALSO
Arabs; Jews

Issei

An Issei is a first-generation Japanese American. The word *Issei* is an adjectival form of the Japanese word for "one." Issei, were, until the passage of the Immigration Act of 1952, "aliens ineligible to citizenship" and ineligible for naturalization. Their U.S.-born children are called Nisei.

SEE ALSO
Immigration Act of 1952; Japanese; Nisei

Italians

- *1990 Population: 14,665,550*
- *Immigration, 1820–1996: 5,427,298*
- *Major periods of immigration: 1880s–1920s, 1960s*
- *Major areas of settlement: New York, Northeast, California,*

Although an Italian named Christopher Columbus "discovered" America, and other Italians such as John Cabot (Giovanni Caboto) were important in its exploration, only 30,000 Italians came to North America before 1870. Some Venetian glassblowers came to Jamestown, Virginia, in 1622; a number of Italian priests tried to convert Indians, while others helped establish Catholicism in the Northwest Territory. Thomas Jefferson arranged for the immigration of some Italian craftsmen to help in the building of his home, Monticello, and, later, Italian quarriers

Italian workers in marble created many buildings and statues in the United States. These are working on the Wisconsin state capitol around 1911.

came to help Vermonters exploit their marble deposits. A few Italians fought in the Revolution, and a larger number formed the Garibaldi Guard in the Union army during the Civil War. One early immigrant, Lorenzo da Ponte, Mozart's librettist, lived in the United States between 1805 and 1838, taught Italian at Columbia University, and supervised building the first opera house in the United States in New York City.

A sizable migration, mostly of northern Italians, took place in the 1870s, and large-scale migration from Italy south of Rome and from Sicily began after 1880. Perhaps 5 million Italians have migrated to the United States, about 4 million of them between 1880 and 1920. From no other ethnic group had so many come so fast. Yet these are but a minor fraction of the estimated 26 million who left Italy between 1871 and 1971; most authorities believe that at least 13 million returned to Italy.

Most Italian immigrants to the United States worked as laborers in railroad and road construction, and in the building trades. Italian American folklore claims that Italians came expecting the streets to be paved with gold but soon discovered, first, that the streets were not paved at all and, second, that *they* were expected to pave them.

By the early 20th century there were large "Little Italys" in New York, Boston, and other large cities, and Italian Americans were subjected to extraordinary prejudice and discrimination. The worst single incident was the 1891 lynching of 11 Italians by a mob in New Orleans. In the 20th century the most famous Italian immigrant victims in America were Nicola Sacco and Bartolomeo Vanzetti, who were tried and eventually executed for robbery and murder in 1927. Because of their politics—they were anarchists—and their

nationality they did not get a fair trial. A number of other Italian immigrants were extremely important as labor organizers, such as Arturo Giovannitti of the radical Industrial Workers of the World (IWW) and Luigi Antonini of the liberal International Ladies Garment Workers Union (ILGWU). The latter union employed thousands of young Italian American women.

Most Italian immigrants, about 75 percent, were workingmen. A minority of Italian immigrants worked in agriculture, most notably in California, where they pioneered the important California wine industry. Many of the urban majority got work through ethnic labor contractors, called *padroni*. The *padroni*, usually immigrants who had been in the United Stats long enough to learn "the ropes," were among the earliest immigrant entrepreneurs. They got

Games are part of immigrant culture. Here a group of Italians play "bocce," a bowling game played on hard dirt, in Connecticut in 1942.

jobs for new immigrants and exploited them by charging them fees, selling them food, etc. Other immigrants found jobs through relatives and friends. An American consular official in Naples reported that when he asked why people were emigrating, the most common answer was: "My friend in America is doing well and he has sent for me."

Because Italy became a unified nation only in 1870, Italian immigrants at first tended to think of themselves as from a village or a region rather than a country, a phenomenon known as *campanilismo*, from the notion that only those who lived within earshot of the local bell tower (*campanile*) were truly one's fellow countrymen.

Italian immigration was much curtailed by the Immigration Act of 1924. During the 1930s a number of distinguished Italian antifascist refugees came to the United States, including the conductor Arturo Toscanini and the physicist Enrico Fermi, a key figure in the invention of the atomic bomb. For a few years after the Immigration Act of 1965, Italians were the most numerous immigrant group, but few have come since then.

SEE ALSO

Campanilismo; Immigration Act of 1924; Padrone system; Refugees

FURTHER READING

Gabaccia, Donna R. *From Sicily to Elizabeth Street: Housing and Social Change among Italian Immigrants, 1880–1930.* Albany: State University of New York Press, 1984.
Hoobler, Dorothy, and Thomas Hoobler. *Italian American Family Album.* New York: Oxford University Press, 1994.
Rolle, Andrew. *The American Italians.* Belmont, Calif.: Wadsworth, 1976.
Vecoli, Rudolph J., ed. *Italian Immigrants in Rural and Small Town America.* Staten Island, N.Y.: Italian American Historical Association, 1981.

Jamaicans

- *1990 Ancestry: 435,024*
- *Immigration, 1986–96: 223,065*
- *Immigration, 1932–96: 536,220*
- *Major period of immigration: 1965+*
- *Major areas of settlement: New York, New Jersey. Florida*

Jamaica is a Caribbean island of 4,232 square miles, about the size of the state of Maine, with a population of more than 2.6 million. People of African descent predominate in Jamaica, some of them of mixed African-European ancestry, as well as small minorities of Asians, particularly Chinese, Asian Indians, and Lebanese. Christopher Columbus saw Jamaica but never landed on it. The Spanish conquered it in 1504. The pre-Columbian residents, Native Americans called Arawaks, were all but wiped out by a combination of warfare and disease. Enslaved Africans were brought in to work the sugar plantations that were established by the Spanish but later taken over by the English, who conquered Jamaica in 1655. Slavery was abolished there in 1838. Although freed, most Jamaicans suffered economic hardship and social and political discrimination. The island's history for more than a century after emancipation was turbulent, as the newly freed blacks, the vast majority of the population, struggled for civil rights. The black population was not granted the right to vote until 1944. Jamaica became fully independent of Britain in 1962.

Although Jamaicans began immigrating to the United States in the 19th century, the overwhelming majority have come since 1965. Perhaps 50,000 Jamaicans came in the first quarter of the 20th century, many of them drawn by the labor shortages experienced during World War I. Unlike many other

Teams of artisans work for months on elaborate costumes for the West Indian Day Parade in Brooklyn, New York, which takes place every Labor Day weekend. Caribbean-type street celebrations have become a tradition in many U.S. cities.

immigrants from the Caribbean, they spoke not Spanish or French, but English, in the musical accents of the West Indies. Most of them and most of more recent immigrants worship in a variety of Protestant churches.

By the 1920s Jamaicans and other Caribbean immigrants were an important part of New York's African American community. A few, like the Jamaica-born, American-educated poet and novelist Claude McKay, were important figures in the famous Harlem Renaissance of the later 1920s. Many individual Jamaican immigrants became African American political and labor leaders in that period. The most influential of these was the black nationalist Marcus Garvey who created the first genuine African American mass movement in the United States. Garvey's Universal Negro Improvement Association (UNIA), which flourished in the 1910s and 1920s, had perhaps 75,000 dues-paying members but influenced hundreds of thousands of African Americans. It successfully advocated black pride and unsuccessfully advocated that African Americans "go back to

Africa." Garvey was convicted—his followers said "framed"—of mail fraud in 1922, sent to the penitentiary, and deported in 1927. This ended the effectiveness of his movement although tiny and isolated fragments of it survive in the 21st century.

The Jamaican immigration since World War II has brought many professionals and well-educated persons, yet many others with little or no education. Large numbers of the latter are part of the uncountable but surely sizeable illegal immigrant population, many of whom work as migratory agricultural workers in the southeastern states. The INS and the Census Bureau estimated in 1996 that there were 50,000 Jamaicans illegally in the United States, the 15th largest number from any country.

Some 55 percent of recent Jamaican immigrants have been female. It is common for Jamaican women to come first, get settled, and then send for their children and husbands. In many cases, however, children are left at home to be educated and taken care of by grandparents or extended family members.

Jamaican Americans are concentrated in three states: New York, New Jersey, and Florida. One in three lives in New York City, and there are also sizable Jamaican communities in Miami, Washington, D.C., and Hartford, Connecticut. In each of these cities Jamaicans have established ethnic enclaves, the largest of which is in central Brooklyn. Most Jamaicans work in low-paying service and clerical jobs. Women are most likely to hold jobs as nurses and other less skilled health care occupations, and as nannies. Men are likely to work in the construction industry, and as drivers.

Although many take great pride in being Jamaicans, they have come to identify also with other English-speaking Afro-Caribbeans in the United States, something that Jamaicans at home do not do. The great cultural occasion is Brooklyn's annual West Indian Carnival, which draws over a million spectators and participants. Jamaican music, reggae, which contains elements of calypso, soul, and rock 'n' roll and is characterized by a strongly accentuated offbeat, has had great influence on the evolution of American popular music.

SEE ALSO

African Americans; Caribbeans; Ethnic enclave; Illegal immigrants

FURTHER READING

Cronon, E. David. *Black Moses: The Story of Marcus Garvey and the Universal Negro Improvement Association.* 2nd ed. Madison: University of Wisconsin Press, 1969.

Foner, Nancy, ed. *New Immigrants in New York.* New York: Columbia University Press, 1987.

Reid, Ira de A. *The Negro Immigrant: His Background, Characteristics, and Social Adjustment, 1899–1937.* New York: Columbia University Press, 1939.

Vickerman, Milton. *West Indian Immigrants and Race.* New York: Oxford University Press, 1998.

Japanese

- *1990 Population: 866,160*
- *Immigration, 1820–1996: 506,399*
- *Major periods of immigration: 1905–24, 1950s*
- *Major areas of settlement: California, Hawaii, Washington*

Although a handful of Japanese were in Mexico in the 17th century and others were shipwrecked on or brought to the Pacific coast in the early 19th century, Japanese immigration to the United States began with a few political exiles in 1869. A year earlier the first Japanese contract laborers were brought to the then-independent Hawaiian Islands; they were followed by thousands of others by the time of American annexation in 1898.

In the meantime, fairly large-scale Japanese immigration to the United States had begun, some of it direct from Japan, some of it from Hawaii. Most of the immigrants to Hawaii before 1900 were contract laborers imported by the Hawaiian Sugar Planters Association. By 1900 there were some 60,000 Japanese in the islands and almost 25,000 in the mainland United States, largely on the Pacific Coast. By the 1920s the numbers were about 110,000 in each place. In Hawaii Japanese were a major component of the population but on the mainland they were but a tiny part of the population. At the time of their highest incidence, Japanese constituted about one-tenth of 1 percent (.001) of the population of the continental United States and just 2.1 percent of the population of California, where most of them lived.

While many Japanese in Hawaii remained plantation laborers for a generation or more, the typical pattern on the mainland was for Japanese to become agricultural proprietors. By

Japanese migrant workers pose with a grape harvest in Florin, California, in the 1920s. Florin, outside of Sacramento, had segregated schools for Japanese children.

1919, although they controlled only about 1 percent of California's farmland, they earned about 10 percent of the state's farm income. The fear of Japanese farmers "taking over" led California and 10 other western states to pass alien land acts to prohibit Japanese and other aliens ineligible to citizenship from owning and in some cases leasing agricultural land.

The hostility that erupted against the Japanese in America can be explained by three factors: they were immigrants and subject to the general prejudice against immigrants called nativism; they were not "white"; and their immigration began just after Chinese were being excluded by law. Later, that hostility would be increased by tensions and then war between the United States and Japan. Japanese suffered from some of the same legal discrimination that Chinese did—they, too, were "aliens ineligible to citizenship"—but Japan, unlike China, was a rising power in the early 20th century.

Although there had been some anti-Japanese agitation in the 1890s, serious troubles began in 1905 when a San Francisco newspaper began a campaign of vilification against Japanese with headlines such as "JAPANESE A MENACE TO AMERICAN WOMEN," and

trade unions, which had led the fight against Chinese immigration, stepped up their agitation against Japanese. A year later the San Francisco School Board ordered the 93 Japanese students in the public school system to attend the long-established segregated school for Chinese in Chinatown.

The Japanese government, which had long feared that its emigrants would suffer the same mistreatment as Chinese and that this would be bad for Japanese prestige, protested to Washington about what the school board had done. President Theodore Roosevelt intervened, persuaded the school board to rescind its order, and opened negotiations with the Japanese government to limit immigration. The result was the so-called Gentlemen's Agreement of 1907–08 in which the Japanese government agreed to stop the immigration of Japanese laborers if the United States agreed not to pass any federal anti-Japanese legislation. The Gentlemen's Agreement contained what were, in effect, family reunification provisions that allowed thousands of women to join husbands already living in America. Some of them were called "picture brides" because they married their husbands after an exchange of pictures without ever having seen each other. Such marriages were legal in Japan. Most got

This bleak desert concentration camp at Mazanar, California, for Japanese Americans during World War II was one of 10 such camps.

married again in the United States.

State and local governments, with California in the lead, were not constrained by the Gentlemen's Agreement and passed many laws and ordinances that discriminated against Japanese and other "aliens ineligible to citizenship." Chief of these were alien land acts passed by California and 10 other states that forbade the purchase, and sometimes the leasing, of agricultural land by such aliens, all of whom were Asian immigrants. The U.S. Supreme Court confirmed in the 1924 case of *Ozawa* v. *U.S.* that Japanese were not eligible for naturalization. Many Japanese immigrant farmers, however, were able either to purchase land in the name of their children who were born in the United States and therefore citizens, or to form U.S. corporations to hold the land for them.

The Tokyo government's worst nightmare would have been the passage of a "Japanese Exclusion Act." That never happened. But in 1924 the United States broke the Gentlemen's Agreement by placing a clause in the Immigration Act of 1924 prohibiting the immigration of "aliens ineligible to citizenship," which was aimed at Japanese without naming them.

By 1924 there were enough Japanese American families established that, unlike Chinese Americans of that era, their community grew steadily by births even though immigration had been stopped. On the eve of the war between the United States and Japan there were about 125,000 Japanese in the United States and 150,000 in Hawaii. Some two-thirds of each group were United States citizens by right of birth on American soil.

In 1942, after the Japanese attack at Pearl Harbor (December 7, 1941) that provoked a declaration of war, the U.S. government incarcerated the entire Japanese American population of the West Coast, both citizen (Nisei) and alien (Issei), in desolate camps behind barbed wire. This action is one of the most unsightly stains on the civil liberties record of the modern United States. On February 19, 1942, more than two months after the Pearl Harbor bombing, President Franklin D. Roosevelt issued Executive Order 9066, which empowered the U.S. Army to move and incarcerate all persons of Japanese birth or ancestry who lived on the Pacific Coast. However, most Japanese living in Hawaii or in the rest of the United States were left free.

A special civilian agency, the War Relocation Authority, was established in 1942 to create what the government called "relocation centers," but which many historians and the government itself now call concentration camps. Unlike the process of internment, which followed due process of law, the process of incarceration was simply a matter of

Japanese American families eat in one of 36 mess halls in the concentration camp at Manzanar, California. Families had to eat all their meals here for more than two years.

race and geography. In 1942, if a person was of Japanese birth or ancestry and lived on the West Coast, he or she had to go. Men, women, and children were incarcerated indiscriminately in 10 desolate wartime camps. These camps were not death camps: more people were born in them than died in them and only a few were killed in "incidents" by the soldiers guarding the camps. The process of incarceration was upheld by the Supreme Court in the case of *Korematsu v. U.S.* (1944).

After the war, the government passed the Japanese American Claims Act in 1948 to compensate some Japanese American property owners for losses suffered while they were prisoners and therefore unable to take care of their own property. Forty years later, the government passed the Civil Liberties Act of 1988, which formally apologized to each survivor and awarded each of 80,000 persons $20,000 tax-free dollars compensation, or what Japanese Americans call "redress."

In 1952 Japanese American resident aliens were finally allowed to become naturalized as the Immigration Act of that year ended the "aliens ineligible to citizenship category" and made the naturalization process "color blind." Relatively few Japanese have immigrated to the United States since the 1950s, so that the vast majority of Japanese Americans, unlike most other Asian American

groups, are of the third or later generation of their families.

SEE ALSO

Alien Land Acts; Aliens ineligible to citizenship; Civil Liberties Act of 1988; Contract labor; Gentlemen's agreement; Hawaii; Hawaiian Sugar Planters Association; Immigration Act of 1924; Immigration Act of 1952; Internment; Issei; Japanese American Citizens League; Japanese American Evacuation Claims Act; *Korematsu v. U.S.*; Nativism; Naturalization; Nisei; *Ozawa v. U.S.*; Picture brides; Sansei; War Relocation Authority

FURTHER READING

Daniels, Roger. *Prisoners Without Trial: Japanese Americans in World War II.* New York: Hill & Wang, 1993.
Kitano, Harry H. L. *Japanese Americans: The Evolution of a Sub-Culture.* 2nd. ed. Englewood Cliffs, N.J., 1976.
Kitano, Harry H. L., and Roger Daniels. *Asian Americans: Emerging Minorities.* 2nd ed. New York: Prentice-Hall, 1995.
Van Sant, John E. *Pacific Pioneers: Japanese Journeys to America and Hawaii, 1850–80.* Urbana: University of Illinois Press, 2000.
Wilson, Robert A., and Bill Hosokawa. *East to America: A History of Japanese in the United States.* New York: Morrow, 1980.

Japanese American Citizens League

The Japanese American Citizens League was founded in 1929 by young Nisei—American citizens—to work for Japanese American civil rights. But it achieved prominence only in 1941–42, when it was informally recognized by many U.S. government officials as the sole representative for Japanese Americans, even though its several thousand members were only a tiny fraction of the Japanese American people. Its policies were highly accommodationist in that it militantly accepted American culture, rejected Japanese culture, and limited membership to United States citizens, thus denying the right of the Issei, Japanese immigrants, who were ineligible for naturalization, to join. The stance was a response to extreme discrimination and is reminiscent of the public posture taken by the African American leader, Booker T. Washington: that is, cooperate with the oppressive society in the hope that it will encourage better—or at least less harsh—treatment. Its most controversial decision was to cooperate with the government in the wartime incarceration of Japanese Americans between 1942 and 1946.

After the war its character gradually changed as it became an advocate for the civil rights not only of Japanese but of all Americans. It lobbied for such things as the granting of naturalization privileges to all legal immigrants, the various civil rights acts of the 1950s and 1960s, and particularly for the Civil Rights Act of 1988, in which the U.S. government formally apologized for the mass incarceration of Japanese Americans during World War II and awarded $20,000 compensation to each survivor. It publishes a semimonthly newspaper, the *Pacific Citizen*, and has some 22,000 members.

SEE ALSO

Aliens ineligible to citizenship; Civil Liberties Act of 1988; Issei; Japanese; Nisei

FURTHER READING

Hosokawa, Bill. JACL: *In Search of Justice*, New York: Morrow, 1981.

Japanese American Evacuation Claims Act

Congress passed the Japanese American Evacuation Claims Act in 1948 to com-pensate Japanese American property owners for some of the losses they incurred while incarcerated between 1942 and 1946. Although, except for fishing boats, the government did not seize property, many Japanese Americans lost their homes and farms because they could not keep up their payments while incarcerated. Others sold their property at bargain basement prices as they were about to be exiled. The government appropriated $38 million to pay all claims, which all authorities now agree was not nearly enough.

FURTHER READING

Daniels, Roger. *Prisoners Without Trial: Japanese Americans in World War II.* New York: Hill & Wang, 1993.

Japanese American incarceration

SEE Japanese

Jews

- *1990 Ancestry: n.a.*
- *1990 Population: around 6,000,000–7,000,000*
- *Immigration, to 1996: around 3,000,000*
- *Major period of immigration: 1880–1914*
- *Major area of settlement: New York*

Jews, unlike most other groups covered in this book, are identified by religion rather than by nationality or ethnicity. This is because, first of all, that is the way that Jews have traditionally identified themselves and have been identified by others, and second, because Jews may be of any nationality, ethnic group, or race. Since the establishment of the state of Israel in 1948, Jews and others (mostly Arabs) migrating from that state have been classified as Israelis by the Immigration and Naturalization Service and the Census Bureau.

Although the overwhelming majority of Jews in the United States are the descendants of people who migrated from Europe, there are Jews in the United States who are either immigrants or descendants of immigrants from every inhabited continent and who represent ethnicities as varied as Chinese and Ethiopian. There are at least three ways of describing the varieties of the American Jewish experience: by national origin, by culture, and by religious practice.

Culturally the vast majority of American Jews have been Sephardic or Ashkenazic. Sephardic Jews originally spoke a language called Ladino, which was a variety of Spanish but usually written in Hebrew characters. Most Ashkenazic Jews spoke either German, if they were from Germany, or Yiddish if they were from eastern Europe. Yiddish is a Germanic language written in Hebrew characters.

Prior to the early 19th century, all observing Jews were what is now called "Orthodox," although there were many regional and local variations of various practices. In the early 19th century a "reform" movement that sought to modernize Jewish beliefs arose in Germany and soon found its greatest strength in the United States. In Cincinnati in 1876, a German-born rabbi, Isaac M. Wise, founded Hebrew Union College, which became the center of Reform Judaism. The chief difference between Orthodox and Reform Jews is they way in which they regard the ancient Jewish law, *halakah*, which governs such things as diet and sabbath observance. Orthodox Jews maintain most if not all traditional practices, whereas Reform Jews perform only

those rituals that they think can promote a Jewish life. A third branch, Conservative Judaism, which arose in the United States in the late 19th century, attempts to compromise between the two. In 1996, Conservative synagogues in the United States claimed 2 million members, Reform 1.3 million, and Orthodox 1 million.

Zionism, the movement to create a Jewish homeland, usually but not always in the "Holy Land," was created in late-19th-century Europe and quickly attracted many American supporters, most of whom were eastern European Jews and their descendants. Many were secular Zionists, that is, people who were not formally religious. Zionism eventually led to the creation of the State of Israel in 1948, which draws financial support from many if not most contemporary American Jews.

The first Jews to settle in what is now the United States probably came to what is now New Mexico in 1585, but, if so, they were Jews who had been forced to hide their religious beliefs by Spanish prejudice. The first Jews who publicly identified themselves were a group of 23 persons who arrived in New Amsterdam (now New York City) in 1654. They had been members of a Dutch colony in Brazil that had been seized by Portugal. These were Sephardic Jews, who were descended from the Jews who were an important community in Iberia (Spain and Portugal) throughout the Middle Ages. They were expelled from Spain in 1492 by Ferdinand and Isabella—the same monarchs who financed Columbus—and from Portugal sometime later. They scattered in the Mediterranean and in western Europe, particularly Holland and England, the colonies of those countries, and in the Islamic world. Their religious beliefs are the same as of other Jews, but their culture was Iberian. They spoke Ladino at home, a language akin to Spanish, but written in modified Hebrew characters.

Jews in colonial New York did not immediately enjoy full religious liberty, but as early as 1656 they were able to establish the first congregation in North America. Other congregations in the colonial era were established in Newport, Rhode Island (1677), Savannah, Georgia (1733), Philadelphia (1745), and Charleston, South Carolina (1750). These were Sephardic congregations.

Beginning in the late 18th century, Jews from Germany began to come to America in the same general movement that brought other Germans. By 1880, of an estimated 250,000 American Jews, perhaps five-sixths were of German origin and most of the rest came from eastern Europe. During the next four decades very large numbers of eastern European Jews came to the United States. By 1924 there were an estimated 4 million American Jews and perhaps five-sixths were of eastern European origin or descent.

Although New York City was the first place in North America where Jews settled, both the Sephardic and the early German immigrants were fairly well dispersed. The former lived primarily in Atlantic seaports and the latter were spread across the country, with large segments in the Midwest and in New York. The eastern European Jews were heavily concentrated in New York City and elsewhere in the northeastern United States. In 1860 perhaps a quarter of American Jews lived in New York; by 1880 it was about a third, and by 1920 nearly half lived in the city. Since that time the concentration in New York has decreased, and by the 1990s fewer than a third of the nation's Jews lived there, with the second-largest contingent in California.

Jewish immigration, from whatever source, has been predominantly a family migration: one authority estimates that 44 percent were female, that 24 percent were children, and that only 5 percent returned to Europe; of these, some eventually came back to the United States.

From the 1880s until the 1930s American Jews tended to be divided by culture but united by resistance to a rising anti-Semitism in American life. There were serious conflicts between the relatively well-established Jews of German origin—often called "uptown Jews" in New York City—and the relative newcomers from eastern Europe—often called "downtown Jews"—most of whom were very poor. The downtown Jews were heavily concentrated on New York's Lower East Side, where an estimated 1.25 million Jews lived in the most densely populated district in the whole country.

Yonah Shimmel's Knish Bakery on the Lower East Side of New York City probably had only Yiddish lettering on its windows when it opened in 1910. By mid-century it used English and Yiddish; today it has its own website.

Max Stein, a Jewish peddler, stands in front of his fruit wagon in Pueblo, Colorado, in 1910. Peddling has often been an immigrant occupation.

The uptown and the downtown Jews made their livings in different ways. The German Jews, like the Sephardic Jews before them, tended to be entrepreneurial, with rather heavy representation in the merchant and professional classes. The downtown Jews, in the first generation, were largely working-class, heavily represented in the garment industry. Most of them worked for manufacturers who were also Jewish. The two groups generally prayed in different synagogues. They formed different organizations to secure their civil rights: the American Jewish Committee for the uptowners, the American Jewish Congress for those living downtown.

But there were many common efforts that the two major Jewish communities shared, particularly when discrimination against Jews became more pronounced after 1880. There had always been some discrimination against Jews in the American colonies and the United States as there was in every predominantly Christian country.

But in the United States, with its tradition of separation of church and state, there was never any national law discriminating against Jews. Some state laws did discriminate against Jews, chiefly by limiting the holding of political office to Christians, but the last of these, in Maryland, was repealed in 1832. But laws were used by individuals to discriminate in housing by means of formal restrictive covenants—provisions placed in deeds to property legally limiting them from being sold to Jews and often other minority groups—and informal arrangements not to rent or sell to Jews; in employment, where as late as the 1940s one could read job ads in the paper that specified "Christians only"; and in higher education, where many of the finest schools, such as Harvard, Yale, and Princeton had quotas for Jewish students. These quotas, unlike so-called affirmative action quotas today, were designed to limit the number of Jews the school would accept. None of these means of restriction were against the law until, in the

1940s, antidiscrimination statutes began to appear on the federal and state law books. The Supreme Court outlawed restrictive covenants in *Shelley* v. *Kraemer* (1948). Although such discrimination today is largely associated with race, in the 19th and the first half of the 20th century, much discrimination was also aimed at white ethnic or religious groups, particularly those who were not Protestants (for example, Irish and Italian Catholics).

During the 1930s and 1940s a significant number of Jewish refugees from Nazi persecution, perhaps 250,000, managed to get into the United States, although an even larger number were denied visas. Although most of these were ordinary, largely middle-class people, the refugee contingent included what some historians have called an "intellectual migration" of Jewish scientists, artists, and professionals of all kinds who greatly enriched American life. One of the first was the German-born physicist Albert Einstein, thought by many to be the most distinguished scientist of the 20th century. It was Einstein's 1939 letter to Franklin D. Roosevelt that helped persuade the President to commission the research that resulted in the splitting of the atom and the production of the first atomic bombs.

After the war many Jews, mostly impoverished survivors of the Holocaust, came to the United States as displaced persons. During some of the cold war (1946–90) and afterward, a large number of Jews came from the Soviet Union. They were a considerable but unknown percentage of the more than 400,000 who came from that country and its successors who came to the United States between 1946 and 1996. Since the destruction of most of European Jewry in the Holocaust, the United States has been home to the largest Jewish community in the world.

SEE ALSO

Anti-Semitism; Displaced persons; Dutch; Georgians; Germans; Hebrew Immigrant Aid Society; Holocaust; Israelis; Nativism; Portuguese; Refugees; Religion; Restrictive covenants; Spanish; United States Memorial Holocaust Museum; Yiddish

FURTHER READING

Diner, Hasia. *Jews in America*. New York: Oxford University Press, 1999.
Feingold, Henry, ed. *The Jewish People in America*. 4 vols. Baltimore: Johns Hopkins University Press, 1992.
Hoobler, Dorothy, and Thomas Hoobler. *The Jewish American Family Album*. New York: Oxford University Press, 1995.
Marcus, Jacob Rader. *The American Jew, 1585–1990: A History*. Brooklyn: Carlson, 1995.
Sachar, Howard M. *A History of the Jews in America*. New York: Knopf, 1992.

Jordanians

SEE Arabs

Khmer

SEE Cambodians

Know Nothing movement

The Know Nothing movement, or the Order of the Star Spangled Banner, was a mass nativist movement of the 1850s directed against immigrants in general and Irish and German Catholic immigrants in particular. It was called the Know Nothing movement by others because the organization was a secret one and members were instructed to say "I know nothing" if asked about it.

An 1852 broadside from Boston announces the publication of the American Patriot, *a short-lived nativist newspaper. The ad states that the paper favors* "sending back Foreign Paupers and Criminals" *and opposes* "Papal Aggression and Roman Catholicism," *among other things.*

The phenomenal growth of the organization in a little more than two years from one that had just 43 members to one that had more than a million members gives evidence of both the popularity of nativism and the unstable politics of the 1850s. Members had to be native-born Protestants who believed in: "resisting the insidious policy of the Church of Rome, and all other foreign influences against the institutions of our country, by placing in all offices in the gift of the people, whether by election or appointment, none but native-born Protestant citizens."

During its meteoric rise in 1854–55, the Know Nothing movement elected eight governors, more than 100 congressmen, the mayors of Boston, Philadelphia, and Chicago, and thousands of other local officials. In 1856 it sponsored the American Party and ran former President Millard Fillmore for President. He managed to carry only Maryland, and the party collapsed partly because it tried to ignore the slavery issue, which came to dominate American politics in the later 1850s. By 1860 the Know Nothing movement had disappeared.

SEE ALSO

Nativism

FURTHER READING

Anbinder, Tyler G. *Nativism and Slavery: The Northern Know Nothings and the Politics of the 1850s.* New York: Oxford University Press, 1992.

Koreans

- *1990 Census: 798,849*
- *Immigration, 1820–1996: 751,582*
- *Major periods of immigration: 1903–5, since 1965*
- *Major areas of settlement: California, New York, Illinois*

The first significant migration of Koreans was to Hawaii during a very brief

submit to exile in 1942. The case, in effect, sanctioned the incarceration of native-born United States citizens of Japanese ancestry in concentration camps. The majority opinion, written by Justice Hugo Black, held that Fred Korematsu, a 24-year-old native of Oakland, California, against whom there was no evidence or charge of disloyalty, had not been unjustly incarcerated: because there were an indefinite number of disloyal people of Japanese ancestry in the country, and because, due to the impossibility of determining loyalty quickly, temporary exclusion of the whole group was deemed by appropriate authorities a military necessity.

The three dissenting justices on the Court held that mass incarceration was unconstitutional and attributed it to racial prejudice, which the majority denied.

Forty-one years later, in 1983, a federal court reversed *Korematsu*'s 1942 conviction for failing to report for exile, because a lawyer-historian demonstrated that in the original case the government had suppressed evidence and thus lied to the Supreme Court. The precedent, however, remains, as Federal Judge Marilyn Hall Patel put it in 1983, "as a constant caution that in times of war . . . the shield of military necessity must not be used to protect government actions from close scrutiny and accountability."

SEE ALSO

Japanese

FURTHER READING

Daniels, Roger. *Prisoners Without Trial: Japanese Americans in World War II.* New York: Hill & Wang, 1993.
Irons, Peter, ed. *Justice Delayed: The Record of the Japanese American Internment Cases.* Middletown, Conn.: Wesleyan University Press, 1989.

Ku Klux Klan (KKK)

An organization called the Ku Klux Klan has flourished in three separate eras of American history. The first arose early in the Reconstruction era (1865–77) and was a movement of white Southerners to prevent the newly freed African Americans from exercising their rights of citizenship with threats and terror, including murder. It was a secret society and its members burned crosses and wore hoodlike masks. In 1915 a technically superior but morally perverted film, D. W. Griffith's *The Birth of a Nation*, glorified the first KKK and was praised by President Woodrow Wilson as "history written with lightning."

At just that time the second KKK was born in Atlanta. Still dedicated to white supremacy and the degradation of the Negro, its major targets became immigrants, Catholics, and Jews. Whereas the first Klan flourished only in the South, the second KKK, with 3 million members, operated in other regions. It was strongest in Indiana and Oregon and had enough support nationally that a resolution to condemn it was narrowly defeated by the 1924 national convention of the Democratic party.

The third Klan arose in 1946 and was centered in the South. It opposed desegregation, often engaging in violence against civil rights activists. Murders of black and white civil rights activists, such as Medgar Evers in Mississippi in 1963, caused public revulsion and helped to create support for the major civil rights legislation of that decade. The contemporary Klan, unlike its predecessors, is fragmentary and dispersed, often, after the 1960s,

Members of the second Ku Klux Klan march, defiantly unmasked, in downtown Washington, D.C., in 1928. They carry flags to stress their claim to be real Americans.

combining with other right-wing extremist organizations.

SEE ALSO

Nativism; Racism

FURTHER READING

Blee, Kathleen M. *Women of the Klan: Racism and Gender in the 1920s.* Berkeley: University of California Press, 1991.

Chalmers, David. *Hooded Americanism: The History of the Ku Klux Klan.* 3rd ed. Durham, N.C.: Duke University Press, 1987.

Jackson, Kenneth T. *The Ku Klux Klan in the City, 1915–1930.* New York: Oxford University Press, 1967.

MacLean, Nancy K. *Behind the Mask of Chivalry: The Making of the Second Ku Klux Klan.* New York: Oxford University Press, 1995.

Kurds

Kurds are a Middle Eastern minority group of perhaps 20 million people whose homeland, sometimes called Kurdistan, is located in the present-day states of southeastern Turkey, northern Iraq, western Iran, and eastern Syria. The Kurds are an ancient warrior people who have been part of many empires. The most famous Kurd was Saladin, the sultan of Egypt and Syria and valiant opponent of England's Richard the Lion-Hearted during the Third Crusade (1189–92); Saladin is widely considered the greatest Muslim hero of all time.

For much of the 20th century, Kurds have been involved in unsuccessful struggles for independence. Almost all Kurds are Sunni Muslims. As late as the mid-1970s there were only an estimated 50 Kurds in the United States. Since that time, however, several thousand Kurds have been admitted to the United States, almost all of them refugees from Saddam Hussein's Iraq, which has waged devastating warfare against the Kurds in that country. Many of these Kurds first found refuge in Iran. They are also involved in armed struggles with the Turks, but few Kurds have immigrated to the United States.

SEE ALSO

Iranians; Iraqis; Refugees; Turks

FURTHER READING

O'Connor, Karen. *A Kurdish Family.* Minneapolis: Lerner, 1996.

Kuwaitis

SEE Arabs

Language maintenance

The term *language maintenance* refers to the degree to which immigrant groups maintain their "mother tongue," the language of their homeland. In general, immigrant groups in the United States have usually lost the use of their native languages within two generations. It is a relatively rare third-generation American who grows up speaking a language other than English.

There are two kinds of circumstances in the American experience that encourage the maintenance of a language other than English: relative isolation and continuous reinforcement. Two prominent cases of isolation that promoted language maintenance are the Acadians (Cajuns) of Louisiana and the Amish, each of whom have maintained outmoded forms of their ancestral language, French in the first case, German in the second. Two cases of continued reinforcement, both by proximity to a border and by constant reinforcement by continued, often circular migration, are the Mexicans of the Southwest and those French Canadians who live close to Quebec.

In 1990 five different non-English languages were spoken at home by at least one million Americans. Spanish led the way with more than 17 million speakers, followed by French with 1.7 million, German with 1.5 million. Italian with 1.3 million, and Chinese with 1.2 million speakers. In 1990, the total number of U.S. residents five years old and over speaking a language other than English at home was 31,845,000, 14 percent of all persons over five years old. It must be emphasized that three out of four of the foreign-language speakers reported that they spoke English "well" or "very well."

SEE ALSO
Acadians; Amish; French Canadians; Media, foreign-language; Mexicans; Mother tongue

Language schools

Language schools are privately run educational institutions, usually held in the late afternoon or on weekends, in which an immigrant language, culture, and sometimes religion are taught. In the late 19th and early 20th centuries, large numbers of these schools existed teaching many immigrant languages. German language schools outnumbered all the rest. In the anti-foreign or nativist reaction during and after World War I, foreign language schools came under attack. By 1923, 24 states had laws outlawing or severely restricting foreign-language schools. The Supreme Court, in a series of cases—the most important of which is an Oregon case, *Pierce* v. *Society of Sisters* (1925)—declared such laws unconstitutional. Most of the Oregon schools were religious in nature, but in *Farrington* v. *Tokushige* (1926), the court upheld a 9th circuit opinion striking down Hawaiian statutes regulating attendance in secular Japanese language schools. The key doctrine, as put forth in *Meyer* v. *Nebraska* (1923), is that "The protection of the Constitution extends to all, to those who speak other languages, as well as to those born with English on the tongue."

Since the 1920s there have been many fewer language schools, although contemporary immigrant groups from

Asia, particularly Chinese and Koreans, have established language schools that are almost completely secular. A different type of school taught in a foreign language has existed since the 1980s: schools for the children of executives of Japanese companies temporarily in the United States, which teach all subjects in Japanese. The parents wish their children to be educated in the Japanese style because they plan to take them back to Japan.

SEE ALSO
Education; *Meyer v. Nebraska*; Nativism; *Pierce v. Society of Sisters*

FURTHER READING
Crawford, James, ed. *Language Loyalties: A Source Book on the Official English Controversy*. Chicago: University of Chicago Press, 1992.

Laotians

- *1990 Census: 149,014*
- *1990 Population: 147,375*
- *Immigration, 1986–96: 86,110*
- *Immigration, 1970–96: around 120,000*
- *Major period of immigration: since 1975*
- *Major areas of settlement: California, Texas, Minnesota*

[There is a certain amount of confusion about Laotians and Hmong in American data. The Immigration and Naturalization Service, which records nationality, includes both groups as "Laotians." The Bureau of the Census, which records ethnicity and asks people what they are, separates the two.]

Laos is a small Southeast Asian nation of about 90,000 square miles without access to the sea. Experts count some 60 ethnic groups in the country's population, estimated at 5

million people. About 60 percent are the lowland Lao, one of whose early kings founded Lan Xang ("land of a million elephants") in 1353. The Lao practice Buddhism, and Buddhist monks were very important in their culture and education. France conquered Laos in 1893, lost it to Japan during World War II, and regained it briefly after the war. Laos achieved independence and was admitted to the United Nations in 1955, but was caught up in a deadly civil war and the growing war in Vietnam as well.

Laotians, like Cambodians and Hmong, have been in the United States such a short time that it is difficult to make meaningful generalizations about their experiences except to note their poverty and their general lack of the kinds of skills which make for success in a high-tech society. Much will depend on what happens to the American-born generation. As of 1990, there were 30,000 of them, or one Laotian American in five. The oldest among them were of college age in the mid-1990s. The fate of this generation and its successors will be crucial for the status of the Laotian American community.

SEE ALSO
Buddhists; Hmong; Refugees; Vietnam War

Some Buddhist temples are elaborate; others, like this one established by Laotians in Des Moines, Iowa, are found inside houses.

FURTHER READING

Hein, Jeremy. *From Vietnam, Laos, and Cambodia: A Refugee Experience in the United States.* New York: Twayne. 1995.
MacDonald, Jeffrey L. *Transnational Aspects of Iu-Mien Refugee Identity.* New York: Garland, 1997.

Latinos

The term *Latino* was first used in the mid-1940s in Texas and, after the 1960s, in the rest of the United States, to describe all persons of Spanish heritage. During those years, and later, the Census Bureau used the term "Spanish surname."

SEE ALSO

Hispanics; Spanish surname

Latvians

- *1990 Ancestry: 100,331*
- *Immigration, 1986–96: 2,737*
- *Immigration, 1820–1996: around 75,000*
- *Major periods of immigration: 1905–13, 1948–51*
- *Major areas of settlement: New York, New Jersey, Massachusetts*

In modern times, Latvia has existed as an independent country only since the end of World War I. Before that it was part of the Russian Empire, and in 1940 it was overrun and annexed as a constituent republic of the Soviet Union. Latvia was occupied by Nazi Germany from 1941 to 1944, when it returned to Soviet control, and it became independent again when the Soviet Union recognized its independence in 1991. Thus, Latvians do not

The Latvian Choral Shield, made up largely of recent immigrants, performs in Grand Rapids, Michigan, in 1958.

appear in American immigration data until after World War I and were often counted as citizens of the U.S.S.R.

Latvians have been coming to American since the 17th century. The first immigrants were members of the multinational Swedish settlements on the Delaware River in 1640; in 1687 a few Latvians, who had emigrated to the West Indies, resettled in Boston. Relatively small numbers continued to come for the next two centuries. In 1900 the U.S. Census reported more than 4,000 Latvian speakers. Perhaps 5,000 more came immediately after the unsuccessful Russian Revolution of 1905. The Latvians settled almost exclusively in northeastern and midwestern cities and worked largely in the construction industry. Most of the early ethnic Latvians were Lutherans, but a considerable number of Catholics and a few Eastern Orthodox were among the post–World War II arrivals.

The most numerous Latvian immigration came as a result of World War II. A few Latvians managed to come during the war (1939–45), but most of the more than 40,000 immigrants of that era came as displaced persons between 1948 and 1951. The residential patterns of these immigrants resembled those of their predecessors, but many of them were skilled and educated professionals. Only rarely did Latvians gather into ethnic enclaves, but generally dispersed into the suburban areas of larger American cities.

A large minority of the early 20th-century Latvian immigrants were political radicals who supported socialist and later communist causes. Perhaps 250 of them departed willingly to settle in the newly founded Soviet Union after 1917, where some of them participated in its leadership. Even more of the immigrants were nationalists. The post–World War II immigrants were nationalists and politically conservative. One of them, Kárlis Ulmanlis, who had been on the faculty of the University of Nebraska, returned to Latvia and served as both its prime minister and president after Latvia regained in independence in 1991.

SEE ALSO

Displaced persons; Ethnic enclave; Refugees

FURTHER READING

Karklis, Maruta, et al., eds. *The Latvians in America, 1640–1973: A Chronology and Fact Book.* Dobbs Ferry, N.Y.: Oceana, 1974.

Lau v. *Nichols*

Lau v. *Nichols* was a 1973 U.S. Supreme Court case in which immigrant Chinese pupils in the San Francisco public schools who had little command of English sued to get public school instruction in the Chinese language. The Court ruled that public schools everywhere had to provide equal education for non–English-speaking children by educating them in their mother tongues while teaching them English as a second language. This program of mandated bilingual education has had mixed success, partly because of the difficulty in securing competent bilingual teachers at the salaries that most public schools pay.

SEE ALSO
Education

Lebanese

SEE Arabs

Literacy test

Beginning in the early 1880s nativist groups, particularly the Immigration Restriction League, agitated for a literacy test as a way to restrict immigration. Bills providing for such a literacy test passed Congress in 1897, 1913, 1915, and 1917, but were vetoed each time by different Presidents. Grover Cleveland's 1897 veto message stressed the fact that the "stupendous growth" of the nation had been "largely due to the assimilation and thrift of millions of sturdy and patriotic adopted citizens." Woodrow Wilson, who vetoed such bills twice, stressed that immigrants came seeking opportunity and the bill would reject them because they did not have education, one of the opportunities many immigrants sought. Wilson's second veto, in 1917, was overridden by Congress and the literacy test became law.

Although many of the literacy test's strongest supporters wanted the requirement to be an ability to read English, the law demanded only an ability to read a brief text in any "language or dialect, including Hebrew or Yiddish" by immigrants over 16 years of

The Literacy Test was a hot issue in Congress for 20 years before it was enacted over a Presidential veto in 1917. This 1916 cartoon opposed it.

THE AMERICANESE WALL, AS CONGRESSMAN BURNETT WOULD BUILD IT.
UNCLE SAM: You're welcome in—if you can climb it!

age. In addition, wives, mothers, grandmothers, widowed or unmarried daughters of a literate male alien, or one already living here, need not be literate. Thus the law had little effect. In 1920–21, when more than 800,000 immigrants were admitted, about 1.5 percent (13,799 persons) were rejected for one reason or another. Only 1,450 of them were barred for illiteracy. Nevertheless the enactment of the literacy test was an important symbolic victory for the forces of nativism, and literacy has remained a requirement in American immigration law, although it can be waived for persons over 65 and for those with physical disabilities.

SEE ALSO
Immigration Act of 1917; Nativism

FURTHER READING
Solomon, Barbara Miller. *Ancestors and Immigrants*. Cambridge, Mass.: Harvard University Press, 1956.

Lithuanians
- *1990 Ancestry: 811,865*
- *Immigration, 1986–96: 3,812*

- *Immigration, 1820–1996: around 330,000*
- *Major periods of immigration: 1890s–1914, 1948–51*
- *Major areas of settlement: Chicago, New York, Boston, Philadelphia, and Cleveland*

Like Latvia, in modern times Lithuania has existed as an independent country only since the end of World War I; unlike Latvia it had been a nation in the Middle Ages. Before 1918 it was part of the Russian Empire. In 1940 it was overrun and annexed as a constituent republic of the Soviet Union. It was occupied by Nazi Germany from 1941 to 1944, when it returned to Soviet control. It became independent again when the Soviet Union recognized its independence in 1991. Thus Lithuanians do not appear in American immigration data until after World War I. After World War II they were often counted as citizens of the U.S.S.R.

Changing conditions in Lithuania, including a railroad boom and a severe famine, set in motion large-scale emigration from Lithuanian villages in the 1860s. While most migrated to other parts of the Russian empire, some went to nearby Germany or to Great Britain and others found their way to America. By the 1890s the movement to the United States had become the most important target of Lithuanian emigration. By the outbreak of World War I perhaps 300,000 had come. During this latter phase perhaps one Lithuanian immigrant in five returned to the homeland.

The immigrants were predominantly male, usually young bachelors or married men who had left their wives and children behind. Most of these men worked in low-skilled industrial occupations, often under dreadful conditions.

Many immigrant men came to the United States without families. This Lithuanian bachelor, who lived in Chicago early in the 20th century, surrounded himself with mementos of home.

The fictional hero of Upton Sinclair's novel *The Jungle* (1905) is a Lithuanian immigrant worker, Jurgis Rudkus, and the hideous working conditions he endures were commonly experienced by Lithuanian and other immigrant industrial workers in that era.

Some of the immigrant families that were reunited or created in America in this era began to experience upward social mobility. A few immigrants became businessmen. There were some 500 Lithuanian-owned businesses in Chicago in 1909: 180 of them were saloons. The saloon keeper was in many instances a community leader, and his premises were often also a social center, boardinghouse, restaurant, bank, travel agency, and employment agency all under one roof. Most Lithuanians were Roman Catholics, and by 1920 there were more than 100 Lithuanian parishes in the United States.

Large numbers of Lithuanian immigrants were socialists before World War I. After the war most Lithuanian American political energy went into supporting the new Lithuanian Republic. After World War II, with Lithuania under Soviet control, some 30,000 refugees and displaced persons settled in the United States. Though they tended to settle in the same places as the earlier Lithuanian immigrants had, many of the newer group were educated professionals, a category underrepresented in the pre–World War I community.

SEE ALSO

Displaced persons; Refugees

FURTHER READING

Fainhauz, David. *Lithuanians in the USA: Aspects of Ethnic Identity*. Translated by Algirdas Dumcius. Chicago: Lithuanian Library, 1991.
Greene, Victor R. *For God and Country: The Rise of Polish and Lithuanian Ethnic Consciousness in America, 1860–1910*. Madison: University of Wisconsin Press, 1975.

Little Russians

SEE Ukrainians

LPC clause

The LPC clause—the letters are short for "likely to become a public charge"—has been a part of American immigration law since 1882. From that time any prospective immigrant adjudged "likely to become a public charge" could be kept from immigrating to the United States. Originally the clause was used only to keep out people who were obviously unable to support themselves, but in the 20th century it was administratively broadened to keep out poor Asian Indians and Mexicans, and then broadened to keep out poor people generally, unless they had affidavits of support from financially responsible individuals or organizations.

SEE ALSO

Asian Indians; Immigration policy; Mexicans

Lusatian Sorbs

SEE Wends

Luxembourgers

- *1990 Ancestry: 49,061*
- *Immigration, 1986–96: 256*
- *Immigration, 1820–1996: around 50,000*
- *Major period of immigration: 1900–14*
- *Major areas of settlement: north central states*

The Grand Duchy of Luxembourg in a tiny, triangular country of 998 square miles between Belgium, France, and Germany, with fewer than 400,000 people in the 1990s. Its language, Luxem-bourgish, is closely related to German and can be understood by most German speakers. More than 90 percent of the people are Roman Catholics. A few Luxembourg immigrants were recorded in Dutch New York in the 17th century, and a few hundred came between then and the 1840s, largely seeking farms.

A rapid increase in population and a system of primogeniture, in which the eldest son inherited all of a family's land, sent many Luxembourgers, mostly younger sons of farming families, abroad in search of land. At a time when farmland in Luxembourg sold for 800 to 2,000 francs a hectare (2.5 acres), a similar-sized plot in northern Illinois or southern Wisconsin could be purchased for the equivalent of 15 or 20 francs. World War I and then American immigration law cut off most Luxembourg immigration, and prosperity in the post–World War II era has limited immigration. Perhaps 300 Jewish refugees from Luxembourg escaped to America before 1940, when the Grand Duchy was temporarily annexed to Nazi Germany.

FURTHER READING

Magocsi, Paul Robert. "Luxembourgers." In *Harvard Encyclopedia of American Ethnic Groups*. Cambridge: Harvard University Press, 1980.

Macedonians

- *1990 Ancestry: 20,365*
- *Immigration, 1994–96: 1,896*
- *Immigration, 1820–1996: 1,996*
- *Major periods of immigration: n.a.*
- *Major areas of settlement: Northeastern cities*

Just who is and who is not a Macedonian is a matter of bitter ethnic dispute that will not be resolved by anything written here. Any definition will be hotly disputed by Greeks, Albanians, Bulgarians and spokespersons for the modern Macedonia. Ancient Macedonia was, in the 4th century B.C., the home of Philip II of Macedon and his son, Alexander the Great. In post–World War II Yugoslavia there was a Macedonian Republic, and in 1991, after the breakup of Yugoslavia, an independent Macedonia was created. It is a country of fewer than 10,000 square miles with about 2 million inhabitants, bordered by Yugoslavia, Bulgaria, Albania, and Greece.

Before World War II most of the perhaps 50,000 Macedonians who had immigrated to the United States thought of themselves, according to the authoritative *Harvard Encyclopedia of American Ethnic Groups*, as Bulgarians or Macedonian Bulgarians, but now some of their descendants think of themselves of Macedonian Americans. Beginning in 1994 the U.S. Immigration and Naturalization Service (INS) began enumerating immigrants from the new Macedonia (a total of 1,896 in the first three years), but many of those were refugees who thought of themselves as something other than Macedonians.

SEE ALSO
Bulgarians

FURTHER READING
Prpic, George J. *South Slavic Immigration in America*. Boston: Twayne, 1978.

Magyars

SEE Hungarians

Manx
- *1990 Ancestry: 6,317*
- *Immigration, 1986–96: n.a.*
- *Immigration, 1820–1996: around 10,000*

- *Major period of immigration: mid-19th century*
- *Major area of settlement: northern Ohio*

Manx are residents of the Isle of Man, an island of 227 square miles in the Irish Sea. The Manx language was a variety of Celtic and was displaced by English in the mid-19th century. Because Manx are British subjects, they have not been listed in immigration reports. Although as recently as 1980 one authority estimated that there were 50,000 persons of Manx descent in the United States, only 6,317 people claimed that lineage in the 1990 census. Although some claim that the Pilgrim Miles Standish was Manx, and it is clear that at least two Manx families were settlers in 17th-century Virginia, most Manx immigrants were farmers and miners who came in the mid-19th century. The largest group settlement was of some 200 families who, after the Erie Canal was opened in 1825, used it and Lake Erie to settle in the Western Reserve of northern Ohio around Cleveland. Manx Americans support at least 12 societies, the largest of which, the North American Manx Association, has 800 members.

Mariel boatlift

The Mariel boatlift was an incident that took place in the spring of 1980 in the midst of a dispute between Cuba and the United States concerning several hundred dissident Cubans who had taken refuge in the Peruvian embassy in Havana, Cuba. The Cuban dictator Fidel Castro unexpectedly announced that anyone who wanted to leave for the

United States—which was forbidden by Cuban law—could do so, if they left almost immediately from the small Cuban port of Mariel, less than 100 miles from Key West, Florida. Many Cuban refugees in the United States chartered small boats and picked up friends and relatives in what became a shuttle service. Although the entrance of the Cubans was illegal under American law, the administration of President Jimmy Carter eventually allowed some 125,000 *marielitos*, as Cubans called them, to enter the United States. A small minority of those who came were criminals whom Castro had released from prison if they would leave. Many of these wound up in American prisons and some of them were eventually sent back to Cuba. Most of the *marielitos*, like most Cuban refugees generally, have successfully entered American society.

SEE ALSO
Cubans; Illegal emigrants; Illegal immigrants; Immigration policy; Refugees

FURTHER READING
Garcia, Maria Cristina. *Havana USA: Cuban Exiles and Cuban Americans in South Florida, 1959–1994.* Berkeley: University of California Press, 1996.
Hoobler, Dorothy, and Thomas Hoobler. *The Cuban American Family Album.* New York: Oxford University Press, 1996.

Maya

The Maya, Native Americans in Central America, created one of the great pre-Columbian civilizations of the New World, which flourished between A.D. 300 and 900. Today there are about 4 million Maya who live in an area stretching from Mexico's Yucatán Peninsula south through El Salvador and northern Honduras. Most live in Guatemala, and perhaps as many as 200,000 have immigrated to the United States since 1970. Although classified by the Census Bureau as "Hispanics," most of them speak one of the 31 Maya languages, although almost all of them have at least some understanding of Spanish.

SEE ALSO
Guatemalans; Hondurans

Mayflower Compact

The Mayflower Compact was a solemn agreement signed by all adult males on board the *Mayflower* just before they landed in Massachusetts in 1620, one of the first and most significant early voyages. We now call this group "Pilgrims" or "Pilgrim Fathers." It begins "In the presence of God and one another [we] combine ourselves together into a civil Body Politick," and is the first document in American history that can be called a constitution.

SEE ALSO
Pilgrims

McCarran-Walter Act

SEE Immigration Act of 1952

Means

Means is a term used by scholars of migration to describe conveniently one of the several factors involved in a person's migrating from one country to another. Means can include the availability of transportation, the ability to purchase or otherwise acquire that transportation, and being able, legally or illegally, to leave the country of origin and to enter the country of destination.

SEE ALSO

Pull; Push

Media, foreign-language

From the 1730s, when German-language newspapers began to be published in Pennsylvania, immigrant communities have utilized whatever media were available to promote their culture and to inform their communities. The most extensive network of publications were maintained by German Americans. Of the roughly 1,000 foreign-language newspapers published in the United States in the 1880s, 800 were in German. The most famous newspaper was the Yiddish-language daily the *Forward* (*Vorwarts*), founded in 1897 and first edited by Abraham Cahan. Almost every ethnic group in America has, at one time or another, published a newspaper, most often a weekly.

In post–World War II America other media are more frequently utilized. Only the more numerous groups can afford to support foreign-language radio and television stations, but in most large cities there are radio stations and, to a lesser degree, television stations, that will devote several hours daily or weekly to broadcasts in one or more foreign languages. In recent decades, videotapes of movies and television programs from foreign countries enable immigrants to keep up with the culture of their homeland.

Benjamin Franklin's Philadelphia Zeitung *was the first foreign-language newspaper in America. This is the front page of the first edition, published in 1732.*

In contemporary America, Spanish-language media of all kinds dwarf those in other foreign languages because Spanish is the mother tongue of so many immigrant groups. Conversely, the multiplicity of languages spoken by Asian Americans has inhibited the growth of any one of them. In addition, the fact that some leading Asian languages use characters rather than letters creates technological difficulties.

SEE ALSO

Language maintenance

FURTHER READING

Danky, James P., and Wayne A. Wiegand, eds. *Print Culture in a Diverse America.* Urbana: University of Illinois Press, 1998.

Miller, Sally M., ed. *The Ethnic Press in the United States: A Historical Analysis and Handbook.* Westport, Conn.: Greenwood, 1987.

Park, Robert E. *The Immigrant Press and Its Control.* New York: Harper, 1922.

Melanesians

Melanesia, a Greek word meaning "black islands," referring to the skin color of the inhabitants, is an area in the southwesten Pacific Ocean, south of the equator and northeast of Australia, and is one of the three main divisions of Oceania. Melanesia includes the Solomon Islands, Vanuatu, New Caledonia, Tuvalu, the Bismarck Archipelago, the Admiralty Islands, and Fiji. New Guinea is sometimes included in Melanesia. The Melanesians are largely of Australoid stock; they speak Malayo-Polynesian languages.

Relatively few people from Melanesia have ever immigrated to the United States, and almost all of those have come since the 1970s. In the 1990s about 1,000 a year came from Fiji, but almost all of those were Asian Indians. The 10 to 20 a year who came from Papua, New Guinea, and an annual handful from the Solomon Islands were probably ethnic Melanesians.

SEE ALSO
Pacific Islanders

Melting pot

The phrase *melting pot* is taken from the title of a 1909 play about immigrant life in America, *The Melting Pot*, by the British writer Israel Zangwill. The phrase implied, incorrectly, that America was a place in which nationalities and ethnic groups would be fused into one entirely new people.

Although Zangwill coined the phrase, the idea was more than a century old. In 1782 Michel-Guillaume-Jean de Crèvecoeur, a French-born writer who became a naturalized U.S.

citizen and the U.S. consul to France, wrote in his *Letters from an American Farmer* that the United States was a place where "individuals of all races are melted into a new race of men, whose labours and posterity will one day cause great changes in the world." Both Crèvecoeur and Zangwill used the word "races" where we, today, would say "ethnic groups." A modern sociologist has written about a religiously oriented "Triple Melting Pot" of Protestant, Catholic, and Jewish faiths.

SEE ALSO
Acculturation; Cultural pluralism; Mosaic; Salad bowl; Triple melting pot

FURTHER READING
Glazer, Nathan, and Daniel P. Moynihan. *Beyond the Melting Pot: The Negroes, Puerto Ricans, Jews, Italians, and Irish of New York City.* 2nd ed. Cambridge: M.I.T. Press, 1970.
Gordon, Milton M. *Assimilation in American Life: The Role of Race, Religion and National Origins.* New York: Oxford University Press, 1964.

Mennonites

Mennonites are a Protestant religious sect whose members live a communal life and are pacifists. The name Mennonite comes from the name of Menno Simons, a Dutch religious reformer. Simons left the Catholic priesthood and became the leader of the Anabaptist movement, which was very strong in Switzerland. Persecution drove many Mennonites to various parts of Germany, and to France and Russia. The first Mennonites in America came from Krefeld in the German Rhineland to found Germantown, Pennsylvania, in 1683. There were an estimated 266,000 Mennonites in the United

Students in a "Deutch" (German language) school attend class in a Mennonite church near Hinkletown, Pennsylvania, in 1942.

States in 1990, and about 114,000 in Canada.

Some Mennonite groups, particularly those known as Amish and Hutterites, live a communal life, largely isolated in rural colonies. Most other Mennonites are also farmers. They tend to be Pacifist and most are conscientious objectors in wartime. They also engage extensively in various kinds of relief work, both overseas and with refugees in the United States.

SEE ALSO

Amish; Germans; Hutterites

FURTHER READING

Bender, H. S., and C. H. Smith, eds. *The Mennonite Encyclopedia.* 4 vols. Hillsboro, Kans.: Mennonite Brethren, 1955–90.

Hostetler, John A. *Mennonite Life.* Scottsdale, Pa.: Herald Press, 1974.

Loewen, Royden. *Family, Church, and Market: A Mennonite Community in the Old and New Worlds, 1850–1930.* Urbana: University of Illinois Press, 1993.

Mestizo

Mestizo is a Spanish word, also used in English since the 1580s, to refer to a person of mixed ancestry, particularly European and Indian. The related French word, used in Canada, is *metis.*

Mexicans

- *1990 Ancestry: 11,586,983*
- *Immigration, 1986–96: 2,968,595*
- *Immigration, 1820–1996: 5,542,625*
- *Major periods of immigration: 17th–18th centuries, 1965+*
- *Major areas of settlement: Southwest, esp. California*

Migrants from Mexico in the 17th and 18th centuries were the founding fathers and mothers of what are now the American states of New Mexico, Arizona, Texas, and California. These and other territories were taken from Mexico in the Texas Revolution of 1835–36 and in the Mexican War of 1847–48. According to the Treaty of Guadalupe Hidalgo (1848), which ended the war, the estimated 80,000 Mexicans living in the territory the United States acquired continued to have residence, property, and other rights. In most of the Southwest, Mexicans were quickly outnumbered by newcomers, but in New Mexico they were the majority until the 1940s.

Mexican Americans have experienced a varied history. There has even been significant variation in what they have called themselves. Although it is now fashionable to use the term *Chicano* to refer to them throughout their history, that term is a relatively recent, post–World War II coinage. In the 19th century before the American conquest, those in Texas, New Mexico, and California called themselves *Tejanos, Hispanos,* and *Californios,* respectively, After that the general term *Mexicano* prevailed for a time. In the 20th century new terms were used: one major Mexican civil rights organization was the League of United Latin American Citizens (LULAC), while the other was the American G.I. Forum, founded by Mexican American veterans (GIs) of World War II. Those in New Mexico tended to call themselves Spanish Americans, while in California the term Mexican American preceded and coexisted with Chicano. More recently, in an attempt to unify the varied Hispanic elements, the term Latino has been used.

Except for much circular migration in border regions, there was little migration from Mexico during the remainder of the 19th century. Then, early in the 20th century, a combination of five factors caused it to increase. The expansion of agriculture in the Southwest, aided by large-scale federal irrigation projects, the cutting off of the immigration of Chinese and Japanese farm workers, and the Mexican Revolution which began in 1909 all created both "push" and "pull" conditions which encouraged immigration from Mexico to the United States. The "pull" was greatly increased by World War I, which cut off European immigration and created labor shortages that Mexicans helped to fill, and the immigration acts of 1921 and 1924, which curtailed European immigration and put no limits on that from the Western Hemisphere, created a vacuum that was filled by New World immigrants, chiefly Canadians and Mexicans.

The official immigration figures, which are certainly too low, as many Mexicans crossed the border informally, show 30,000 Mexican immigrants between 1900 and 1909, 185,000 between 1910 and 1919, and nearly 500,000 from 1920 to 1929. In the Depression decade of the 1930s, many more Mexicans left than arrived. Some simply returned to Mexico; others were

sent back through informal deportation procedures. Many were stopped from coming by an administrative reinterpretation of the LPC clause. This clause, first introduced into U.S. law in 1882, originally kept out only persons who were unable to support themselves and so "likely to become a public charge." The new interpretation kept out poor people, particularly persons of color.

During these years and after, Mexican Americans suffered from severe discrimination in the Southwest, where almost all of them then lived. In many places in Texas and California schools were segregated, employment opportunities were limited, available housing was inferior, and many public facilities were either closed to them or available only on a limited basis. In southern California, for example, public swimming pools were open to Mexican Americans one day a week—usually the day *before* the pool was cleaned. Conditions for Mexican Americans were worst in Texas where, among other things, the state police, the much-touted Texas Rangers, have long record of systematic mistreatment of Mexican Americans.

World War II created more labor shortages. The federal government in cooperation with the Mexican government created a Bracero program to supply much needed agricultural workers. The term *bracero*, ("one who swings his arms"), derives from *brazo*, the Spanish word for arm, and refers to someone who does manual labor. The Bracero program brought some 200,000 Mexican workers to the United States between 1942 and 1947. About half of them worked in California, the rest in 20 other states. The program was started again in 1951 during the Korean War and continued until 1964, long after the war was over. The heaviest single years was 1959, when nearly 450,000 braceros were brought in. Braceros were supposed to be short-term workers in the United States—they were not counted as immigrants—whose return fare to Mexico was paid. Most did go back, but some stayed, illegally. Others continued to come during the growing season, often working on the same farms and ranches year after year.

The ending of the Bracero program in 1964 did not mean the end of Mexicans coming to work temporarily in the United States; temporary workers have continued to come, both legally and illegally. Most of the temporary workers who come legally live close to the border. Many have employment authorization, usually called a green card. Thousands of such persons commute daily from such Mexican cities as Ciudad Juárez and Tijuana to American cities such as El Paso, Texas, and San Diego, California. Many work in factories making clothing or assembling electronic components.

The illegal temporary workers usually come for longer periods, often many months. Many of them work in southwestern agriculture, but they migrate all over the United States in search of agricultural work. These are almost all semiskilled and unskilled jobs, with long hours, low pay, and few, if any, benefits. Like earlier European and Asian sojourners, most of them are trying to save money to send to their families in Mexico.

Over the course of time, many of these migrants have decided to live in the United States full-time. Some of them apply for and obtain visas; others stay without legal sanctions and become illegal permanent residents. Still other Mexicans, as the immigration figures show, simply immigrate in the normal way: 60,000 did so in the 1940s; 300,000 in the 1950s; 450,000 in the 1960s; 640,000 in the 1970s;

1.65 million in the 1980s; and a somewhat larger number in the 1990s. On the other hand, the INS and the Census Bureau believed that in 1996 there were 2.7 million illegal Mexican immigrants in the United States, more than half of the estimated total of 5 million illegal immigrants present in that year.

With all of the emphasis on illegal immigrants from Mexico it is easy to forget that nearly 6 million Mexicans have immigrated here legally. Moreover, two-thirds of the 13.5 million persons of Mexican birth or ancestry in the 1990 census were native-born American citizens; and of the 6.2 million foreign-born Mexicans the Census Bureau recorded in 1994 (which includes many illegal immigrants), almost 900,000 were naturalized citizens and very large numbers are naturalizing every year. In addition, between 1986 and 1996, under the provisions of the Immigration Act of 1986 (IRCA), more than 2 million Mexicans who had entered illegally went through the complex process of legalization and become United States citizens.

Mexican Americans, although concentrated in the Southwest, now live in every part of the United States. Although they are thought of as rural

The Mexican laborer in California pictured on this identification card was admitted to the United States in a special WW I–era program. Most immigrants workers then did not have cards.

Mexican American dancers reenact a traditional folk dance. They are dressed in the kinds of costumes used in Mexico.

agricultural workers, the overwhelming majority are city dwellers like most other Americans. Like the Hispanic population generally, they are an extremely young population. About 70 percent of the Hispanic population in 1990 was under 35, as opposed to about 50 percent for others in the population, and only 5 percent of Hispanics were over 65 as opposed to 13 percent for others. Although language retention is relatively strong among Mexicans, more than a quarter of them do not speak Spanish at home, and more than half of those checked the box of their census form that said they spoke English "very well."

The vast majority of Mexicans are Roman Catholics, but their presence has not always been embraced by American church leaders. Many Mexicans brought both a deep religious faith and an anticlericalism from Mexico. The historian George Sánchez reports interviewing a mature Mexican American in 1976 who remembered that his grandmother had told him early in the century, "My son, there are three things that pertain to our religion: the Lord, Our Lady of Guadalupe, and the Church. You can trust in the first

two, but not the third." It should also be noted that three things that the American Catholic Church regarded as essential—financial support of the church, religious instruction, and regular attendance at Mass—were not things that Mexican Catholics were used to. On the other hand, the Virgin of Guadalupe, the central icon of Mexican Catholics, was used as a rallying symbol by the American-born labor leader Cesar Chavez, perhaps the most effective leader the Mexican American people have produced.

Although most immigrants from Mexico have been speakers of Spanish, millions of Mexicans either do not speak Spanish or do not speak it very well; they speak, instead, a variety of Native American languages. Scholars estimate, for example, that in 1990 more than half a million of Mexico's inhabitants were speakers of one of the more important of these languages, Zapotec. Observers have noted in recent years that a growing minority of immigrants from Mexico are more comfortable in Zapotec or Maya or some other Amerindian language, although United States census data does not record this phenomenon. Most of these immigrants understand some Spanish.

The rapid growth of the Mexican American population has yet to be translated into political power commensurate to their presence in the population, but there is every reason to believe that this will not be the case for very long.

SEE ALSO

Bracero program; Circular migration; Hispanics; Illegal immigrants; Immigration Act of 1986; LPC clause; Pull; Push; Sojourners; Spaniards

FURTHER READING

Camarillo, Albert. *Chicanos in California: A History of Mexican Americans in California.* San Francisco: Boyd & Fraser, 1984.

Cardoso, Lawrence A. *Mexican Emigration to the United States, 1897–1931.* Tucson: University of Arizona Press, 1980.

Sánchez, George J. *Becoming Mexican American: Ethnicity and Acculturation in Chicano Los Angeles, 1900–1943.* New York: Oxford University Press, 1992.

Meyer v. Nebraska

Mr. Meyer, a teacher in the Zion Parochial School in Hamilton County, Nebraska, was convicted in a Nebraska court in 1920 for teaching the "subject of reading in the German language to Raymond Parpart, a child of ten years," which was against the law in Nebraska because Raymond had not yet reached grade eight. The United States Supreme Court, in *Meyer* v. *Nebraska* (1923), declared the law unconstitutional. This 1919 Nebraska law and similar statutes in other states passed during and after World War I were part of a nativist attack on all things German and on foreign cultures in general. The Court's opinion in this and similar cases, particularly *Pierce* v. *Society of Sisters*, was an important defense of the rights of people to educate their children in the culture of their homeland, and of academic freedom generally.

SEE ALSO

Education; Language schools; Nativism; *Pierce* v. *Society of Sisters*

Micronesians

Micronesia, whose name is a Greek word meaning "tiny islands," is located in the western Pacific Ocean, north of the equator. Micronesia includes the Caroline Islands, Marshall Islands, Mariana Islands, Gilbert Islands, and Nauru. The inhabitants are ethnically Australoid and Polynesian and speak Malayo-Polynesian languages. Small but increasing numbers of Micronesians immigrated to the United States after 1965, along with other Pacific Islanders.

SEE ALSO

Pacific Islanders

Montenegrins

- *1990 Ancestry: n.a.*
- *Immigration, 1986–96: n.a.*
- *Immigration, 1820–1996: around 30,000*
- *Major period of immigration: 1880–1914*
- *Major areas of settlement: northeast, esp. Pennsylvania*

Montenegrins are mostly a Serbian people, but have long been recognized as a separate group, largely because of their special history. Although the Ottoman Turks overran and dominated the Balkan Peninsula after their defeat of the Serbs in the battle of Kosovo in 1389, they never succeeded in conquering Montenegro. Montenegro, which means "black mountain," is a heavily mountainous region that became a republic of Yugoslavia in 1946, and, in 1992, joined with Serbia to form the Federal Republic of Yugoslavia. There were perhaps 600,000 Montenegrins in 1994.

Relatively few Montenegrins came to the United States, and many of those who came were sojourners. One authority estimates about 20,000 were present just before 1914, but that represented nearly a tenth of Montenegro's population. And, since most of them were young adult males, it represented a much greater proportion of the most economically active part of the population. In most respects, the experience of Montenegrins in the United States has been similar to that of Serbs and other Balkan peoples.

SEE ALSO
Serbs; Yugoslavia

Mormons

Between 1849 and 1887, the Mormon Church—properly speaking the Church of Jesus Christ of Latter-day Saints— actively engaged in a program of converting Europeans to its religion and then transporting them to the Mormon homeland, Deseret, which eventually became the state of Utah. The Mormon religion had begun in 1830 under the leadership of Joseph Smith, Jr. in upstate New York. Smith and his followers moved in stages to Nauvoo, Illinois. Some of the Mormon practices, especially plural marriage (polygamy), as well as their communal economic success, were violently opposed by many "gentiles," the Mormon term for all non-Mormons, some of whom persecuted Mormons. Shortly after Smith was lynched by a mob in Illinois in 1844, the Mormons decided to emigrate outside the United States and settled, without permission of Mexico, in Mexican territory near the Great Salt Lake in 1847. However the United States "followed and caught" them by annexing their new home after the Mexican War of 1846–48. (Unlike many communal religious groups, the Mormons are not pacifists: a Mormon Battalion fought as part of the United States forces during the Mexican War.) Shortly after that war, the Mormon mission to Europe, which had begun with an effort directed at England in 1837, became well organized and financed. It was most successful in Denmark and England. With the aid of a Perpetual Emigration Fund (1850–87), the church leaders financed and organized what was almost certainly the most efficient "immigrant travel service" of the 19th century. By the time the Perpetual Emigration Fund was seized by the U.S. government in 1887 as part of its attempted suppression of Mormonism, it had brought some 50,000 persons, largely in families, to Utah. The Fund not only arranged for and financed the Atlantic crossing and the overland travel to Utah, but also settled them, usually on farms, and saw that they had enough supplies to get started. Today Mormons send missionaries all over the world and some of their converts do emigrate to the United States, but there have been no more large-scale, church-sponsored migrations.

SEE ALSO
Religion

FURTHER READING
Mulder, William. *Homeward to Zion.* Minneapolis: University of Minnesota Press, 1957.
Taylor, Philip A. M. *Expectations Westward: The Mormons and the Emigration of their British Converts in the Nineteenth Century.* Ithaca, N.Y.: Cornell University Press, 1966.

Mosaic

Mosaic is a term that some scholars feel would be more appropriate than "melting pot" to describe the ways that ethnic and cultural groups acculturate in immigrant societies. They argue that a mosaic, whose individual pieces retain their shape and color while forming part of a picture or image, is a more accurate metaphor. The term has had little acceptance in the United States but is popular in Canada. "Salad bowl" is another metaphor for a similar idea.

SEE ALSO

Acculturation; Melting pot; Salad bowl; Triple melting pot

FURTHER READING

Morrison, Joan, and Charlotte Fox Zabusky. *American Mosaic: The Immigrant Experience in the Words of Those Who Lived It.* New York: Dutton, 1980. Porter, John. *The Vertical Mosaic: An Analysis of Social Class and Power in Canada.* Toronto: University of Toronto Press, 1965.

Mother tongue

The mother tongue is the language that a person learns first as a child. Some U.S. censuses, for example that of 1910, recorded "mother tongue," which is one of the ways we have of calculating the number of immigrants in the country of many ethnic groups, such as Poles or Jews, who did not have a national state at that time.

SEE ALSO

Language maintenance

Music, ethnic

Every group that has come to America has brought with it, as part of its culture, some kind of music. Almost every ethnic group that comes to America brings, as part of its culture, its music, songs, dances, and instruments, and quickly absorbs some aspects of other cultures' music and helps shape the American musical experience. Some of this music has been religious; the first book printed in New England was a book of psalms, or religious songs. Other songs have been songs of work, of politics, or of recreation. Some of

Mexican American musicians perform at an outdoor fiesta in New Mexico sometime in the 1930s. In that southwestern region, Mexican and American cultures have been interacting for more than a century and a half.

these songs, particularly if they are in English, are called folk songs. Others, deriving from African American Christianity, are called spirituals.

Jazz, thought by some to be the most distinctively American music, clearly has Afro-Caribbean roots. Reggae from the West Indies and salsa from Mexico have become very popular with nonethnic audiences and have influenced contemporary American music. The polka, a central European form, has become fully Americanized, and many who enjoy it are unaware of its origins. The Cajun music called zydeco is really an amalgam of tunes of French origin and music of Caribbean origin and the blues. Other forms, like the Mexican *corrido*, or song of topical political comment, have remained within the ethnic community.

FURTHER READING

Greene, Victor R. *A Passion for Polka: Old-time Ethnic Music in America.* Berkeley: University of California Press, 1992.

Limón, José Eduardo. *Mexican Ballads, Chicano Poems: History and Influence in Mexican-American Social Poetry.* Berkeley: University of California Press, 1992.

Parades, Américo. *"With his pistol in his hand": A Border Ballad and Its Hero.* Austin: University of Texas Press, 1971.

Sablosky, Irving. *American Music.* Chicago: University of Chicago Press, 1985.

Musicians, immigrant

Although few professional musicians came to America before the mid-19th century, some people associated with churches and synagogues were trained musicians, often organists and cantors. The first immigrant whom one can call a professional musician was Johann Christian Gottlieb Graupner, a German-born musician who came to America in 1798 and settled in Charleston, South Carolina, in 1793, and after three years as a traveling musician, settled in Boston in 1796, where he was a founder of the city's Handel and Haydn Society, which still exists. He also organized, about 1810, a Philharmonic Society that did not survive.

Well into the 20th century, European-born and -trained conductors and other musicians were the backbone of most classical orchestras in the United States. Clearly the most important of these was the German-born Theodore Thomas, who organized orchestras in New York, Cincinnati, and Chicago. Although few if any immigrant composers achieved prominence in that era, some of the most famous composers, including the Austrian Gustav Mahler and the Czech Antonín Dvořák spent time as conductors in America, and the latter lived for part of one year in a Czech settlement in Iowa where he wrote the "American Quartet."

But the truly extraordinary influx of musicians of talent and genius came in the 1930s and 1940s, as many of the best and the brightest European musicians fled Hitler and found refuge in the United States, where most of them continued to work. A partial listing of composers must include the Germans Arnold Schoenberg and Paul Hindemith, the Russian Igor Stravinsky, the Frenchman Darius Milhaud, the Czech Bohuslav Martinů, the Englishman Benjamin Britten, and the Hungarian Béla Bartók. Many conductors came, as well, of whom the most notable was the Italian Arturo Toscanini.

As for prominent foreign performers there are far too many to list, but from the time of Jenny Lind, the Swedish soprano who toured pre–Civil War America, to the more recent Beatles and Spice Girls from Britain, foreign performers, some of whom have settled in the United States, have been a staple of American music.

FURTHER READING

Fleming, Donald, and Bernard Bailyn, eds. *The Intellectual Migration; Europe and America, 1930–1960.* Cambridge: Harvard University Press, 1969.

Jackman, Jarrell C., and Carla M. Borden, eds. *The Muses Flee Hitler: Cultural Transfer and Adaptation, 1930–1945.* Washington, D.C.: Smithsonian Institution Press, 1983.

Sablosky, Irving. *American Music.* Chicago: University of Chicago Press, 1969.

Muslims

Muslims, an Arabic word meaning "ones who submit," are followers of the religion of Islam. Islam is an Arabic word meaning "submission to God [Allah]." It is a world religion founded by the prophet Muhammad in the early 7th century A.D. In 1990 there were an estimated 935 million Muslims worldwide. The two principal sects among the Muslims are the Shiite and Sunni. About a fifth of all Muslims are Arabs.

Islam is the principal religion of much of South and Southeast Asia, including Indonesia (which has more Muslims than any other single nation), Pakistan, Bangladesh, and a sizable minority in India. Several of the successor states of the former Soviet Union are Muslim and there are areas of western China that are highly Muslim. In the Middle East all countries except Israel have Muslim majorities. In Africa there are Muslim majorities in Egypt, Algeria, Tunisia, Djibouti, Gambia, Guinea, Libya, Mali, Mauritania, Morocco, Niger, Senegal, Somalia, and Sudan, with sizable populations also in Chad, Eritrea, Ethiopia, Ghana, Tanza-

nia, and Nigeria. In Europe, Albania is predominantly Muslim, and, historically, Bulgaria, Bosnia, Macedonia, and Georgia have had Muslim populations. Elsewhere in Europe, immigrant communities of Muslims from North Africa, Turkey, and Asia exist in France, Britain, and Germany.

In the Americas the Islamic population has increased substantially since 1970, both from conversions and the immigration of adherents from other parts of the world; 20 percent of the population of Suriname, on the northern coast of South America, is Muslim. The best estimate is that there were about 5 million Muslims in the United States at end of the 1990s. Mosques are now a common sight in most large American cities and in some small ones. The greatest U.S. center of Muslim population is Detroit.

SEE ALSO

Arabs; Bosnian Muslims; Iranians; Pakistanis; Religion

FURTHER READING

Haddad, Yvonne Y., ed. *Muslim Communities in North America.* Albany: State University of New York Press, 1994.

Moore, Kathleen M. *Al-Mughtaribun: American Law and the Transformation of Muslim Life in the United States.* Albany: State University of New York Press, 1995.

Muslim men bow before prayer rugs during Ramadan at a park in Brooklyn, New York. Ramadan is the ninth month of the Muslim calendar, in which many Muslims fast during daylight hours.

Nationality

Nationality refers to the nation or political entity to which an individual maintains citizenship or owes legal allegiance. It is this legal relationship that determines a person's nationality. Ethnicity, which depends upon the culture a person acquires, is something different. In some cases, nationality and culture are the same. A Norwegian immigrant from Norway, for example, would be recorded in the American census and by immigration officials as having Norwegian nationality or national origin, and would also have Norwegian ethnicity. But a Polish immigrant, arriving at a time when a Polish state did not exist, would be listed in American records as having the nationality of the nation she came from—usually Russia, Austria or Germany—but would have Polish ethnicity. If these immigrants became naturalized, both would acquire American citizenship and nationality and be considered Norwegian American or Polish American.

SEE ALSO
Citizenship; Ethnicity; Naturalization

National Origins Act

SEE Immigration Act of 1924

Nativism

Nativism is the policy of favoring established residents as opposed to recent or prospective immigrants.

Organized nativism has a long history in the United States. In the 1750s, for example, Benjamin Franklin expressed fears that the German immigrants would take over Pennsylvania and replace the English language with the German language. (Franklin later became a supporter of all kinds of immigration.) Major nativist movements in the United States have included the Know Nothings of the 1840s and 1850s, the American Protective Association of the 1880s and 1890s, and the Ku Klux Klan of the 1920s. Historians have defined 19th- and early 20th-century nativism as intense opposition to an internal minority because of its foreign connections.

Special targets of nativists have been Roman Catholics, Jews, Asians and other foreigners of color, and immigrants generally. Most contemporary nativist organizations, such as the Federation for American Immigration Reform (FAIR), no longer revile immigrant groups but argue for immigration restriction on broad economic, social, and sometimes ecological grounds.

SEE ALSO
American Protective Association; Discrimi-

This 1891 nativist cartoon blames immigrants for radicalism, crime, and poverty. The well-dressed man is telling Uncle Sam to restrict immigration.

nation; Immigration Restriction League; Know Nothing movement; Ku Klux Klan; Prejudice; Racism; Stereotype

FURTHER READING

Higham, John. *Strangers in the Land: Patterns of American Nativism, 1860–1925.* New Brunswick, N.J.: Rutgers University Press, 1955.

Reimers, David M. *Unwelcome Strangers: American Identity and the Turn Against Immigration.* New York: Columbia University Press, 1998.

Naturalization

A certificate of naturalization from 1923 for a Polish immigrant named Bronek Rafalka lists the names and ages of his five children, gives his address in Pennsylvania, and indicates that he had a tatoo on his right hand.

Naturalization is the legal process by which foreigners obtain citizenship. To become naturalized a person must have lived in the United States for five years, be of good character, and pass a citizenship examination requiring a knowledge of U.S. history and government. Sample questions include history: "Who was the first President of the United States?"; current events: "Who is the Vice President today?"; and civics: "Can the Constitution be changed?" A sample of the test may be found online (http://www.ins.usdoj.gov/graphics/services/natz/require.htm).

At certain times special provisions have allowed foreigners serving in the United States Armed Forces to become citizens more quickly, and exceptions may be made for persons over 65 or with disabilities. Naturalization is supervised by the Immigration and Naturalization Service, but the actual process of naturalization takes place in a ceremony conducted by a federal judge.

Naturalized citizens have all of the rights of birthright citizens except that they are not eligible to become President or Vice President. Naturalized citizens have been elected to both houses of Congress and appointed as cabinet members and Supreme Court justices.

Not all immigrants wish to be naturalized. Of the 352,070 immigrants admitted in 1977, just over half—52.8 percent—had been naturalized 20 years later. Immigrants from some countries were more likely to become citizens than those from others. More than three-fifths of all 1977 immigrants from China, Colombia, Cuba, Guyana, India, Korea, the Philippines, and the former Soviet Union had been naturalized by 1997, while fewer than a third of those from Canada, Germany, Italy, Mexico, and the United Kingdom had done so. In 1997 598,225 people were naturalized.

SEE ALSO

Alien; Citizen; Nationality; Naturalization policy

FURTHER READING

Bredbenner, Candice Lewis. *A Nationality of Her Own :Women, Marriage, and the Law of Citizenship.* Berkeley: University of California Press, 1998.

United States Department of Justice, Immigration and Naturalization Service. *A Guide to Naturalization.* Washington, D.C.: The Service, 1998.

Naturalization policy

Naturalization policy, which governs the way foreigners may obtain citizenship, begins with the U.S. Constitution, Art. 1, Sec. 8, which empowered Congress to "establish a uniform Rule of Naturalization." In 1790 the first naturalization act provided for the naturalization of "free white persons"; Congress clearly meant to bar naturalization of indentured servants and blacks. In 1868, the 14th Amendment to the Constitution, adopted after the Civil War, made the former slaves who had been born in the United States citizens: "all persons born or naturalized in the United States . . . are citizens of the United States and of the State wherein they reside."

In 1870 Congress expanded those eligible for naturalization to include all "white persons" and "persons of African descent." Congress specifically rejected a proposal by Senator Charles Sumner of Massachusetts to open naturalization to all. Asians were still ineligible for naturalization, and the fact that they were "aliens ineligible to citizenship" made certain kinds of legal discrimination, such as limiting their ability to own land or enter certain professions, easier. In 1943 the right of naturalization was extended to Chinese, in 1946 to Filipinos and "natives of India," and in 1952 to members of all ethnic and racial groups so that naturalization was, for the first time, "color blind."

SEE ALSO
Aliens ineligible to citizenship; Chinese Exclusion Acts; Citizenship; 14th Amendment; Immigration Act of 1952; Nationality; Naturalization

Nicaraguans

- *1990 Ancestry: 177,077*
- *Immigration, 1986–96: 79,763*
- *Immigration, 1820–1996: n.a.*
- *Major period of immigration: 1970s+*
- *Major areas of settlement: Florida, California*

Nicaragua, a nation in Central America, has a population of nearly 4.5 million in a country of 49,579 square miles, which makes it a little bigger than Pennsylvania. The people are almost all mestizo, that is, of European and indigenous descent. Spanish is almost universally spoken and the overwhelming majority are Roman Catholics. Nicaragua was conquered by the Spanish in 1522, and after its independence in 1821 was first part of Mexico and then of a short-lived Central American Federation before declaring itself a separate country in 1838.

From the mid-19th century both Britain and the United States sought influence in Nicaragua, and well into the 20th century there were projects, never realized, for an isthmian canal through Nicaragua from the Caribbean to the Pacific. (It was built in Panama instead.) U.S. Marines occupied Nicaragua almost continuously between 1912 and 1933. During much of that time the United States was opposed by guerrilla forces led by a prominent politician, Augusto César Sandino. Shortly after the Marines left, the Somoza family arranged the murder of Sandino and soon seized power in Nicaragua and instituted a brutal dictatorship that lasted more than 40 years. It was overthrown in 1979 by a coalition.

Eventually a radical faction known as the Sandinistas (after Sandino) seized power and soon came into conflict with the United States, which threw its support to anti-Sandinista counterrevolutionary forces popularly known as the Contras. The Sandinistas were defeated in an election in 1990, which installed a democratic government but did not end the turmoil and violence.

Opposition to the Somoza regime in the 1970s and to the Sandinista regime created intolerable conditions for many Nicaraguans and led to the first numerically significant immigration to the United States. That immigration has come in three distinct phases: the first and smallest group came in the 1970s as opponents of the Somoza regime. After the Sandinista victory in 1979 came many supporters of the former regime, including members of the Somoza family, and, after 1990, many supporters of the Sandinistas left. More than 25,000 Nicaraguans have been granted refugee and asylee status since the late 1970s, many more than from any other New World country except Cuba. The INS and the Census Bureau have estimated that there were 70,000 Nicaraguans illegally in the United States in 1996, ranking it ninth among the nations from which such immigrants came.

SEE ALSO

Asylees; Central Americans; Hispanics; Illegal immigrants; Mestizo; Panama; Refugees

FURTHER READING

Cruz, Arturo J., and Jaime Suchliki. *The Impact of Nicaraguans in Miami.* Coral Gables, Fla.: Institute of Interamerican Studies, University of Miami, 1990.
Hart, Dianne Walta. *Undocumented in L.A.: An Immigrant's Story.* Wilmington, Del.: SR Books, 1997.

Nisei

A Nisei is the American-born child of an immigrant from Japan—in other words, a second-generation Japanese American. The word *Nisei* is an adjectival form of the Japanese word for "two" that literally means "second generation." Unlike their Issei parents, Nisei were birthright citizens. Persons of subsequent generations are called *Sansei*, *Yonsei*, and *Gosei*, forms of the words for "three," "four," and "five."

SEE ALSO

Issei; Japanese Americans

Norwegians

- *1990 Ancestry: 3,869,395*
- *Immigration, 1986–96: 5,199*
- *Immigration, 1820–1996: 804,813*
- *Major period of immigration: 1865–1930*
- *Major areas of settlement: Minnesota, Wisconsin, North Dakota; Pacific Northwest; Brooklyn, New York*

The first "Norwegians" to come to America were the Vikings who came with Leif Eriksson to the short-lived colony in Newfoundland, Canada around A.D. 1000. In modern times Norwegian immigration dates from the early 19th century. Nowhere else in

A group of Norwegian immigrants rowed out to a ship to begin their journey to America in 1906.

Norwegian American children form a Norwegian flag at the Minnesota State Fair in 1925 to commemorate 100 years of Norwegian immigration.

19th-century Europe was the pressure of population on arable land as severe as in Norway. Although not a small country—its 125,000 square miles make it about the size of New Mexico —only about 4 percent of its mountainous land can be farmed. A 50 percent increase in population during the first half of the 19th century meant that by 1850 an absolute majority of Norway's rural population owned no land, and there were few urban employment opportunities in Norway.

Although some Norwegians came to the United States in the decades before the Civil War, the major period of their migration was after 1865. They came primarily to the rural regions of the north central states—particularly Wisconsin, Minnesota, and the Dakotas—which were being developed at that time and where land could be obtained free or at very little cost. Until about 1890 almost all Norwegian settlement in America was agricultural, as was much of it after that. There was a flurry of Norwegian immigration in the years after World War II, when nearly 50,000 came between 1945 and 1970, but relatively few have come after that.

The major urban concentration of Norwegians was in Brooklyn, New York, where a community of perhaps 50,000 Norwegians developed. Most of them were people involved in seafaring—Norway had a very large merchant marine—and many Norwegians migrated to American informally as seamen who simply walked off their ships and never went back.

Almost all Norwegians and Norwegian Americans are Protestants. In the United States Norwegian Americans churchgoers are usually members of one of the many Lutheran synods.

Norwegians tended to put down roots in specific areas where they were often in a majority so that they were able rather soon after their large migration to elect members of their community to state and federal political office. In 1910 just more than half of all Norwegian-born persons lived in just three states: a quarter in Minnesota, a sixth in Wisconsin, and an eighth in North Dakota.

Norwegians created a large cultural apparatus in America. There were some 800 Norwegian-American publications, most of them published in Dano-Norwegian, as were large numbers of plays, short stories, and novels. Most were not memorable, but one Norwegian immigrant, Ole E. Rolvaag, is one of the rare authors who, while living in the United States, wrote important works of literature in a non-

English language. His novels, the most important of which is *Giants in the Earth* (English translation 1927), are realistic depictions of the struggles, both physical and psychological, of Norwegian families on the American prairies. When some called his books "emigrant literature," he replied that they were "American literature in the Norwegian language."

Norwegians founded a number of colleges, beginning with Luther College in Decorah, Iowa, in 1861. Although these were established to train ministers—as Harvard and Yale were in the 17th century—many have endured to become essentially secular institutions. The most prestigious college founded by Norwegians is St. Olaf's, which opened in Northfield, Minnesota, in 1874 and is currently rated as one of the finest private colleges in the Midwest.

SEE ALSO
Scandinavians

FURTHER READING
Blegen, Theodore C. *Norwegian Migration to America*. Northfield, Minn.: Norwegian-American Historical Association, 1931.
Gjerde, Jon. *From Peasants to Farmers: The Migration from Balestrand, Norway to the Middle West*. New York: Cambridge University Press, 1985.
Overland, Orm. *The Western Home: A Literary History of Norwegian America*. Urbana: University of Illinois Press, 1996.

Omanis

SEE Arabs

Order of the Star Spangled Banner

SEE Know Nothing movement

Orientals

Once commonly used to describe both Asians and Asian Americans, "Orientals" is now regarded as derogatory and an aspect of anti-Asian stereotypes.

SEE ALSO
Asian Americans; Stereotype

Ozawa v. *U.S.*

Ozawa v. *U.S.* was a Supreme Court case of 1922 that denied the right of Takao Ozawa, an acculturated immigrant from Japan, to become a naturalized citizen, purely on the grounds of his race. The Court's decision was based on the naturalization law of the United States, which at that time limited naturalization to "white persons" and "persons of African descent." The Court made this decision even though it granted that, in every other way, Ozawa, who had been in the United States since 1894 and had been trying to become a citizen since 1902, was a good candidate for citizenship except for his race.

This decision settled the question of naturalization for Japanese until the law was changed in 1952. A few Japanese who had fought in the U.S. Army were allowed to be naturalized because Congress had passed a law granting an accelerated right to citizenship to any alien who served during World War I. The dual significance of the *Ozawa* case was that Japanese—and by extension other Asians—could not become naturalized citizens and that it was "safe" for Congress and the states to discriminate against immigrant Asians by using the "aliens ineligible to citizenship" formula, which had been used since 1913 by California and other western states chiefly as a means of blocking Asian immigrants from acquiring farmland. The decision would be slightly modified in *U.S. v. Thind*.

SEE ALSO

Aliens ineligible to citizenship; Citizen; Japanese; Nationality; Naturalization; Naturalization policy; *U.S. v. Thind*

Pacific Islanders

- *1990 Census: 365,054*
- *Major areas of settlement: Hawaii, California*

In 1990 the U.S. Census Bureau listed 24 different "Pacific Islander" ethnicities under three umbrella headings: Polynesian, Micronesian, and Melanesian. Polynesians included Hawaiians, Samoans, Tahitians, and Tongans. Micronesians included Guamanians, Saipanese, and Tinian Islanders. Marshalese included Marshall Islanders, Eniwetok Islanders, Bikini Islanders, Kwajalein Islanders, and a number of other groups. Melanesians included Fijians and several other groups. The most numerous Pacific Islander groups in the United States in 1990 were Hawaiians (211,014), Samoans (62,964), Tongans (17,606), and Guamanian (6,808). Most Pacific Islanders live either in Hawaii (162,000) or California (111,000). This arbitrary grouping of people—who have little in common except for a similarity in their geographical location—is useful to government bureaucrats and no one else.

SEE ALSO

Guamanians; Hawaiians; Melanesians; Micronesians; Polynesians; Samoans

FURTHER READING:

Barkan, Elliott R. *Asian and Pacific Islander Migration to the United States: A Model of New Global Patterns*. Westport, Conn.: Greenwood, 1992.

Padrone system

A *padrone*, from the Italian word for "patron" or "boss," was an ethnic labor contractor who served as a middleman between English-speaking employers and non–English-speaking workers. Although some padrones were American-born, most were immigrants who had been in America long enough to learn the language and "the ropes." Padrones assisted immigrants in finding employment, for which they charged the immigrants a fee.

Some merely exploited immigrants; others performed a useful function for both employers and workers. The most notorious padrones were those, most often Italians and Greeks, who in the late 19th and early 20th century exploited very young immigrant youths.

SEE ALSO

Contract labor; Greeks; Italians

FURTHER READING

Saloutos, Theodore. *A History of the Greeks in the United States*. Cambridge: Harvard University Press, 1964.
Zucchi, John. *The Little Slaves of the Harp: Italian Child Street Musicians in Nineteenth-Century Paris, London, and New York*. Montreal: McGill–Queen's University Press, 1992.

Page Act

SEE Chinese Exclusion Acts

Pakistanis

- *1990 Ancestry: 99,974*
- *Immigration, 1986–96: 105,967*
- *Immigration, 1954–96: 163,131*
- *Major periods of immigration: 1900–17, 1965+*
- *Major area of settlement: California*

Pakistan did not exist as a nation until 1947, when the former British colony of India was divided into two nations, India and Pakistan. Before that time there had been small numbers of immigrants from what is now Pakistan who are included in the article on Asian Indians. Pakistan is a large country of more than 300,000 square miles—15 percent larger than Texas—with 135 million people. It is a Muslim state, but a significant minority of those who have immigrated from what is now Pakistan are Sikhs. In addition, since Pakistan is usually the nation of first asylum for Afghans, many of the Afghan refugees who have settled in the United States have come via Pakistan.

Little has been written about Pakistani Americans, but their socioeconomic profile is somewhat similar to that of Asian Indians. Whereas the earliest immigrants were largely agricultural laborers with a sprinkling of merchants, recent immigrants have tended to be professionals, particularly physicians.

SEE ALSO

Afghans; Asian Indians; Muslims; Sikhs

FURTHER READING

Kitano, Harry H. L., and Roger Daniels. *Asian Americans: Emerging Minorities.* New York: Prentice-Hall, 2nd ed., 1995.
Leonard, Karen I. *The South Asian Americans.* Westport, Conn.: Greenwood, 1997.

Palestinians

SEE Arabs

Panamanians

- *1990 Ancestry: 88,649*
- *Immigration, 1986–96: 30,592*
- *Immigration, 1820–1996: n.a.*
- *Major periods of immigration: 1914–20s, 1965+*
- *Major areas of settlement: New York, New Orleans, Boston*

Panama, the Panamanian homeland, is a narrow isthmus connecting Central and South America. Fewer than 3 million people live in its 29,760 square miles, making it a little smaller than South Dakota. Much of it is still wilderness. The population is ethnically diverse, owing largely to the building of the Panama Canal (1904–14), which brought workers from all over the world, but particularly blacks from the Caribbean, to Panama. Perhaps 70 percent of the population is mestizo, 14 percent is of Afro-Caribbean descent, 10 percent Euro-American, and 6 percent Native American. Spanish is the official language, and some 85 percent are Roman Catholics and the remainder Protestant.

Panama was visited by Christopher Columbus and settled by the Spanish early in the 16th century. The native American population was all but wiped out by the Spanish and the diseases they brought with them. In 1513 Vasco Núñez de Balboa crossed the isthmus and became the first European to see the western shore of the New World. The isthmus became important as a way of transporting the Inca treasure of

clear how the misnomer arose, but perhaps in the 18th century someone asked a German immigrant what he was and received the answer, "*Ich bin Deutsch*" ("I am German"), and thought *Deutsch* was "Dutch." In any event, the phrase stands, and, in late 19th- and early 20th-century America it was common to nickname a German or German American person "Dutch," or "Dutchy."

SEE ALSO
Amish; Germans; Mennonites; Swiss

Persians

SEE   Iranians; Zoroastrians

Peruvians

- *1990 Ancestry: 161,866*
- *Immigration, 1986–96: 109,299*
- *Immigration, 1820–1996: n.a.*
- *Major periods of immigration: 1970s+*
- *Major areas of settlement: New York, Los Angeles, Miami, Washington, D.C., San Francisco*

Peru, which has a population of about 25 million, is a country on the Pacific side of South America covering 496,220 square miles, almost twice the size of Texas. It was the home of the Incas, who developed one of the most advanced pre-Columbian civilizations. Its people today are about 45 percent Incan and other native American groups, 37 percent mestizo, 15 percent of European ancestry, with smaller numbers of descendants of African, Japanese, and Chinese minorities. Both Spanish and Quechua, the language of the Incas, are official languages and almost all Peruvians are Roman Catholic.

Peru was conquered by the Spanish in 1532 and much of its great wealth was looted. It became independent in 1821. Its ruling classes, both European and mestizo, imported some African slaves and, from the mid-19th century on, first Chinese and then Japanese indentured servants.

Almost none of the Peruvian immigrants to the United States have been of Native American descent. The first immigrants from Peru came in the California gold rush of 1849–50, although there were not very many of them. For almost the next century most Peruvians who went overseas went to Europe. During World War II the U.S. government brought some 1,800 Japanese Peruvians to the United States and interned them in Immigration and Naturalization camps. After the war Peru would not take them back, and many were sent to Japan; others remained in the United States and many of them became American citizens. Many were resettled in Seabrook, New Jersey. In 1998 the U.S. government paid each surviving Japanese Peruvian who had been interned a token compensation of $5,000. Ironically, a Peruvian-born Japanese, Alberto Fujimori, was elected president of Peru in 1990.

Relatively heavy immigration from Peru to the United States began in the 1970s, spurred by chaotic conditions in Peru and made easier by the Immigration Act of 1965. The migration of Peruvians has been largely of middle-class families, most of whom have come legally, although 17,802 received amnesty under the 1986 Immigration Act. In 1995 the INS estimated that another 30,000 Peruvians were in the country illegally. Because Peru is so far away, illegal immigration can be very expensive: one scholar has reported that in the early 1990s Peruvians were paying $5,000 to $7,000 for a trip from Peru to New York City.

Like many other middle-class Latin American families, Peruvians in the United States have a special celebration for their daughters at or close to their 15th birthday. Called a *quinceañera,* the party is similar to the "sweet sixteen" parties celebrated by many other Americans.

SEE ALSO

Illegal immigrants; Immigration Act of 1965; Immigration Act of 1986; Indentured servants; Internment; Japanese; Mestizo; Slave trade; South America

FURTHER READING

Gardiner, C. Harvey. *Pawns in a Triangle of Hate: The Peruvian Japanese and the United States.* Seattle: University of Washington Press, 1981.

Picture brides

The term *picture bride* was coined in the first decade of the 20th century to describe a procedure by which Japanese men in the United States and Hawaii arranged for marriages with women in Japan whom they had never seen. The two would exchange photographs, a legal proxy marriage—a marriage in which one or both partners is not present—would take place in Japan, and the bride would cross the Pacific to join her new husband. Korean immigrants in Hawaii used the same term and practice.

Although the term was coined in the 20th century, heavily male immigrant communities had been importing brides since the English residents of the Jamestown colony did so early in the 17th century.

SEE ALSO

Japanese; Koreans; Women

Pierce v. *Society of Sisters*

The Oregon legislature was opposed to both Catholic schools and instruction in foreign languages, so it barred all private schools in an attempt to get around previous Supreme Court decisions, especially *Meyer v. Nebraska,* that had ruled that it was unconstitutional to bar instruction on those grounds. The U.S. Supreme Court, in the case of *Pierce* v. *Society of Sisters* in 1925, declared the law unconstitutional. In the 1920s Oregon was one of the strongholds of the Ku Klux Klan.

SEE ALSO

Education; Ku Klux Klan; Language schools; *Meyer v. Nebraska*; Nativism; Parochial schools

Photos like these of Fumi and Kentaro Akashi, a Japanese picture bride and her husband, were for use by immigration officials.

Pilgrims

The Pilgrims were a group of Protestant separatists, or dissenters from the Church of England, living in the village of Scrooby, in Nottinghamshire, who in 1607 emigrated to Leiden in what is now the Netherlands. They believed that they could practice their version of Christianity more freely there. Although not persecuted in Leiden, many felt out of place and, in 1620, a part of that congregation embarked for America via England. They traveled on the ship *Mayflower*.

The 32 Pilgrims from Leiden were only a minority of its 102 passengers, and many of the others were not separatists. But the well-organized Leiden group was clearly in charge. The Pilgrims sometimes referred to themselves as "Saints" and called the other passengers "Strangers." In December 1620, not exactly the best time of year to move to New England, they landed and established the Plymouth Colony. Although they were not the first English settlers in North America and were soon overshadowed by the more numerous and influential Puritans, the Pilgrims enjoy a special place in American history and mythology. They were the first group of colonists to come primarily for religious motives, and their gentle image and untypical good relations with Indians make them a group Americans like to remember. A harvest festival first celebrated with the neighboring Wampanoag Indians in October 1621 is the feast commemorated as Thanksgiving.

Their agreement of government, the Mayflower Compact, a document signed just before they landed, is the earliest American document that can be called a "constitution." The most

notable Pilgrim was William Bradford, who was elected governor 30 times and wrote the *History of Plymouth Plantation*, the most important history written in 17th-century America (although it was not published until 1856).

SEE ALSO

English; Mayflower Compact; Protestants; Puritans; Religion

FURTHER READING

Morison, Samuel E., ed. *Of Plymouth Plantation*. New York: Modern Library, 1967.
Willison, George F. *Saints and Strangers*. New York: Reynal & Hitchcock, 1945.

A postage stamp from 1920 commemorates the 300th anniversary of the Pilgrims' landing. Many contemporary historians feel that traditional histories have overemphasized the Pilgrims.

Pluralism

SEE Cultural pluralism

Poles

- *1990 Ancestry: 9,366,106*
- *Immigration, 1986–96: 191,338*
- *Immigration, 1820–1996: around 3.2 million*
- *Major period of immigration: 1880s–1920*
- *Major areas of settlement: Great Lakes states, New York*

Except for about 100 soldiers who fought for American independence, such as Casimir Pulaski and Tadeusz Kósciuszko, few Poles came to the United States before the end of the 18th century. In 1795, after a series of wars, the territory of the Poles was divided between Prussia (later Germany), Russia, and the Austro-Hungarian empire. It remained divided until the re-creation of the Polish state in 1919. Thus the 2.5 million Poles who came between those years did not appear in the American immigration statistics, which record nationality but not ethnicity.

A few thousand Poles came in the first half of the 19th century. About 1,000 refugees from a failed revolution in Russian Poland in 1830–31 were the largest group. The first Polish group settlement in 1854, led by a Franciscan priest, created a farming community southeast of San Antonio, Texas, named Panna Maria for the Virgin Mary.

From then until the early 1890s some 400,000 came, largely from German Poland. Most Poles from Austria and Russia came after 1890. Perhaps 800,000 came from Austria, half of them in the 1890s; another 800,000 came from Russian Poland, about four-fifths of them after 1900. The different migration patterns were caused largely by the availability of transportation and by differing laws in the three countries. Most Poles came to America through one of the two great German emigration ports, Hamburg and Bremen, although a sizable minority came through Trieste, then an Austrian seaport.

Except for the soldiers and the political refugees, who were from elite groups, most migrating Poles were devoutly Catholic, upwardly mobile peasants or workers. Poles came, as they put it, *za chlebem* ("for bread").

Unlike the persecuted Jews or the often desperately poor Irish, most Poles believed that they would return to their homeland. Many considered themselves sojourners only temporarily in America, intending to work hard to earn enough money to buy land—or more land—back in Poland. Sojourners generally adapted to American life more slowly than immigrants who come intending to stay. Of course, some who came to sojourn never went back to Poland, although large numbers, perhaps a third, did return.

While family groups came, often in serial migration, about two-thirds of Polish immigrants were male. Although almost all had been peasants in Poland, only about 10 percent were able to settle on the land in America. Like most immigrants of their era, they settled in cities. Chicago quickly became, and remains, the "capital" of American Polonia. Estimates for 1920 show 400,000 Polish Americans there, 200,000 in New York, and 100,000 or more in four other cities: Pittsburgh, Buffalo, Milwaukee, and Detroit.

Most Poles earned their bread in factory work and mining, often hard, dirty, and dangerous work. A Polish folk song of this era, "When I Journeyed from America," is about a father

This 1888 Pittsburgh newspaper illustration, captioned "'Moving In' during a Rainstorm—An Incident of Polish Miners' Life in Pennsylvania," documents some of the hardships endured by working-class immigrants.

who leaves his family, goes to America, works in a foundry, and returns, via New York and Hamburg, finally arriving in Krakow where

> . . . my wife was waiting for me,
> And my children did not know me,
> For they fled from me, a stranger,
> "My dear children, I'm your papa;
> Three long years I have not seen you.

The two cultural traits most commonly associated with Polish Americans are a strong nationalism and a devout Catholic faith. The nationalism can be seen in immigrant support for various nationalistic organizations, such as the Polish National Alliance and the Polish Roman Catholic Union, which both lobbied for an independent Poland. Yet support for Poland and for these organizations did *not* mean a lack of loyalty to America, any more than did Irish or Jewish support for Ireland or Israel. As was the case with other Slavic ethnic groups under Austrian domination, Poles organized sokols, gymnastic organizations that had important social and patriotic functions, and established them in America.

Almost all ethnic Poles were Catholics, and their support for Catholicism was exceptional in several ways. In 1921 about two-thirds of all Polish American schoolchildren attended one of the more than 500 Polish parochial schools. In most of them the teaching was in Polish, often by nuns who knew little English. This slowed acculturation to American society. The combination of high degrees of nationalism and devoutness produced, ironically, the only significant schism or heresy ever developed within American Catholicism.

The schism developed from the resentment Polish Americans felt about Irish American domination of the church. As one Polish-born American

priest who did *not* break away put it just after 1900, there ought to be "Polyglot Bishops for a Polyglot Church." ("Polyglot" means "many languages.") What they wanted were Polish American bishops, but none were appointed. One priest, the Reverend Francis Hodur in the mining region of Pennsylvania, founded the breakaway Polish National Catholic Church in 1904, which still exists, largely in Pennsylvania. It has perhaps 250,000 communicants. By comparison, some 5 million Polish Americans are Roman Catholics. Not surprisingly, the first Polish American Catholic bishop, Paul Rhode, was appointed in 1908.

Electoral success for Polish American politicians came more slowly for than some ethnic groups. Edmund S. Muskie, longtime United States senator from Maine who was the Democratic nominee for Vice President in 1968 and served as secretary of state in 1980, has

This building at Division and Noble Streets in Chicago housed a Polish American ethnic organization, the Kosciusko Guards. American flags show their patriotism.

been the most successful Polish American politician.

During and immediately after World War II some 150,000 Poles came to America, largely as displaced persons, and throughout the Cold War era a small but steady stream of refugees from Poland settled in the United States, often joining relatives and friends in Chicago and other centers of Polish American population. Similar immigration has continued in recent years.

SEE ALSO

Austro-Hungarian Empire; Jews; Sokols

FURTHER READING

Bukowczyk, John J. *And My Children Did Not Know Me*. Bloomington: Indiana University Press, 1987.

Greene, Victor R. *The Slavic Community on Strike: Immigrant Labor in Pennsylvania Anthracite*. Notre Dame, Ind.: University of Notre Dame Press, 1968.

Pula, James S. *Polish Americans: An Ethnic Community*. New York: Twayne, 1995.

Polish National Catholic Church

Formed in 1904 in Nanticoke, in the coal region of Pennsylvania, the Polish National Catholic Church is the result of the only enduring schism from the Roman Catholic Church that has occurred in the United States. In the mid-1960s it claimed 500,000 adherents, about a tenth of the 5 million Polish American Catholics at that time. Although a standard history of American Catholicism dismisses the church as a formation resulting from quarrels about church property and ecclesiastical jurisdiction, it was really a result of Polish American nationalism and a feeling that, within the church, Polish Americans

were not adequately represented. It is not insignificant that, four years after the church was founded, the first Roman Catholic church appointed its first Polish American bishop, Paul Rhode.

SEE ALSO

Poles; Religion; Roman Catholics

FURTHER READING

Ellis, John Tracy. *American Catholicism*. 2nd ed. Chicago: University of Chicago Press, 1969.

Wldarski, Szczepan. *The Origin and Growth of the Polish National Catholic Church*. Scranton, Pa.: Polish National Catholic Church, 1974.

Polynesians

- *1990 Census: 296,145*
- *Major areas of settlement: Hawaii, California*

Polynesia, a Greek word meaning "many islands," is the name imposed on a number of ethnically and linguistically similar peoples who speak Malayo-Polynesian languages. Polynesia is one of the three main divisions of Oceania in the South and central Pacific Ocean. The larger islands are volcanic; the smaller ones are generally coral formations. The principal groups are the Hawaiian Islands, Samoa, Tonga, and the islands of French Polynesia. Ethnologically, though not geographically, the Maori, the first settlers of New Zealand, are Polynesian, but New Zealand is not considered a part of Polynesia.

The three major groups of Polynesians in the United States in 1990 were Hawaiians (211,014), Samoans (62,964), and Tongans (17,606). Polynesians are grouped by the Census Bureau with Micronesians and Melanesians as "Pacific Islanders."

SEE ALSO
Hawaiians; Pacific Islanders; Samoans

Portuguese

- *1990 Ancestry: 1,153,351*
- *Immigration, 1986–96: 35,791*
- *Immigration, 1880–1996: 731,892*
- *Major periods of immigration: 1900–24, 1958+*
- *Major areas of settlement: New England, especially Massachusetts, and California.*

[This article does not consider Cape Verdeans, who were Portuguese until 1975 and are included in the data above. They are discussed at "Cape Verdeans."]

Although Portugal was one of the great maritime nations from the 15th century onward, its energies in the New World were chiefly directed not to North America but to Brazil, which remained a Portuguese colony until 1822. The earliest people of Portuguese birth we know about in colonial America were Sephardic Jews, such as the Newport, Rhode Island, merchant Aaron Lopez. The earliest ethnic Portuguese immigrants were almost certainly sailors who signed on to American whalers that stopped in the Azores, nine Atlantic islands about 800 miles off the coast of Portugal. The Portuguese had colonized the Azores in the 15th century. In any event, "Portygees" were a small but prominent part of New England's maritime population, as reflected by the Portuguese among the crew of the *Pequod* in Herman Melville's novel *Moby-Dick* (1851).

Whaling ships took Portuguese islanders not only to New England but also to Hawaii. A numerically significant Portuguese migration to Hawaii

A Portuguese American ship chandler in Provincetown, Massachusetts, dips fishing nets into a wax preservative, which prevents rotting.

began about 1878; for a time Portuguese were contract laborers but soon took and intermediary role as overseers, or *lunas*, between Asian contract workers and American managers. One scholar reports that in 1915, Portuguese workers there averaged $2.24 a day, while Japanese received $1.86 and Americans got $3.82. Many Portuguese, discouraged by the labor conditions in the Islands, remigrated to California, while others returned home, although a minority made the Islands their permanent home.

A small group of persons from Madeira (an island about 400 miles off the Atlantic coast of Morocco) who had become converted to Protestantism emigrated in the 1840s, first to Trinidad and them to central Illinois. Although Portuguese Atlantic islanders predominated in the relatively small Portuguese immigration—fewer than 30,000 persons before 1890—there was some immigration from Portugal proper. A grandfather of the American novelist John Dos Passos, for example, emigrated to Baltimore about 1830.

In the 1890s a much heavier immigration set in, and more than 200,000 persons came between then and 1924. Much of this migration was triggered by political change in their homeland.

The last king of Portugal fled to England in 1910, and the early years of the new republic were difficult. This flow was increased in 1916 when Portugal entered World War I on the side of the Allies, which caused many to leave to avoid military service. The immigrants of this period settled largely in New England, and many Portuguese worked and were recruited for New England textile mills. Later Portuguese exiles from political upheavals in 1926 and 1974 went to Brazil rather than to the United States.

After World War II a number of factors contributed to continued Portuguese immigration. One was the breakup of the Portuguese colonial empire. One small group, perhaps 4,000 strong, were from Macao, a Portuguese possession in China from 1557 to 1999, which is just a 40-mile ferry ride southwest of Hong Kong, Most of this group, who are ethnically Chinese or part Chinese and call themselves "Luso-Sino-Americans" (Portuguese Chinese Americans) settled in California. These are well-educated people who have become entrepreneurs and professionals in America. They have

their own small organization, Uniao Macaense Americana (American Macao Union), with chapters in four California cities. Other Portuguese persons came later from Portugal's dissolving empire in Africa. A third group of Portuguese came from the Azores after devastating volcanic eruptions and earthquakes in 1958: Congress passed a special bill enabling perhaps 5,000 to come; these immigrants began a chain migration process that is still continuing.

Portuguese are predominantly Roman Catholics and some 40 Portuguese "national parishes" have been created since the first was established in New Bedford, Massachusetts in 1869. All but a handful of these parishes have been in New England and in recent years many have been named "Our Lady of Fátima," after the Portuguese village of Fátima at which, in 1917, a vision of the Virgin Mary was reported to have appeared to three shepherd children. Because the Portuguese Cape Verdeans were a racially mixed group of both African and European origins, they and to a lesser degree other Portuguese Americans have been and are subjected to racial prejudice in the

These Portuguese American children are in a Catholic school in New Bedford, Massachusetts, a center of Portuguese America.

United States. This has caused some Portuguese Americans of European heritage to deemphasize or even deny their Portuguese heritage. Perhaps for this reason there are relatively few Portuguese American organizations. The largest is a fraternal benefit association, the Portuguese Continental Union of the United States.

SEE ALSO

Cape Verdeans; Chain migration; Jews; Refugees

FURTHER READING

Baganha, Maria Ioannis Benis. *Portuguese Emigration to the United States, 1820–1930.* New York: Garland, 1990.

Pap, Leo. *The Portuguese Americans.* Boston: Twayne, 1981.

Preference system

The preference system has been established by Congress and is a fundamental part of American immigration policy. It dictates which immigrants have priority for visas to enter the United States. The United States has had such a system since 1921. Since fiscal 1992 the following preferences have been in effect, but they ignore immigrants who enter outside of the preference system: spouses and minor children of U.S. citizens and refugees, including asylees. The two basic categories of preferences are family related and job related.

Family preferences are, in rank order: unmarried adult sons and daughters of U.S. citizens; spouses, children, and unmarried sons and daughters of permanent resident aliens; married sons and daughters of U.S. citizens; and brothers and sisters of U.S. citizens.

Job-related preferences, also in rank order, are: priority workers (per-

sons of extraordinary ability, outstanding professors and researchers, and certain executives and managers of multinational companies); professionals with advanced degrees or aliens with exceptional abilities; skilled workers, professionals (without advanced degrees), and needed unskilled workers; special immigrants; and employment-creation immigrants (people who agree to invest a specific amount of money in employment-creating businesses).

In 1996, of a total of 915,900 immigrants admitted, 713,763, or 77.9 percent, were admitted under the preference system. Of these, 596,264 (65.1 percent of all immigrants) came in as family members, while 117,499 (12.8 percent) entered on employment-based preferences. Another 58,790 (6.4 percent) entered under diversity programs, and 143,163 (15.6 percent) immigrants entered outside of the preference system.

SEE ALSO

Diversity programs; Immigration policy

FURTHER READING

Daniels, Roger. *Coming to America: A History of Immigration and Ethnicity in American Life.* New York: HarperCollins, 1990.

Prejudice

Prejudice literally means pre-judgment, or the formation of an opinion (usually unfavorable) without knowledge or sound reasoning. It is something that most newcomer groups in American society have faced from the colonial era to the present. Prejudice has focused on mainly on religion, ethnicity, and, above all, on race. It should be noted that groups and individuals that have

In 1834 this Massachusetts convent was burned because of rumors of a nun being held there against her will. Between 1834 and the mid-1850s more than a dozen Catholic churches were destroyed nationwide.

been the subjects of prejudice often have prejudices of their own. Prejudice is primarily an attitude, but it is an attitude that often leads to discrimination. Discrimination can be defined as prejudice in action.

SEE ALSO
Discrimination; Nativism; Racism; Stereotype

FURTHER READING
Montagu, M. F. Ashley. *Man's Most Dangerous Myth: The Fallacy of Race.* New York: Harper, 1952.

Protestants

Protestant is the name given to the followers of the religious reformers such as the German Martin Luther and the French John Calvin, who set off what Protestant historians call the Protestant Reformation and Catholic historians call the Protestant Revolt. The vast majority of the Europeans who came to what is now the United States in the colonial period, and for half a century thereafter, were Protestants of various denomina-

tions; most of them were extremely anti-Catholic, while most Catholics of that era were extremely anti-Protestant. The nativist movements of the 19th and early 20th centuries had a decided Protestant (anti-Catholic) cast.

SEE ALSO
Nativism; Religion

Puerto Ricans

- *1990 Ancestry: 1,955,323*
- *1990 Census: 2.7 million*
- *Major period of migration: since 1945*
- *Major areas of settlement: New York City and vicinity*

Strictly speaking, Puerto Ricans have not been immigrants since 1898, when the United States annexed their Caribbean island homeland, although there had been a few hundred immigrants before that date. Most of these early immigrants were elite political exiles who hoped to make Puerto Rico an independent nation. When the United States seized Puerto Rico from Spain, the island had a population just

The Puerto Rican Day Parade has taken place in New York City every summer since 1958. In 1999, an estimated 100,000 people marched in the parade and 3 million spectators attended. The flags are Puerto Rican flags.

below 1 million; by the mid-1990s the population was almost 4 million, and approximately 2.7 million persons of Puerto Rican birth or ancestry lived in the United States, about half of them in New York City.

The status of Puerto Rico and Puerto Ricans has changed several times since 1898. For two years after conquest the island was under American military rule. An act of Congress in 1900 gave the islanders some self-government and made them American nationals (the same status held by Filipinos at that time). In 1917 another act of Congress made Puerto Ricans American citizens. Until 1948 the President of the United States appointed the governors of Puerto Rico; since that time they have been elected. In 1952 Puerto Rico became an "*estado libre asociado*," literally, "associated free state," but always translated as Commonwealth.

There has been a Puerto Rican independence movement since the mid-19th century—which has sometimes resorted to terrorism—but in several elections Puerto Ricans have overwhelmingly rejected independence. Under the Commonwealth status agree-ment, Puerto Rico is affected by most federal laws, but neither individuals nor corporations in Puerto Rico pay federal income tax. People living in Puerto Rico elect their own officials but cannot vote for President or send senators and representatives to Washington. They do elect a "resident commissioner" who sits in Congress but has no vote. Puerto Ricans who reside in the United States have all the legal rights and obligations of other U.S. citizens.

Puerto Rico is an island ravaged by great poverty: "the stricken land," was what its last non–Puerto Rican governor, Rexford Guy Tugwell, called it. But Puerto Rico's poverty is relative. On a Caribbean scale, Puerto Ricans have one of the highest, if not the highest, per-capita incomes in the region. But on an American scale, Puerto Rico is poorer than any American state. And it is Puerto Rico's poverty that partly explains its massive migration.

But the ease of that migration is a product of the post–World War II air age. Prior to 1945, travel between Puerto Rico and the American mainland was expensive, slow, and irregular. Some Puerto Ricans did migrate to

New York City during the labor-short World War I years and, by the 1930s there were two small Puerto Rican neighborhoods there, one in Brooklyn and the other on Manhattan's Upper East Side, centered on East 116th Street, which remains the heart of *El Barrio*, as New York's Puerto Ricans call it. Surplus World War II transport planes provided frequent direct air travel between San Juan, the island's capital, and New York City at a price, $50 in the late 1940s, that was equivalent to two weeks' wages. This low and quick air fare also made it possible for many Puerto Ricans to participate in a circular migration in which they went back and forth between the island and the mainland.

In any event the great Puerto Rican migration was on in the later 1940s, and it presaged the migration of other millions from various parts of Latin America in the last half of the 20th century. Few migrant populations have grown so fast. In 1950 there were about 300,000 Puerto Ricans on the mainland; in 1970 almost 1.4 million and about 2.7 million in 1990. Although the 1990 poverty rate for Puerto Ricans in the United States proper was high, it was not as high as the rate in Puerto Rico. On the mainland about three out of ten Puerto Rican families were below the poverty line in 1990, as opposed to about two out of ten Hispanic families, and about 1 out of 10 non-Hispanic families.

Two issues are related to Puerto Rican poverty: race and language. Many Puerto Ricans are of mixed or mestizo ancestry, chiefly European, with a considerable African and a slight Taino (a native Caribbean group) mixture. In Puerto Rico race/color is much less significant than in the United States, and many darker Puerto Ricans encounter a degree of racial discrimina-

tion in the United States unknown on their island. In addition, Puerto Rico is a Spanish-speaking commonwealth, although English is now one of its two official languages. But while many in Puerto Rico grow up able to speak English, usually with a distinct accent, all speak Spanish. Thus, although native-born American citizens, most Puerto Ricans experience severe and immediate culture shock, as most immigrants do, when they come to the mainland. More than a third of the Puerto Ricans living on the mainland in 1990 reported to the Census that they did not speak English "very well." Some children of Puerto Rican migrants who were involved in the circular migration of their parents and went to school in both the United States and Puerto Rico do not speak either language "very well."

On the other hand, many Puerto Rican families of the second and third generation, perhaps a quarter, do not usually speak Spanish at home. As is the case with most persons in poverty and/or of Hispanic ancestry in the United States, the educational achievements

A Puerto Rican nurse (right) attends to a baby in a New York City health clinic. Immigrant medical professionals and paraprofessionals are vital to the American health system, particularly in urban areas and the hospitals that serve them.

of Puerto Ricans are below the national norm, although in recent years their academic profile has improved. In 1970 only 2 percent of Puerto Ricans on the mainland had finished college; in 1990 the figure was almost 10 percent. It is quite noticeable that in Puerto Rican communities outside of the greater New York area, the degree of acculturation to English and of measurable socioeconomic success is higher than in the greater New York area, where "Nuyoricans"—that is, New York- or mainland-born Puerto Ricans, a term that many use—associate largely with others of their own community.

In religion Puerto Ricans are overwhelmingly Roman Catholics but, as was true with many earlier Catholic groups, their style of Catholicism did not also fit comfortably into the American Roman Catholic mode: Puerto Ricans were not in the habit of attending Mass regularly and were not accustomed to supporting local parishes financially. In addition, relatively few Puerto Ricans, either on the island or on the mainland, chose religious vocations. Even in Puerto Rico, the majority of the Roman Catholic clergy are not Puerto Ricans.

Puerto Ricans are an important segment of the growing Hispanic element of the American population and their influence and impact on American life will surely increase as time goes by.

SEE ALSO
Circular migration; Citizen; Filipinos; Hispanics; Mestizo

FURTHER READING
Korrol, Virginia Sánchez. *From Colonia to Community: The History of Puerto Ricans in New York City.* Westport, Conn.: Greenwood, 1983.
Rodriguez, Clara E., and Virginia Sánchez Korrol, eds. *Historical Perspectives on Puerto Rican Survival in the U.S..* Princeton, N.J.: Markus Weiner, 1996.

Pull

Pull is a term used by scholars of immigration to describe the forces that cause people to want to immigrate to a certain country. These forces include economic opportunity, religious and political liberty, peaceful conditions, the presence of family, friends and neighbors who are established there, and an attractive climate. Many immigrants have inaccurate and often too optimistic notions of what life in the new country will be like: the often-stated notion that "in America the streets are paved with gold" is a good example. Even unrealistic expectations, when people act on them, are pull factors.

SEE ALSO
Means; Push

Puritans

The Puritans were a group of 17th-century English Protestant reformers. Unlike the Pilgrims and many other dissenters, they did not wish to separate from the Church of England, but to reform it. A large number of Puritans emigrated to America, and they represent not only one of the largest but also the most influential single religious group to immigrate to colonial America. They came to establish God's commonwealth, what their leader John Winthrop called "a city on a hill." Puritans were in Virginia from the beginnings of settlement there in 1607 and some were in every North American colony, but it is in New England in general and Massachusetts in particular that Puritan numbers and influence were the strongest. In the so-called "Great Migration" between 1628 and 1640, some 20,000 English Puritans settled in Massachusetts and began to build what they believed to be a Bible commonwealth. It leaders, like its first governor John Winthrop, tended to treat the Indians harshly and were intolerant of other religious views. Some leading Puritans, such as Roger Williams and Anne Hutchinson, were exiled for their religious beliefs. Williams, who founded Rhode Island as a haven for religious toleration, believed that "every one should have liberty to worship God according to the light of their consciences." Conversely, most Puritans believed that it was wrong to tolerate religious error. When radical Quakers insisted on preaching and protesting in Massachusetts, they were punished and driven out. When they came back, several, including one woman, were hanged.

Much of what is commonly called "Puritanical" in American culture—such as abstinence from alcohol—has nothing to do with 17th-century Puritan practice. However, even though few historians today would endorse the views of an early 20th-century historian who claimed that "the Puritans provided the leaven which caused the whole loaf of the American people to rise," the ongoing influence of some general Puritan ideals, including respect for education, devotion to public service, and diligence in business, continues to be important in contemporary American life.

SEE ALSO
English; Pilgrims; Protestants; Religion

FURTHER READING
Morgan, Edmund S. *The Puritan Dilemma: The Story of John Winthrop*. Boston: Little, Brown, 1958.
Morison, S. E. *The Builders of the Bay Colony*. 2nd ed. Boston: Houghton Mifflin, 1930.

Push

Push is a term used by scholars of immigration to describe the forces existing in a country that cause people to emigrate from it. These forces include economic hardship, persecution, warfare, desire to avoid military service, and natural disasters.

SEE ALSO
Means; Pull

Qataris

SEE Arabs

Quota Acts

SEE Immigration Act of 1921; Immigration Act of 1924; Immigration Act of 1952; Quota system

Quota system

A quota system, eventually called the National Origins Quota System, was a policy that largely governed immigration to the United States between 1921 and 1965. The quota system assigned numerical annual quotas, or limits on the number of permissible immigrants, to each country. This quota was supposedly based on the number of immigrants who had previously come from that country. It was designed to favor immigrants from northwestern Europe and did not affect immigrants from independent countries of the New World and Canada. During the era of the quota acts there was a parallel system that provided entry without numerical restriction for certain relatives of American citizens.

SEE ALSO

Immigration Act of 1921; Immigration Act of 1924; Immigration Act of 1952; Immigration policy

Racism

Racism is the belief that a particular race or ethnic group is superior and that some others, or all others, are inferior. Its most common and almost universal aspect can be called *ethnocentrism*: the belief that one's own group is the best.

In many "primitive" languages, the particular tribe or group refers to itself as "the people" and all others are called something else. In other words, one's own group is "human" and all others are less than that. In modern times racism has been directed largely at "non-white" groups—particularly blacks, reds, and yellows. Europeans justified their largely successful attempts at imperial conquest by insisting on their own superiority to native peoples in Africa, North and South America, Asia, and Australia and New Zealand.

Slavery and the African slave trade were, in the final analysis, based upon and rationalized by racism, as was its successor, the "coolie trade," which used an indentured labor system as a "new kind of slavery" after the slave trade was abolished in the 19th century.

In the United States, segregation, developed after slavery was abolished,

was based on racism, as was its more extreme form, apartheid, in 20th-century South Africa. In 20th-century Europe, anti-Semitism, the fear and hatred of Jews, which has a centuries-long history, produced under the Nazi regime in Germany (1933–45) the Holocaust, in which at least 6 million people, mostly Jews but including other despised groups such as Gypsies and homosexuals, were put to death with industrial precision and brutality.

SEE ALSO

Discrimination; Nativism; Prejudice; Stereotype

FURTHER READING

Bauer, Yehuda. *A History of the Holocaust.* New York: Franklin Watts, 1982.
Carnes, Jim. *Us and Them: A History of Intolerance in America.* New York: Oxford University Press, 1995.
Montagu, M. F. Ashley. *Man's Most Dangerous Myth: The Fallacy of Race.* New York: Harper, 1952.
Woodward, C. Vann. *The Strange Career of Jim Crow.* 3rd rev. ed. New York: Oxford University Press, 1974.

Redemptioners

Redemptioners is a term used to describe some Scotch-Irish and German indentured servants in the 18th and early 19th centuries who came expecting to be able to buy—or redeem—their freedom before their full terms were served. Unlike other indentured servants who were usually single and worked for the full term of their indenture, the redemptioners tended to be family migrants. Often some of the family came as free people while others came as servants under indentures, expecting that the free members of the family would soon earn enough to buy the freedom of the indentured members, usually children.

SEE ALSO
Indentured servants

FURTHER READING
Salinger, Sharon V. *"To Serve Well and Faithfully": Labor and Indentured Servitude in Pennsylvania, 1682–1800.* New York: Cambridge University Press, 1987.

Refugee Act of 1980

The Refugee Act of 1980, sponsored by the administration of President Jimmy Carter, sought to regularize what had become a disorderly procedure in the admission of refugees. It also broke new ground by creating a new category of refugee, the asylee, a person who fits all the definitions of a refugee but is already in the country, either on a temporary visa of some kind, or illegally. The law placed a theoretical annual numerical cap of 50,000 on refugees and one of 5,000 by asylees, but these were almost immediately exceeded by unforeseen events and court orders.

Within five weeks of the 1980 act becoming law, Cuba's Fidel Castro set off the Mariel boatlift which allowed 125,000 Cubans to leave for the United States by small boats. Although this immigration was illegal under American law, the Carter administration eventually allowed them to remain in the United States. The numbers of refugees and asylees have regularly exceeded the limits set in the law. In 1996, for example, 74,491 refugees and 18,566 asylees were admitted. The Refugee Act, following international precedent, speaks of "a well-founded fear of persecution" as the major criterion for asylum. This can be a very subjective and variable standard, as a comparison of the experience of Haitian and Cuban refugees shows.

Most Haitian applicants have been evaluated as fleeing poor economic conditions, and thus not eligible under the INS definition, while almost all Cubans, regardless of their circumstances, have been favorably evaluated. The initial judgments are made by Immigration and Naturalization Service employees, who are called "immigration judges" but are in fact administrative officers who can be fired for making decisions their supervisors do not like. Increasingly, however, adverse decisions have been appealed to the federal courts who have often overruled the INS.

SEE ALSO
Asylees; Cubans; Haitians; Immigration and Naturalization Service (INS); Immigration policy; Mariel boatlift; Refugees

FURTHER READING
Haines, David W., ed. *Refugees in America in the 1990s: A Reference Handbook.* Westport, Conn.: Greenwood, 1996.

Refugees

A refugee is a person who, because of religious or political—or in some instances personal—persecution, seeks refuge in a foreign country. The term was first used to describe the Huguenots (French Protestants) who fled France after the revocation in 1685 of the Edict of Nantes, a policy that had given them some protection in a mainly Catholic land. In addition to Huguenots, the term *refugee* has been applied to the Tory supporters of the British who left the United States in the era of the American Revolution, to slaveholders and their slaves who fled to the United States after the successful slave revolt in Haiti in 1804, and to former slaves after the American Civil War.

In the early 20th century it was applied to Armenians fleeing Turkish persecution and to Russians escaping the Bolshevik Revolution of 1917. The rise of the Nazis in Germany and other fascist regimes in Europe in the 1930s created a large refugee exodus, but it was World War II and the cold war that followed it (called "cold" because it was not a "hot," or shooting war) that produced millions of refugees—so many, in fact, that some historians have argued that the 20th century should be called the century of the refugee.

Refugees who manage to get out of their own country also become immigrants. Until after World War II, American immigration law made no distinction between immigrants and refugees, and hundreds of thousands of potential refugee immigrants were denied admission to the United States—most often by American consuls abroad—before, during, and just after World War II. Among the some 200,000 refugees who did enter the United States in that era, however, were the most distinguished

and talented immigrants ever to come. These included, to name only a handful, scientists Albert Einstein and Enrico Fermi, author Thomas Mann, composers Béla Bartók and Arnold Schoenberg, and the artists Marc Chagall and Piet Mondrian.

Beginning with the Displaced Persons Acts of 1948 and 1950, American immigration law and policy have enabled millions of refugees from Europe, Asia, Latin America, and Africa to come to the United States. The Refugee Act of 1980, which for the first time provided asylum as well as refuge, still largely governs American refugee policy.

SEE ALSO

Displaced Persons Acts; Huguenots; Immigration policy; Refugee Act of 1980

FURTHER READING

Fleming, Donald, and Bernard Bailyn, eds. *The Intellectual Migration; Europe and America, 1930–1960.* Cambridge: Harvard University Press, 1969.

Haines, David W., ed, *Refugees in America in the 1990s: A Reference Handbook.* Westport, Conn.: Greenwood, 1996.

Jackman, Jarrell C., and Carla M. Borden, eds. *The Muses Flee Hitler: Cultural Transfer and Adaptation, 1930–1945.* Washington, D.C.: Smithsonian Institution Press, 1983.

These two women, Bosnian and Vietnamese, work in a garment factory in Ilion, New York, that employs many refugees. This is a typical immigrant job. The workplace, in this 1992 photograph, seems better lit than most.

Religion

Religion is part of the culture of almost every immigrant and is likely to be the most durable aspect of that culture. Although language tends to disappear in a generation or so, and most aspects of ethnicity fade quickly, religion remains durable for generations and can be regarded as semipermanent. The religious historian Martin Marty put it well when he wrote that "religion is the

A German-language Protestant church in Lawrence, Massachusetts, decorated for a "Dank-Fest" (Festival of Thanks) in 1923.

skeleton of ethnicity," meaning that, in the final analysis, it is often religion that holds ethnicity together over generations. An alternative view holds that, in many instances, "ethnicity is the skeleton of religion."

SEE ALSO

Amish; Buddhists; Copts; Eastern Orthodox churches; Eastern Rite churches; Hinduism; Huguenots; Jews; Language maintenance; Mormons; Muslims; Pilgrims; Polish National Catholic Church; Protestants; Puritans; Roman Catholics; Sikhs; Triple melting pot; Zoroastrians

FURTHER READING

Ahlstrom, Sydney E. *A Religious History of the American People.* New Haven: Yale University Press, 1972.
Marty, Martin E. "Ethnicity: The Skeleton of Religion in America." *Church History* 41 (1972): 5–21.

Remittance

A remittance is money sent by an immigrant in the United States or elsewhere to someone back home, usually a relative or close friend. Although immigrants from most immigrant groups have sent back remittances since the 19th century, the practice has been particularly prevalent among Chinese, Italians, and Dominicans. The latter are currently estimated to be sending back $1 billion annually. In addition, many immigrants of all kinds have purchased tickets to enable friends and family to follow them to the United States, a form of chain migration.

Conversely, a much smaller number of immigrants to the United States have been assisted, typically in the early months or years of migration, by payments sent by family or friends in the old country. An even smaller number of people, largely British, were called "remittance men." For one reason or another, these men were an embarrassment to their families, who were willing to pay them a regular remittance or allowance as long as they would stay abroad—often, but not always, in the United States.

SEE ALSO

Chain migration; Chinese; Dominicans

Restrictive covenant

A restrictive covenant is an agreement, placed in a deed to real estate property, binding the buyer or owner not to sell to certain kinds of persons. The most common restrictive covenant was an agreement to sell to "whites only." These flourished from the late 19th century until 1948. Other covenants—and there could be more than one group restricted in one covenant—barred selling to Jews ("Christians only")—and some were written to screen out particular ethnic groups, such as Chinese, Japanese, Italians, and Armenians.

These covenants were enforceable in many state courts until 1948, when the U.S. Supreme Court, ruling in *Shelley* v. *Kramer*, declared them unconstitutional. The case involved the Shelleys, a black family who purchased a home that was subject to a racially restrictive covenant, and the neighbor who sued to enforce the covenant against them. Many real estate deeds still contain restrictive covenants but they are legally null and void.

SEE ALSO
Discrimination; Prejudice; Racism

Return migration

One of the great myths of American immigration is that everyone wants to come to the United States but no one wants to leave. The fact of the matter is that large numbers of immigrants came planning to return, and, from the earli- est days of European and Asian settle- ment in America, large numbers did so. The U.S. government, however, did not begin to count returning immigrants until 1908. Most authorities believe that during the period of heavy immigration between 1820 and 1908, perhaps one immigrant in three returned home. However, many who returned came back again. Sometimes the process was repeated several times, and, in circular migration, very many times. In the first 90 years of the 20th century it is esti- mated that some 38 million immigrants arrived, while 12 emigrated or returned home, a return rate of almost one in three. During the worst years of the Great Depression, 1930–34, more peo- ple actually emigrated from the United States than entered it.

Since the 1960s the return migra- tion flow has been lower: in the 1980s it was estimated at just over 2 in 10. There are many reasons for return migration. The most common, perhaps, is that the immigrant came intending to sojourn— that is, stay for a while, and then return home. A second reason is disappoint- ment with life in the United States. A third reason is that many immigrants— especially since the creation of the Social Security system in the 1930s—spend a

A group of immigrants pre- pares to return to Europe with their baggage stacked beside them in 1902 or 1903. Per- haps one immi- grant in three in this era went back.

working life in the United States and then return home to retire. Their Social Security checks, which they have earned, are sent to them.

And, just as immigration is not always permanent, neither is return migration. That is, there are people who migrate, return home, and then migrate again.

SEE ALSO

Circular migration; Emigration from the United States; Sojourners

FURTHER READING

Caroli, Betty Boyd. *Immigrants Who Returned Home.* New York: Chelsea House, 1990.
Warren, Robert, and Ellen Percy Kraly. *The Elusive Exodus: Emigration from the United States.* Washington, D.C.: Population Reference Bureau, 1985.
Wyman, Mark. *Round-trip to America: The Immigrants Return to Europe, 1880–1930.* Ithaca, N.Y.: Cornell University Press, 1993.

Revolutions of 1848

The successful February 1848 revolution in France that overthrew the monarchy and established the Second French Republic is thought to have provided the spark that set off revolutions, ultimately unsuccessful, in Germany, Austria, Hungary, what is now the Czech Republic, and Italy. Many of the revolutionary leaders fled, some of them, largely Germans, to the United States.

These German exiles in the United States were called "forty-eighters." The most prominent of these was Carl Schurz, who was a general in the Union Army during the Civil War, a Republican senator from Missouri, and secretary of the interior in Rutherford B. Hayes's cabinet (1877–81).

SEE ALSO

Exiles; Germans; Refugees

FUTHER READING

Evans, R. J. W., and Hartmut Pogge von Strandmann, eds. *The Revolutions in Europe, 1848–1849: From Reform to Reaction.* Oxford: Oxford University Press, 2000.
Trefousse, Hans L. *Carl Schurz, a Biography.* Knoxville: University of Tennessee Press, 1982.

Roman Catholics

Although there were Roman Catholics in Britain's North American colonies from early in the 17th century, mainly in the colony of Maryland, the overwhelming majority of immigrants in the colonial era were Protestants—many of them, like the New England Puritans, fiercely anti-Catholic. The first English-language schoolbook in the colonies, the *New England Primer* (around 1690), called the Pope a "man of sin."

The long series of wars between Britain and France in the 17th and 18th centuries, which in the New World culminated in the French and Indian War (1754–63), increased the fear of Catholics as a subversive influence. During the "long century" of immigration, from 1820 to 1924, an absolute majority of immigrants were Catholics, and the small Roman Catholic church in the United States, which had been composed chiefly of old-stock Americans, soon became an immigrant church. The earliest mass anti-immigrant movement, the Know Nothing movement of the 1840s and 1850s, while opposed to all immigrants, focused on Roman Catholics, particularly the Irish.

In the years after 1870, while the immigration of Irish and German

Puerto Rican Catholics in New York City perform the stations of the cross in a vacant lot on the Lower East Side during the Easter season, 1991. They are enacting an ancient, traditional ritual in a modern, untraditional setting, which is not uncommon for immigrant religious groups.

Catholics continued, much larger numbers of Catholics came from southern and eastern Europe, particularly from Italy and Poland. In the 1880s and 1890s a second anti-immigrant, anti-Catholic mass movement, the American Protective Association, enjoyed a brief notoriety. And, in the 1910s and 1920s, the second Ku Klux Klan focused its hatred on immigrants and Roman Catholics even more than on African Americans.

One of the issues that continues to cause dissent between Catholics and other Americans is education. In the 19th century most Catholics resented the clear Protestant bias in the public schools, and widespread support for private parochial schools was the result. By the 20th century, Roman Catholicism had become the largest single denomination in the United States, a position it continues to hold. Most Catholic immigrants since World War II have come from Latin America, particularly Mexico and Cuba.

While there has been a general cohesion among American Roman Catholics, there have been many ethnic antagonisms within the church. Early in the 19th century those tensions were chiefly between old-stock Americans and Irish and German Americans. After Irish Americans achieved a kind of hegemony, both because of their numerical prominence among the laity and among the clergy (a majority of whom were foreign-born), rivalries and conflicts arose between Irish and Germans, and then between Irish and Germans on one side and southern and eastern Europeans on the other.

One of the issues they fought over was the use of languages other than English for sermons and the conduct of church business. One of the solutions was the establishment of so-called national parishes, in which members of a given non–English-speaking ethnic group, in places in which they predominated, could hear sermons in the language of their homeland and be ministered to by religious of their own ethnicity. In the years since World War II the ethnic strains within the church have been largely between Spanish-speaking communicants and those speaking English.

SEE ALSO

American Protective Association; Education; Know Nothing movement; Ku Klux Klan; Language; Nativism; Parochial schools; Polish National Catholic Church; Religion; individual ethnic groups

FURTHER READING

Dolan, Jay P. *The American Catholic Experience: A History from Colonial Times to the Present.* New York: Doubleday, 1985.

Dolan, Jay P. *The Immigrant Church: New York's Irish and German Catholics, 1815–1865,* Baltimore: Johns Hopkins University Press, 1975.

Ellis, John Tracy. *American Catholicism.* 2nd rev. ed. Chicago: University of Chicago Press, 1969.

Fisher, James T. *Catholics in America.* New York: Oxford University Press, 2000.

Romanians

- *1990 Ancestry: 365,544*
- *Immigration, 1986–96: 49,943*
- *Immigration, 1880–1996: 233,997*

- *Major periods of immigration: 1900–10, 1921–24*
- *Major areas of settlement: Middle Atlantic and Midwestern cities*

Romania became independent only in 1878; before that Romania was divided between the Ottoman, Austro-Hungarian, and Russian empires, and its boundaries have been changed often.

Few Romanians came to the United States before the 1870s, and there are no U.S. immigration data on those who came before 1880. We do know that there were Romanians in the California gold rush of 1849 and that two Romanian military officers fought in the Union Army during the Civil War: one of them, General Gheorge Pomutz, rose to the rank of brigadier general and later served as U.S. consul general in St. Petersburg, Russia.

The official immigration figures are quite confused. On the one hand, many of the 85,000 entrants recorded as having come before 1920 were not ethnic Romanians but Jews. On the other hand, many ethnic Romanians were counted as Hun-

garians, Austrians, or Russians. There have been relatively few Romanian immigrants since the 1924 restrictions on immigration, although some 10,000 did come in as displaced persons in the years following World War II.

The major reasons for immigrating to America were poverty in Romania, and, for those who lived in Russia or Austria-Hungary, the desire to avoid military service. The overwhelming majority of these immigrants were unskilled and drawn to the industrial areas of Middle Atlantic and Midwestern cities such as Chicago, Cleveland, Detroit, New York, Philadelphia, and Pittsburgh. Since most of these immigrants came from villages that were ethnically mixed, they tended to live among other recent immigrants rather than in enclaves they could call their own. Perhaps a third of all the Romanian immigrants who came before 1920 eventually returned to Europe.

Large numbers of these sojourners—as well as many Romanian immigrants who stayed—lived in boardinghouses that were often used exclusively by members of the same ethnic group. As was true of many immigrant groups,

Around 1918, these Romanian American amateur actors in Philadelphia put on a play in Romanian whose title translates as "The Matchmaker." The play addressed a major issue in immigrant life: how to find a mate in a strange land.

the chief institutions established by Romanian immigrants were churches and fraternal benefit societies. Even though some 90 percent of ethnic Romanians were of the Orthodox faith, Romanian believers in America were badly divided. For a variety of reasons, the Romanian Orthodox churches in America have had a history punctuated by almost perpetual quarrels. No large Romanian American fraternal benefit society seems to have survived.

SEE ALSO

Austro-Hungarian Empire; Displaced persons; Fraternal benefit societies; Hungarians; Jews; Sojourners

FURTHER READING

Barton, Josef J. *Peasants and Strangers: Italians, Rumanians, and Slovaks in an American City, 1890–1950*. Cambridge: Harvard University Press, 1975.
Wertsman, Vladimir. *The Romanians in America, 1748–1974: A Chronology & Factbook*. Dobbs Ferry, N.Y.: Oceana, 1975.

Roms

SEE Gypsies

Russians

- *1990 Ancestry: 2,952,987*
- *Immigration, 1992–96: 70,433*
- *Immigration, 1880–1996: 3,752.811*
- *Major period of immigration: 1905–14*
- *Major areas of settlement: Northeastern and midwestern cities; Brighton Beach, New York City*

The vast majority of the nearly 3 million Americans who reported themselves to be of "Russian" ancestry in the 1990 census were not ethnic Russians but Jews who had emigrated from Russia or the Soviet Union. ("Jewish"

was not an option that the census accepted.) This article will deal only with ethnic Russians who were one of the peoples of the Russian and later Soviet Empires. (See "Jews," for discussion of Jewish immigrants.) Even today there are many ethnic groups in post-Soviet Russia, and many if not most of the 70,000 immigrants who came between 1992 and 1996 were not ethnically Russian, either.

The earliest ethnic Russians to settle in North America came to Alaska in the late 18th century as part of the eastward expansion of the Russian Empire. In 1784 they established their first settlement on Kodiak Island, Alaska. They eventually established more than 40 permanent settlements, including one at Ft. Ross, about 100 miles north of present-day San Francisco. Russia surrendered its claims south of Alaska to the United States in 1819, and, in 1867, sold Alaska to the United States. The Russian settlements were never large, and the most permanent impact was on many of the native peoples, some 12,000 of whom, such as the Aleuts, were converted to the Russian Orthodox Church. An even greater number of their descendants still follow the Orthodox faith.

A much more numerous Russian presence on the West Coast came in the early 20th century when perhaps

Buffalo Bill's Wild West shows, which started with Indians and cavalry, eventually used European horsemen too. These are Russian Cossacks in 1901.

Documentary photographer Lewis Hine took this picture of steel workers outside their Russian boarding house in Homestead, Pennsylvania, in 1907.

5,000 Molokans, members of a dissident, pacifist Russian religious sect, emigrated to California, chiefly to Los Angeles and San Francisco. A much larger number of members of the sect migrated to Canada, particularly to its prairie provinces.

Meanwhile, larger movements of Russians, in several distinct increments, settled in the eastern and midwestern cities of the United States. The first of these involved some 90,000 people, most of whom arrived between 1905 and the outbreak of World War I in 1914: these were primarily unskilled immigrants whose profile was quite similar to that of other eastern European immigrants of the era.

A second period of migration occurred as a result of the Bolshevik Revolution of 1917 and the civil war that followed. Between 1920 and 1922 more than 2 million people fled from what became an oppressive dictatorship; about 30,000 came to the United States, some directly, others after sojourns in western European countries. Included in this migration were many highly skilled individuals, professionals, former aristocrats, Tsarist officials, and a number of intellectuals and artists.

Other groups of Russians came after World War II. Between 1945 and 1955 these were chiefly displaced persons who were opposed to the Soviet regime and did not want to return to the Soviet Union. Emigration from the Soviet Union itself was extremely difficult before 1969. After that, periodic "thaws" allowed several hundred thousand people to emigrate before the breakup of the Soviet Union in 1991. Most of these were Jews who chose to go to Israel, but substantial contingents of Soviet Jews came to the United States, as did a few thousand ethnic Russians. Ironically, there were even instances of Russians pretending to be Jews in order to be able to emigrate.

Since the breakup of the Soviet Union, almost 15,000 people have come to the United States from Russia each year, but not all of these have been ethnic Russians. The largest single enclave of these new Russian Americans is in Brighton Beach, in Brooklyn, New York. Its inhabitants call it "Little Odessa." According to the U.S. government, a number of Russian immigrants since the early 1990s have been connected with Russian organized crime and "money laundering."

Most ethnic Russians have been members of the Russian Orthodox Church, which moved its American headquarters first from Alaska to San Francisco in 1867, and then to New York City in 1903, with the curious territorial title of Diocese of the Aleutian Islands and North America. After the Russian Revolution of 1917, the church in America became snarled in political disputes over control from Moscow, and the church split into three distinct parts that have not been rejoined even after the fall of communism.

SEE ALSO

Displaced persons; Ethnic enclave; Jews; Soviet Union; Ukrainians

FURTHER READING

Hardwick, Susan W. *Russian Refuge: Religion, Migration, and Settlement on the North American Pacific Rim.* Chicago: University of Chicago Press, 1993.
Magocsi, Paul R. *The Russian Americans.* New York: Chelsea House, 1996.

Rusyns

SEE Carpatho-Rusyns; Ukrainians

Ruthenians

SEE Ukrainians

Salad bowl

"Salad bowl" is a term sometimes (but infrequently) used as a substitute for "melting pot" in discussing acculturation and assimilation. The idea is that in a salad, although many elements are mixed, they generally retain some or all of their identity. In the "melting pot" metaphor, by contrast, the individual elements are fused into one. Other metaphors include "mosaic" and "triple melting pot."

SEE ALSO

Acculturation; Assimilation; Melting pot; Mosaic; Triple melting pot

Salvadorans

- *1990 Ancestry: 499,153*
- *Immigration, 1986–96: 319,369*
- *Immigration, 1932–96: 421,687*
- *Major period of immigration: mid-1970s+*
- *Major areas of settlement: Los Angeles, New York, Washington, D.C., San Francisco, Houston*

El Salvador, the homeland of the Salvadorans, is a small Central American nation of 8,260 square miles, about the size of New Jersey, with a population of some 5.7 million, nearly 95 percent of whom are mestizo and most of the rest Native Americans. Salvadorans speak Spanish and about 75 percent are Roman Catholics, with a number of Protestant groups accounting for the rest. El Salvador, settled in the early 16th century by the Spaniards, gained independence in 1831.

Coffee production on large plantations became the mainstay of the economy in the late 19th century, which made the country's prosperity dependent on the fluctuating world price for coffee beans. The plantation owners tended to dominate politics, which were traditionally unstable. The chronic instability erupted into a bloody civil war in 1979, and over the next 12 years an estimated 75,000 Salvadoran civilians were killed by soldiers, many of them deliberately murdered.

The INS believes that until the

This Salvadoran restaurant in Los Angeles advertises its ethnicity and its menu in Spanish but tells English-language speakers that they too can eat breakfast or lunch there. The small sign in the window on the right says that it also sells a Spanish-language newspaper, La Opinion.

1970s no more than 30,000 Salvadorans had ever migrated to the United States. More than three times that many came in the 1970s, and the civil war that devastated El Salvador between 1979 and 1982 sent at least half a million refugees to the United States, most of whom entered illegally. Under the "amnesty" program introduced by the Immigration Act of 1986, 153,447 Salvadorans had their entry into the United States legalized. They represented 5.7 percent of all the participants in the program, the second-largest national group. A 1996 INS estimate put the number of illegal Salvadoran immigrants in the country at 335,000, also the second-largest national group.

Not surprisingly, most Salvadoran Americans are quite poor: their average per capita income has been put at about half of the American average, and more than a fifth of all Salvadoran families are below the government's poverty line. Predominantly peasants in El Salvador and overwhelmingly urban in the United States, large numbers of adult Salvadorans are illiterate in Spanish, which makes learning effective English more difficult. Until 1991 the federal government generally refused to give Salvadorans refugee status, insisting that they came for "economic" rather than for "political" reasons, even though most

experts testified that it was the civil war that was the chief cause of the massive post-1979 immigration. Only 5,052 Salvadorans have ever been granted refugee status, which is not even two-tenths of one percent of the refugees admitted between 1946 and 1996.

Salvadoran ethnic neighborhoods in the United States tend to be distinct from those of other Hispanic groups. In greater Los Angeles, where nearly half of Salvadoran Americans live, the largest ethnic enclaves, such as the one in the Union Pico district in downtown Los Angeles, have many small businesses, including many *pupuserias* (restaurants). Other large enclaves are in Hempstead, a suburb of New York City, and in the Columbia Road area of Washington, D.C.

SEE ALSO

Asylum; Central Americans; Ethnic enclave; Hispanics; Immigration Act of 1986; Mestizo; Refugees

FURTHER READING

Coutin, Susan Bibler. *Legalizing Moves: Salvadoran Immigrants' Struggle for U.S. Residency.* Ann Arbor: University of Michigan Press, 2000.

Mahler, Sarah J. *Salvadorans in Suburbia: Symbiosis and Conflict.* Boston: Allyn and Bacon. 1996.

Menjívar, Cecilia. *Fragmented Ties: Salvadoran Immigrant Networks in America.* Berkeley: University of California Press, 2000.

Samoans

- *1990 Ancestry: 55,419*
- *1990 Census: 39,520*
- *Immigration, 1986–96: 3,045*
- *Immigration, 1820–1996: n.a.*
- *Major period of immigration: since 1950*
- *Major areas of settlement: California, Hawaii*

Samoa, the homeland of Samoans, consists of a chain of volcanic islands extending for about 350 miles in the South Pacific about halfway between Honolulu, Hawaii, and Sydney, Australia. The Samoans are Polynesians believed to have arrived in the islands as early as 1000 B.C. During its imperial 19th-century expansion in the Pacific, the United States acquired what is now called American Samoa, the easternmost islands that comprise only 77 of the total 1,200 square miles of the chain. This includes the port of Pago Pago and 47,000 of the islands' 220,000 people.

The rest of the chain was divided between Great Britain and Germany. During World War I, New Zealand troops captured the German part and administered all of the non-U.S. territory until 1962. In that year, Samoa, formerly known as Western Samoa, became an independent nation. Only its citizens are included in the immigration data above, as the residents of American Samoa are "American nationals." This means that they have the right to come to and live and work in the United States but are not American citizens. If they wish to become citizens they must become naturalized as if they were aliens.

Like many other Pacific ethnic groups, Samoans migrated first to Hawaii and only later to the American mainland. The first such group migration came in 1920 when Samoan members of the Mormon church were brought to Hawaii to help build the Mormon Temple at Laie, near Honolulu. Migrations of individuals and families continued.

A second group migration occurred in 1950 when, as a result of the transfer of the administration of American Samoa from the U.S. Navy to the U.S. Department of the Interior, many Samoans who had worked for the navy came to Honolulu and to bases in California to continue their employment.

As of 1990 almost half of the Samoans in the United States, 45.8 percent, lived in California and more than a third, 36.3 percent, lived in Hawaii.

Most Samoan families in the United States are still headed by first-generation immigrants and still maintain many island customs. At work a Samoan man might dress and behave like most of his fellow Americans, but at home he will take off his shoes, put on a *lava lava* (a long wraparound skirt), sit on the floor, and expect his teenage children to prepare the evening meal. Samoans are physically large, and a number of them have done very well as wrestlers and as professional football players.

SEE ALSO

American nationals; Mormons; Pacific Islanders; Polynesians

FURTHER READING

Janes, Craig R. *Migration, Social Change, and Health: A Samoan Community in Urban California.* Stanford, Calif.: Stanford University Press, 1990.
Macpherson, Cluny, et al., eds. *New Neighbors: Islanders in Adaptation.* Santa Cruz: University of California, Santa Cruz, Center for South Pacific Studies, 1978.

Saudis

SEE Arabs

Scandinavians

Scandinavians is an umbrella term that encompasses people from Denmark, Iceland, Norway, and Sweden.

Although Scandinavian languages are similar enough that all these people

Lodgers of a "Skandinavisk" (Scandinavian) boarding house in Des Moines, Iowa. The two women on the roof of the porch probably ran it.

can understand one another, Icelandic and Swedish are distinct languages, while Danish and Norwegian are so similar that the term Dano-Norwegian is generally used.

SEE ALSO

Danes; Icelanders; Norwegians; Swedes; Vikings

FURTHER READING

Hoobler, Dorothy, and Thomas Hoobler. *The Scandinavian American Family Album.* New York: Oxford University Press, 1997.

Skardal, Dorothy B. *The Divided Heart: Scandinavian Immigrant Experience through Literary Sources.* Lincoln: University of Nebraska Press, 1974.

Scientists, immigrant

Three different types of immigrant scientists have been important in the development of science and technology in the United States: immigrants who came to the United States in their youth and achieved prominence only after immigrating; immigrants who were established scientists before they came to the United States as exiles or refugees; those who were established scientists before they came to the United States and immigrated because they believed that opportunities for research and advancement were better in the United States, including scientists who were recruited for work for which they were uniquely qualified. (This last phenomenon is part of what is sometimes called a "brain drain," the "siphoning off" of talent from one country to another.)

Michael Idvorsky Pupin, a Serb born in Hungary, is a good example of the first type. A professor at Columbia University most of his life, Pupin not only made important inventions having to do with the telegraph, the telephone, and X rays, but he also wrote a Pulitzer Prize–winning autobiography. Examples of the second category would include Joseph Priestley, the English chemist who discovered oxygen and fled Britain in 1793 because of his radical political views, and the German Jewish physicist

NONQUOTA
Immigration Visa

Nonquota
Relative— — — — — — — Section 4(a)
Returning alien — — — — — " 4(b)
Native of — — — — — — " 4(c)
(Country of birth)
Minister or professor — " 4(d)
Student — — — — — — " 4(e)
Expatriate — — — — — — " 4(f)

No. 19

Date: May 28, 1935

Passport No. 173329/571 , issued by
Swiss Consul General at New York
on the 21
day of September , A. D. 1934 , valid
until the 21 day of September
A. D. 1939

SEEN: May 28, 1935
The Bearer, Albert Einstein , who
is of Swiss nationality, having
(Citizen or subject)
been seen and examined, is classified as a Nonquota
Immigrant under Subdivision (D) of Section 4 of the
Immigration Act of 1924, as amended, and is granted
this Immigration Visa pursuant to the provisions of
said act.

The validity of this Immigration Visa expires on
the 27 day of September
A. D. 1935

Charles H. Heisler
Consul of the
United States of America.

Immigrant identification card No. 831234
issued

Charles H. Heisler,
Consul.

Albert Einstein's second U.S. visa was issued in 1935. With it, he left the United States briefly in order to change his immigration status. He later became a U.S. citizen.

Albert Einstein, who fled Nazi Germany in 1933. Examples of the third type include the German engineer John A. Roebling, one of America's greatest civil engineers before and after the American Civil War, who designed the Brooklyn Bridge and other bridges.

SEE ALSO

Brain drain; Exiles; Refugees

FURTHER READING

Fermi, Laura. *Illustrious Immigrants: The Intellectual Migration from Europe, 1930–1941.* Chicago: University of Chicago Press, 1968.
McCullough, David. *The Great Bridge.* New York, 1972.
Pupin, Michael I. *From Immigrant to Inventor.* New York: Scribners, 1923.

Scotch-Irish

- *1990 Ancestry: 5,617,773*
- *Immigration, 1986–96: n.a.*
- *Immigration, 1820–1996: aroumd 2 million*

- *Major periods of immigration: 1770s, 1815–45, 1851–99*
- *Major areas of settlement: Pennsylvania, Piedmont area of Virginia and the Carolinas*

Scotch-Irish is a term invented in the United States in the late 17th century and used nowhere else. It is applied to the approximately 2 million people of Irish nationality and Protestant religion who migrated to America in the 17th, 18th, and 19th centuries, and their descendants. They, in turn, were descended from perhaps 200,000 Scots who migrated to northern Ireland, or Ulster, from lowland Scotland in the 17th century. The term did not gain wide acceptance until the 1840s, when Scotch-Irish in America adopted it with enthusiasm to differentiate themselves from the unpopular Catholic Irish who were emigrating to the United States in unprecedented numbers. The term is not used to describe 20th-century Protestant immigrants from Northern Ireland, who appear in American immigration data as British.

Perhaps 100,000 Scotch-Irish came to America before the Revolution, some 40,000 of them in the 1770s. Most left because of miserable economic conditions in Ireland and were attracted by the availability of land. As relative latecomers in the colonial era, most Scotch-Irish settled along the frontier, largely in Pennsylvania and to the south. Their main internal migration route was along what was called the Great Philadelphia Road, which went from southeastern Pennsylvania down through Virginia's Shenandoah Valley to the North Carolina Piedmont and on into South Carolina. This path had been pioneered by Germans in the early 18th century. Although we have been taught to think of American migration as running from east to west, this north-to-south migration stream was the principal internal migration route of the late colonial era. It led from the chief immigrant port of Philadelphia down through hundreds of thousands of acres of relatively uninhabited land east of the Appalachian Mountains.

Partly because they spoke English and had some familiarity with the political process, large numbers of Scotch-Irish quickly made their mark in American politics. Three Presidents, Andrew Jackson, James Buchanan, and Chester A. Arthur were sons of Scotch-Irish immigrants, and four others—James K. Polk, William McKinley, Woodrow Wilson, and Ronald Reagan—were of Scotch-Irish descent.

Scotch-Irish immigrants also brought the Presbyterian form of Protestant Christianity to the British colonies, and it was primarily Scotch-Irish ministers who organized the first presbytery, the group organization of Presbyterian churches, in the New World at Philadelphia in 1706. An important step in assuring the growing number of Presbyterian churches with educated ministers was the founding of the "Log College" near Philadelphia in 1726–27. This modest establishment was the seed from which grew the College of New Jersey (1746): it became Princeton University in 1896.

Although most of the Scotch-Irish had been farmers and linen weavers in Ireland, there were also large numbers of craftsmen in their migration, including carpenters, tailors, shoemakers, and wheelwrights. Many of these immigrants, with or without trades, came as indentured servants. In the early 18th century one friendly Ulster bishop estimated that only 1 in 10 of those going to America could afford a ticket.

During the American Revolution, in which Scotch-Irish immigrants and

their sons fought on both sides, immigration ceased. But as soon as peace was declared in 1783 it resumed, and for the rest of the century about 5,000 a year came. Most of these postwar immigrants were able to pay for their own passage, and by 1800 the trade in indentured servants had died out. Beginning in 1801 British laws and regulations made it difficult for Scotch-Irish to emigrate, and the War of 1812 with Britain temporarily cut off access to the United States, but not to Canada. The end of that war in 1815 set off a great increase in immigration: by 1845 some half a million more Scotch-Irish had come. This emigration marks the beginning of prepaid passages: people in the United States could buy "tickets" from shipping agents for family members and friends to join them. This system would be used later by many immigrant groups, particularly in the age of the steamship after the mid-1850s.

The great potato famine of the later 1840s had relatively little effect in Ulster, where potato culture did not predominate and a growing industrialism provided non-agricultural ways for making a living. Yet Scotch-Irish immigration continued to be important. From 1851, when British statistics first began to identify Irish emigrants by the province from which they came, until 1899, more than a million left from Ulster, some 90 percent of them for the United States.

Whereas most 18th- and early 19th-century Scotch-Irish immigrants were involved in farming, only a small minority of the post-1815 immigrants were. Many were weavers and craftsmen, while a smaller but substantial number became businessmen of various kinds. Some made great fortunes: the most prominent of these was Thomas W. Mellon. Brought to the United States at age five, Mellon established

As rebellions and political disorder were persistent in 17th- and early 18th-century Scotland, hundreds of the losers in these struggles were exiled to America. Before the 1730s more Scots may have come to America as punishment than came voluntarily. During the English Civil War of the 1660s, hundreds of Scottish prisoners were sent to America, as were the followers of the Earl of Argyll's rebellion in 1685; the same fate awaited more than 1,400 supporters of the Jacobite risings in 1715 and 1745. Large numbers of other Scots came throughout the colonial period as indentured servants.

Most Scots came as individuals, but there were examples of group settlement. From the Lowlands small groups of Scots Quakers and Presbyterians settled in 1683–84, the former in New Jersey and the latter in South Carolina. Larger numbers of Highlanders came shortly before the American Revolution, many of them led by persons called tacksmen, large leaseholders who had organized the fighting forces of the clans in earlier, more warlike times. The most significant of these tacksmen brought about 5,000 persons, mostly families, from the Isle of Skye in the Hebrides to the Cape Fear region of North Carolina.

Some historians believe that at the time of the American Revolution, in which Scots fought on both sides, there may have been more Tories (loyalists to the British crown) than patriots among the Scots in America. If that is true, they are they only ethnic group with a majority opposed to the American Revolution. On the other hand, Scots were more prominent in patriot politics than their number in the population would suggest. Of the 56 members of the Second Continental Congress that adopted the Declaration of Independence, 11, nearly a fifth, were of Scots birth or ancestry. The most prominent of these

Andrew Carnegie became perhaps the most famous 19th-century immigrant. His "rags to riches" story was American myth come true.

was James Wilson of Pennsylvania, who also played a major role in the Constitutional Convention of 1787 and served as a justice of the Supreme Court of the United States.

In the 19th century, particularly after 1850, Scots immigration was steady, with at least several thousand coming every year. There are few generalizations that one can make about these emigrants except that they came seeking economic opportunity, which large numbers of them found, thanks in part to the excellent educational system in Scotland and the fact that most could speak English. The most spectacularly successful Scots immigrant was Andrew Carnegie, the poor immigrant boy who organized the American steel industry and became one of the richest men in the world. Carnegie, like a number of other Scots emigrants before and after him, used some of his wealth to endow institutions in Scotland, although Carnegie's gifts to America, chiefly in the form of a system of public libraries, were much, much greater.

While Scots Americans seem to be highly aware of their heritage, there are few other enduring cultural links. Gaelic, the language that provided cohesion for Highlanders, had died out in America by 1860. The more numerous Scotch-

Irish tended to dominate the Presbyterian churches that most Lowlanders attended. Scots seem to have intermarried with members of other groups more rapidly and more often than did many other ethnic groups. Many Scots founded St. Andrews's Societies—St. Andrew is the patron saint of Scotland—wherever they lived, and, although dozens of them still exist, they have very small memberships. In addition to their other contributions, there are two sports that Scots brought with them: curling—a kind of bowling on ice that is very popular in Canada—and golf, which took root in America and, eventually, in much of the rest of the world.

SEE ALSO
Irish; Scotch-Irish

FURTHER READING
Donaldson, Gordon. *The Scots Overseas.* London: R. Hale, 1966.
Graham, Ian C. C. *Colonists from Scotland: Emigration to North America, 1707–1783.* Ithaca, N.Y.: Cornell University Press, 1956.

Serbs

- *1990 Ancestry: 116,795 [Yugoslavian: 257,994]*
- *Immigration, 1986–96: [Yugoslavia: 42,795]*
- *Immigration, 1820–1996: around 300,000–400,000*
- *Major periods of immigration: 1880–1914, 1948–75*
- *Major areas of settlement: Great Lakes area, especially Pittsburgh*

[Because there is no immigration data for Serbs specifically, the statistics for Yugoslavia are given in brackets above. Many of those were Serbian immigrants and their descendents.]

Serbs are a Slavic people who were a major component (some 40 percent) of the people of the former Yugoslavia, and are the overwhelming majority in the Federal Republic of Yugoslavia created in 1992. Serbs and their neighbors, the Croatians and the Slovenes, share a common language, called Serbo-Croatian, but the Serbs use the Cyrillic alphabet while the others use the Latin alphabet, a variance that reflects their different religious and cultural heritages.

Serbs are Orthodox, and Croatians and Slovenes are Catholics. Serbian Orthodoxy is related to but different from the Orthodoxy of other Slavic groups. It most distinctive form is the *slava*, or family patron saint, which is inherited in the male line and symbolizes the family's conversion to Christianity.

The Serbs have often been at odds with the Croats and Slovenes. During World Wars I and II, Serbian leaders supported Russia, while Croat and Slovene leaders supported Austria and Germany.

Serbia itself was an independent state between 1878 and 1918. Since the mid-19th century, almost half of the Serbs in Europe have lived outside of Serbia proper, and it is from this outside

Serb immigrants Ilija Jovanovich (left) and Danilo Nomchilovich pose in the regalia of their Serbian Benevolent Lodge, St. Stephen Nemanja, in Bisbee, Arizona, around 1905. They were almost certainly copper miners in everyday life.

area that most Serbian immigration has come. For example, neither of the two most prominent Serbians ever to come to America, the inventors Nikola Tesla and Michael Idvorsky Pupin, came from Serbia proper. Tesla was from Croatia and Pupin from the Hungarian Banat.

Although it is almost certain that Serbian sailors visited the United States in the 18th century, the first Serbian immigrant in America who can be identified by name is Djorde Sagic, who arrived in Philadelphia in 1815 as an indentured servant and took the name George Fisher. The first to come in significant numbers were seamen and others who were numerous enough in New Orleans to establish a small Serbian colony there in the 1830s. There were also small groups of Serbians in gold-rush California in the 1850s.

Most of the 200,000 to 300,000 Serbs who came to the United States before World War II arrived during the decades just before World War I. Most did heavy industrial work and many were sojourners. Though Serbs still went to the far West and the South—the first Serbian Orthodox churches in America were built in the 1890s in Jackson, California, and Galveston, Texas—most went to the industrial heartland between western Pennsylvania and Chicago. It has been claimed, for example, that around 1900 one area of Pittsburgh's South Side was so heavily Serbian that you could walk for blocks, passing dozens of Serbian retail businesses, and hear Serbo-Croatian spoken all the way. Even before World War I disrupted European immigration patterns beginning in 1914, thousands of Serbs had returned to Europe to fight in the Balkan Wars (1912–13) that resulted in a larger Serbia.

Between 1914 and the end of World War II in 1945, few Serbs came to the United States, as the two wars,

restrictive immigration legislation, and the Great Depression of the 1930s brought most American immigration to a halt. Shortly after the end of World War II, Serbian immigration resumed as more than 80,000 persons identified as Yugoslavs were admitted, largely as displaced persons and as refugees. Since the breakup of Yugoslavia in 1991–92, the Serbs dominate the Federal Republic of Yugoslavia, which includes only Serbia and Montenegro.

SEE ALSO

Austro-Hungarian Empire; Croatians; Displaced persons; Eastern Orthodox churches; Montenegrins; Refugees; Religion; Slavs; Slovenes; Sojourners; Yugoslavia

FURTHER READING

Kisslinger, Jerome. *The Serbian Americans*. New York: Chelsea House, 1990.

Serial migration

SEE Chain migration

Shiites

SEE Muslims

Sikhs

Sikhs are believers in Sikhism, and while non-Sikhs can be converted to Sikhism, the overwhelming majority of the world's 16 million Sikhs are either residents of the Punjab, a region in South Asia now divided between India and Pakistan, or their descendants. Sikhism is a monotheistic religion created by the religion's founder, Nanak, that combines elements of both Hinduism and Islam. Sikhs are identifiable by the turbans the men wear, their beards, the iron metal bracelet they wear, and the small dagger they carry. Many of the earliest Asian Indians to migrate to the United States were Sikhs, but they are now a small minority of the 800,000 Asian Indians in the United States. A Sikh immigrant, Dalip Singh Saund, was the first Asian American elected to Congress; he represented a California district including much of San Diego from 1957 to 1963.

SEE ALSO

Asian Indians; Hindus; Muslims; Pakistanis; Religion

FURTHER READING

Jensen, Joan M. *Passage from India: Asian Indian Immigrants in North America.* New Haven: Yale University Press, 1988.
Saund, Dalip Singh. *Congressman from India.* New York: Dutton, 1960.
Tweed, Thomas A., and Stephen Prothero, eds. *Asian Religion in America: A Documentary History.* New York: Oxford University Press, 1999.

Slave trade

The modern African slave trade began around 1450, about a half-century before the "discovery" of America. The trade initially supplied labor for sugar plantations established by Europeans on offshore African islands and, to a lesser degree, for work in Spain and Portugal. After the European conquest of the New World, at least 11 million Africans were brought to the New World. However, fewer than 500,000 of them were brought to what is now the United States; more than 3.5 million went to Brazil and even more went to European colonies in the Caribbean.

TO BE SOLD on board the Ship *Bance-Island*, on tuesday the 6th of *May* next, at *Ashley-Ferry*, a choice cargo of about 250 fine healthy **NEGROES**, just arrived from the Windward & Rice Coast. —The utmost care has already been taken, and shall be continued, to keep them free from the least danger of being infected with the SMALL-POX, no boat having been on board, and all other communication with people from *Charles-Town* prevented.
Austin, Laurens, & Appleby.

N. B. Full one Half of the above Negroes have had the SMALL-POX in their own Country.

Slavery was legal in every American colony and was recognized by the Constitution of the United States. In 1808 Congress outlawed further importation of slaves, although slaves could still be traded between those states that allowed it. Historians believe that perhaps 50,000 slaves were brought into the United States, largely from the Caribbean, between 1808 and the Civil War. They were the first illegal immigrants. All slavery ended in the United States with the adoption of the 13th Amendment to the Constitution in 1865.

SEE ALSO

Africans; Illegal immigrants

FURTHER READING

Berlin, Ira. *Many Thousands Gone: The First Two Centuries of Slavery in North America.* Cambridge: Harvard University Press, 1998.
Curtin, Philip D. *The African Slave Trade: A Census.* Madison: University of Wisconsin Press, 1969.
Palmer, Colin A. *The First Passage: Blacks in the Americas, 1502–1617.* New York: Oxford University Press, 1995.

This advertisement of slaves for sale in South Carolina claims that a new shipment has just arrived from the "rice coast" of Africa, presumably bringing with them valuable agricultural skills.

Slavs

Slavs are people who speak Slavic or Slavonic languages. Perhaps 400 million people today have a Slavic language as a mother tongue: most of them live in Russia and Ukraine. There are three linguistic divisions, East, West, and South Slavic. Russian, Ukrainian, and Belorussian are East Slavic; Polish, Czech, and Slovak are the chief West Slavic tongues; and Serbo-Croatian, Slovenian, Macedonian, Bulgarian and Church Slavonic are the West Slavic languages. Millions of immigrants have come to America speaking Slavic languages—more than 3 million spoke Polish—but, apart from some use in church serviced, these languages have only rarely endured past the first generations of immigrants.

SEE ALSO
Belorussian; Bulgarians; Croatians; Czechs; Macedonians; Poles; Russians; Serbs; Slovaks; Slovenes; Ukrainians

Slovaks

- *1990 Ancestry: 1,882,897*
- *Immigration, 1993–96: 248*
- *Immigration, 1820–1996: around 500,000*
- *Major period of immigration: 1880–1914*
- *Major areas of settlement: Great Lakes states (particularly Pennsylvania)*

Until the creation of the Slovak Republic in 1993, American immigration data had never enumerated Slovaks separately. From 1919 until 1993 they were listed under Czechoslovakia, and before that under the Austro-Hungarian

Empire. During the period of their greatest migration in the late 19th and early 20th century, most Slovaks, a Western Slavic people, lived in the Hungarian part of the Austro-Hungarian Empire, and, from the 1840s, had to put up with a policy that tried to impose the Hungarian language upon them. The Slovaks were almost all peasants living under harsh economic conditions, and most of those who came to America did so to escape poverty. These immigrants were predominantly young men, and large numbers of them came as sojourners. Some were able to send for wives or sweethearts, others returned home, and still others spent their lives in America sending money back to families they would never see again. The Slovak Republic has some 5 million inhabitants in a territory of almost 19,000 square miles, about twice the size of Massachusetts.

Although a few individuals surely came earlier, significant migration of Slovaks to the United States began in

Most of the workers posed with this massive generator frame that they have made are Slovak immigrants. Their supervisors— the men in suits and bowler hats— are not. Those jobs went either to native-born men or immigrants from the British Isles or Germany.

the 1870s, when some 5,000 came in response to recruiting by American railroads and steel mills. This recruitment set off a chain of migration from Slovak villages that peaked when an estimated 50,000 Slovaks came in 1905 alone. The vast majority worked at hard, dirty, and dangerous industrial jobs, more than half of them in Pennsylvania. A gripping description of Slovak American life in early 20th-century Braddock, Pennsylvania, may be found in the 1941 novel *Out of This Furnace*, by the Slovak American novelist Thomas Bell (born Belejcak).

Slovaks were members of four distinct religious denominations: Roman Catholic, Lutheran, Calvinist, and Greek Catholic. One authority writes that as of 1930, more than 300 Slovak churches had been established, 241 of them Roman Catholic, 48 Lutheran, 9 Calvinist, and a smaller number of Greek Catholic. As was the case with many other ethnic groups, for perhaps two generations there were clashes between Slovak Roman Catholics and the American Catholic hierarchy, often over the matter of lay control over or ownership of the church buildings and other property that the contributions of the laity had paid for. By the 1960s, these disputes were no longer a major issue and American Slovak Catholics have largely acquiesced in the hierarchy's view that these buildings are owned by the bishop as surrogate for the church.

SEE ALSO

Austro-Hungarian Empire; Czechoslovakia; Czechs; Slavs; Sojourners; Sokols

FURTHER READING

Alexander, June Granatir. *The Immigrant Church and Community: Pittsburgh's Slovak Catholics and Lutherans, 1880–1915.* Pittsburgh: University of Pittsburgh Press, 1987.
Stolarik, M. Mark. *The Slovak Americans.* New York: Chelsea House, 1988.

Slovenes

- *1990 Ancestry: 124,437 [Yugoslavian: 257,994]*
- *Immigration, 1992–96: 2,277*
- *Immigration, 1820–1996: around 300,000*
- *Major periods of immigration: 1880–1914, 1949–56*
- *Major areas of settlement: Great Lakes states, Cleveland*

Until the creation of the Republic of Slovenia in 1991, American immigration data had never separately enumerated Slovenes. From 1919 until 1991 they were listed under Yugoslavia, and before that under the Austro-Hungarian Empire. Slovenes are a South Slavic people who are linguistically related to their neighbors, the Croatians and the Serbs. They share a common language, called Serbo-Croatian, but the Slovenes and the Croatians use the Latin alphabet while the Serbs use the Cyrillic alphabet, a variance that reflects their different religious and cultural heritages. The Slovenes and the Croatians are Roman Catholic, while the Serbs are Orthodox.

The first Slovenes in the United States whom we know about were Roman Catholic priests who came in the early 19th century as missionaries to the Indians. The best known of these is Rev. Frederick Baraga, who came in 1831. Baraga County in Michigan's Upper Peninsula is named for him. By 1880 there were perhaps 1,000 Slovenes in the United States, many of them working as miners in Michigan and Minnesota.

After the 1890s, although some Slovenian immigrants continued to work as miners, most new arrivals got factory jobs, as did most of their fellow southern and eastern European immigrants.

A 1951 publicity picture for Frank (Frankie) Yankovic, the popular Slovene American musician, dubbed both "America's Jukebox King," and, more frequently, the "Polka King."

By the mid-1890s Cleveland, Ohio, had become the focal point of Slovenian settlement: by the 1920s it was estimated the 30,000 to 40,000 Slovenian immigrants and their children lived in and around Cleveland. By the 1930s, one Slovenian immigrant, Louis Adamic had become a popular American writer whose books, such as *From Many Lands* (1940), recorded the experience of all immigrants, not just Slovenes or Yugoslavs. Even more influential was the Cleveland-born, second-generation Slovene Frankie Yankovic, the "Polka King," and one of the most influential American ethnic musicians.

The overwhelming majority of Slovenes are Roman Catholics, although there is a small group of Lutherans in the population.

SEE ALSO

Austro-Hungarian Empire; Croatians; Serbs; Slavs; Yugoslavia

FURTHER READING

Adamic, Louis. *From Many Lands*. New York: Harpers, 1940.

Govorchin, Gerald Gilbert. *Americans from Yugoslavia*. Gainesville: University of Florida Press, 1961.

Greene, Victor R. *A Passion for Polka: Old-time Ethnic Music in America*. Berkeley: University of California Press, 1992.

Sojourners

Sojourners are people who emigrate but intend to return to their native country. Millions of immigrants to the United States came with this intention, especially between 1865 and 1914 when perhaps one immigrant in three went back to the home country. Not all who came intending to be sojourners actually went back, however, and many who expected to stay in the United States eventually returned. Also, many persons came and went more than once. Sojourners were typically young adult males hoping to earn enough money to buy a new farm back home or to be able to purchase more land for an existing one.

A Hungarian-language newspaper published in Cleveland wrote of Hungarian sojourners in 1901: "The majority of our people do not want to adjust to the conditions here, do not like it here, yet do not want to return home [because they had not yet saved enough money]."

Yet, whatever they intended, many thousands of Hungarians immigrants did stay in Cleveland, which became one of the centers of Hungarian-American life. The same would be true for many other ethnic groups in many other cities.

SEE ALSO

Emigrants; Return migration

FURTHER READING

Caroli, Betty Boyd. *Immigrants who Returned Home*. New York: Chelsea House, 1990.

Warren, Robert, and Ellen Percy Kraly. *The Elusive Exodus: Emigration from the United States*. Washington, D.C.: Population Reference Bureau, 1985.

Wyman, Mark. *Round-trip to America: The Immigrants Return to Europe, 1880–1930*. Ithaca, N.Y.: Cornell University Press, 1993.

Sokol

Sokols were gymnastic organizations, but with important social and patriotic

functions, first organized in Prague by Czechs in 1862. Sokols (the word also means "falcon") quickly spread among other Slavic nationalities in the Austro-Hungarian Empire and to Slavic communities overseas. The first Czech sokol in the United States was established in St. Louis in 1865. The existing sokols in America are now largely social and without significant political content.

SEE ALSO

Austro-Hungarian Empire; Turnverein

Sorbs

SEE Wends

South Americans

- *Immigration, 1986–96: 615,986*
- *Immigration, 1820–1996: 1,595,971*

Although very little has been written about them, there have been immigrants from South America coming to the United States since early in the country's history. Many of them, like the 23 Sephardic Jewish immigrants expelled from Brazil who came to New Amsterdam (now New York City) in 1654, were people who emigrated to South America only to remigrate relatively quickly. In the 19th and early 20th centuries, many of those from Argentina were Italian immigrants and their children.

Between 1924 and 1965, when American immigration law contained no quotas for immigrants from the New World, many immigrants from Europe and the Middle East came to the United States via South and Central American countries. Until the early

1930s no separate national records were kept for immigrants from South America. A total of 1,595,971 immigrants have been recorded from South American sources since 1820: the three leading nations have been: Colombia, 375,479; Ecuador, 201,195: and Argentina, 149,995. Fewer than 13,000 of these immigrants came before 1900. Some 900,000 came between 1901 and 1986. In recent years the volume has increased greatly: nearly 600,000— about 38 percent of the total—came in the 11 years 1986–96.

SEE ALSO

Argentinians; Brazilians; Colombians; Ecuadorians; Immigration Act of 1924; Immigration policy; Jews

South Asians

SEE Afghans; Asian Indians; Bangladeshis; Pakistanis; Sri Lankans

Soviet Union

Created out of the turmoil of World War I, the Russian revolutions, and the ensuing civil war, the Soviet Union—or, formally, the Union of Soviet Socialist Republics (USSR)—was created in 1922 and dissolved in 1991. In theory its constituent republics were semiautonomous, but they had little power. In its final configuration (1940–91) the USSR had constituent republics that today are largely independent nations. They were: Armenia, Azerbaijan, Belorussia (Belarus), Estonia, Kazakhstan, Kirghizia (Kyrgyzstan), Latvia, Lithuania, Moldavia (Moldova), Russia, Tadzhikistan (Tajikistan), Turmenistan, Ukraine, and Uzbekistan.

The Russians were the largest and dominant ethnic group.

During most of its history the USSR made it very difficult for people to leave, whether as tourists or emigrants, and many of those who left were illegal emigrants. In the 1970s and 1980s many Jews were allowed to emigrate, often after enduring much persecution. After 1992 it was nationalities that wanted to leave Russia and on-going wars in the Caucasus region are largely about the desire of some groups, particularly Chechens, for independence.

SEE ALSO

Illegal emigrants; Russians

Spaniards

- *1990 Ancestry: 2,384,939 [Spaniard 360,935; Spanish 2,024,004. These were self-identifications on 1990 census forms. Clearly, many who chose the latter were indicating their language and not an identification with Spain.]*

- *Immigration, 1986–96: 17,354*
- *Immigration, 1820–1996: 297,033*
- *Major periods of immigration: before 1848, 1911–20*
- *Major areas of settlement: Southwest, especially California and New Mexico; New York City; Tampa, Florida*

Spaniards and people of Spanish descent were the original European settlers of Florida and of the American Southwest before its conquest by the United States in 1848: these pioneers are *not* reflected in American immigration statistics. The Spanish settlement of St. Augustine, Florida, in 1665— 42 years before Jamestown, 55 years before the Plymouth colony—involved only handfuls of people. In 1830, the first census of Florida after American annexation in 1819, there were 34,000 people there, perhaps half of them of Spanish origin. (Indians were not then counted by the census.)

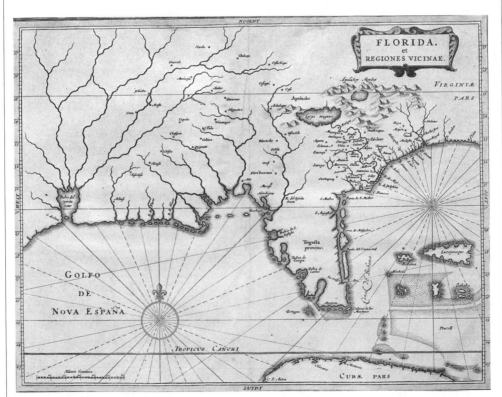

A 16th-century Spanish map of Florida and the region around it has the general shape of Florida, but is misleading about the east coast north of Florida.

Artist Jose Vives-Atsara was born in Spain in 1919 and educated there at the Barcelona School of Fine Arts. He and his wife emigrated to Venezuela in 1947, then to Mexico, and, in 1956, to San Antonio, where they have remained. It is not unusual for immigrants to move to more than one country before settling permanently.

But the settlement of New Mexico, begun in 1598, resulted by 1848 in a population of possibly 50,000 people of Spanish or part-Spanish descent. At the same time, in California, whose Spanish settlement began in 1769, there were perhaps 13,000 such people who called themselves *Californios*. In Texas, there were perhaps 4,000 *Tejanos* (Spanish for "Texans") before American immigration there began in 1821. In Texas and in California mass immigration from the rest of the United States and Europe soon swamped the Spanish-speaking pioneers and their descendants, but in New Mexico Spanish-speaking persons were a majority of the population until about 1940. Reflecting that heritage, New Mexico is the only state today that has two official languages, Spanish and English.

Between 1820 and 2000 nearly 300,000 Spaniards came to the United States, about half of them between 1900 and 1925. But the overwhelming majority of Spaniards who emigrated went to Latin America, particularly to nations of its southern cone, Argentina, Chile, and Uruguay. In addition, large numbers of the Spaniards who came to the United States—57 percent, according to one authority—eventually left, either to return to Spain or to move somewhere in Latin America.

In the 19th century the centers of Spanish immigration were New York City and California; in the early 20th century several thousand Spaniards settled in Tampa, where they were important in the cigar manufacturing industry. As a result of the Spanish Civil War of 1936–39 a small number of refugees came to the United States, while many more went to Mexico. Many of these refugees were distinguished and talented. Among the most outstanding were the master cellist Pablo Casals and the historian Américo Castro.

Spaniards in the United States have organized largely on regional lines—as Basques or as Galicians, for example—rather than as Spaniards. The first organization founded with a national identity in mind was the fraternal benefit society, Centro Español, founded in New York City in the mid-19th century.

SEE ALSO

Basques; Hispanics; Latinos; Mexicans; Refugees

FURTHER READING

Mormino, Gary R., and George E. Pozzetta. *The Immigrant World of Ybor City: Italians and their Latin Neighbors.* Urbana: University of Illinois Press, 1987.

Weber, David J. *The Spanish Frontier in North America.* New Haven: Yale University Press, 1992.

Spanish surname

A term invented by the Census Bureau in an attempt to enumerate persons of Hispanic ancestry used in the 1950 and 1960 censuses, which tabulated 2.3 million and 3.5 million persons of "Spanish surname."

It was a most inaccurate method because of name changes, marriages, etc.

SEE ALSO
Hispanics

Sri Lankans

- *1990 Ancestry: 14,448*
- *Immigration, 1986–96: 10,386*
- *Immigration, 1970–96: 16,570*
- *Major period of immigration: since 1980*
- *Major area of settlement: California*

Sri Lanka, an island nation formerly known as Ceylon, has a population of nearly 20 million in a territory of some 25,000 square miles, about the size of West Virginia. The majority of its population, about 75 percent, are Sinhalese and practice Buddhism. A significant minority, nearly 20 percent, are Tamils who are descended from immigrants from India and practice Hinduism. The Tamils are concentrated in the northern part of the pear-shaped island, the part closest to India. Since 1983 there has been a bloody civil war between the Sinhalese-dominated government and the Liberation Tigers of Tamil Eelam, generally known as the Tamil Tigers. Most of the minority refugees have gone to India, but between 1987 and 1996, 261 Sri Lankans had been granted refugee or asylee status in the United States. Little has been written about the Sri Lankans in the United States, of whom many first came as students.

SEE ALSO
Asylees; Refugees; South Asians

FURTHER READING
Leonard, Karen I. *The South Asian Americans*. Westport, Conn.: Greenwood, 1997.

Statue of Liberty

The Statue of Liberty was originally intended to be a tribute to the idea of liberty and to Franco-American friendship, but it has also become the preeminent symbol of immigration, as well as one of the most evocative symbols of the United States itself. The huge statue, 151 feet tall, on a pedestal 154 feet high, was created by the French sculptor Frédéric-Auguste Bartholdi, who named it "Liberty Enlightening the World." It was completed in Paris in 1884 and was a gift to the United States from the people of France. It was taken apart and shipped to the United States in 214 large packing cases. Reassembled, it was placed on a large pedestal that was built in the United States and partly paid for by the contributions of American schoolchildren. The statue was erected on Bedloe's Island (now Liberty Island) in New York Harbor and was dedicated on October 22, 1886, by President Grover Cleveland. Emma Lazarus's poem "The New Colossus," placed on the statue's pedestal in 1903, helped transform "Miss Liberty" into a symbol of welcome for immigrants:

> Not like the brazen giant of
>   Greek fame,
> With conquering limbs astride
>   from land to land;
> Here our sea-washed, sunset
>   gates shall stand
> A mighty woman with a torch,
>   whose flame
> Is the imprisoned lightning, and
>   her name
> Mother of Exiles. From her
>   beacon-hand
> Glows world-wide welcome; her
>   mild eyes command
> The air-bridged harbor that twin
>   cities frame.

"Keep ancient lands, your storied
pomp!" cries she
With silent lips. "Give me your
tired, your poor,
Your huddled masses yearning to
breathe free,
The wretched refuse of your
teeming shore.
Send these, the homeless, tempest-
tost to me:
I lift my lamp beside the golden
door!"

In the early 1980s the statue and neighboring Ellis Island underwent an extensive restoration and renovation and
reopened in 1986, the centennial of the
statue's dedication.

SEE ALSO
Ellis Island

FURTHER READING

Bell, James B., and Richard I. Abrams. *In
Search of Liberty: The Story of the Stat-
ue of Liberty and Ellis Island.* New York:
Doubleday, 1994.
Holland, F. Ross. *Idealists, Scoundrels, and
the Lady: An Insider's View of the Statue
of Liberty–Ellis Island Project.* Urbana:
University of Illinois Press, 1994.
Moreno, Barry. *The Statue of Liberty
Encyclopedia.* New York: Simon &
Schuster, 2000.

Steamship lines

Beginning in the late 19th century, special passenger ships were built for the
immigrant trade. European firms dominated the Atlantic trade, and three of
them carried the majority of the millions of European passengers. Most
came in "steerage," as opposed to the
more expensive and comfortable "cab-
ins" on the upper decks.

Two German lines and one British
dominated immigrant trade. The Hamburg-Amerika and the Bremen-based

North German Lloyd lines were the
most important continental companies,
while the British Cunard Line, based in
Liverpool, served many continental
passengers as well as those from the
British Isles.

In the Pacific the Japanese NYK
line was dominant in bringing Japanese
not only to the United States and Canada but also to Peru and Brazil.

SEE ALSO
Steerage

Steerage

Steerage consisted of the lowest, most
uncomfortable passenger decks on
steamships in the immigrant trade.
Steerage fares were the least expensive,
and most immigrants in the steamship
age traveled in that mode. Most passengers who paid for cabin class did
not have to go through Ellis Island.

*A 1906 cross-
section drawing
of the Ham-
burg-Amerika
liner "Deutsch-
land" (Ger-
many). "Zwis-
chendeck,"
(steerage), is
where 280 pas-
sengers, usually
immigrants,
had to cook,
eat, and sleep
in one cramped
area. On the
right-hand side
of steerage is
the roomy bar-
bershop for
first class pas-
sengers. The
next four decks
up are devoted
to the first-class
passengers.*

SEE ALSO

Ellis Island; Steamship lines

Stereotype

A stereotype was originally a printing plate designed to make identical images. By extension, stereotypes have come to mean standardized images, usually of ethnic groups, usually but not always negative. Thus, Irish were portrayed as ignorant, pugnacious drunkards, Italians as scheming and treacherous, Jews as cowardly and avaricious, etc. Stereotypes are standard "thought-clichés" of prejudice, as they help form a prejudgment without the inconvenience of thinking, or seeing people as individuals.

SEE ALSO

Discrimination; Nativism; Prejudice

Students

Although during the 19th century and well into the 20th many of the most important American scholars had received important parts of their training overseas—mostly in England, Germany, and France—by the late 19th century many students from Asia and Latin America were coming to American institutions for both undergraduate instruction and advanced degrees. The first and most famous group were the 120 Chinese youths sent to Connecticut who constituted the Chinese Educational Mission of 1872–80. Although the purpose of the mission was to train students who would help in the modernization of China, a number of the students

Top 15 countries sending students to the United States in 1998–99	
China	51,001
Japan	46,406
Korea	39,199
India	37,482
Taiwan	31,043
Canada	22,746
Thailand	12,489
Indonesia	12,142
Malaysia	11,557
Mexico	9,641
Germany	9,568
Turkey	9,377
Hong Kong	8,735
Brazil	6,982
United Kingdom	7,534
All Countries	490,933

Institute for International Education, *Annual Report, 1999.*

remained in the United States permanently, as did its co-director, Yung Wing, who had been the first Asian to earn an American college degree (Yale, 1854). That many students sent to a developed country would choose to stay there is not surprising, and students who originally came to study but stayed on to become permanent residents and citizens are today an important minor component of American immigration. Most foreign students, do return home. In 1998–99, 490,933 persons were admitted to the United Sates as students: they are classified as "nonimmigrants" and are therefore not included in immigration numbers. More than half, 56 percent, were from Asia.

Foreign students are dispersed widely across the United States. While foreign students represent about 3 percent of all U.S. higher education enrollments, they are enrolled in greater proportions at higher academic levels. International students represent about 2 percent of all four-year undergraduate enrollments and more than 11 percent of graduate enrollments. The percentages of foreign students at some institutions, in some academic fields, and especially at the graduate level, are high. The Institute of International Education, which compiles statistics on foreign students, has calculated that during 1998–99, international education contributed $13 billion to the U.S. economy.

Sunnis

SEE Muslims

Swedes

- *1990 Ancestry: 4,680,863*
- *Immigration, 1986–96: 11,637*
- *Immigration, 1820–1996: 1,292,657*
- *Major period of immigration: 1870–1910*
- *Major areas of settlement: Minnesota, Illinois, Washington State*

The largest and most populous of the Scandinavian countries, Sweden has almost 9 million people spread over more than 170,000 square miles. A few Swedes came to New Sweden, the short-lived 17th-century colony on the Delaware near what is now the city of Wilmington. A few other Swedes came to other colonies. Before the mid-1840s perhaps a thousand Swedes had come to America. Sweden's greatest contribution to colonial America was not its people, but the log cabin, a form of home construction developed in heavily forested Sweden and later adopted as the primary frontier housing type on the early American frontier.

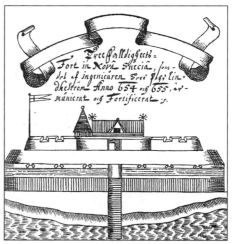

Peter Lindeström's Geographia Americae, 1625, contained this engraving of Fort Trinity in New Sweden. It was on the present-day site of Wilmington, Delaware.

In the mid-1840s began the immigration of farmers seeking agricultural land, and between then and the outbreak of the Civil War in 1861 some 20,000 Swedes came to the United States. A Swedish novelist, Vilhelm Moberg, wrote a three-book historical novel called *The Emigrants* (1949–59) about these early immigrants. And, although Moberg had never been to America, his novels and the movie *The Emigrants*, based on them, provide vivid and accurate pictures of life in Sweden and in America.

Swedish immigration continued and grew in the 1860s and 1870s when another 150,000 Swedes came. These immigrants arrived largely in family groups and settled mostly in the American wheat belt of the upper Middle West. But the image of the Swedish farmer must not obscure the fact that a significant minority settled in American cities, chiefly Chicago. In 1900 some 150,000 Swedish Americans were nearly 9 percent of Chicago's population and the Windy City was, after Stockholm, the largest "Swedish city" in the world. Swedes also become the largest ethnic group in the Twin Cities, Minneapolis and St. Paul.

A short but severe famine in Sweden in the late 1860s also spurred immigration. In just one year of the famine, 22 Swedes of every thousand died. Even heavier immigration

A whole rural neighborhood, many of them immigrant Swedes, got together to "raise" this large barn on the Rainy River in Minnesota about 1900. Such cooperative ventures were common in rural America at that time.

occurred later in the 19th century, and the composition of the immigration changed from farmers traveling in family groups to predominantly male industrial workers. At the end of the 1890s and during World War I more Swedish women than men emigrated, some of then to join—or find—husbands, and others in search of employment. The 1910 American census, taken when Swedish immigration began to wane, showed nearly a fifth of all Swedish immigrants in Minnesota and just over a sixth in Illinois.

After the 1890s a number of second-generation Swedes and Swedish immigrants migrated westward to the Pacific Northwest via the Great Northern and Northern Pacific railroad. They are concentrated in Washington State, which by 1930 had the second-largest concentration of Swedish Americans.

Both Swedes and Swedish Americans are overwhelmingly Lutherans. In 1860 Swedes in America founded the Augustana Synod jointly with Norwegians, but the latter soon left. In 1860 and 1862 Swedish Lutherans founded their first two denominational colleges, Augustana College in Sioux Falls, South Dakota, and Gustavus Adolphus College in St. Peter, Minnesota. Another noteworthy aspect of Swedish culture in America is the large number of books—perhaps as many as 10,000 titles—published in the Swedish language by a variety of ethnic publishing concerns, many of them church-related.

Swedish Americans, thanks in part to their heavy concentration in certain regions, have had a great deal of success in American politics. Partly because of the slavery issue and partly because of generous Republican land policies, including the Homestead Act of 1862, Swedes were almost universally Republicans in the later 19th and early 20th centuries. Before World War I there may have been more Swedish socialists than Swedish Democrats.

Like many ethnic midwesterners, Swedes tended to oppose American entry into World War I, although once the battle was joined, they supported the war effort like most other Americans. A number of factors, including agrarian discontent in the wheat belt and the Great Depression of the 1930s turned many Swedes away from Republicanism and, in Minnesota in particular, large numbers of them found a home in the state's Democratic-Farmer-Labor party and supported such Democratic stalwarts as Franklin D. Roosevelt and Minnesota's Hubert H. Humphrey. Over the years thousands of Swedish Americans have held political office including more than 25 governorships (10 of them in Minnesota) and dozens of members of Congress. At the beginning of World War II many Swedish Americans opposed American intervention, but after Hitler invaded Denmark and Norway most supported intervention.

Swedish Americans have made a very successful acculturation to American life, but the decline of Swedish immigration and the virtual disappearance of Swedish as a viable language has made continued Swedish American ethnicity largely a matter of tradition and nostalgia. Its once thriving fraternal associations, such as the Vasa Order of America, are now greatly reduced in size and have lost much of their influence.

SEE ALSO

Scandinavians

FURTHER READING

Anderson, Philip J., and Dag Blanck, eds. *Swedish-American Life in Chicago: Cultural and Urban Aspects of an Immigrant People*. Urbana: University of Illinois Press, 1992.

Runblom, Harald, and Hans Norman, eds. *From Sweden to America: A History of the Migration*. Minneapolis: University of Minnesota Press, 1976.

Swiss

- *1990 Ancestry: 1.045,495*
- *Immigration, 1986–96: 9,275*
- *Immigration, 1820–1996: 366,654*
- *Major period of immigration: 1880s*
- *Major areas of settlement: Pennsylvania*

Switzerland is a truly multicultural country and its unity depends on neither language nor religion but on the successful history of the Swiss as a nation. It is a small, mountainous country of nearly 16,000 square miles, of which a fifth is uninhabitable. The 7.2 million Swiss speak four official languages: 72 percent speak German, 20 percent speak French, 6 percent speak Italian, and about 1 percent speak Romansch, an ancient Celtic language spoken nowhere else. While most are members of either the traditional Protestant Reformed or the Catholic Church, there are smaller numbers of more radical Protestants who call themselves Brethren, a term that unites former Amish and Mennonites who remain separate in the United States.

There was at least one "Switzer" in the Jamestown, Virginia, colony, and individual French- and German-speaking Swiss are reported in several colonies before 1710. In that year Christopher de Graffenreid led some 650 Germans and 100 Swiss to North Carolina, where they founded New Bern. In the same year, radical German-speaking Swiss Protestants, including Mennonites, began settling in southeastern Pennsylvania. Amish, who had split off from the Swiss Mennonites in 1690, began to settle in Pennsylvania in 1738. These immigrants numbered in the hundreds. Even larger numbers (perhaps 20,000) of Swiss members of the state Reformed church settled in Pennsylvania in the 18th century. All have been included under the blanket term Pennsylvania Dutch.

Other Swiss, both German- and French-speaking, established at least three group settlements in South Carolina. At the end of the colonial period, in 1780, Albert Gallatin arrived from Geneva and became the most illustrious Swiss immigrant. He settled in Pennsylvania, represented it for three terms in Congress, was secretary of the Treasury

Swiss-born star racing driver and engine designer Louis Chevrolet, here in a 1909 car, came to the United States in 1905. The cars he made were high-performance luxury models. General Motors bought his name and he had nothing to do with their line of low-cost popular models that still bear his name.

under Presidents Jefferson and Madison, and, because of his study of American Indians, is often called the "father of American ethnology."

Of the some 200,000 Swiss who came in the 19th century, most settled in rural areas, largely in Indiana, Illinois, and Wisconsin, One Swiss German settlement, in New Glarus, Wisconsin, has an annual Swiss festival that is said to attract 30,000 tourists annually. In California, one Swiss colonizer, Johann August Sutter, founded New Helvetia (*Helvetia* was the Latin name for Switzerland) and became famous when gold was discovered in 1848 near his sawmill, which set off the gold rush of 1849. Perhaps 20,000 Italian-speaking Swiss came to California, where they were instrumental in laying the foundations for the California wine industry, although much of the initial labor was done by Chinese workers.

In the late 19th and 20th century, Swiss immigration was largely one of individuals, many of whom have achieved success in various businesses and professions. No Swiss name has become as well known as that of the mechanic-inventor Louis Chevrolet, although the man and his original nationality are all but unknown. Swiss Americans have few national organizations: the best-known is the North

American Swiss Alliance, a fraternal benefit insurance society.

SEE ALSO
Amish; Mennonites; Pennsylvania Dutch

FURTHER READING
Hoelscher, Steven D. *Heritage on Stage: The Invention of Ethnic Place in America's Little Switzerland.* Madison: University of Wisconsin Press, 1998.
Schelbert, Leo, ed. *America Experienced: 18th and 19th Century Accounts of Swiss Immigrants to the United States.* Camden, Me.: Picton, 1996.

Syrians

SEE Arabs

Taiwanese

- *1990 Ancestry: 192,973*
- *Immigration, 1986–96: 140,907*
- *Immigration, 1820–1996: n.a.*
- *Major period of immigration: since 1965*
- *Major areas of settlement: California (especially Monterey Park), New York*

Taiwan, an island of almost 14,000 square miles, has a population of 21 million, larger than that of Australia, which has almost 3 million square miles. The overwhelming majority of its inhabitants are ethnic Chinese, but there is a minority of indigenous Taiwanese. Almost all of Taiwan's immigrants to the United States have been ethnic Chinese. The island was known as Formosa during the half-century of Japanese occupation, 1895–1945, but after the establishment of the communist People's Republic of China in 1949, Taiwan became the Republic of China when Chiang Kai-shek, the ousted leader of Nationalist China, and millions of his followers fled there from the mainland. Both nations claim to be the proper government of China. Until December 1978 the United States recognized the government on Taiwan as the "true" government of China; at that time it recognized the People's Republic of China and no longer has formal diplomatic relations with Taiwan, although economic relations remain strong. There is a continuing conflict between Beijing and Taipei; Beijing insists that Taiwan is a "rebel province of China," while Taipei insists that Taiwan is independent.

For more than half a century the two Chinas have coexisted, and Chinese people emigrate to the United States from each. Most of the numerous immigrants from Taiwan have been skilled professionals, businesspeople, and investors.

SEE ALSO
Chinese

FURTHER READING
Chen, Hsiang-Shui. *Chinatown No More: Taiwan Immigrants in Contemporary New York.* Ithaca, N.Y.: Cornell University Press, 1992.
Ng, Franklin. *The Taiwanese Americans.* Westport, Conn.; Greenwood, 1998.
Saito, Leland. *Race and Politics: Asian Americans, Latinos, and Whites in a Los Angeles Suburb.* Urbana: University of Illinois Press, 1998.

Thais

- *1990 Ancestry: 112,117*
- *Immigration, 1986–96: 74,174*
- *Immigration, 1820–1996: n.a.*
- *Major period of immigration: 1965+*
- *Major areas of settlement: California*

Thailand is a Southeast Asian nation of nearly 200,000 square miles and some 60 million people. Unlike its neighbors, Laos, Cambodia, and Vietnam, Thailand was not the scene of recent warfare, so the thousands of Thais who have emigrated to the United States since 1965 have not been refugees. A significant number of Thai women have married American servicemen stationed at U.S. air bases in Thailand and have come to America when their husbands returned. Most other Thai immigrants have been young professionals, including a large number of nurses. Some Thai immigrants are merchants, and more than a few have opened restaurants. Most Thais are Buddhists.

SEE ALSO
War brides

Third World

The *Third World* is a term coined in 1956 to describe those countries of the world, primarily in Africa, Asia, and Latin America, that were aligned with neither the communist nor the noncommunist bloc. Usage quickly changed, however, and the term is now used to describe the economically underdeveloped or poorer countries of the world without regard to political alignment.

With the disappearance of the Communist bloc in the early 1990s, the term has been broadened to include some of the poorer countries, such as Romania, once included in the Communist bloc, or "Second World." The "First World" refers to the more developed nations—principally the United States and Western Europe, Australia, and South Africa—and including some developed countries in Asia, such as Japan. Before the 1960s the majority of immigrants to the United States had come from the First World. Since then the majority have come from the Third.

Tibetans

- *1990 Ancestry: n.a.*
- *Immigration, 1986–96: n.a.*
- *Immigration, 1820–1996: n.a.*
- *Major period of immigration: 1990+*
- *Major area of settlement: New York*

[Tibetans do not appear in official American immigration data because the United States does not recognize Tibet as an independent nation but accepts Chinese sovereignty over it. Tibetan refugee organizations estimated in 1995 that 1,970 Tibetans had taken up residence in the United States.]

Tibet is a vast and remote country of more than 470,000 square miles in the Himalayan Mountains between India and China. It has a population of more than 2 million, many of whom are recent Chinese immigrants. Sometimes called "the roof of the world," its capital, Lhasa, is more than two miles high, and the plateau on which most Tibetans live averages almost three miles above sea level. Claimed by China for centuries, Tibet, because of its geographical isolation, was essentially self-governing

Tibetans and others protest Chinese domination of Tibet in front of the Consulate General of the People's Republic of China in Chicago in 1998.

until a Chinese invasion in 1950 resulted in it becoming a "national autonomous region" of China, now called the "Tibetan Autonomous Region." Ethnic Tibetans are of Mongolian stock and speak a distinct language which is written in an alphabet rather than in ideograms or characters as Chinese and Japanese are.

Buddhism, the religion of Tibet, came to it from India in the 8th century. In Tibet Buddhism developed in a special way so that the lamas—the name given to Buddhist priests in Tibet and neighboring Mongolia—governed. The chief priest, or Dalai Lama, governed the country. In theory, Tibet remains governed by the lamas, but in fact is run by a commission appointed by the government in Beijing which encourages the immigration of ethnic Chinese to Tibet. A revolt by Tibetans against Chinese rule in 1959 was brutally suppressed and the Dalai Lama and more than 100,000 Tibetans fled—mostly to India where they set up a government in exile in Dharamsala.

The first Tibetans in the United States were a trade delegation which came in 1947. The next year, a Tibetan scholar, Telopa Rimpoche, was invited to teach at Johns Hopkins University in Baltimore. After the Chinese invasion the American Central Intelligence Agency brought some Tibetans to Colorado to train as guerrillas, but the project was abandoned without significant result. After the Dalai Lama's visit to the United States in 1989, Congress provided for Tibetan refugees in a special provision of the Immigration Act of 1990.

SEE ALSO

Buddhism; Immigration Act of 1990; Refugees

FURTHER READING

Minority Rights Group. *The Tibetans.* London: Minority Rights Group, 1983.
Nowak, Margaret. *Tibetan Refugees: Youth and the New Generation of Meaning.* New Brunswick, N.J.: Rutgers University Press, 1984.

Trinidadians

- *1990 Ancestry: 76,270*
- *Immigration, 1986–96: 63,567*
- *Immigration, 1820–1996: n.a.*
- *Major periods of immigration:*
- *Major areas of settlement: Northeast; New York, especially Brooklyn and Queens*

Trinidadians come from the islands of Trinidad and Tobago in the Caribbean, just off the coast of Venezuela. Nearly 1.3 million people live in the nation's 1,980 square miles, which makes it smaller than Rhode Island. Spanish settlement followed a visit by Columbus in 1498; later the islands were taken over by the Dutch and then the French until the British seized them in 1797. Sugar plantations became the major economic activity, and at first enslaved Africans were brought and then, after the end of the slave trade, indentured laborers from India came to cultivate the fields and produce the sugar. Trinidad became an independent nation in 1962. Its people today are 42 per-

cent of African ancestry, 40 percent of Asian Indian ancestry, with the rest of the population of European, Asian, Middle Eastern, and mixed ancestry. Almost a third of the population is Roman Catholic, more than a quarter Protestant, and nearly a quarter Hindu.

Trinidadians, largely Afro-Caribbeans, began immigrating to the United States in the 19th century, but records are scanty. Some scholars estimate that, by the early 1920s, perhaps a third of the residents of New York's Harlem were West Indians, with a large number of Trinidadians among them. The passage of the restrictive Immigration Act of 1924 cut off most immigration for 40 years. Both legal and illegal immigration resumed after the passage of the Immigration Act of 1965, and the majority of those who identify themselves as Trinidadians have come since then. It is likely that, when asked about ancestry, Trinidadians of Asian Indian ancestry identify themselves as Indians. The INS, whose records list nation of origin, not ancestry, believed that there were some 50,000 Trinidadians illegally in the United States as of 1996. A good estimate is that, by the late 1990s, there were perhaps 150,000 persons of Trinidadian origin in the United States, three-quarters of Afro-Caribbeans ancestry and almost all of the rest of Asian Indian ancestry.

Heavily concentrated in the New York area, Afro-Caribbean Trinidadians live largely in enclaves in Brooklyn, while Asian Indian Trinidadians are similarly clustered in Queens. Trinidadians have been active in American politics: a prominent member of the House of Representatives, Mervyn Dymally (Democrat–California), and the black power advocate, Stokely Carmichael, both emigrated from Trinidad. Carmichael was of Afro-Caribbean ancestry, whereas Dymally has both

African and Asian ancestors.

Although Trinidad is a very poor country, large numbers of Trinidadians in the United States, particularly of the American-born generations, are professionals and relatively well off. One Trinidadian, Derek Walcott, who taught at Boston University, received the Nobel Prize for literature in 1992, and another, V. S. Naipaul, is one of the most highly regarded writers of English prose.

SEE ALSO

Africans; Asians; Caribbeans; Immigration Act of 1924; Immigration Act of 1965; Indentured servants; Slave trade

FURTHER READING

Foner, Nancy, ed. *New Immigrants in New York*. New York: Columbia University Press, 1987.

Vickerman, Milton. *Crosscurrents: West Indian Immigrants and Race*. New York: Oxford University Press, 1999.

Triple melting pot

The *triple melting pot* is a term invented in 1944 by the sociologist Ruby Jo Reeves Kennedy, who argued that, instead of a "melting pot" in which ethnicity disappeared after a generation or so, there was in the modern United States a triple melting pot. Studying the marriages of European immigrants who lived in Connecticut from 1870 to 1940, she noted that most marriages occurred within one of the three larger religious frameworks—Catholic, Protestant, or Jewish. For the first generation or so almost all Irish Catholics married only other Irish Catholics, Italian Catholics married only other Italian Catholics, etc. But, she argued, after two generations the ethnic continuity was less important but that the religious continuity

remained important. Almost all marriages continued within the larger religious context, but Irish, Italian, and Polish Catholics intermarried frequently.

SEE ALSO

Melting pot; Religion

FURTHER READING

Herberg, Will. *Protestant, Catholic, and Jew; An Essay in American Religious Sociology*. Rev. ed. Garden City, N.Y.: Anchor, 1960.

Kennedy, Ruby Jo Reeves. "Single or Triple Melting Pot? Intermarriage Trends in New Haven, 1870–1940." *American Journal of Sociology* 49 (1944): 331–39.

Turks

- *1990 Ancestry: 83,850*
- *Immigration, 1986–96: 25,130*
- *Immigration, 1820–1996: 436,742*
- *Major period of immigration: 1965+*
- *Major area of settlement: New York, esp. Brooklyn*

The official immigration statistics from Turkey actually include many more non-Turks than Turks. Because the Ottoman

Two Turkish American women pose, knitting, on their stoop in Boston, in 1909. The man is smoking a water pipe, or narghile.

Empire that preceded the present-day Turkish republic was a multinational empire, fewer than 10 percent of the 360,000 immigrants listed as coming from Turkey between 1820 and 1950 were ethnic Turks. Most were Greeks, and a significant number were Armenians and members of other ethnic groups. Modern Turkey is a secular republic of 300,000 square miles and is larger than Texas. Its 62 million people are 80 percent Turks and 20 percent Kurds. All but tiny fractions of both groups are Muslim.

Prior to the end of World War II the majority of the Turks in the United States worked in unskilled and semi-skilled jobs, and they were predominantly male. Some merchants, professionals, and technicians immigrated, as did a number of outstanding professional wrestlers. After 1923 the new Turkish Republic, anxious to build a modern state, urged its nationals living abroad to return and in some cases paid for their tickets. It also offered attractive incentives in terms of jobs to well-educated overseas Turks, many of whom did return. Since World War II there has been a slow but steady "brain drain" of professionals, particularly engineers and physicians, from Turkey to the United States. These have generally come as family migrants. Within the United States Turks have engaged in propaganda wars with Armenians about the history of Armenian suffering in Turkey and with Greeks over the Mediterranean island of Cyprus, which is divided between Greeks and Turks and has been the scene of intermittent fighting and constant bitterness since 1963.

SEE ALSO
Armenians; Cypriots; Greeks; Kurds

FURTHER READING
ATA-USA : Bulletin of the Assembly of Turkish American Associations. Washington, D.C.: The Association, 1980+.

Turnverein

Turnverein are gymnastic organizations, but with important social and patriotic functions. They were first organized in Germany in 1811 and spread to the United States and other places where Germans settled in significant numbers. The first Turner Hall in the United States, the meeting places for these societies, was built in Cincinnati in 1850.

SEE ALSO
Sokols

Ukrainians

- *1990 Ancestry: 740,803*
- *Immigration, 1992–96: 92,220*
- *Immigration, 1820–1996: around 500,000*
- *Major period of immigration: 1880s–1914*
- *Major areas of settlement: New York, Pennsylvania, New Jersey*

The homeland of the Ukrainians gained its independence from the Soviet Union

3,000 Milwaukee gymnasts, members of Milwaukee Turnvereins, perform exercises in 1892.

only in 1992. Prior to World War I the territory had been divided between the Russian and Austro-Hungarian empires, and between 1919 and 1940 some of the Ukraine had been part of Poland. A large country, bigger than France but less populous, Ukraine has more than 50 million people in its 232,000 square miles.

Ukrainians are a Slavic people whose language is related to but distinct from Russian. They are generally divided in religion between the Ukrainian Catholic and the Eastern Orthodox churches. The term Ukrainian was not used as an ethnic designation until after World War I, and most of the quarter million Ukrainians who came to the United States before that were known by other names. Many called themselves Rusyns or Ruthenians, while outsiders sometimes called them "Little Russians," which most Ukrainians regarded as an ethnic slur used by others.

Individual Ukrainian names may be found on various colonial American documents, as in the muster rolls of George Washington's army—but no extensive immigration occurred before the 1880s. Probably 85 percent of the quarter million Ukrainians who immigrated to the United States before World War I were from the lands governed by the Austro-Hungarian Empire. Labor recruitment, cheap railroad and steamship fares, poor economic conditions at home, and a desire to avoid military service were all factors pushing Ukrainians to leave. Very little migration to the United States took place after the immigration restriction legislation of the early 1920s; instead, many emigrated from the Ukraine to Canada in the years between the world wars.

In the decades after World War II, perhaps 85,000 Ukrainians came to the United States, most of them displaced

persons who had been driven from their homes by either German or Soviet armies. The USSR discouraged emigration but since the establishment of an independent Ukraine there has been a renewed migration, as there has been from other parts of the former Soviet Union. Both the absence of restraint and the poor economic conditions are major factors.

Although the overwhelming majority of Ukrainian immigrants had been of agrarian background, in the 1880–1914 period almost all went to work in American factories, as did many of their fellow immigrants in those years. The post–World War II immigrants presented a very different profile: almost 40 percent of them were professionals, entrepreneurs, and skilled workers.

In addition to the many Ukrainian churches, the immigrant community created a large number of fraternal associations that provided both insurance and a heightened sense of ethnic solidarity. The most important of these is the Ukrainian National Association.

These dancers from the Ukraine and Uzbekestan, photographed in 1995, perform with the Brighton Beach Ballet Theatre in New York. Brighton Beach is a major enclave for immigrants from the former USSR.

Ukrainian Americans have concentrated most of their political energies on problems of their homeland. This was particularly true during the long years of Soviet rule, from 1919 to 1992, when most community organizations took a decided anti-Soviet stance. In the brief period since Ukraine became independent, there has been an increased feeling of pride in the homeland and a renewed immigration to the United States, which, if it continues will probably transform the Ukrainian American community.

SEE ALSO

Austro-Hungarian Empire; Displaced Persons; Eastern Rite churches; Immigration Act of 1921; Immigration Act of 1924

FURTHER READING

Kuropas, Myron B. *Ukrainians in America*. Rev. ed. Minneapolis: University of Minnesota Press, 1996.

Undocumented persons

SEE Illegal immigrants

United Arab Emirates

SEE Arabs

United Nations High Commissioner for Refugees, Office of (UNHCR)

The UNHCR is a permanent organization of the United Nations created in 1951 to succeed the International Refugee Organization. It mission is to protect and provide shelter for refugees until they can be resettled in either their former countries or in new countries. Initially its efforts were concentrated on the resettlement of European refugees of World War II (1939–45), but since then it has operated throughout the world, particularly in Africa. It was awarded the Nobel Peace Prize in both 1954 and 1981.

A small minority of refugees it helps eventually come to the United States. As a major supporter of the United Nations, the United States is partly responsible for the UNHCR and other UN agencies.

SEE ALSO

International Refugee Organization; Refugees; United Nations Relief and Rehabilitation Administration

FURTHER READING

Holborn, Louise W. *Refugees, a Problem of Our Time: The Work of the United Nations High Commissioner for Refugees, 1951–1972*. Metuchen, N.J.: Scarecrow, 1975.
Patterson, Charles. *The Oxford 50th Anniversary Book of the United Nations*. New York: Oxford University Press, 1995.
Zarjevski, Yéfime. *A Future Preserved: International Assistance to Refugees*. New York: Pergamon, 1988.

United Nations Relief and Rehabilitation Administration (UNNRA)

UNRRA was the first of three organizations of the United Nations that cared for and resettled refugees. Unlike its two successors, it had broad responsibilities for wartime and postwar relief to war-ravaged nations. It was established in 1943 and went out of existence in 1947. UNRRA's refugee work was taken over by the International Refugee Organization, which in turn was replaced by the permanent United Nations High Commissioner for Refugees. Many of the displaced persons who came to the United States in 1948–52 came from camps established by UNRRA.

SEE ALSO

Displaced persons; International Refugee Organization; Refugees; United Nations High Commissioner for Refugees; War Refugee Board

FURTHER READING

Patterson, Charles. *The Oxford 50th Anniversary Book of the United Nations.* New York: Oxford University Press, 1995.

United Nations Relief and Rehabilitation Administration. *UNRRA: The History of the United Nations Relief and Rehabilitation Administration.* New York: Columbia University Press, 1950.

United States Immigration Commission

The U.S. Immigration Commission, sometimes known as the Dillingham Commission, for its chair and instigator, Senator William P. Dillingham, made the first large-scale U.S. government study of immigration. A so-called Presidential commission, its members were appointed by President Theodore Roosevelt and congressional leaders to investigate immigration and recommend future immigration policy.

The Commission was in existence between 1907 and 1910 and published its massive report in 41 volumes in 1911. Though much of the data gathered by its investigators has been most useful to scholars, the Commission's major conclusions were that the immigrants then coming to America, chiefly from Eastern and Southern Europe, were inferior in education, ability and genetic makeup to most of those who had come previously. This came from the preconceived ideas of the commissioners— appointed by politicians— rather than from the data in the report. Speaking of Italians, Jews, Poles and others it argued that:

> The old immigration movement was essentially one of permanence. The new immigration is very largely one of individuals, a considerable proportion of whom apparently have no intention of permanently changing their residence, their only purpose in coming to America being to temporarily take advantage of the greater wages paid for industrial labor in this country.

The commission's report recommended that a new and generally restrictive and ethnically discriminating immigration policy be instituted. The report was a major impetus to the general immigration restriction that followed in 1917, 1921, and 1924.

SEE ALSO

Immigration Act of 1917; Immigration Act of 1921; Immigration Act of 1924; Immigration policy

FURTHER READING

Daniels, Roger. *Coming to America: A History of Immigration and Ethnicity in American Life.* New York: HarperCollins, 1990.

United States Immigration Commission. *Reports of the Immigration Commission.* Washington, D.C.: Government Printing Office, 1911.

U.S. v. *Thind*

Bhagat Singh Thind, a Sikh immigrant from India, was denied citizenship on

the basis of his race and sued in federal court in a attempt to become an American citizen. In the case of *Ozawa v. U.S.*, decided just three months before, the Court had held that "the words 'white person' are synonymous with the words 'a person of the Caucasian race'" in denying naturalization to a Japanese immigrant.

Mr. Thind, although quite dark in complexion, was, in ethnological terms, a Caucasian. The very same Supreme Court justice, George Sutherland, himself an immigrant from England, who wrote the Ozawa opinion, now ruled that "the words 'free white persons' are words of common speech, to be interpreted in accordance with the understanding of the common man. . . ." This decision, *U.S. v. Thind*, in 1923, settled the question of naturalization for "natives of India" until the law was changed to make them eligible in 1946.

SEE ALSO

Aliens ineligible to citizenship; Asian Indians; Immigration policy; Japanese; Naturalization; *Ozawa v. U.S.*

FURTHER READING

Daniels, Roger. *The History of Indian Immigration to America: An Interpretative Essay.* New York: The Asia Society, 1989.

Vietnamese

- *1990 Ancestry: 535,825*
- *1990 Population: 593,213*
- *Immigration, 1986–96: 477,939*
- *Immigration, 1952–96: 646,263*
- *Major period of immigration: since 1960*
- *Major areas of settlement: California, Texas*

Vietnamese immigration is almost entirely due to American military involvement in Vietnam during the years after the end

A Vietnamese woman sells vegetables at the Dane County Farmer's Market in Madison, Wisconsin, in 1997. Small fruit and vegetable stands like hers have been established recently by immigrants of various ethnicities as an alternative to huge supermarkets.

of World War II and continuing through the Vietnam War of the 1960s and 1970s. Almost all of those coming from Vietnam have been refugees from that war and its ongoing aftermath. Only a few thousand came before 1970, and most of the rest have come since the American withdrawal in 1975.

The pre-1975 refugees tended to be more westernized: Catholics slightly outnumbered Buddhists, and nearly half had attended college. Among those who came in the decade after 1975, Buddhists greatly outnumbered Catholics and only about 30 percent had attended college. Although the war is long over, the refugees continue to come. In the decade 1987–96, 250,000 came, 42,000 of them in 1996. An almost equal number came in as family members of persons already here. Large numbers of the refugees and other immigrants who have come from Vietnam were not ethnic Vietnamese, but of other nationalities, mainly Chinese. The immigration figure above includes these people. The population figure above represents ethnic

Vietnamese, including their American-born children. People born in Vietnam represented about 75 percent of the latter figure; the rest are the children born in the United States or in refugee camps elsewhere.

Most Vietnamese refugees arrived with little or no possessions and no assets, but a small minority of the Vietnamese elite, mostly high-ranking military officers and politicians, came with significant amounts of cash and other assets. Former Air Vice Marshal Nguyen Cao Ky, for example, is the proprietor of an upscale liquor store–delicatessen in a Northern Virginia suburb of Washington, D.C.

But most Vietnamese came to the United States after spending time in refugee camps in Southeast Asia and many endured terrible hardships as "boat people" in the South China Sea, where they were subject not only to the natural hazards of voyaging in small, overcrowded boats, but they were also often stripped of their possessions by pirates and venal officials in the neighboring countries of first asylum.

Not surprisingly, one in four Vietnamese in America in 1990 lived in poverty; the group's average per capita income was only $9,032, compared with a national average of $14,143. However, most Vietnamese have been in the United States for a very short time, and studies have shown that prosperity for immigrants of the same ethnic group tends to be directly proportional to the time that they have spent in the country. A study based on 1979 data showed that full-time Vietnamese workers who had been in the country before 1970 had a median income of $12,120, while those who had come since 1975 earned only $9,179. Family income data was even more striking. Only 6.8 percent of families who had immigrated before 1970 were below the poverty

line, while 35.7 percent of those who migrated after 1975 were.

Vietnamese, many of whom came from urban environments, were generally more successful than other Southeast Asian refugee groups. One special group of Vietnamese refugees, fishermen and their families, have made a successful transition to fishing on the Gulf Coast, although there was significant opposition to them from already established fishermen, as Louis Malle's film, *Alamo Bay*, depicts clearly.

SEE ALSO

Asylees; Cambodians; First asylum; Hmong; Laotians; Refugees; Vietnam War

FURTHER READING

Freeman, James M. *Hearts of Sorrow: Vietnamese-American Lives*. Stanford, Calif.: Stanford University Press, 1989.

Hein, Jeremy. *From Vietnam, Laos, and Cambodia: A Refugee Experience in the United States*. New York: Twayne, 1995.

Vietnam War

The war in Vietnam, which went on from 1945 to 1975, is regarded by Vietnamese as their war for independence. Americans were deeply involved during its last 12 years. More than 50,000 American soldiers were killed there, as were millions of Asians. That war has brought more refugees to the United States than all of its other wars combined. One special group of refugees were the Amerasians, children fathered by Americans, mostly soldiers, in Vietnam. Congress passed Amerasian Acts in 1982 and 1987 to facilitate their entry.

All told, more than 2 million refugees left Vietnam, Laos, and Cambodia because of the war. About 1.5

million have been resettled in western nations, chiefly the United States, France, and Australia.

SEE ALSO

Amerasian Acts; Amerasians; Cambodians; Chinese; Laotians; Refugees; Vietnamese

FURTHER READING

Herring, George C. *America's Longest War: The United States and Vietnam, 1950–1975*. 3rd ed. New York: McGraw-Hill, 1996.

Karnow, Stanley. *Vietnam: A History*. New York: Viking, 1983.

Vikings

The Vikings—the word means "men of the Viks" [fiords, narrow inlets of the sea between cliffs]—were Norse seafarers who, around the year 1000, were the first European immigrants in North America. Based in Greenland and led by Leif Eriksson, a small band settled briefly at a place they named Vinland, which has been identified by archaeologist Helge Ingstad as a site in Newfoundland called L'Anse aux Meadows. They were driven off by Indians, and the settlement had no influence on later immigration. The fact that Leif Eriksson called his settlement Vinland (meaning "land of vines," suggesting a mild climate) and his father had named a large snow- and glacier-covered island Greenland, suggests that, in addition to being explorers, they were the first American real estate salesmen. There have been several notorious frauds perpetrated by people trying to "prove" a more significant role for the Vikings in America. Most notable were the Kensington Stone, "planted" in Minnesota with fake "ancient inscriptions," in 1898 and a "Vinland Map," which Yale University Press published and then had to disavow as a forgery. But the settlement was real: in addition to the archaeological evidence, there is literary evidence in some of the Icelandic sagas written shortly after the Norse abandoned America.

This is a page from an Icelandic saga of the Middle Ages. Such sagas are a major source of information about the Vinland colony.

FURTHER READING

Fitzhugh, William, and Elizabeth I. Ward. *Vikings: The North Atlantic Saga*. Washington, D.C.: Smithsonian Institution Press, 2000.

Ingstad, Helge. *Westward to Vinland: The Discovery of pre-Columbian House-sites in North America*. London: Jonathan Cape, 1969.

Wahlgren, Erik. *The Kensington Stone: A Mystery Solved*. Madison: University of Wisconsin Press, 1958.

Washburn, Wilcomb E., ed. *Vinland Map Conference: Proceedings*. Chicago: University of Chicago Press, 1971.

Visa

A visa is a document, usually placed in a person's passport, indicating legal permission to enter a country on certain terms. Visas have been required for immigrants to the United States since 1924. The U.S. government issues visas to foreigners at its embassies and consulates all over the world.

Visas currently issued by the United States are of many types. The most desirable is the immigrant visa, which entitles the holder to permanent residence in the United States. Other important kinds of visas are the visitor's visa, good for a specified term, and the student visa, good for as long as its holder continues in good standing at a recognized educational institution. Before the 1920s, visas were not required to enter the United States. Unlike a green card, a visa is not an authorization to work, although a holder of an immigrant visa is entitled to apply for one.

SEE ALSO
Green card; Immigration policy; Passports

VOLAGS

VOLAGS is the acronym for Voluntary Agencies Responsible for Refugees. Beginning with the Displaced Persons Act of 1948, various private voluntary agencies, many of them religious in orientation, such as the Lutheran Resettlement Service, Catholic Refugee Committee, and the Hebrew Immigrant Aid Society, were given official status by congress as agencies of refugee sponsorship and resettlement. Before 1948 sponsorship had to be by individuals who had to assume financial responsibility for any refugee they wanted to help.

Sponsorship includes providing food, shelter, clothing, and health care; helping refugees adjust to new surroundings; finding employment and schooling when appropriate; and doing whatever else is necessary to help the refugees get established.

SEE ALSO
Displaced persons; Refugees

Walloons

SEE Belgians

War brides

War brides is the term given during and after World War II to foreign women who married American military personnel serving overseas. Special legislation—the War Brides Act of 1945 and the G.I. Fiancées and Fiancés Act of 1946 made it possible for European women—mostly British—who were married or engaged to American soldiers to enter the United States without regard to immigration quotas. A few handfuls of foreign men who married female American personnel also came.

During and after World War I, perhaps 10,000 European women came: because there were no quotas for Europeans at that time, no special legislation was necessary. In the immediate aftermath of World War II, much larger numbers came, perhaps 70,000 from Britain and 30,000 from the European continent. The continued worldwide military

The Belgian war bride on the right immigrated to Terre Haute, Indiana, in 1946. The woman on the left may be her new mother-in-law.

presence of the United States has made marriages between its military personnel commonplace not only in Europe but also in Asia, especially during the occupation of Japan after World War II and the wars in Korea and Vietnam.

SEE ALSO
Women

FURTHER READING
Shukert, Elfrieda B., and Barbara S. Scibetta. *War Brides of World War II*. New York: Penguin, 1989.
Virden, Jenel. *Goodbye Piccadilly: The American Immigrant Experience of British War Brides of World War II*. Urbana: University of Illinois Press, 1996.

War Refugee Board

The War Refugee Board was created by an Executive Order of President Franklin D. Roosevelt in January 1944. The major efforts of the Board were directed toward easing the lot of refugees in Europe and North Africa by setting up refugee and later displaced persons camps in those places. Its one venture in bringing refugees to America was an experiment urged by Roosevelt in which nearly a thousand refugees, most of whom were Jewish, were brought from United Nations Relief and Rehabilitation Administration (UNNRA) camps in Europe and North Africa to a government facility at Oswego, New York, as "parolees," not immigrants. Presumably they were to be sent back to Europe after the war was over, but in fact they were eventually allowed to enter the United States as immigrants. Ironically, the facility was placed under the control of the War Relocation Authority, whose main purpose was the incarceration of Japanese Americans. The "parole authority" device was later incorporated into the Immigration Act of 1952 and used to bring Hungarian "freedom fighters" and other cold war refugees into the United States.

SEE ALSO
Displaced persons; Immigration Act of 1952; Immigration policy; Jews; Refugees; United Nations Relief and Rehabilitation Administration (UNNRA); War Relocation Authority

FURTHER READING
Lowenstein, Sharon. *Token Refuge: The Story of the Jewish Refugee Shelter at Oswego 1944–1946*. Bloomington: Indiana University Press, 1986.

War Relocation Authority

The War Relocation Authority was created by an Executive Order of President Franklin D. Roosevelt's in March 1942. The Authority was responsible for running the camps in which some 120,000 Japanese Americans and nearly 1,000 European refugees were kept.

their more numerous German neighbors, a Texas Wendish Heritage Society was established to celebrate Wendish culture and traditions.

SEE ALSO
Slavs

FURTHER READING
Grider, Sylvia Ann. *The Wendish Texans*. San Antonio: Institute for Texas Cultures, 1982.
Nielsen, George R. *In Search of a Home: Nineteenth Century Wendish Immigration*. College Station: Texas A & M University Press, 1989.

West Indies

Collective name for the islands of the Caribbean. The name stems from Columbus's mistaken notion that the islands were just off the coast of India (which was his intended destination). The term *West Indian* is sometimes uses for Caribbean Islanders, especially those from British or former British possessions.

SEE ALSO
Caribbeans

FURTHER READING
Vickerman, Milton. *Crosscurrents: West Indian Immigrants and Race*. New York: Oxford University Press, 1999.

Wetback

Derogatory term used to describe illegal immigrants, usually Mexicans. The term comes from the notion that most illegal Mexicans swam or waded across the Rio Grande to get into America. Actually most overland entrants cross on dry land in the desert Southwest, and the Rio Grande is often so shallow that only a crosser's feet would get wet.

SEE ALSO
Illegal immigrants; Mexicans

Women

Historically women were a distinct minority of immigrants to the New World. Even among groups that migrated as families, such as the Pilgrims, Puritans, and German sectarians in the colonial period, more men came than women. In the 19th century in particular, when large numbers of immigrants were sojourners intending to stay only a short time, women were perhaps a third of all who came. Conversely, women were more likely to stay once they did come, and therefore less likely to become return migrants.

Probably the first ethnic group to have more women immigrants than men was the Irish in the late 19th century. By the mid-20th century an absolute majority of all immigrants were women, although men continued to predominate among some groups. In the 1990s about 54 percent of all immigrants were female.

Even during the period when male immigrants were more numerous, the presence of immigrant women was crucial to the establishment and survival of immigrant communities. Sending for brides from the old country was a clear sign of the intent to become permanent settlers as opposed to sojourners. In addition to their obvious contribution to biological survival, their economic

This 1932 pageant in Chicago supposedly presented "girls of all nations"; however, it is clear that women from Asia and Africa have been left out.

and cultural contributions were also crucial in the establishment and survival of immigrant cultures.

SEE ALSO

Irish; Picture brides; Sojourners; War brides

FURTHER READING

Diner, Hasia R. *Erin's Daughters in America: Irish Immigrant Women in the Nineteenth Century.* Baltimore: Johns Hopkins University Press, 1983.

Gabaccia, Donna. *From the Other Side: Women, Gender, and Immigrant Life in the U.S., 1820–1990.* Bloomington: Indiana University Press, 1994.

Pozzetta, George E., ed. *Ethnicity and Gender: The Immigrant Woman.* New York: Garland, 1991.

Yemenis

SEE Arabs

Yiddish

A Germanic language, written in Hebrew characters, spoken by the Jews of eastern Europe, the ancestors of most of today's American Jews. The derogatory term *Yid* derives from this, but is not limited to Jews of eastern European background.

SEE ALSO

Germans; Jews; Religion

Yugoslavia

Yugoslavia—the name means "southern Slavs"—was created in the aftermath of World War I in late 1918 as the "Kingdom of Serbs, Croats, and Slovenes." Other major ethnic groups in the country included Montenegrins, Bosnian Muslims, and Albanians. The last two groups are largely or partly Muslim in religion; most of the others are Eastern Orthodox or Roman Catholic. In 1929 the country's name was changed to Yugoslavia, sometimes spelled Jugoslavia. Overrun during World War II by Nazi Germany in 1941, Yugoslavia was the scene of bitter guerrilla warfare until 1945, warfare that was not only between Yugoslavs and Germans, but between armies of different ethnic groups and ideologies. By the end of the war, the communist guerrilla leader Josip Broz Tito took power and ruled Yugoslavia until his death in 1980. Although himself a Croat, Marshal Tito was a nationalist leader who held the country's various ethnic groups together. After his death the six constituent republics—Serbia, Croatia, Bosnia and Herzegovina, Macedonia, Slovenia, and Montenegro—could not agree. The largest, Serbia, tried to dominate, and a civil war marked by savage fighting and appalling atrocities went on from 1991 to 1995. Yugoslavia no longer exists. There are, instead, independent republics of Slovenia, Croatia, Bosnia and Herzegovina, Macedonia, and a "federal republic of Yugoslavia" that includes a dominant Serbia and Montenegro. This part of the Balkan Peninsula has been unstable for centuries, and the arrangements described above may or may not be lasting.

SEE ALSO

Albanians; Bosnian Muslims; Croats; Montenegrins; Serbs; Slavs; Slovenes

FURTHER READING

Denitch, Bogdan Denis. *Ethnic Nationalism: The Tragic Death of Yugoslavia.* Minneapolis: University of Minnesota Press, 1994.

Zoroastrians

Zoroastrians are an ethnocultural religious group with perhaps a few thousand followers in the United States, most of whom are recent immigrants from Iran or India or their children. The religion was founded by Zoroaster (also Zarathustra) in Persia, present-day Iran. After the Islamic conquest of Persia in the 7th century, most Zoroastrians either fled to India or kept out of public life. In India, where they are called Parsees (from Persian), many became prominent, particularly in Bombay. Perhaps the first Zoroastrian family to come to the United States were the Soroushians, who established a carpet business in New York City in the 1920s. One ethnic journal estimated in 1996 that there were 3,000 Zoroastrians in the United States and Canada. Today the most celebrated Zoroastrian in the United States is the renowned orchestra conductor Zubin Mehta, a native of Bombay.

SEE ALSO

Iranians; Religion

FURTHER READING

Leonard, Karen I. *The South Asian Americans.* Westport, Conn.: Greenwood, 1997.

APPENDIX 1

IMPORTANT DATES IN AMERICAN IMMIGRATION HISTORY

40,000–10,000 B.C.

Scholars assume that during this period the Western Hemisphere was first settled by humans who migrated from eastern Asia to Alaska and points east and south. These were the ancestors of the various Native American peoples. No evidence has been discovered that indicates any prior human settlement.

1565

Spaniards settle St. Augustine, Florida, the first permanent European settlement in what is now the United States

1598

Spanish invasion and settlement of New Mexico begins

1607

First permanent English settlement in Jamestown, Virginia

1619

First African Americans brought to Jamestown; slavery later established throughout British North America

1620

The Pilgrims, English settlers, land at Plymouth Rock, Massachusetts

1624

Dutch settle New Netherland, now New York

1624

Maryland established as a refuge for Catholics

1654

The first Jews, refugees from a former Dutch colony in Brazil, settle in New Amsterdam (New York City)

1683

First large German settlement established at Germantown near Philadelphia

1685

Louis XIV's revocation of the Edict of Nantes, tolerating Protestantism, sends many French Protestants, called Huguenots, into exile; many come to America

1717

Britain begins exiling convicts to America

1718

Large-scale "Scotch-Irish" migration of Irish Protestants begins; most go to Pennsylvania and the southern backcountry

1755

British force French-speaking Nova Scotians, called Acadians, from their homes; many later go to French Louisiana, eventually becoming Cajuns

1788

Constitution calls for liberal treatment of immigrants; orders Congress to set up a "uniform system of naturalization"

1790

Congress passes law permitting the naturalization of "free white persons"

1798

The short-lived Aliens Act is passed, the first federal anti-immigrant law

1808

Congress bars the importation of foreign slaves; despite this, perhaps 50,000 slaves are brought in illegally between then and the abolition of slavery in the United States in 1865

1818

Black Ball Line begins the first regular passenger service from Liverpool to New York

1825

First group of Norwegian immigrants arrives on sloop *Restaurationen*

1834–44

Sporadic anti-Catholic riots from Massachusetts to Pennsylvania

1840

Cunard steamship line founded in Liverpool

1845–49

Irish potato famine accelerates Irish emigration

1848

Failed democratic revolutions in much of central Europe send thousands of political refugees, mostly Germans, to the United States

1849

In the *Passenger Cases* the U.S. Supreme Court strikes down state laws regulating immigration; says that only federal government can do this

1849–50

Chinese immigration, largely to California, begins; it is the first sizable migration of Asians to the United States

1850

For the first time U.S. Census tabulates foreign-born persons; almost 10 percent of the non-Indian population is foreign-born

1854–56

Know Nothing movement, an anti-immigrant, anti-Catholic mass organization, at its height

1855

First major immigrant depot, Castle Garden, opened on lower Manhattan

1861–65

American Civil War; ethnic regiments of foreign-born soldiers play significant roles in both Union and Confederate armies

1868

Fourteenth Amendment establishes a national birthright citizenship: "all persons born or naturalized in the United States . . . are citizens of the United States and of the state wherein they reside." Passed to protect the rights of former slaves, it protected the rights of the native-born children of Asian immigrants in the years before 1952, and, in more recent years, those of the native-born children of illegal immigrants.

1870

Naturalization Act allows naturalization of "persons of African descent"

1882

Chinese Exclusion Act passed; first restriction of free immigrants

1886

Statue of Liberty dedicated

1892

Ellis Island opens

1894

Immigration Restriction League founded; it was an effective anti-immigrant pressure group for 30 years, partially responsible for the immigration acts of 1917, 1921, and 1924

1905–14

Heaviest 10-year period in American immigration history: 10,116,000 legal immigrants admitted

1907–08

Gentlemen's Agreement between U.S. and Japan restricts Japanese immigration

1911

U.S. Immigration Commission report recommends slowing immigration

1914–18

World War I disrupts flow of European immigration

1917

Literacy test and "barred zone" acts passed

1921

Emergency Quota Act passed, temporarily limiting immigration and beginning quota system

1922–23

Ozawa (*Ozawa v. U.S.*) and Thind (*U.S. v. Bhagat Singh Thind*) cases confirm ineligibility of Asian immigrants for U.S. citizenship

1924

National Origins Act passed; limits immigration from southern and eastern Europe with quotas and ends Asian immigration

1930–40

Great Depression limits most immigration

1933–45

Adolf Hitler in power as leader of Germany; anti-semitic policies of his Nazi party create refugee crisis and lead to the Holocaust

1939–45

World War II curtails immigration

1943

Chinese Exclusion Act repealed

1945

War Brides Act passed

1948 and 1950

Displaced Persons Acts admit 450,000 European refugees

1949

Peoples Republic of China proclaimed; United States begins to accept Chinese refugees

1950–53

Korean War; few refugees immediately admitted, but "war brides," and after 1965, large numbers of other immigrants from Korea come to the United States

1952

McCarran-Walter Act ends racial discrimination in naturalization; quota system continued

1953

Refugee Relief Act continues to provide for refugees from Communist countries

1954

Ellis Island closes

1956

Failed Hungarian revolution sets off small refugee crisis; 39,000 admitted to the United States

1959

Fidel Castro seizes power in Cuba; a continuing migration of Cubans begins

1963–75

Major U.S. involvement in Vietnam War; more than 1 million Southeast Asian refugees—chiefly Vietnamese, Cambodians and Laotians—come to the United States in subsequent years

1965

Immigration Act ends quota system and accelerates immigration from Asia, Latin America, and the Caribbean

1980

Refugee Act recognizes asylum, the right of persons illegally in the United States to claim legal status if they can demonstrate "a well-founded fear of persecution"

1986

Immigration Reform and Control Act seeks to stem illegal migration and creates amnesty program which legalizes nearly 2.7 million persons who had previously entered the United States illegally; also provided, at the urging of trade unions, "employer sanctions" against those "knowingly" employing illegal immigrants

1989–91

Collapse of the Soviet Union and its hold on eastern Europe creates increased immigration from eastern Europe

1989–98

Second heaviest 10-year period in U.S. immigration history: 7,527,000 new legal immigrants admitted plus nearly 2.7 million earlier illegal immigrants legalized

1990

Immigration Act increases emphasis on family- and employment-based immigration

1993

North American Free Trade Agreement (NAFTA) lowered economic barriers and some immigration barriers between the United States, Canada, and Mexico

1996

INS records 915,900 legal immigrants, the largest number since 1914, when 1,218,480 were recorded

1996

Three separate statutes mark the short-lived "turn against immigration" which penalized legal immigrants who had not yet become citizens from most federal and state social services. Many of these provisions were struck down by the federal courts; others were repealed or modified prior to the 2000 Presidential elections.

1998

Non-Citizen Benefit Clarification Act continued or partially restored eligibility to legal aliens for benefits that had been ended or curtailed by the 1996 act listed above

1998–2000

The INS, which had grown from some 8,000 employees in the late 1970s to more than 30,000 in the late 1990s, comes under heavy attack for all sides. Rated by Syracuse University's respected survey as the "least effective" large federal agency, it survives congressional efforts to abolish it.

2000

In a reversal of its traditional anti-immigrant posture, the Executive Council of the AFL-CIO, the largest American labor federation, calls for blanket amnesty for illegal immigrants and ending of employer sanctions which it had supported in 1986. The labor movement had been anti-immigrant since just after the Civil War.

APPENDIX 2
IMMIGRATION, ETHNIC, AND REFUGEE ORGANIZATIONS

Immigration History and Policy

IMMIGRATION HISTORY

The Immigration and Ethnic History Society
http://www.libertynet.org/balch/iehs

Founded in 1965, it consists of scholars interested in the field of human migration, particularly to the United States and Canada. It publishes a scholarly magazine, *The Journal of American Ethnic History.* Before 1998 it was known as the Immigration History Society.

IMMIGRATION POLICY

Federation for American Immigration Reform (FAIR)
1666 Connecticut Avenue, NW,
  Suite 400
Washington, DC 20009
202-328-7004
http://www.fairus.org

Founded in 1979, it is one of the most active organizations lobbying for a more restrictive immigration policy. It has 70,000 members and "seeks to establish a five year moratorium on all legal immigration, excluding spouses and minor children of U.S. citizens" and advocates efforts "to help leaders in source countries deal with the overpopulation and underdevelopment that result in emigration pressures." It publishes a monthly *FAIR Immigration Report.*

Ethnic Organizations

ACADIANS

Acadian Cultural Society
P.O. Box 2304
Fitchburg, MA 01420
978-342-7173
http://www.angelfire.com/ma/1755

Founded in 1985 to preserve and promote Acadian heritage among people of Acadian descent and to conduct educational programs; it publishes a quarterly newsletter, *Le Reveil Acadien*, in English and French.

AFGHANS

Afghan Community in America
P.O. Box 311
Flushing, NY 11352
516-756-9198

Founded in 1980 to increase public awareness of conditions in Afghanistan through press releases, demonstrations, walks, and radio and television messages and to help Afghan immigrants adjust to American conditions.

ARABS

American-Arab Anti-Discrimination Committee
4201 Connecticut Avenue, NW, Suite 300
Washington, DC 20008
202-244-2990
http://www.adc.org

Founded in 1980, this self-styled grassroots organization seeks to protect the rights of people of Arab descent; it works through its action network and media monitoring groups to end stereotyping of Arabs in the media and discrimination against Arab Americans in employment, education, and politics.

ARMENIANS

Armenian Assembly of America
122 C Street, NW, Suite 350
Washington, DC 20001
202-393-3434
http://www.aaainc.org

Founded in 1972 to collect and disseminate information about Armenian Americans and to serve as an information bureau for the Armenian American community. Its publications include the free *Armenia This Week/Assembly This Week.*

BALTIC AMERICANS
(Estonians, Latvians, and Lithuanians)

Joint Baltic American National Committee
P.O. Box 4578
400 Hurley Avenue
Rockville, MD 20850
301-340-1954
http://jbanc.org

Founded in 1961, this coordinating organization was long dedicated to securing the freedom from Soviet domination of the three Baltic peoples: Estonians, Latvians, and Lithuanians. The committee is affiliated with the Estonian American National Council, the American Latvian Association in the United States, and the Lithuanian American National Council. Since these countries regained their independence in the early 1990s, the committee now serves largely as a lobbying and informational organization. It publishes a quarterly, The *JBANC Chronicle,* and the *JBANC Annual Report.*

BUDDHISTS

American Buddhist Association
301 West 45th Street
New York, NY 10036
212-489-1075
http://www.americanbuddhist.com

Founded in 1980 to support and unify Buddhists in the United States, this group encourages the study of Buddhism and the relationship between Buddhism and American culture, seeks to foster interreligious cooperation, and assists individuals in locating Buddhist groups. It serves as a link among American Buddhist groups, disseminates information, maintains a speakers' bureau, and publishes a monthly magazine, *The American Buddhist.*

CARPATHO-RUSYNS

Greek Catholic Union of the U.S.A.
5400 Tuscarawas Road
Beaver, PA 15009
724-495-3400
http://www.gcuusa.com/

A fraternal benefit society founded in

Wilkes Barre, Pennsylvania, in 1892 as the Greek Catholic Union of Rusyn Brotherhoods. Few if any of its 52,000 members are of Greek ethnicity. It publishes a free monthly magazine, *The Messenger.*

CATHOLICS

Knights of Columbus
1 Columbus Plaza
New Haven, CT 06510
203-772-2130
http://www.kofc.org

A fraternal organization of Catholic men 18 years of age or over with more than 1.5 million members. It was founded in 1882 at a time when Catholics, both immigrant and native-born, were generally discriminated against and functioned partly as a defense organization. It publishes a monthly magazine, *Columbia,* in English, French, and Spanish; has a reference library; and maintains a museum.

COPTS

American Coptic Association
P.O. Box 9119 G.L.S.
Jersey City, NJ 07304
201-451-0972

Founded in 1974 and dedicated to helping immigrant Copts (Egyptian Christians) in the United States and defending the human rights of the Copts in Egypt. It publishes a quarterly journal, *The Copts.*

CUBANS

Cuban American National Foundation
[Formerly: (1983) Cuban American Public Affairs Committee; (1987) Cuban American Freedom Coalition; (1997) Cuban American Foundation]
1312 SW 27th Avenue, Suite 301
Miami, FL 33145
305-592-7768
http://www.canfnet.org/

The Cuban American Foundation was established in 1983 and is the most influential of the numerous Cuban exile organizations in the United States. It describes itself as "a grass roots lobbying organization

• O R G A N I Z A T I O N S •

promoting freedom and democracy in Cuba" and publishes a newsletter, the *Cuban Monitor*, eight times a year.

CZECHS

CSA Fraternal Life
(formerly Czechoslovak Society of America)
122 West 22nd Street
Oak Brook, IL 60522
630-472-0500
http://www.csafraternallife.org

A fraternal benefit society founded in 1854 with some 30,000 present members, it maintains a museum, biographical archives, and a 1,500-volume library of magazines and Czech books dating back to the 1860, and publishes the *CSA Journal* (in Czech and English) 11 times a year.

DUTCH

Holland Society of New York
122 East 58th Street
New York, NY 10022
212-758-1675
hhtp://members.aol.com/hollsoc/

An organization devoted to preserving the "Old Dutch" heritage. Although membership is reserved to "descendants in the direct male line of settlers in the Dutch colonies in North America prior to 1675," it maintains a reference library that may be used by the public. It publishes a quarterly, *De Halve Maen* (The Half Moon): *Magazine of the Dutch Colonial Period in America*.

EDUCATION

Institute of International Education
809 United Nations Plaza
New York, NY 10017
212-883-8200
http://www.iie.org/

Founded in 1919, it has a budget of $90 million and is the major clearinghouse for information about international education. It is concerned with both foreign students who study in the United States and American students who study abroad. It publishes a wide variety of information about both kinds of students and programs.

ESTONIANS

Estonian American National Council
Estonian House
243 East 34th Street
New York, NY 10016
212-685-0776
http://www.estosite.org/

Founded in 1952, it coordinates political, ethnic, and cultural affairs and human rights activities of Estonian Americans and maintains liaison with governmental agencies and other organizations.

FINNS

Finnish-American Historical Archives
Finlandia University
601 Quincy
Hancock, MI 49930
906-487-7347

Founded in 1932, it is devoted to the collection and preservation of the history and culture of the Finns in the United States and maintains a library that is open to the public.

GEORGIANS

Georgian Association in the United States of America
1224 Centre West, Suite 200B
Springfield, IL 62704
217-698-7071

Founded in 1931 or 1932, it has just 400 members. It is the voice of the small Georgian American community and maintains a library and publishes a semi-annual newsletter in English.

GREEKS

American Hellenic Educational Progressive Association (AHEPA)
1909 Q Street, NW, Suite 500
Washington, DC 20009
202-232-6300
http://www.ahepa.org

A fraternal association composed almost exclusively of persons of Greek descent.

Members must be U.S. citizens or have declared their intention to become citizens. Founded in 1922, it stressed Americanization and unlike some rival organizations, it conducted its business in English rather than in Greek. Today it promotes charitable, cultural, and social activities in the United States and works to educate the American public on issues relating to Greece and Cyprus. It has about 50,000 members in 700 chapters and publishes a quarterly magazine, *The Ahepan*.

HUNGARIANS

American Hungarian Foundation
300 Somerset Street
P.O. Box 1084
New Brunswick, NJ 08903
732-846-5777
http://www.ahfoundation.org

Founded in 1954, it is devoted to furthering an understanding and appreciation of the Hungarian cultural and historical heritage in the United States. It maintains a Hungarian Heritage Center with library and museum collections of 40,000 books and 500 paintings, rare volumes, and manuscripts. Among its publications is a triennial magazine, *Hungarian Heritage*.

ITALIANS

Order Sons of Italy in America
219 East Street, NE
Washington, DC 20002
202-547-2900
http://www.osia.org

The largest Italian American organization, with half a million members, was founded in 1905. It is now "a fraternal society for American men and women of Italian descent." It works to keep alive the cultural heritage of Italy, and founded the separate Commission for Social Justice, the antidefamation arm of the Italian American movement. It publishes a quarterly magazine, *Italian America*.

JAPANESE

Japanese American Citizens League
1765 Sutter Street
San Francisco, CA 94115
415-921-5225
http://www.jacl.org

Founded in 1929, this educational, civil, and human rights organization has more than 20,000 members. It works to defend the civil and human rights of all peoples, particularly Japanese Americans, and seeks to preserve the cultural and ethnic heritage of Japanese Americans. It publishes *The Pacific Citizen* every other week.

JEWS

American Jewish Committee
Jacob Blaustein Building
165 East 56th Street
New York, NY 10022
212-751-4000
http://www.ajc.org

Founded in 1906, it was originally an organization of the then more established Jews of German origin, many of whom were second- and third-generation Americans. Its leaders are sometimes referred to as "uptown" Jews, as opposed to the "downtown" Jews of eastern European origin, in reference to the parts of Manhattan in which they then lived.

Today those ethnic differences have largely disappeared. The committee now describes itself as conducting programs "of education, research, and human relations" and being concerned with the protection "of religious and civil rights." It has 70,000 members and publishes the influential magazine *Commentary*.

American Jewish Congress
15 East 84th Street
New York, NY 10028
212-879-4500
http://ajcongress.org/

Founded in 1918 by the Hungarian-born Rabbi Stephen S. Wise, this was originally an organization supported largely by eastern European Jewish immigrants. It saw itself, in part, as a more liberal alternative to the longer established American Jewish Committee. Today those ethnic differences are barely perceptible. The Congress describes itself as composed of "American Jews opposed to all forms of racism and committed to the unity, security, dignity, and creative survival of Jews . . . wherever they may be threatened." It publishes *Congress Monthly Magazine* and *Judaism: A Quarterly Journal of Jewish Life and Thought*.

B'nai B'rith
1640 Rhode Island Avenue, NW
Washington, DC 20036
202-857-6500
http://bnaibrith.org
Anti-Defamation League
823 United Nations Plaza
New York, NY 10017
212-490-2525
http://www.adl.org

Founded in 1843 as a Jewish fraternal organization, B'nai B'rith ("Sons of the Covenant") now has overseas branches and a membership of 500,000. It also has a number of component organizations, the best known of which is its Anti-Defamation League, a research and advocacy group that monitors and combats discrimination, largely but not exclusively against Jews.

Hadassah, The Women's Zionist Organization of America
50 West 58th Street
New York, NY 10019
212-355-7900
http://www.hadassah.org

Founded in 1912, Hadassah—the name is the Hebrew version of the biblical hero, Esther—is a women's, Zionist, and Jewish organization with more than 300,000 members that supports health care and medical research facilities, educational and youth institutions, and park projects in Israel. In the United States it promotes health education, Jewish education and research, volunteerism, social action, and advocacy. Its semi-annual newsletter, *Hadassah*

Associates Advisor, disseminates information about Hadassah of interest to its male associate members.

YIVO Institute for Jewish Research
The Center for Jewish History
15 West 16th Street
New York, NY 10011
212-246-6080
http://www.yivoinstitute.org

Major center for the study of eastern European Jews and Yiddish culture—in Europe and in the United States. It provides access to its library and archives, to Jewish genealogical resources, to resources for studying the Holocaust, and to links to other Jewish libraries and archives.

MANX

North American Manx Association
c/o John Cormode
13085 Franklin Avenue
Mountain View, CA 94040
http://www.isle-of-man.com/interests/genealogy/nama

Founded in 1928 in Cleveland for individuals of proven Manx birth, marriage, or descent. Works to establish a closer union of all Manx people to stimulate ties with the Isle of Man through the World Manx Association. It publishes the North American Manx Association *Bulletin*, quarterly.

POLES

Polish National Alliance of the United States of North America
6100 North Cicero Avenue
Chicago, IL 60646
773-286-0500
http://www.pna-znp.org/

Founded in 1880, this fraternal benefit society has more than 230,000 members in 966 local groups. It publishes the *Polish Daily News* and conducts Saturday classes on the Polish language, heritage, and culture.

**Polish Roman Catholic
Union of America**
984 North Milwaukee Avenue
Chicago, IL 60622
773-782-2600
http://www.prcuofa.org

A fraternal benefit society founded in 1873, it has 90,000 members in 529 local groups. It conducts language classes, publishes a bimonthly newspaper, *Narod Polski,* and maintains the Polish Museum of America at its headquarters.

PORTUGUESE

**Portuguese Continental Union
of the United States**
30 Cummings Park
Woburn, MA 01801
781-376-0271
http://members.aol.com/upceua

A fraternal benefit organization with nearly 7,000 members founded in 1925 for persons of Portuguese birth or descent. In addition to its insurance functions, it sponsors cultural and educational events, offers scholarships, and publishes a bulletin.

PUERTO RICANS

National Puerto Rican Coalition
1700 K Street, NW, Suite 500
Washington, DC 20006
Phone:(202) 223-3915
http://www.bateylink.org/

Founded in 1977, this coordinating and advocacy group for over 100 local and national Puerto Rican organizations fosters the social, economic, and political well-being of Puerto Ricans. It publishes a bimonthly newsletter, *NPRC Reports.*

RUSSIANS

**Russian Brotherhood Organization
of the U.S.A.**
1733 Spring Garden Street
Philadelphia, PA 19130
215-563-2537

A fraternal benefit life insurance society with about 8,000 members founded in

1900 for persons of Russian or Slavic descent. It publishes *The Truth,* a monthly tabloid covering news of interest to those of Russian or Slavic descent, with emphasis on the Orthodox church.

SCANDINAVIANS
(Danes, Finns, Icelanders, Norwegians, and Swedes)

American-Scandinavian Foundation
58 Park Avenue
New York, NY 10016
212-879-9779
http://www.amscan.org

Founded in 1910, it seeks to foster understanding between the peoples of the United States and Scandinavian countries through educational and cultural exchanges, publications, and public programs such as art exhibitions and lectures. It publishes *Scan,* a quarterly, and *Scandinavian Review,* three times a year.

SCOTS

St. Andrew's Society
215 South 16th Street
Philadelphia, PA 19102

The traditional ethnic organization for Scots Americans. (St. Andrew is the patron saint of Scotland.) Chapters once existed in many large cities and at least two dozen still exist, although with very small memberships. Their chief present function is an annual dinner, usually on November 30, St. Andrew's festival. The oldest, the St. Andrew's Society of Philadelphia, was founded in 1747 and has 470 members.

SERBS

Serb National Federation
One Fifth Avenue
Pittsburgh, PA 15222
412-642-7372
http://www.serbnatlfed.org

A fraternal benefit life insurance society founded in 1910, with about 15,000 present members. It publishes a semimonthly newspaper, *The American Srbobran,* which has a national circulation.

SLOVAKS

First Catholic Slovak Union of the U.S.A. and Canada

6611 Rockside Road
Independence, OH 44131
216-642-9406
www.fcsu.com/index.htm

A fraternal benefit life insurance society for Catholic Americans of Slovak descent, founded in 1890.

National Slovak Society of the United States of America

333 Technology Drive, Suite 112
Canonsburg, PA 15317
724-873-1953
www.nssusa.org/index.htm

A fraternal benefit life insurance society of 15,000 members founded in 1890; it maintains the Slovak Hall of Fame.

Sokol U.S.A.

276 Prospect Street
P.O. Box 189
East Orange, NJ 07019
973-676-0280

A fraternal benefit life insurance society for Slovak Americans that also promotes physical fitness. Founded in 1896, it has 12,000 members. Also known as the Slovak Gymnastic Union Sokol of the U.S.A., it publishes a monthly, *Sokol Times*, in English and Slovak.

SLOVENES

Slovene National Benefit Society

247 West Allegheny Road
Imperial, PA 15126-9786
724-695-1100
http://www.snpj.com

A fraternal benefit life insurance society that offers many social and cultural activities. Founded in 1904, it has 40,000 members and publishes *Prosveta*, a weekly, and the *Voice of Youth*, a monthly.

SWISS

North American Swiss Alliance

7650 Chippewa Road, #214
Brecksville, OH 44141
440-526-2257

Founded in Cincinnati in 1865 as the Grütli-Bund, this is a fraternal benefit life insurance society for persons of Swiss birth or ancestry and friends of the Swiss. It has 3,000 members and publishes a bimonthly magazine, *Swiss-American*.

TIBETANS

U.S.-Tibet Committee

241 East 32nd Street
New York, NY 10016
212-481-3569
http://www.ustibet.org/

Founded in 1978 as an organization of Americans and Tibetans advocating the human rights of the Tibetan people in Tibet and in exile, it coordinates activities to achieve lawful correction of human rights violations against the Tibetan people; sponsors commemoration of Tibetan National Day on March 10; and conducts mail and cablegram campaigns to U.S., United Nations, and world leaders soliciting support for a halt to human rights violations in Tibet and elsewhere. It maintains a library, free and open to the public, at its New York headquarters, and publishes a free *USTC Newsletter*.

TURKS

Federation of Turkish-American Associations

821 United Nations Plaza, 2nd floor
New York, NY 10017
212-682-7688
http://www.ftaa.org

Founded in 1956 and composed of 35 separate Turkish American organizations, it provides information and maintains the Turkish Cultural Center. Its purpose is to maintain and preserve knowledge of the cultural heritage of Turkey and the United States.

UKRAINIANS

Ukrainian National Association
2200 Route 10
Parsippany, NJ 07054
973-292-9800

The largest and one of the oldest of the Ukrainian fraternal organizations in the United States, It provides life insurance and conducts cultural and educational activities. Founded in 1894, it has 62,000 members and publishes two newspapers—*Svoboda,* in Ukrainian, and the *Ukrainian Weekly*, in English—and an encyclopedia about the Ukraine.

Refugee Organizations

American Jewish Joint Distribution Committee
711 3rd Avenue
New York, NY 10017
212-687-6200
http://www.jdc.org

Founded in 1914, it is one of the oldest American refugee organizations and provides health, welfare, and social programs for needy Jews in nearly 60 countries in Asia, Africa, Europe, the former Soviet Union, and Latin America. It publishes a free annual report.

American Refugee Committee (ARC)
430 Oak Grove Street
Minneapolis, MN 55403
612-872-7060
http://www.archq.org

Founded in 1929, it works for the survival, health, and well-being of refugees, displaced persons, and those at risk. It publishes a quarterly newsletter, *Bridges*.

Hebrew Immigrant Aid Society (HIAS)
333 7th Avenue
New York, NY 10001
212-967-4100
http://www.hias.org

Founded in 1880 to assist Jewish immigrants to the United States, today it focuses on assisting refugees and immigrants from Europe, North Africa, the Middle East, and other troubled areas to resettle in the United States, Canada, Latin America, and Australia. It publishes a free monthly newsletter, *Headlines and Highlights*. Their website has an large number of links to other websites about refugees.

United Nations High Commissioner for Refugees (UNHCR)
C.P. 2500
1211 Geneva 2
Switzerland
+41-22-739-8111
http://www.unhcr.ch/

The UNHCR is a permanent organization of the United Nations created in 1951 to succeed the International Refugee Organization. Its mission is to protect and provide shelter for refugees until they can be resettled in either their former countries or in new countries. Initially its efforts were concentrated on the resettlement of the European refugees of World War II (1939–1945), but since that time it has operated throughout the world, particularly in Africa. It publishes a number of periodicals—including a magazine, *Refugees*—reports, and maps, which can be read and downloaded from its website.

DOING RESEARCH ON IMMIGRATION AND ETHNICITY:
FURTHER READING, MUSEUMS, AND WEBSITES

Further Reading

Overviews of Immigration

Archdeacon, Thomas. *Becoming American: An Ethnic History.* New York: Free Press, 1983.

Bodnar, John. *The Transplanted: A History of Immigrants in Urban America.* Bloomington: Indiana University Press, 1985.

Daniels, Roger. *Coming to America: A History of Immigration and Ethnicity in American Life.* New York: HarperCollins, 1990.

Handlin, Oscar. *The Uprooted: The Epic Story of the Great Migrations That Made the American People.* Boston: Little, Brown, 1951.

Jones, Maldwyn A. *American Immigration.* 2nd ed. Chicago: University of Chicago Press, 1992.

Levinson, David, and Melvin Ember, eds. *American Immigrant Cultures: Builders of a Nation,* 2 vols. New York: Simon & Schuster Macmillan, 1997.

Reimers, David M. *Still the Golden Door: The Third World Comes to America.* 2nd ed. New York: Columbia University Press, 1992.

Simone, Roberta. *The Immigrant Experience in American Fiction: An Annotated Bibliography.* Metuchen, N.J.: Scarecrow Press, 1994.

Thernstrom, Stephan, ed. *Harvard Encyclopedia of American Ethnic Groups.* Cambridge: Harvard University Press, 1980.

Ethnicity

Glazer, Nathan, and Daniel Patrick Moynihan. *Beyond the melting pot; the Negroes, Puerto Ricans, Jews, Italians, and Irish of New York City.* 2nd. ed. Cambridge: M.I.T. Press, 1970.

Gordon, Milton M. *Assimilation in American Life: The Role of Race, Religion, and National Origins.* New York: Oxford University Press, 1964.

Hutchinson, John, and Anthony D. Smith, eds. *Ethnicity.* New York: Oxford University Press, 1996

Vecoli, Rudolph J., contributing ed. *Gale Encyclopedia of Multicultural America,* 2 vols. Detroit: Gale Research, 1995.

Genealogy

Carmack, Sharon DeBartolo. *A Genealogist's Guide to Discovering Your Immigrant & Ethnic Ancestors.* Cincinnati, Ohio: Betterway Books, 2000.

Colletta, John Philip. *They Came in Ships: A Guide to Finding Your Immigrant Ancestor's Arrival Record.* Rev. ed. Salt Lake City, Utah: Ancestry, 1993.

Szucs, Loretto Dennis. *They Became Americans: Finding Naturalization Records and Ethnic Origins.* Salt Lake City, Utah: Ancestry, 1998.

Tepper, Michael. *American Passenger Arrival Records: A Guide to the Records of Immigrants Arriving at American Ports by Sail and Steam.* Rev. ed. Baltimore: Genealogical Publishing, 1993.

Whyte, Donald. *Dictionary of Scottish Emigrants to the United States,* 2 vols. Baltimore: Magna Carta, 1972–1986.

Wolfman, Ira. *Do People Grow on Family Trees? Genealogy for Kids & Other Beginners: The Official Ellis Island Handbook.* New York: Workman, 1991.

Immigration Law

Bredbenner, Candice Dawn. *A Nationality of Her Own: Women, Marriage, and the Law of Citizenship*. Berkeley: University of California Press, 1998.

Hutchinson, E. P. *Legislative History of American Immigration Policy, 1798–1965*. Philadelphia: University of Pennsylvania Press, 1981.

LeMay, Michael C., and Elliott R. Barkan, eds. *U.S. Immigration and Naturalization Laws and Issues: A Documentary History*. Westport, Conn.: Greenwood. 1999.

Immigration Policy

Baron, Dennis. *The English-Only Question*. New Haven: Yale University Press, 1990.

Bhagwati, Jagdish. *A Stream of Windows: Unsettling Reflections on Trade, Immigration, and Democracy*. Cambridge: M.I.T. Press, 1998.

Briggs, Vernon M. *Mass Immigration and the National Interest*. 2nd ed. Armonk, N.Y.: M. E. Sharpe, 1996.

Daniels, Roger, and Otis Graham. *Debating American Immigration*. Lanham, Md.: Rowman & Littlefield, 2001.

Higham, John. *Strangers in the Land: Patterns of American Nativism, 1860–1925*. 2nd ed. New Brunswick, N.J.: Rutgers University Press, 1988.

Reimers, David M. *Unwelcome Strangers: American Identity and the Turn Against Immigration*. New York: Columbia University Press, 1998.

Solomon, Barbara Miller. *Ancestors and Immigrants*. Cambridge: Harvard University Press, 1956.

Tatalovich, Raymond. *Nativism Reborn: The Official English Language Movement and the American States*. Lexington: University of Kentucky Press, 1995.

U.S. Commission on Immigration Reform. *U.S. Immigration Policy: Restoring Credibility*. Washington, D.C.: Government Printing Office, 1994.

Zucker, Norman L., and Naomi F. Zucker. *The Guarded Gate: The Reality of American Refugee Policy*. San Diego, Calif.: Harcourt, 1987.

Museums

Balch Institute for Ethnic Studies
18 South 7th Street
Philadelphia, PA 19106
215-925-8090
http://www.balchinstitute.org/

This Philadelphia institution is a leading research collection for immigrant and ethnic history. Pictures and exhibits are on view at the institute and on the website; the website also contains the Immigration and Ethnic History Society. Among its resources are syllabi for immigration history courses and reading lists.

Ellis Island Immigration Museum
Statue of Liberty/Ellis Island
   National Monument
Liberty Island
New York, NY 10004
212-363-3206
http://www.ellisisland.org/ellis.html

The premier immigration museum in the world, located in New York harbor and operated by the National Park Service. It features the historic Great

Hall where immigrants awaited processing, as well as extensive displays of historic artifacts, photographs, maps, and oral histories.

Lower East Side Tenement Museum
40 Orchard Street
New York, NY 10002
212-431-0233
http://www.tenement.org/index.html

Housed in a surviving 19th-century tenement; devoted to showing how urban immigrants lived a hundred years ago and more. It features reconstructed apartments from the 1870s and 1930s. The website offers a tour, photographs, and other information about the museum.

United States Holocaust Memorial Museum
100 Raoul Wallenberg Place SW
Washington DC 20024
202-488-0400
http://www.ushmm.org/index.html

The United States Holocaust Memorial Museum is the best possible single source of information about the Holocaust: the murder of some 6 million Jews and numerous others in death camps during World War II. The museum was created by a unanimous act of Congress in 1980 and is adjacent to the National Mall in Washington, D.C. The museum describes its goals as follows:

> The Museum's primary mission is to advance and disseminate knowledge about this unprecedented tragedy; to preserve the memory of those who suffered; and to encourage its visitors to reflect upon the moral and spiritual questions raised by the events of the Holocaust, as well as upon their own responsibilities as citizens of a democracy.

Websites

There is a vast and growing amount of sites concerning immigration available on the web. Some of these sites contain straightforward information, some contain accurate information organized and slanted to portray a particular point of view, and others simply contain so much misinformation that they are worse than worthless. The sites below may contain an occasional error—nobody is perfect—but they are conducted and maintained by responsible organizations both governmental and non-governmental.

American Memory
Part of a large Library of Congress site, the collection contains photos, documents, maps, sound recordings, and bibliographies. It is sometimes difficult to use but still worthwhile.
http://memory.loc.gov/

Angel Island
A guide to the former Immigration Station in San Francisco Bay used primarily to detain immigrants from Asia.
http://www.a-better.com/asians.htm

Center for Migration Studies
This institution, on Staten Island in New York City, is an important center for immigration history operated by the Scalabrini Fathers, a Roman Catholic order. Its excellent specialized library and archives are searchable online.
http://www.cmsny.org/

Church of Jesus Christ of Latter-Day Saints (LDS) [The Mormons]
The LDS Church maintains the largest genealogical collection in the world in its Salt Lake City headquarters. Its microfilm collections may be used, free

of charge, at LDS reading rooms all over the United States and the world. There is a step-by-step program on its site—"Family History: How Do I Begin? The first steps to success in tracing your family history"—that provides an excellent beginning guide for anyone wishing to do family history. www.lds.org

Digital Librarian: History

A descriptive and well-chosen list of sites dealing with history of all kinds. Many are relevant to immigration and ethnic history. http://www.digital-librarian.com/history.html

Immigration History Research Center

This University of Minnesota-Twin Cities site contains exhibits, photos, and a unique set of links to other sites. For example, under "Family History Research" is a list of internet sites for several dozen different ethnic groups. http://www1.umn.edu/ihrc/

Making of America

This University of Michigan site is a digital library of primary sources in American social history concentrating on the period from the 1840s to the 1880s. Steadily expanding, in 2000 the collection contained approximately 1,600 books and 50,000 journal articles from the 19th century. http://moa.umdl.umich.edu/

Statistical Abstract of the United States

Reissued annually, the Census Bureau publication has much detailed information. Recent and current data on immigration, immigrants, and the foreign-born may be found in Section One. http://www.census.gov/statab/www/

United States Bureau of the Census

Contains detailed statistical information. Search under "foreign born" for statistical data about immigrants. Within the site there is a useful series of pamphlets, "We, the Americans" (http://www.census.gov/apsd/www/wepeople.html) which can be downloaded. http://www.census.gov/

United States Immigration and Naturalization Service (INS)

There are a number of useful sites operated by the INS. All have detailed instructions. The following are some of the most useful:

Historical Research Tools

Provides a general introduction to what is available on the INS site with links to everything listed below and more. http://www.ins.usdoj.gov/graphics/aboutins/history/tools.html

Ports of Entry

Provides records of not just the major ports of entry such as New York and San Francisco, but also of minor ports of entry in almost every state, the District of Columbia, and Canada. http://www.ins.usdoj.gov/graphics/aboutins/history/poelist/poe.htm

Arrival Records

Provides statistical information about immigrant arrivals by year and by country. http://www.ins.usdoj.gov/graphics/aboutins/history/immrecs/immrec.htm

Naturalization Records
Provides detailed information about naturalization, including copies of forms and samples of individual records.
http://www.ins.usdoj.gov/graphics/aboutins/history/natzrec/natrec.htm

Chinese Immigration Files
Provides access to a variety of records associated with the era of Chinese Exclusion, 1882–1943, including sample records.
http://www.ins.usdoj.gov/graphics/aboutins/history/chinese.html

United States National Archives: The Genealogy Page
Genealogists are the most numerous users of the Washington, D.C., research rooms and 13 regional facilities of the National Archives and Records Administration (NARA). This site provides many of the finding aids, guides, and research tools that can prepare you for a visit to one of its facilities or for requesting records from NARA.
http://www.nara.gov/genealogy/
The same is true for a link from that page, which treats immigration records similarly.
http://www.nara.gov/genealogy/immigration/immigrat.html

United States National Park Service (NPS): History in the Parks
This portion of the vast NPS website can be searched for any ethnic group. It has separate sections on African American, Asian American, Hispanic, and Pacific Islander American Heritage.
http://www.cr.nps.gov/catsig.htm

INDEX

PICTURE CREDITS

American Jewish Historical Society, Waltham, Massachusetts, and New York, New York: 172; Anthracite Museum, Scranton, Pa.: 272; Reprinted with permission of the Anti-Defamation League: 33; Archives of the Archdiocese of Boston: 161, 219; Courtesy of the Arizona Historical Society, Tucson: 243 (AHS# 62860); E. M. Avery, *A History of the United States*: 269; Joyce and Michael Axelrod collection: 233; Balch Institute for Ethnic Studies: 37, 128, 235 (Eliot Barkman Photographs), 75 (Estampas Colombianas Photographs), 231 (George Ardelean Photographs), 83 (Sokol USA, Lodge 56 Photographs), 13 (Temple University); Courtesy of the Bancroft Library, University of California, Berkeley: 152; Basque Library, University of Nevada, Reno: 49; Courtesy of the Ira M. Beck Memorial Archives, Special Collection at Penrose Library, University of Denver: 173; Bishop Museum: 176; Courtesy of the Boston Public Library, Print Department: 262; Brown Brothers: 63; Anne S. K. Brown Military Collection, Brown University Library: 133; Courtesy of the California History Room, California State Library, Sacramento, California: 193; © Jordan Cassway: 35; Courtesy of the Chicago Cubs: 90; Chicago Historical Society: 57, 58, 72, 185, 214, 228, 275; Chinatown History Museum, New York: 70; Cincinnati Historical Society: 97; City Lore: cover (top left), 18, 165, 199, 220, 230; © J. Michael Craig: 241; Denver Public Library, Western History Collection: 232; By Courtesy of the Ellis Island Immigration Museum: 14, 28, 67, 69, 81, 93, 98, 99, 105, 151 (top and bottom), 154, 163, 194, 201, 216; Erie Canal Museum, Syracuse, N.Y.: 159; Courtesy of Finlandia University (formerly Suomi College) at Hancock, Michigan: 111; Florida State Archives: 80, 115, 250; Courtesy of Foto Farm: 84; The Historic New Orleans Collection: 19 (accession no. 1974.25.31.210); Historical Museum of Southern Florida: 47, 131; Collection of Immigrant City Archives, Lawrence, Mass.: 227; Immigration History Research Center, University of Minnesota: 141 [Janossy Family Orchestra, "IHRC Photograph Files," (Hu) 12A], 182 (Latvian Chorus Shield, Grand Rapids, MI 1958, "Latvian Chorus Shield Records," Box 3, Folder "82-80 Photos"); Indiana Historical Society: 271; The Library Company of Philadelphia: 246; Library of Congress, Geography and Map Division: 10 (G3701.E27 1853.Z5 TIL); Library of Congress, New York World Telegram & Sun Collection: 23, 41, 242, 248, 258; Library of Congress, Prints & Photographs: cover (bottom), 12 (USZ62-22399), 15 (USZ62-44049), 30 (USZ62-104027), 76 (USZ62-116241), 88 (USZ62-93707), 92 (USZ62-17525), 101 (USZC4-5546), 127 (USZ62-102814), 146, 147, 175 (PC/US-1852.F37), 179 (USZ62-38617), 184 (USZ62-52584), 191 (USF 34-82441-E), 198, 200 (USZ62-114829), 213 (USZ62-60849), 217 (USW-3-2204-D), 245, 255 (USZ62-5139), 261; University of Massachusetts Lowell Center for Lowell History: 117; © Paul T. McMahon: 267; Photo courtesy of the Milwaukee County Historical Society: 263; Minnesota Historical Society: 11, 26, 125 (Photo by Edmund A. Brush), 129, 204, 256; Courtesy Murphy Library, University of Wisconsin-La Crosse: 122; © Museum of the City of New York: 65; National Archives: 25, 31, 53, 168, 169, 211 (Pacific Region--San Francisco), 253; Courtesy of The National Japanese Historical Society: 167; National Postal Museum, Smithsonian Institution: 212; New England Historic Genealogical Society: 119; © Collection of the New-York Historical Society: 2 (neg. no. 41800), 123 (neg. no. 41921A); New York Public Library Picture Collection: 7, 100, 189; Norwegian Folk Museum: 203; Courtesy of Orthodox Church in America Archives: 64; The Pluralism Project, Harvard University: 181; Private Collection: 68; © Mel Rosenthal: 22, 59, 136, 221, 226, 264; Shades of L.A. Archives/ Los Angeles Public Library: 109, 157; Ante Sikic: 79; Photo courtesty State Historical Society of Iowa--Des Moines: 237; State Historical Society of Wisconsin: 162 (WHi X3 11515); Tibetan Alliance of Chicago: 260; U.S. Immigration and Naturalization Service: 238; U.S. Military History Institute, Carlisle, Pa.: 140; Union Pacific Museum Collection: 55; The UT Institute of Texan Cultures at San Antonio: 85 (No. 72-723), 251, 273 (No. 90-457); Courtesy Ursuline Archives & Museum: 116; JimWestPhoto.com: cover (top right), 73.

Roger Daniels, Charles Phelps Taft Professor of History at the University of Cincinnati, holds a Ph.D. from the University of California, Los Angeles. He has written or co-authored 13 books, including *The Politics of Prejudice* (1962), *American Racism: Exploration of the Nature of Prejudice* (1970), *The Bonus March (1971), Concentration Camps, USA* (1971), *The Decision to Relocate the Japanese Americans* (1975), *Concentration Camps, North America* (1981), *Asian Americans: Emerging Minorities* (1987), *Asian America: Chinese and Japanese in the United States since 1850* (1988), *Coming to America (1990), Prisoners Without Trial* (1993), *Not Like Us: Immigrants and Minorities in America, 1890–1924* (1997), and *Debating American Immigration* (2001). He has also edited more than 75 volumes. Professor Daniels is a past president of the Immigration and Ethnic History Society and of the Society for Historians of the Gilded Age and the Progressive Era. He has been a consultant to a number of public bodies including the Presidential Commission of the Relocation and Internment of Civilians and is a member of the history committee which helped to plan the Immigration Museum on Ellis Island. He has frequently taught in Europe and Canada at the Universities of Hamburg and Munich, and Martin Luther University in Germany; the University of Innsbruck in Austria; and Toronto and Calgary in Canada. Professor Daniels has lectured widely, and consulted for and appeared in a number of public television programs.

William H. Chafe is Alice Mary Baldwin Distinguished Professor of History and Dean of the Faculty of Arts and Sciences at Duke University. His numerous publications include *Civilities and Civil Rights: Greensboro, North Carolina and the Black Struggle for Freedom* (winner of the Robert F. Kennedy Book Award); *A History of Our Time: Readings in Postwar America* (edited with Harvard Sitkoff); *The Unfinished Journey: America Since World War II; The Paradox of Change: American Women in the Twentieth Century; Never Stop Running: Allard Lowenstein and the Struggle to Save American Liberalism* (winner of the Sidney Hillman Book Award); and *The Road to Equality: American Women Since 1962*. Professor Chafe is currently the president of the Organization of American Historians.